BJ
1469
.K54
1995
Copy 2

$12⁰⁰

12/95

KILLING AND LETTING DIE

D1430685

WITHDRAWN

Media Center (Library)
Elizabethtown Community College
Elizabethtown, KY 42701

KILLING
AND LETTING DIE

Second Edition

Edited by
BONNIE STEINBOCK
and
ALASTAIR NORCROSS

Fordham University Press
New York

Copyright © 1994 by Fordham University Press
All rights reserved
LC 94-16793
ISBN 0-8232-1562-8 (hardcover)
ISBN 0-8232-1563-6 (paperback)
Second printing 1995

Library of Congress Cataloging-in-Publication-Data

Killing and letting die / [edited] by Bonnie Steinbock and
Alastair Norcross. — 2nd ed.
    p.   cm.
Includes bibliographical references.
ISBN 0-8232-1562-8 : 27.00. — ISBN 0-8232-1563-6 :
$16.95
    1. Life and death, Power over.   2. Euthanasia.   3.
Medical ethics.
    I. Steinbock, Bonnie.   II. Norcross, Alastair.
BJ1469.K54   1994   94-16793
179'.7—dc20   CIP

PUBLICATION OF THIS BOOK
WAS AIDED BY A GRANT FROM
THE HENRY AND IDA WISSMANN FUND

Printed in the United States of America

To our parents,
Elmer and Natalie Steinbock
and
Lawrence and Margaret Norcross

CONTENTS

ACKNOWLEDGMENTS

I have received help and encouragement from more people than can be listed here. But I would like to offer special thanks to Bernard Williams for stimulating my interest in killing and letting die; Jonathan Bennett and N. Ann Davis, from whom I have learned more than I can ever acknowledge; Gerald Dworkin, Bruce Russell, Peter Singer, and Richard Wasserstrom, all of whom made helpful suggestions; Helen Somich for flawless typing; Norwell F. Therien, Jr. and all the people at Prentice-Hall, Inc. who helped to produce this book. Most of all I thank my husband, David Pratt, who helped immeasurably with the research, was a patient and meticulous editor, spent hours discussing difficult legal concepts with me, and whose idea the anthology was.

Bonnie Steinbock

ACKNOWLEDGMENTS FOR THE SECOND EDITION

I would like to offer thanks to Jonathan Bennett for teaching me how to think clearly about philosophy in general and about the issues of this book in particular; Bonnie Steinbock for inviting me to coedit the book and for making the collaboration such a fruitful one; Christopher Coniglio for invaluable help with the bibliography; Mary Beatrice Schulte, Kathy Moreau, and all the people at Fordham who helped to produce this book. Most of all I thank my wife, Diana, for her support, her assistance, and especially for her existence.

Alastair Norcross

Introduction to the Second Edition

Alastair Norcross

IN THE FOURTEEN YEARS since the publication of the first edition of *Killing and Letting Die*, the issues treated in the book have remained at the forefront of public, legal, medical, and philosophical discussion. There has been enough excellent new scholarly work devoted to these topics to fill several volumes. Instead of issuing an entirely new collection, however, we have chosen to retain most of the readings from the first edition, many of them philosophical classics, and to add nine new selections. Our decisions concerning what to add and what to retain were influenced by both the quality of the articles and their influence on the field. Bonnie Steinbock's introduction to the first edition provides an excellent discussion of the religious, legal, medical, and philosophical aspects of the controversy surrounding killing and letting die. I will not attempt here to cover the same ground, except where it is relevant to a discussion of one of the new selections. Rather, I will highlight some of the most significant developments in recent years, and I will discuss, in some detail, the articles that are new to the second edition.

ACTIVE AND PASSIVE EUTHANASIA

A legal and medical consensus has gradually emerged in the United States that "termination of life support is legitimate under certain circumstances."[1] The consensus is grounded in the right of both competent and incompetent patients to refuse treatment. The most significant recent legal challenge to this consensus occurred when the United States Supreme Court considered the case of *Cruzan v. Director, Missouri Department of Health* (1990). Nancy Beth Cruzan was reduced to a persistent vegetative state by an

1

automobile accident. Her parents were granted permission by a
Missouri trial court to terminate her artificial nutrition and hydration, but the Missouri Supreme Court reversed the decision on
the grounds that there wasn't clear and convincing evidence that
Nancy Cruzan would have wanted the termination. The U.S.
Supreme Court upheld, by a five-to-four decision, the judgment
of the Missouri Supreme Court. This was the first so-called "right
to die" case to reach the U.S. Supreme Court. At issue was the
constitutionality of the Missouri Supreme Court requirement for
incompetent patients that, "in the absence of the formalities required under Missouri's Living Will statutes," there be "clear and
convincing, inherently reliable evidence" (p. 81) of the patient's
wishes regarding the termination of life-prolonging procedures.
As Justice Rehnquist wrote in the majority opinion:

> Here, Missouri has in effect recognized that under certain circum-
> stances a surrogate may act for the patient in electing to have hydra-
> tion and nutrition withdrawn in such a way as to cause death, but
> it has established a procedural safeguard to assure that the action
> of the surrogate conforms as best it may to the wishes expressed
> by the patient while competent. Missouri requires that evidence of
> the incompetent's wishes as to the withdrawal of treatment be
> proved by clear and convincing evidence. The question, then, is
> whether the United States Constitution forbids the establishment
> of this procedural requirement by the State. We hold that it does
> not [p. 84].

Perhaps the most significant piece of reasoning used to reach this
decision was the following:

> Finally, we think a State may properly decline to make judgments
> about the "quality" of life that a particular individual may enjoy,
> and simply assert an *unqualified interest in the preservation of human
> life* to be weighed against the constitutionally protected interests
> of the individual [p. 85; emphasis added].

It is important to stress that the Court's decision does not *require*
states to employ a particularly stringent standard of proof in ascer-
taining the wishes of incompetent patients, but it certainly *permits*
the use of such standards. In this respect, the decision itself is a
fairly narrow one, and does not seriously threaten the legal consensus over the withdrawal of life-support. However, the stress

on the "unqualified interest in the preservation of human life" may invite further restrictive legislation in certain states that could have an impact on the consensus. (It could also invite particularly restrictive abortion legislation in some states.) Also of interest is the possible impact of the decision on so-called "futility" cases. An increasing number of litigated cases involve doctors attempting to remove life-support from incompetent patients on the grounds that it is futile. A number of these cases involve patients who are not merely incompetent, but who have never been competent—an anencephalic infant, for example. Clearly, the Missouri Supreme Court's requirement could not be satisfied in such a case.

The consensus also recognizes a clear distinction between active euthanasia and assisted suicide on the one hand, and forgoing life-sustaining treatment, sometimes referred to as "passive euthanasia," on the other. This distinction, often identified with the distinction between killing and letting die, is seen as a vital element in maintaining the consensus.

> A bedrock assumption on which the consensus is grounded is that there is a fundamental distinction between a patient's death from forgoing life-sustaining treatment and active intervention to end life. The courts have manifested an unflagging insistence on establishing and maintaining a bright line between active euthanasia and passive euthanasia . . . , even when it seriously strains reasoning to do so. . . . The pressures for legalizing mercy killing are intended to extend the consensus about forgoing life-sustaining treatment. Rather than resulting in the acceptance of mercy killing, the pressure to dissolve the distinction between killing and letting die—between active and passive euthanasia—could easily boomerang and undermine the entire consensus.[2]

Though the legal consensus is that there is a sharp distinction between active and passive euthanasia,[3] there is by no means a public consensus on this point. The activities of Dr. Jack Kevorkian, who has assisted numerous suicides in recent years, command as much public admiration as condemnation. In 1992, a ballot measure in California empowering doctors to give lethal injections to terminal patients in some circumstances received 46 percent of the vote. A year earlier in Washington State a similar measure received an equal level of support. In fact, many voters seem to get cold feet (or dirty hands?) when it comes time to vote, because opinion polls show significant *majorities* of Americans supporting the proposition that doctors should help terminally ill patients commit suicide or give them lethal injections if they request them. Organizers of the losing ballot initiatives realize that they have been trying to change too much too soon in what is, by the standards of Western industrialized nations, a very conservative country, and believe that they need to change tactics. One possible approach, inspired by recent developments in the Netherlands, is to push for the approval of guidelines for doctors that prosecutors could also use to determine which doctors to prosecute.

In February 1993, the Dutch Parliament enacted legislation that gave that country the world's most permissive policy on active voluntary euthanasia. Under the new law, active euthanasia and assisting suicide remain illegal, but doctors are protected from prosecution if they notify the coroner of any death they have deliberately caused, and provide a detailed account of the circumstances based on an official checklist. The new law put an official stamp of approval on a practice that had been more or less openly tolerated, when practiced under recognized professional guidelines, since the 1970s. In opinion polls, about 80 percent of the Dutch public express approval of voluntary euthanasia for the terminally ill. Government surveys estimate that there are about 2300 deaths from euthanasia per year, and about 400 cases of physician-assisted suicide.

While the Netherlands is the first European country to guarantee doctors immunity from prosecution in certain cases of active euthanasia, there is evidence that the practice is fairly well established and accepted in Britain, France, and Scandinavia. A recent case in Britain received a good deal of public attention. Dr. Nigel Cox administered a lethal dose of potassium chloride to a terminally ill patient who was in severe and unremitting pain, and who had asked to die. The matter would never have been brought to the attention of the police if he hadn't dutifully entered the injection in the hospital log, where it was spotted by a nurse, who eventually informed the police. Dr. Cox was charged and convicted of attempted murder in September 1992. (The body had already been cremated by the time the nurse reported the incident. Because it could not be proved that the injection was the cause of death, Dr. Cox could not be charged with murder.) Despite the gravity of the charge, he did not go to prison, but received a 12-month suspended sentence. The British public were, for the most part, supportive of his actions, so much so that the nurse who reported him was widely vilified.

Doubts about the significance of the distinction between active and passive euthanasia have not been confined to public opinion. There has been a great deal of philosophical debate on the issue. One of the classic attacks on the distinction is James Rachels' "Active and Passive Euthanasia," reprinted in both editions of this book. Rachels claims that the American Medical Association policy statement on euthanasia endorses the doctrine that there is an important moral difference between killing and letting die. He further argues that there is no such difference, and thus that the AMA policy is seriously flawed. Both Bonnie Steinbock in "The Intentional Termination of Life" and Thomas Sullivan in "Active and Passive Euthanasia: An Impertinent Distinction?" argue that Rachels has misread the AMA policy. The policy does not make the distinction between killing and letting die, they claim, but rather it makes two further distinctions: (i) between intending and foreseeing a death; and (ii) between the cessation of ordinary and extraordinary means of prolonging life. Here is the policy statement:

> The intentional termination of the life of one human being by another—mercy killing—is contrary to that for which the medical profession stands and is contrary to the policy of the American Medical Association.
>
> The cessation of the employment of extraordinary means to prolong the life of the body when there is irrefutable evidence that biological death is imminent is the decision of the patient and/or his immediate family. The advice and judgment of the physician should be freely available to the patient and/or his immediate family.

Against Rachels' claim that the cessation of treatment in cases where death is known to ensue simply is the intentional termination of life, both Steinbock and Sullivan argue that life-support may be terminated without the intention to terminate life, although such a termination will be foreseen. Sullivan writes:

But we all know that it is entirely possible that the unwillingness
of a physician to use extraordinary means for preserving life may
be prompted not by a determination to bring about death, but by
other motives. For example, he may realize that further treatment
may offer little hope of reversing the dying process and/or be excruciating, as in the case when a massively necrotic bowel condition in a neonate is out of control. The doctor who does what he
can to comfort the infant but does not submit it to further treatment or surgery may foresee that the decision will hasten death,
but it certainly doesn't follow from that fact that he intends to
bring about its death [pp. 135–36].

In "More Impertinent Distinctions and a Defense of Active
Euthanasia" Rachels replies to Sullivan. He doesn't concede that
the killing/letting die distinction isn't involved in the AMA policy, but rather than argue that point, he argues that neither the
intending/foreseeing distinction nor the ordinary/extraordinary
means distinction can bear the moral weight required by Sullivan's
position. The role of intentions in morality is a fiercely debated
topic, with implications far beyond the question of euthanasia. I
will, therefore, confine my discussion to the intending/foreseeing
distinction, although both Rachels and Sullivan have very interesting things to say about the ordinary/extraordinary means distinction. Rachels considers two doctors, Dr. White and Dr. Black,
each faced with the necrotic neonate of Sullivan's example. Dr.
White ceases treatment because he regards it as pointless, and
thinks that it will only increase the suffering. He foresees that
death will occur, but he doesn't "seek, choose, or plan that death,
so it is not part of his intention that the baby dies." Dr. Black
also realizes that further treatment is pointless and will only increase the infant's suffering. But his intentions are different: "He
decides that it is better for the baby to die a bit sooner than to go
on suffering pointlessly; so, with the intention of letting the baby
die, he ceases treatment" (p. 142). According to Sullivan's interpretation of the AMA doctrine, Dr. Black's action is impermissible, because it is the intentional termination of the infant's life.
Dr. White's action, on the other hand, appears to be permitted
by the doctrine. But their actions cannot differ in permissibility,
says Rachels, since they did "*the very same thing*." More generally,

Rachels claims that intentions never affect the moral status of actions, but only that of the character of agents.

In "Coming to Terms: A Response to Rachels," written specially for this book, Sullivan continues the debate. He argues that Rachels has to establish a very strong claim to support his position that the difference between intending and foreseeing a death is morally irrelevant. Rachels has to establish the claim that *all* intentions are irrelevant to the moral status of actions. If only some intentions are irrelevant, "it is by no means obvious or even plausible that deadly intentions are among those irrelevant to the evaluation of deadly acts" (p. 156). But how can we maintain that intentions are never relevant? "If we draw out of an act *all* the motivating intention, the residue seems not to be the same act, if it is, properly speaking, any act at all" (p. 156). As for the example of Dr. Black and Dr. White, Sullivan points out that each does something intentionally—he withholds treatment. "For whatever else they intend, they intend not to treat; in the absence of intention there would be nothing properly depictable as a human act and nothing left to evaluate" (pp. 157–58). Therefore, claims Sullivan, Rachels cannot show that *all* intentions are irrelevant to the evaluation of acts.

If we agree with Sullivan that there are no intentionless acts, does it follow that at least some intentions must be relevant to the moral evaluation of acts? I don't think so. Consider the following reasoning: the shape of a piece of clay must, at least in some instances, be relevant to its weight, since there could not be a piece of clay with no shape at all; there would be nothing to weigh. Even if it is true that all pieces of clay must have some shape or other, it doesn't follow that differences in shape are relevant to differences in weight. Likewise, even if it is true that all acts must be accompanied by some intention or other, it doesn't follow that differences in intention are ever relevant to differences in moral status. It may be true that differences in intention are relevant to differences in the *identity* of acts. If so, Rachels should not have claimed that Dr. Black and Dr. White did the very same thing. However, he could claim that the difference in intention affects only the identity of the acts and not their moral status.

Sullivan doesn't address the strongest point in Rachels' argument against the moral relevance of intentions, which is the example itself. Even if we grant that Dr. Black and Dr. White do different things, how could we possibly claim that one is permissible but the other isn't? Look at it from the point of view of the infants themselves. Are we going to refuse Dr. Black's patient relief from suffering because she had the bad luck to get stuck with a doctor who aimed at her death rather than merely foresaw her death? When she complains (metaphorically) that the patient in the next bed, who seems to be in the same condition, is being treated differently, and more humanely, and asks why Dr. Black isn't allowed to do the same for her, we'll explain that her neighbor has Dr. White for a neonatologist, and that what would appear to be the same treatment from Dr. Black would actually be different, because of certain of Dr. Black's mental states. This difference in the mental states of the two doctors, we continue, explains why she must suffer far more excruciating pain than her neighbor.

The fact that the actions of Dr. Black and Dr. White differ only with respect to certain of the mental states that are involved points to a serious problem, namely, one that involves intentions. Even if the difference in the doctors' mental states does render one act permissible and the other impermissible, there will be problems enforcing a policy based on this distinction. Dr. Black will be aware of the policy. If he really wants his patient to die, he will simulate the intentions of Dr. White. How are we to know that his decision to stop treatment is really aimed at the death of his patient, if he doesn't tell us?

There are even deeper and more complex problems with the use of intentions in moral theory that I can only sketch here. The notion of intention is often explicated in terms of explanations of actions. My intent in doing something is what explains my doing it; it is the point or the aim of my action. Consider what Bonnie Steinbock says about a decision not to perform a simple life-saving operation on an infant with Down's syndrome:

> Withholding treatment in this case is the intentional termination of life because the infant is deliberately allowed to die; that is the point of not operating. But there are other cases in which that is not the point. If the point is to avoid inflicting painful treatment on a patient with little or no reasonable hope of success, this is not the intentional termination of life [p. 126].

Consider actual and proposed cases of active euthanasia. How often is the death of the patient really the point of the procedure? In most of those cases which the public tends to approve (at least until they reach the ballot box), but the medical and legal professions deem impermissible, isn't the point of the procedure basically the same as in the permissible cases of terminating life-support? The point of administering a lethal injection to a terminally ill patient who has nothing but the prospect of excruciating pain ahead of him is not to end his life, but to end his suffering. For some patients, the only way to end suffering is to end life, but this doesn't make the point of the action the ending of their lives. Similarly, we know for sure that some patients will die if their life-support is removed, but that in itself doesn't make the point of such removal the ending of their lives. It will be claimed in response to this that the death in the former case is the means to the real point of the action, whereas the death in the permissible cases of terminating life-support is a mere by-product. Even if this is true, it is hard to see how it could be morally relevant. As I said above, the problems surrounding the role of intentions in moral theory are too complex to explore in detail here. For now, I simply state my suspicion that the whole concept of intention may prove to be too fragile to bear the weight required to affect the permissibility of actions.

DOING AND ALLOWING

The distinction between killing and letting die is usually regarded as a specific instance of a more general distinction, variously described as the distinction between doing and allowing, making and allowing, acting and refraining, action and inaction, action and omission, etc. A common tactic in arguing either for or against the moral significance of such a distinction is to present a matched pair of cases in which behavior leads to an upshot, usually harmful. It is then claimed that the evident moral difference or equivalence between the two actions demonstrates that the distinction is or is not morally significant.

Judith Lichtenberg in "The Moral Equivalence of Action and Omission" employs the tactic of presenting a matched pair of

cases to argue her conclusion, but she also criticizes the use of the
tactic by philosophers who attempt to demonstrate a difference
between action and omission. Lichtenberg distinguishes between what she calls "practical" and "necessary" differences
between types of behavior. If there is a necessary moral difference between action and omission, "given a pair of cases parallel
in every respect except that one requires positive action and the
other requires forbearance, . . . the latter [is] more morally binding than the former" (p. 213). There may, however, be morally
relevant characteristics that are contingently connected—highly
correlated—with the action/omission distinction. If we are presented with a pair of cases which differ with respect to the action/
omission distinction, and which differ morally, we may be able
to trace the moral difference to a difference in the contingently
connected characteristics:

> Morally relevant features fall under two general headings: (1) cer-
> tainty or probability of the connection between an act or omission
> and the harm to be avoided; and (2) sacrifice or cost to the agent in
> having to forbear or to act. The idea that there is a moral difference
> between action and omission comes from comparing cases that are
> asymmetrical with respect to these features; when comparable cases
> are compared, the gulf disappears [p. 211].

Lichtenberg presents a pair of cases in which the only difference
is between action and omission. In each case a person is stranded
on a desert island with no source of sustenance and no provisions
left. A ship arrives full of provisions, providing an easy way to
return to the human world, and a sailor comes ashore. In the first
case, the sailor refuses to share his provisions or to take the
stranded man on board, and is ready to leave without him. In the
other case, the sailor attempts to kill the stranded man. Lichtenberg claims that the former sailor's refusal of aid is morally
equivalent to the latter sailor's killing. In fact, she also claims that
the stranded man in the former case would be justified in killing
the sailor, if that were the only way to save his life, just as the
stranded man in the latter case would be justified in killing in self-
defense. Since the distinction between action and omission makes
no moral difference here, the distinction is not morally relevant
in itself.

In "Negation and Abstention: Two Theories of Allowing" Jonathan Bennett returns to the distinction he first presented in "Whatever the Consequences," and later developed at much greater length in his 1980 Tanner Lectures. Bennett labels his distinction the "making/allowing" distinction, but he doesn't claim that it always corresponds to the ordinary usage of those terms. An agent makes an upshot come about if her behavior is "positively relevant" to the upshot; she allows it to come about if her behavior is "negatively relevant" to it. The positive/negative distinction "does not distinguish two kinds of action: there are no negative actions" (p. 232). It is, rather, a distinction between two kinds of propositions, and thus also facts. The propositions in question concern how an agent behaves at one time, specifically, how she moves her body. A negative proposition about an agent's behavior at time T is a very uninformative proposition. What is it for a proposition about behavior to be uninformative? We are to imagine all the different possible movements of an agent's body at T represented on a Venn diagram. If we divide the diagram very unequally, so that most of the possibilities are in the larger portion and relatively few are in the smaller, the larger portion represents a negative fact about the agent's behavior and the smaller portion represents a positive fact. The negative fact is uninformative, because it doesn't tell us very much about the agent's behavior. It merely excludes a few possibilities. We can now see what it is for an agent's conduct to be positively or negatively relevant to a particular upshot. Suppose that an upshot U comes about at T_2, and furthermore that an agent, called Agent, could have behaved so that it didn't come about. Let T_1 be the latest time at which Agent could have behaved differently so that U would not have occurred. What we look for is the weakest fact A about Agent's conduct at T_1 which, when added to a description of Agent's environment, yields a complete causal explanation of U. If A is negative, Agent's conduct at T_1 is negatively relevant to U, that is, she allows U to occur. If A is positive, her conduct is positively relevant to U, that is, she makes U occur.

Consider an example that illustrates both sides of the distinction. Let's say you throw a baseball at T_0, as a result of which a window breaks at T_2. Intuitively, this is a case of making the window break rather than allowing it to break. Bennett's account agrees. The weakest fact about your behavior at T_0 that is needed for an explanation of the window breaking is a fairly specific fact about your throwing the baseball in a certain manner. That you threw the ball in that manner excludes most of the bodily movements you could have made at T_0. It excludes most of the ways you could have thrown the ball, not to mention all the other things you could have done that didn't involve throwing the ball. Now consider my role in the window-breaking episode. We were playing catch. You threw the baseball at T_0, and I could have caught the ball in my mitt as late as T_1. The weakest fact about *my* behavior that explains the breaking of the window is the very weak fact that I didn't interpose my mitt at T_1. This is a very weak fact, because it excludes hardly any of my possible body movements. It tells us very little about what I *was* doing at T_1. Again, Bennett's account fits our intuitions about this case. Even though you, fairly clearly, *made* the window break, I, just as clearly, *allowed* it to break.

When Bennett first presented his distinction in "Whatever the Consequences," he presented it in terms of the distinction between killing and letting die. In fact, the distinction fits the vast majority of cases of killing and letting die. However, it was a fairly easy matter for opponents to concoct examples that seem to involve killing, but are judged otherwise by Bennett's account. I will consider such an attack by Warren Quinn later. In the light of these attacks, Bennett no longer claims to have provided an analysis of our ordinary uses of "kill" and "let die," or, more broadly, "make" and "allow." His purpose is to present a distinction that underlies much of our thinking on these matters and to show that it cannot be of moral relevance. Few, if any, would dispute his claim that his distinction cannot bear any moral weight. Those who think that there is a morally significant distinction between making and allowing must come up with an alternative account. In "Negation and Abstention" Bennett presents what he considers to be the most considerable rival to his account, provided by Alan Donagan, and argues both that the two accounts collaborate in shaping our intuitions, and that alternative accounts, when viable, are best understood as versions of Donagan's account.

Donagan defines an action as "a deed done in a particular situation or set of circumstances; . . . [consisting] partly of [the agent's] own bodily and mental states."[4] He continues:

> Should he be deprived of all power of action, the situation, including his bodily and mental states, would change according to the laws of nature. His deeds as an agent are either interventions in that natural process or abstentions from intervention. When he intervenes, he can be described as causing whatever would not have occurred had he abstained; and when he abstains, as allowing to happen whatever would not have happened had he intervened. Hence, from the point of view of action, the situation is conceived as passive, and the agent, *qua* agent, as external to it. He is like a *deus ex machina* whose interventions make a difference to what otherwise would naturally come about without them.[5]

In considering what would have happened if Agent hadn't acted, Donagan asks what would have happened in "the course of nature" (his phrase). The course of nature can include not only Agent's physical presence, but also changes in her "bodily and mental states." It is the exercise of human agency that gives Agent the option to intervene in the course of nature or to allow nature to take its course. All of Agent's deeds are either interventions or abstentions. Those that make a difference to the course of nature, or what would have happened anyway, are interventions; those that leave the course of nature unchanged are abstentions.

Bennett contends that his making/allowing distinction and Donagan's active/passive distinction both underlie common-sense intuitions about making and allowing:

> I conclude that Donagan and I are both right. When people use the locutions that express the making/allowing distinction, they may be guided by the abstention thought or by the negativeness thought or by both at once. . . . In the form in which most people have it, the making/allowing distinction does not equip them to deal with the odd cases where only one of those thoughts is available [pp. 249–50].

Bennett admits that Donagan's active/passive distinction is not so obviously devoid of moral significance as his own making/ allowing distinction. However, it is hard to see how it *can* carry moral weight. If my behavior leads to a harmful upshot, and I could have behaved so that the upshot did not occur, what differ-

ence does it make whether the upshot would have occurred if I
hadn't exercised my agency at all? Bennett therefore places the
burden of proof on those who would invest Donagan's distinction
with moral weight. If we are to show that the difference between
making and allowing is morally significant, we must either explain why Donagan's distinction carries moral weight, or provide
a different account of the distinction and an explanation of how
that account is morally relevant.

In "Killing and Letting Die" Phillipa Foot presents a distinction
that focuses on the question of whether someone is "the agent"
of harm to someone else. When the harm in question is death,
this distinction corresponds roughly to the killing/letting die distinction. She illustrates her distinction with the following two
stories: In Rescue I we can save either five people in danger of
drowning in one place or one person drowning somewhere else.
In Rescue II, we can save the five drowning people only by driving
over and killing someone who is trapped on the road. In Rescue
I we act permissibly if we save the five, even though the one dies
as a result. We let the one die. In Rescue II we do not act permissibly if we save the five. The only way to save the five involves
killing the one. The distinction, according to Foot, is between
originating or sustaining a fatal sequence on the one hand, and
allowing such a sequence to run its course on the other. It is often
permissible, she claims, to bring about a harm by the latter
method that could not permissibly be brought about by the former. What explains this moral difference? Foot's answer harks
back to one of the themes of her earlier paper "The Problem of
Abortion and the Doctrine of the Double Effect." The different
types of agency receive their moral significance via their connection with different types of right:

> For there are rights to noninterference, which form one class of
> rights; and there are also rights to goods or services, which are
> different. . . . Typically, it takes more to justify an interference
> than to justify the withholding of goods or services . . . [p. 284].

Originating or sustaining a harmful sequence will usually involve
the violation of a right to noninterference, whereas allowing such
a sequence to run its course will, at most, involve the violation
of a right to goods or services. The former type of right is

stronger than the latter, so the former type of agency is less likely to be permissible than the latter. Notice that this way of arguing for the moral significance of the distinction does not imply that the distinction always matters morally. There may be circumstances in which a particular harmful result cannot permissibly be brought about by either interference or withholding aid. Even if a right to noninterference is stricter than a right to be given aid, it will often be the case that neither right can permissibly be violated.

This could provide an answer to Lichtenberg's pair of cases. Perhaps the stranded man's right not to be killed is stricter than his right to be saved, but neither right is overridden in the examples. That the sailor acts impermissibly in each case, and the only difference between the cases is the difference between action and omission, does not in itself demonstrate the moral equivalence of action and omission. Lichtenberg could, perhaps, reply that if there were a moral difference between action and omission, we could expect to find *some* moral difference between the two sailors' actions, even if not a difference in permissibility. We might expect to find that one impermissible action was actually worse than the other. Foot, of course, might reply that this is so, and any temptation to judge the two actions entirely morally equivalent comes from our recognition that they are both morally impermissible. There is a general point that could be made here about the use of pairs of cases. If we present a pair of cases, in each of which the protagonist acts very badly, it may be difficult for our intuitions to detect a moral difference between the cases, even when there is one. Our intuitions are drowned out, so to speak. Similarly, if I ask who was the worse dictator, Hitler or Stalin, you might not be able to tell the difference, even though it is highly likely that one was worse than the other.

Foot's claim about the relative strictness of positive and negative rights and duties has a good deal of intuitive support. My right not to be poisoned does seem stronger than my right, if any, to be given the food I need to survive. However, as an explanation of a morally significant difference between killing and letting die, this appeal to different types of rights simply diverts the question. If the moral difference between positive and negative rights is to provide a satisfactory explanation of the moral difference between killing and letting die, we also need an explanation of the former difference. *Why* is my right not to be poisoned stronger than my right to be given the food I need to survive? The answer that springs most readily to mind is that it is worse to kill me than to let me die. But this can be of no help to Foot's approach, since it merely takes us in a circle. Perhaps a theory of rights can be given that explains the relative strength of positive and negative rights without any appeal to an alleged moral difference between making and allowing. Such a theory, if plausible, could provide Foot's approach with the explanatory power it needs.

Warren Quinn in "Actions, Intentions, and Consequences: The Doctrine of Doing and Allowing" criticizes both Bennett's and Foot's accounts of the doing/allowing distinction. His criticism of Bennett is directed against Bennett's 1980 Tanner Lectures, but it would also apply to Bennett's more recent work. Quinn complains that Bennett's account gives the wrong results in cases involving immobility:

> Bennett imagines a situation in which if Henry does nothing, just stays where he is, dust will settle and close a tiny electric circuit which will cause something bad—for example, an explosion that will kill Bill. If Henry does nothing, he is by Bennett's criterion positively instrumental in Bill's death. . . . But suppose Henry could save five only by staying where he is—suppose he is holding a net into which five are falling. Surely he might then properly refuse to move even though it means not saving Bill. . . . Bennett also misses the opposite case. Suppose the device will go off only if Henry makes some move or other. In that case his instrumentality in the death would, for Bennett, be negative. But those who would rule out Rescue II would surely not allow Henry to go to the rescue of five if that meant setting off the device. For his agency in the death of Bill would in that case seem positive [p. 362].

Bennett's answer to what he calls "the immobility objection" is to admit that if Henry does nothing (in the first example), he allows the dust to fall. This, he claims, "is an example of how the detailed meaning of the word 'allow' is a poor guide in our present problem area" (p. 239). In their ordinary uses of such locutions as "make" and "allow," says Bennett, "people are guided by a clean, deep concept, but only imperfectly, because they sometimes drift away from it and use the terminology of making/

allowing in ways that have no solid conceptual support" (p. 241). Bennett, unlike most others who write on the topic, is not attempting to give an account of a distinction between making and allowing that fits *all* our intuitions about particular cases. These intuitions, according to Bennett, are shaped by so many factors that there isn't a single clear distinction to explain them all. His distinction, and Donagan's, do seem to lie behind a vast number of our intuitive judgments. Bennett also points out that immobility will usually fall on the negative, or allowing, side of his line. Almost every actual case of immobility leading to a harmful upshot will be a case of allowing. Our intuitions might be conditioned by this almost constant conjunction of immobility to allowing to judge even positive cases of immobility as allowings. We might, to use Lichtenberg's terminology, be mistaking a practical difference for a necessary one.

Bennett's complaint that we can be led astray by too much attention to the ordinary usage of "allow" seems to be borne out by Quinn's judgment of another case. Quinn considers a variation on the second Henry example. In this variation, Henry's movement triggers an explosion by allowing dust to settle on a spot he was shielding with his body. In this case, according to Quinn, Henry does not so much set off the explosion as allow it to be set off. It is, therefore, permissible for Henry to go to the rescue of the five, even though Bill is blown up as a consequence. Clearly something has gone wrong here. Quinn seems to be making the permissibility of Henry's going off to save the five dependent on the mechanics of the triggering device of the bomb that will kill Bill.

Quinn's criticism of Foot's account is more successful. He points out that Foot will have to appeal to the distinction between action and inaction to explain the difference between allowing a sequence to complete itself and keeping it going when it would otherwise have stopped. Quinn also points to a problem with the strategy of identifying already existing fatal sequences. Suppose I have always fired up my aged neighbor's furnace before it runs out of fuel. An emergency arises involving five other neighbors, whom I can save only if I rush off and let my neighbor freeze. Have I simply allowed an already existing fatal sequence to polish off my neighbor? She wasn't in any danger before I rushed off.

Perhaps we could say that she was in danger, because I might have failed to do something to help her. This strategy will have to rely on the distinction between action and inaction in order to avoid the conclusion that we are all constantly in danger from already existing fatal sequences. There is a fundamental problem here for any approach to the distinction between making and allowing that relies on the notion of a pre-existing threat or harmful sequence.

Quinn's own position is stated as follows:

> Harmful positive agency is that in which an agent's most direct contribution to the harm is an action, whether his own or that of some object. Harmful negative agency is that in which the most direct contribution is an inaction, a failure to prevent the harm [p. 367].

Furthermore, the notion of direct contribution is explained as follows:

> An agent's *most direct contribution* to a harmful upshot of his agency is the contribution that most directly explains the harm. And one contribution explains harm more directly than another if the explanatory value of the second is exhausted in the way it explains the first [p. 366].

Quinn's account thus relies on the notions of action and inaction. He is not, of course, claiming that an agent has to be inactive in order to allow something to happen. It is, rather, an agent's inactivity in a particular respect that is important. I might be exceedingly active at the time that I allow some harm to befall you, but my inactivity with respect to preventing the harm is my most direct contribution to the harm. It is my failure to prevent the harm that most directly explains the harm. This sounds very much like Bennett's account. That I failed to prevent a harm at a particular time is most likely a very uninformative fact about me. Quinn's notion of more and less direct explanation could be read in terms of Bennett's stress on the weakest fact necessary to explain an upshot. Although such a reading of Quinn seems to make a lot of sense on its own terms, it is clearly not what Quinn intended. He explicitly rejects Bennett's approach in terms of facts about behavior. On the other hand, it is hard to see how to make Quinn's approach work without recourse to facts. If we imagine that an agent's behavior consists of actions and inactions, we need to be able to explain the difference between the two. Ordinary language won't be of any help. We can just as easily describe my failure to save the one in Foot's Rescue I as my consigning him to his fate. Is this piece of behavior an action or an inaction? Likewise, my driving over the one in her Rescue II could be described as my failure to avoid him. We might employ a theory of action according to which my failure to save the one and my consigning him to his fate are actually two different pieces of behavior, the one an inaction and the other an action. This won't help Quinn's analysis, though, since the inaction in this case doesn't explain the death of the one any more directly than does the action. If Quinn's account is best understood as a version of Bennett's account, it clearly can't explain how harmful positive agency is morally worse than harmful negative agency. Even if it is not a version of Bennett's account, it is hard to see how to get moral significance from the distinction. Why should it matter whether my most direct contribution to a harm is an action or an inaction?

Jeff McMahan in "Killing, Letting Die, and Withdrawing Aid" declares that "The concepts of killing and letting die are not evaluatively neutral. Yet their use, while reflecting certain moral beliefs, is nevertheless governed primarily by empirical criteria" (p. 383). The task of uncovering the empirical criteria is particularly important:

> For, since the empirical criteria determine a way of applying the concepts that we recognize as having moral significance, it seems that the criteria themselves must have moral significance. Mapping our use of the concepts helps to reveal the contours of common-sense morality. Discovering the criteria for their use helps to reveal the deeper foundations of that morality [p. 383].

To reveal the foundations of a morality is not necessarily to justify it, though. In fact, one of McMahan's aims is to cast doubt on the moral relevance of the killing/letting die distinction by revealing what underlies it.

Instead of attempting to analyze the concepts of killing and letting die in general, McMahan focuses on problem cases involving the removal or withdrawal of life-supporting aid or protection. He concludes that a variety of factors conspire to render a case one of killing or one of letting die. These factors most notably include the following: (i) whether the person who withdraws the aid is the person who initially provided it; (ii) whether the aid is operative or as-yet-inoperative when it is withdrawn; (iii) whether the aid is self-sustaining or requires further intervention from the agent.

Whether aid is self-sustaining could well be a vague matter, leading to uncertainty as to how to classify some cases. The classic problem case involving a doctor turning off a mechanical life-support mechanism that she herself provided is just such a case. Many, perhaps most, people classify this as a case of letting die, but a significant number judge it to be a case of killing. McMahan suggests that the difficulty in classifying this case stems from "a lack of clarity about whether or not a life-support machine counts as a self-sustaining form of aid" (p. 400). A life-support machine does, after all, require monitoring and maintenance. Interesting as this suggestion is, I don't think it is correct. The invention of a completely reliable maintenance-free life-support machine would not affect the uncertainty involved in judging this case.

The question of whether aid is operative or as-yet-inoperative may also involve uncertainty. One of McMahan's examples of operative aid is given in the following example:

> *The Pipe Sealer.*—An earthquake cracks a pipe at a factory, releasing poisonous chemicals into the water supply. Before a dangerous amount is released, a worker seals the pipe. But a year later he returns and removes the seal. As a result, numerous people die from drinking contaminated water [p. 389].

McMahan claims that this is clearly a case of killing, since the seal on the pipe is both operative and self-sustaining. An example of as-yet-inoperative aid is a safety net positioned below a person who has jumped from a burning building and is still in the air. If the person who positioned the net immediately repositions it to save two others, he does not kill the first jumper, but only lets him die. The aid here is self-sustaining, but it is as-yet-inoperative, if moved before the first jumper hits it. These cases may seem clear enough, but consider the following: a plumber installs a totally reliable maintenance-free water filter designed to remove a specific type of toxic particle from a household water supply. A year later, he removes the filter, and soon afterwards the residents die from poisoned water. Does the plumber kill the people? The case, as described, seems just like the pipe sealer, in which case the answer should be yes. Let me add one more detail. Throughout the year in which the filter is in place, there are no toxic particles in the water coming into the house, so the filter doesn't actually remove any. Soon after the plumber removes the filter, purely coincidentally, toxic particles show up for the first time. Was the filter operative or as-yet-inoperative aid when it was removed? It was designed to catch toxic particles, and it hadn't ever done so. In this respect it seems just like the safety net. And yet this added detail makes no difference to our assessment of the plumber's behavior. Do we really think that the plumber kills the residents if he removes the filter just after the toxic particles start coming into the house, but that he merely lets them die if he removes it just before? Perhaps we could say that the filter was operative all along because it was catching any toxic particles that passed through it. There just didn't happen to be any. The problem with this suggestion is that it could just as easily be applied to the safety net to render it operative.

The problems I have raised for two of McMahan's suggested criteria do not prove that they play no role in our ordinary thinking about killing and letting die. The situation is, as McMahan says, very complicated. However, the ease with which it is possible to invent counterexamples to suggested criteria for the uses of "kill" and "let die" may ring warning bells concerning the whole enterprise of supplying such criteria. It could be that there simply is no systematic way to characterize the ordinary uses of these terms, no matter how much complication we are prepared to endure. Part of the problem is that there is a good deal of disagreement about particular cases, unrelated to an uncertainty as to how to apply McMahan's criteria. A lot of the disagreement arises from the fact that many people are guided in their application of the terms, at least in part, by their moral judgments of the cases themselves.

McMahan has a different explanation for the complexity of the task he has undertaken:

> Our intuitions about killing and letting die are indeed based on considerations that are relatively simple. . . . But, because of the

unruly complexity of reality, it is often difficult to determine what these considerations imply about the classification of a particular case [p. 402].

And what are these relatively simple criteria?

> In short, the fundamental intuitive difference between killing and letting die is that in cases of killing we assign primary causal responsibility for a person's death to an agent's intervention in the person's life, whereas, in cases of letting die, primary responsibility for the death is attributed to factors other than any intervention by the agent [p. 411].

This seems very similar to Donagan's active/passive distinction, which is also couched in terms of "intervention." And, like Donagan's distinction, it doesn't clearly bear moral weight. As McMahan says, "it is difficult to believe that the way in which an agent is instrumental in the occurrence of an outcome could be more important than the nature of the outcome itself" (p. 413). Thus, he claims, a deeper understanding of the distinction between killing and letting die may reveal that intuitions that are "central to any morality that we could bring ourselves to accept" are "apparently ungrounded" (p. 413).

I suspect that McMahan is right to claim that the intuition that there is a morally significant difference between killing and letting die is ungrounded. It is less clear that this intuition is central to any morality that we could bring ourselves to accept. However, if we reject the moral significance of the distinction between killing and letting die, we will most likely have to accept more than just the permissibility of active euthanasia. If there is no morally significant difference between killing and letting die, it is that much harder to justify our neglect of the underprivileged, both in our own country and abroad. We might well be forced to conclude that most of us who possess even modest resources are seriously at fault for not doing more to help others. This conclusion could certainly be painful. The unpleasantness of a moral conclusion is, however, neither evidence for its falsity nor even its unacceptability. If we have to choose between a position that is ungrounded and one with painful implications, we should grit our teeth and choose the latter.

NOTES

1. Alan Meisel, "The Legal Consensus About Forgoing Life-Sustaining Treatment: Its Status and Its Prospects," *Kennedy Institute of Ethics Journal*, 2, no. 4 (December 1992), 309–45.

2. *Ibid.*, 326, 331.

3. The legal consensus recently received a blow in the form of a decision by U.S. District Judge Barbara Rothstein which struck down as unconstitutional a Washington state law against assisted suicide. Judge Rothstein said that the law placed an undue burden on the 14th Amendment liberty interests of terminally ill, mentally competent adults. More significant for the issues of this book, she said that it unconstitutionally distinguishes between two similarly situated groups, since Washington allows terminally ill patients to hasten their deaths by removing life-support, but bans physicians from giving medication at their patients' request to achieve the same result. She said that from a constitutional perspective the distinction between refusing life-sustaining medical treatment and physician-assisted suicide by an uncoerced, mentally competent, terminally ill adult cannot be made.

4. Alan Donagan, *The Theory of Morality* (Chicago: The University of Chicago Press, 1977), p. 42.

5. *Ibid.*, pp. 42–43.

Introduction

Bonnie Steinbock

The Controversy

THAT IT IS ONE THING to kill someone and quite another to let that person die is a common assumption. Precisely how to distinguish killing from letting die might be a task best left to philosophers, but the assumption that there is a distinction, and that the distinction has moral significance, is clearly reflected in our law, in religious discussions, and in contemporary medical writing.

It seems to be generally true that it is worse to kill a person than to let him or her die. When Kitty Genovese was stabbed to death on a New York street, thirty-eight people heard her screams and did nothing at all—not even call the police—to help her. Depending on their degree of awareness of the situation (that she was in danger of death) and their ability to do something about it, it seems probable that at least some of the thirty-eight could be said to have let her die. But under our legal system, they are guilty of no crime. And from a moral point of view, their behavior, while reprehensible, isn't as bad as that of her killer.

Philosophers have begun to question the moral significance of the killing/letting die distinction. They ask, first, how the distinction should be characterized, and secondly, whether the distinction provides support for our moral judgments. In general, killing someone involves actually doing something to the person which causes his or her death. Causing death by stabbing, drowning, poisoning—these are clearcut examples of killing. Letting die usually involves *refraining* from doing something that could save a person in mortal danger: not calling the police, not throwing the lifeline, not operating. But there can be cases of killing in which the killer does nothing (e.g., killing by starving to death), and there can be cases of letting die which involve doing something (e.g., hiding the lifeline that could save the drowning person). We see, then, that even characterizing the distinction correctly is a

24

difficult task. Even more difficult is determining its moral relevance.

Should the fact that a form of behavior is more correctly characterized as a killing or as a letting die affect our judgment of its rightness or wrongness? The answer may seem to be obviously yes. After all, it is clearly against the law to kill another person (with certain exceptions, such as self-defense); and with certain exceptions, the law is indifferent to letting die. Secondly, the Sixth Commandment explicitly prohibits killing (or wrongful killing) but is silent about letting die. And while the Hippocratic Oath explicitly enjoins doctors from giving deadly medicine to anyone, it does not provide clear guidance concerning when treatment may be omitted and a patient allowed to die. In three areas, then— law, religion, and medicine—the moral significance of the killing/ letting die distinction seems to be upheld.

Most philosophers who question the moral significance of the killing/letting die distinction are not denying that often it does make a difference. Rather, they maintain that it is certain features usually connected with, but not essential to, the distinction which make the moral difference. One of these features is the *motivation* of the agent. The motivation of a person who kills someone is generally, though not always, more evil than the motivation of a person who merely lets someone die. Another feature is the *certainty of the outcome*. A death is usually more certain if one is trying to kill than if one is merely refraining from preventing a death.

These features help to explain why it is generally thought that killing is worse than letting die, and why letting die may be permissible where killing would be wrong. But what if, in certain cases, these features are irrelevant or symmetrical? Does the killing/letting die distinction have moral significance then? This question is important in our thinking about euthanasia and infanticide.

Often a distinction is drawn between active and passive euthanasia. Active euthanasia involves intentionally killing the patient for reasons of compassion. Passive euthanasia involves refraining from doing something that could prolong or save a human life, for reasons of compassion. Many members of the medical profession acknowledge engaging in, and support the idea of, passive euthanasia, while strongly rejecting the idea of active euthanasia. But why? The motivation—compassion—is the same, as is the end result. Are there other morally relevant features which differentiate active and passive euthanasia?

Some doctors might appeal to the law in their support of passive and rejection of active euthanasia. The legal attitude toward active and passive euthanasia will be discussed in detail in the following section. But even if it were true that the law allowed passive euthanasia while forbidding active euthanasia (and this is not quite accurate), this does not necessarily imply that there is a moral difference between the two. Outlawing one kind of behavior and allowing another can be a result of legal reasons which have nothing to do with morality.

The Hippocratic Oath might be cited in support of the active/passive euthanasia distinction. But mere allegiance to an oath without critical thought will not do—perhaps the oath should be revised? In any event, the Hippocratic Oath is consistent with regarding any sort of euthanasia as wrong, as opposed to supporting a distinction between active and passive euthanasia.

Michael Tooley and James Rachels are two philosophers who maintain that the active/passive euthanasia distinction rests on the killing/letting die distinction. They attack that distinction in order to show that the active/passive euthanasia distinction is without moral significance. More important, they believe that the maintenance of this distinction can lead to appalling results—e.g., leaving a defective infant to starve to death slowly rather than killing it quickly and painlessly.

In order to show that the distinction between killing and letting die is itself without moral importance, both Tooley and Rachels construct parallel cases which are supposed to be exactly alike except that one involves killing and the other letting die. They then ask whether this difference makes any difference to moral assessment and both conclude that it makes no difference at all. Where the motive and the intention are the same, the distinction between killing and letting die is without moral significance. Intentionally letting die, according to Tooley, is as bad (or as good) as intentionally killing, and the belief that there is a critical moral difference reflects either "confused thinking" or a "moral point of view unrelated to the interests of individuals."

The American Medical Association rejects the intentional termination of the life of one human being by another, but allows, in certain cases, for the cessation of treatment. Clearly, the AMA does not regard all cases of cessation of treatment as intentionally ending a life. To this Rachels responds, "This is where the mistake comes in, for what is the cessation of treatment, in these circumstances, if it is not 'the intentional termination of the life of one human being by another'? Of course it is exactly that, and if it were not, there would be no point to it."

The question, then, is not whether the distinction between killing and letting die is in itself morally significant, but what *is* the intentional termination of a life? Is foreseeing the death as certain sufficient to characterize a doctor's ceasing treatment as intentional termination of life? Or must doctors cease treatment *in order to* cause death for their action to be so described? This second condition is not always met. It may be that the doctor discontinues treatment in order to comply with the patient's request. Even if the patient wants to die, this does not mean that this is the doctor's reason for terminating treatment.

A doctor may also refrain from initiating or continuing treatment because she or he thinks that the benefits of treatment do not justify the amount of suffering that will be inflicted on the patient. This is particularly so when treatment prolongs life but cannot cure or ameliorate the condition. Many doctors would want to distinguish between foreseeing that death will occur without treatment and intending that the patient die. It may be that this distinction cannot be drawn or that it lacks moral significance, but this is not obvious and would have to be shown.

The killing/letting die controversy is of interest to philosophers engaged in normative ethics. But it is also of interest to philosophers interested in theory of action and meta-ethics, because it raises questions about other distinctions: acts/omissions, acts/consequences, intention/foresight, to name a few. It also raises questions about *responsibility for an action* which are fundamental to any moral theory. Finally, it is of the utmost significance to moral philosophers for its role in the dispute between consequentialism and absolutism.

Consequentialism is a type of ethical theory (of which the most famous representative is utilitarianism) which determines the rightness or wrongness of actions ultimately (and perhaps solely) in terms of the goodness or badness of their consequences. Opponents of consequentialism have maintained that there are morally relevant features besides the goodness or badness of the consequences (whatever the standard of goodness or badness), including *how* the consequences are brought about. In particular, absolutists have maintained that there are some ways of bringing about consequences (certain types of action, that is) which are absolutely forbidden—killing the innocent is a paradigm. Even when refraining from killing the innocent would have worse consequences than killing (e.g., more deaths), absolutists hold that it is still impermissible to kill the innocent. This seems to commit absolutism to a belief in the moral significance of the killing/letting die distinction. Indeed, in "Whatever the Consequences" Jonathan Bennett claims that absolutism depends on this distinction and maintains that if this distinction can be shown to be without moral force, absolutism (he calls it "conservatism") can be shown to be muddled. Bennett, then, uses the killing/letting die question as part of a larger attack on absolutism. To know if his strategy works, we will have to ask ourselves whether he shows the distinction between killing and letting die to be morally insignificant and if absolutism does indeed rest on the killing/letting die distinction.

At this point, it will be helpful to understand the legal, medical, and religious background to the controversy. Each area will help in our attempt to understand why the distinction has been thought to have moral significance and to evaluate that belief.

THE LEGAL ASPECT

Our obligation to refrain from killing our fellow human beings is fairly precise. What about our legal obligation to prevent death, to give aid, to save? The law in several European countries subjects to penal liability anyone who knowingly fails to assist a helpless person, where such assistance can be rendered without danger to himself or others. By contrast, one is not in general required by Anglo-American law to give aid to strangers—even if one could do so without hardship to oneself or others.

The situation is changed where there is a special relationship between the one needing aid and the one in a position to give aid.

A doctor has a special responsibility for a patient; a parent is obligated to care for a child. Roles can impose moral obligations from which legal duties arise. However, there are situations in which a moral obligation is clearly present and there is no legal obligation. (Kitty Genovese is a case in point.)

Although Anglo-American law does not require one to give aid to strangers, it does require that one refrain from harming them. It also recognizes the possibility that harm can be caused by omission as well as by commission. The extent to which criminal liability can be founded on a failure to act in the absence of a special relationship is, except in the case of various relatively minor statutory offenses, the subject of much debate among legal scholars. The orthodox view is that "a homicide resulting from an omission is noncriminal, even though intentional, unless there is a duty to act."[1] The duty to act may be created by statute or assumed by contract, and the courts have imposed it as an incident of some special relationship where there is dependence on one side and support on the other. The dependency to impose such a duty has increased somewhat in recent decades.

A more innovative view is that there is no difference in principle in criminal liability between causing a death by a positive act and causing a death by omission.[2] In both cases, according to this view, criminal responsibility is established by causal responsibility for the death and *mens rea* (a guilty mind; criminal intent), the actual or imputed intent to cause harm. The requirement of *mens rea* does not necessitate showing that the defendant's intentions were malicious but only that he or she believe that harm was likely to occur as a result of what he or she did. Normally one causes harm by a positive act, but one can equally cause harm by "cooperating with"external elements. Hall gives the example of a man who, wanting his wife dead, does nothing to help her when she has caught her foot on a railroad track and is trapped by an oncoming train, although he easily could free her at no risk to himself. Although the man does nothing, Hall thinks that he is causally and criminally responsible for her death.

If, however, the same man were not married to the trapped woman, it is unlikely he would be held criminally responsible for her death, even if he wanted her dead and refrained from helping her for that reason alone. This means either that (a) a special

relationship is evidentially necessary to establish *mens rea* or (b) a
duty to act (deriving from statute, contract, or a special relationship) is logically necessary to establish causal responsibility or (c)
causal responsibility and *mens rea* are not sufficient to establish
criminal responsibility in the case of homicide by omission, in the
absence of a duty to give aid. Therefore, it seems that a specific
duty to give aid is essential for criminal responsibility in the case
of omissions and this, it would seem, is enough to distinguish
homicide by omission and homicide by commission.

One important relationship which gives rise to a legal obligation to give aid when needed is that between doctor and patient. In "Prolonging Life: Some Legal Considerations," George
Fletcher says, "The factor of reliance and responsible expectation
that the doctor will render aid means that the doctor is legally
obligated to do so. His failure to do so is then tantamount to an
intentional infliction of harm." Motivation here, as in the case of
assertive killing, is irrelevant in analyzing liability for omitting to
render aid when one is obligated to do so. But when is a doctor
obligated to give aid? This is determined in part by the requirements of the relationship and on prevailing medical standards and
practices. Failure to render aid on the part of a doctor will probably not be construed as tantamount to an intentional infliction
of harm unless the doctor has fallen short of prevailing medical
standards.[3]

The difference, then, between acts and omissions is crucial. If
the case is an act, the relationship between doctor and patient is
irrelevant. If an omission, the relationship is extremely important
in determining the doctor's duty. Suppose, for example, a doctor
fails to put a comatose patient with little or no brain activity on
a mechanical respirator. If this is standard practice (and consistent
with societal and legal norms), the doctor will not be criminally
or civilly liable, should the patient die. But what about turning
the respirator off after the patient has been put on? Is this homicide? Fletcher argues that, depending on the state of the patient,
we might regard this as an omission rather than an act. If the
patient is beyond recovery and on the verge of death, it would be
more accurate to describe turning off the respirator as "permitting
death to occur" than as "causing death."

Although Fletcher does not say so, it seems clear that the characterization of turning off the respirator in this type of situation as an omission depends not only on the permitting/causing harm distinction but also on the special relationship between doctor and patient. For if someone without authority—a relative, say— turned off the respirator, and death of the patient ensued, he or she could be criminally liable. It appears that just as the special relationship imposes obligations from which liability can incur, so it also affords special protection.

The question of whether a physician can be liable for criminal homicide in removing a comatose terminal patient from a life-support machine was crucial in the case of Karen Ann Quinlan, who became comatose in April 1975 and was placed on a respirator to assist her breathing. Her condition was characterized as a "chronic persistent vegetative state." Although not dead by prevailing legal or medical criteria, her brain was so damaged as to preclude any reasonable hope for her returning to cognitive, sapient existence, and there was no form of treatment that could cure or improve her condition. When Karen's family became reconciled to the certainty of her impending death, they requested that the doctor remove her from the life-support mechanism. The doctor, however, refused, in accordance with his conception of medical standards, practice, and ethics. Karen's father then sought to be appointed the guardian of her person and property and sought the express power of authorizing the discontinuation of all extraordinary procedures for sustaining her vital processes.

The Superior Court of New Jersey refused to appoint Joseph Quinlan guardian of his daughter's person and ruled that it was a reasonable construction of the homicide law of New Jersey that implementation by the physician of the authorization would constitute homicide. Judge Muir wrote:

> The common law concept of homicide, the unlawful killing of one person by another, is reflected in our codified law. The intentional taking of another's life, regardless of motive, is sufficient grounds for conviction. . . . Humanitarian motives cannot justify the taking of a human life. . . . The fact that the victim is on the threshold of death or in terminal condition is no defense to a homicide charge. . . .

It is difficult to reconcile this statement with his prior holding that the decision as to whether Karen should be removed from the respirator was a medical decision, not a judicial one.

While it is true that the terminal condition of a victim is no *defense* to a homicide charge, Fletcher's point is that the patient's being on the threshold of death might incline us to view the removal from a respirator as an omission rather than an act, and therefore (if within guidelines provided by standard medical practice) not as a homicide at all. That Judge Muir failed to understand this is revealed when he alludes to Fletcher's point and dismisses it, saying, "An intricate discussion on semantics and form is not required since the substance of the sought-for authorization would result in the taking of the life of Karen Quinlan when the law of the State indicates that such an authorization would be homicide."

On appeal, the Supreme Court of New Jersey held that, while removing Karen Quinlan from the respirator would undoubtedly hasten her death, "the ensuing death would not be homicide but rather expiration from existing natural causes." Chief Justice Hughes went on to say that even if it were to be regarded as homicide, it would not be unlawful, for the constitutional right to privacy includes the right to refuse treatment. The termination of treatment pursuant to this right would be ipso facto lawful. "There is a real and in this case determinative distinction between the unlawful taking of the life of another and the ending of artificial life-support systems as a matter of self-determination." Although Karen's physical condition precluded her asserting the right to privacy herself, the Court decided that it was reasonable to assume that Karen—or anyone—would prefer to be spared a few months of vegetative existence with no realistic possibility of returning to any semblance of cognitive or sapient life, and that in these circumstances the right to privacy could be asserted by her parents on her behalf.

The Court recognized the State's interest in preserving life, but held that this interest weakens and the individual's right to privacy grows as the degree of bodily invasion increases and the prognosis dims. Since Karen's prognosis was extremely poor and the bodily invasion very great, it was held that her rights overrode the State's interest.

The Quinlan case is interesting in relation to the killing/letting die question in several respects. First, it reveals the difficulty of applying the distinction in any clear way. If turning off the respirator is viewed as a positive act, as killing, then it is homicide, and may be prohibited. Both Karen's doctor and Judge Muir regarded it in this way. Chief Justice Hughes, however, agreed with Fletcher in classifying the process of turning off the respirator when the patient is beyond recovery and on the verge of death as an omission, as permitting rather than causing death to occur. (In fact, upon removal from the respirator, Karen Quinlan did not die immediately, but lived on, in a persistent vegetative state, for about ten years.) Hughes' and Fletcher's interpretation clearly stresses the importance of causal responsibility rather than, say, movement/nonmovement, to the acts/omissions distinction. But when can one be said to be causally responsible for a death? An analysis of causal responsibility is a knotty philosophic problem but it is absolutely essential for both legal theorists and moral philosophers. Establishing causal responsibility for outcomes would seem to be necessary for ascribing moral responsibility. At the same time, the judgment that A caused B may be, in the case of A's deliberately refraining from doing something that would have prevented B, a function of a moral judgment that A ought to have prevented B. It may be that in the case of omissions, causal and moral responsibility are hopelessly intertwined and that the one cannot serve as a basis for the other.

There is another way in which the Quinlan case bears on the killing/letting die question. One of the justifications for removing Karen from the respirator was her right to privacy, interpreted as the right to refuse treatment. In general, this right has been restricted to competent adults, but the interesting question is whether such a right implies "a right to die." If so, then one might plausibly argue that it is arbitrary to restrict this right only to those who will die quickly without intervention. In other words, the right to privacy might be thought to include, at least in some cases, a right to be killed. Some legal theorists[4] carefully distinguish the right to reject medical treatment, even where such a choice means the patient's death, from suicide and, by implication, euthanasia. But in a discussion of the legality of euthanasia, writer Edward M. Scher asks:

> What justifies such a diametrically different treatment for euthanasia? It is the contention of this paper that no such justification

exists, because the distinction between a refusal of compulsory lifesaving treatment and euthanasia is all but illusory.[5]

In Scher's view, if a patient may refuse lifesaving treatment, he or she ought also to be allowed to request euthanasia. Whereas our discussion so far has concerned the distinction between killing and letting die, our focus is now on being killed versus being allowed to die. Scher sees no justification for different treatment apparently because in both cases, death is the intended end result.

However, it is not always the case that a patient refuses lifesaving treatment *in order to* die. Treatment may be refused because, offering no hope for a cure, it merely prolongs the patient's suffering. Such was the case of Mrs. Carmen Martinez, a 72-year-old Miami resident suffering from terminal hemolytic anemia, who refused "cut-down" transfusions and the removal of her spleen. The court ruled that Mrs. Martinez could not be forced to undergo the surgery and she died in less than a day. In the decision, the court affirmed the right of a conscious adult patient who is mentally competent to refuse medical treatment, even when the best medical opinion deems it essential to save her life. Noting the carefully circumscribed language of the *Martinez* court as a caveat against overextension, one legal commentator warns that it would be "erroneous to expand the *Martinez* application of the right of bodily self-determination into a broad right to die by whatever means one may choose."[6]

Even where the patient does refuse treatment in order to die, it is not clear that the right to refuse treatment can be expanded into a right to die. The right to refuse treatment, whether derived from the right to bodily self-determination or the right to privacy, is essentially a right against the invasion of one's own body. In general, one cannot be forced to undergo medical treatment. Because of this, one may be said to have a right to be left alone, even at the risk of death. But unless a substantially broader interpretation of the right to bodily self-determination is taken by the courts, one cannot be said to have the right to die, much less the right to be killed.

THE MEDICAL ASPECT

Members of the medical profession generally reject the idea of euthanasia, seeing their role as healing and prolonging life rather than ending it. However, doctors cannot always cure, and there are times when the prolonging of life is of questionable value. Indeed, in some cases, prolonging life might be seen as prolonging dying. At some point, it may be appropriate for doctors to stop staving off death. But at what point?

As we noted earlier, Anglo-American law does not recognize "mercy killings." Doctors may not actively kill their patients, even with the kindest of motives. They have more discretion in the area of omissions, for what they are required to do to save or prolong life is determined in part by contemporary medical practice. What contemporary medical practice is, however, is not always clear. In addition, such practice is no doubt influenced by doctors' interpretation of the law, since doctors are not likely to do what they believe is prohibited by law. Determining criminal liability of omissions by referring to contemporary medical practice, then, can be a somewhat circular practice. It was partly for this reason that the Supreme Court of New Jersey ruled on the question of whether doctors could be held criminally liable for removing terminal patients with no reasonable hope of recovery from respirators.

The American Medical Association apparently supports the active/passive euthanasia distinction. It is important to be careful here, however, for not all cases of stopping or refraining from life-prolonging treatment can reasonably be viewed as euthanasia. The New Jersey Supreme Court's decision regarding Karen Quinlan, for example, should not be seen as approval of passive euthanasia.

A clearcut approval in one type of situation is revealed by the following testimony from a neurologist called by the plaintiff in the Quinlan case: "No physician that I know personally is going to try and resuscitate a man riddled with cancer and in agony and he stops breathing. They are not going to put him on a respirator. . . . I think that would be the height of misuse of technology." Since the patient could presumably be revived by the respirator (unlike Karen Quinlan), failing to put him on a respirator can be seen as causing his death, or passive euthanasia. If this is in accord with standard medical practice, the doctor would probably not be guilty of criminal neglect, much less homicide. The law is clear, however, that giving a lethal dose to a man in precisely the same condition described above, but who has not stopped breathing, would be homicide. But is there a moral difference? We might ask whether the man who does not stop breathing (call him Jones) really wants to die, in spite of his agony. But exactly the same question might be asked about the man who has stopped breathing (call him Smith), for no mention was made of his requesting that treatment be terminated. We might ask if the doctors can really be sure that there is no hope of a cure for Jones. But again, this question can be asked about Smith. The justification for failing to resuscitate Smith is to spare him a few pain-filled months. But this consideration applies equally to Jones. Is there any moral reason why it should be permissible to fail to resuscitate Smith but not give Jones a lethal dose? The latter, of course, is prohibited by law while the former may not be, but perhaps the law should be changed.

Sometimes defective newborns are neglected in order that they might die. In such cases, death is viewed as preferable to life for the infants, and this may be a reasonable attitude, considering the quality of care too often prevalent in the United States. The question is, however, why it is thought preferable to let these babies die rather than to kill them quickly and painlessly. Defective newborns have even been left to starve to death, which seems morally worse than killing them quickly. Of course, doctors and nurses are prohibited by law from directly killing defective newborns, whatever the motivation, but it should be noted that they are also prohibited from leaving them to starve. Doing so is at least criminal neglect and possibly homicide.

The situation is changed when there is no neglect, but rather a decision not to treat a specific condition. "Testimony before a congressional committee included estimates that several thousand mentally and physically defective babies are allowed to die annually."[7] Judicial treatment of such matters is sparse, but in general the courts have been reluctant to accord guardians authority to terminate treatment necessary to sustain life, and physicians who withhold care for defective infants, even with parental permission, risk criminal liability.

It is apparently not uncommon for doctors to leave children with certain diseases (such as spina bifida and meningomyeloceles) unoperated. While a certain percentage die within the first year of life, many do not die quickly, but slowly over months or years, dying of meningitis, hydrocephalus, or renal disease. Some people maintain that the decision not to operate is, in effect, a decision that the child shall die. They ask if, having made this decision, on the grounds that it is in the child's best interest, it would not be better to alleviate pain and suffering by accelerating death.

Other doctors would insist that the decision to "let nature take its course" is not a decision that the child shall die. They would distinguish between foreseeing that the child will die, if untreated, and intending that it should die. We will return to this distinction in the following sections. Does it embody a significant moral difference? Or is the distinction sophistical, a way of avoiding "dirty hands"?

Some people fear that active euthanasia lends itself more readily to abuses than passive euthanasia. "The crucial difference between euthanasia and allowing to die is that the self-restraint imposed by the latter choice is more consistent with ethical and legal norms that physicians and parents do no harm to the infant."[8] Neglecting an infant, of course, is doing harm to it, but neglect aside, an infant can only be left to die if it is dying or requires extraordinary care. Thus the "pool" of babies available for passive euthanasia is smaller than those who might be considered candidates for active euthanasia. This is why the risk of abuse is thought to be greater for active than for passive euthanasia. The correct approach, however, may not be in distinguishing active from passive euthanasia, but in carefully determining criteria for either killing or letting die defective newborns.

Another factor to be considered is the effect on those delegated to doing the killing. An argument against active euthanasia and infanticide is that it will have a brutalizing effect on those who carry it out. Others deny that this will happen and argue that a quick and painless death is often in the best interests of a defective newborn. The truth of this depends on the amount of unavoidable pain the infant will be forced to suffer if left untreated. If pain can be alleviated and the infant is not neglected, it is not clear why a quick death should be thought preferable to allowing to die. Allowing a child to die can be accompanied by loving care by hospital staff and parents. This might have psychological benefits for the people involved, such as reducing feelings of guilt. Such an approach is also more in line with traditional conceptions of the role of doctors, and a change in the conception could conceivably have adverse effects on the doctor-patient relationship. In other words, there seem to be good utilitarian reasons for maintaining the active/passive euthanasia distinction.

THE RELIGIOUS ASPECT

Jews and Christians believe that life is a sacred gift from God. This does not mean that all killing is forbidden, or even that all killing of human beings is forbidden. Some writers claim that the Sixth Commandment, usually rendered as "Thou shalt not kill," actually prohibits only the wrongful killing of human beings. This has generally been interpreted to include murder, suicide, and active euthanasia. From religious writings on euthanasia, we may be able to glean Judeo-Christian attitudes toward killing and letting die.

Jewish ethics are most clearly articulated in Jewish law. Wherever possible, abstract moral generalizations are translated into particular legal obligations. The important questions concern what is forbidden, what is obligatory, and what is permissible. The prevalent view is that a physician may not actively cause a patient's death, even if requested, even to end great suffering, even if there is no hope of recovery.

> According to Jewish law, "A dying man is regarded as a living person in all respects." Active euthanasia—causing or accelerating his death in any way—is considered murder. Maimonides, in his classical legal code, wrote: "One who is in a dying condition is regarded as a living person in all respects. . . . He who touches him (thereby causing him to expire) is guilty of shedding blood."[9]

However, a physician is not required to treat a terminal patient, thus providing the possibility for a quicker, easier death. Furthermore, "One is permitted but not obliged to remove any artificial means keeping a terminal patient alive because such activity is not considered a positive action (Yoreh Deah)."[10] Apparently, writers of the classical texts reasoned in the same way as Fletcher and Chief Justice Hughes that an action that does not cause but merely permits death is to be classified as an omission, rather than a commission. In general, a commission that causes a death is forbidden by Jewish law, while an omission that permits a death to occur may or may not be forbidden.

Some writers have drawn from this a generalization about the Jewish view toward acts and omissions. Certain acts are forbidden by Jewish law, so this theory goes, but if no act is committed, no law is broken. "Omission is thus seen as 'less severe,' somehow, than commission, and benign neglect becomes more palatable."[11] There is some truth in this because of the deontological and legalistic nature of Jewish ethics. However, it is as much an oversimplification of Jewish ethics as it would be of Anglo-American law. Jewish law prohibits causing death and, as we have seen, it is possible for a death to be caused by an omission. Such an omission would no doubt be regarded as severely as an act that caused death.

The Catholic position toward euthanasia is similar to the Jewish one. In a Papal *allocutio* delivered in 1957, Pope Pius XII indicated that there is no obligation for Roman Catholics to use "extraordinary" means of preserving life. Refraining from or stopping extraordinary treatment is permissible (though not obligatory) and should not be regarded as euthanasia. In view of this address and other Catholic teachings, Bishop Joseph Casey supported Joseph Quinlan's decision to request the discontinuation of life support mechanisms for his daughter as a "morally correct decision."

The ordinary/extraordinary distinction (itself by no means clear) applies to the permissibility of omissions likely to result in death. What is the Catholic position on acts that result in death? Are these ever permissible? In general, the Judeo-Christian tradition forbids the killing of the innocent. However, an exception is sometimes made for killings that are "indirect." The distinction between "direct" and "indirect" killing is essential to what has become known as the *doctrine of the double effect* (DDE), a rule of conduct used to determine when a person may lawfully perform an action that has both good and bad effects. The permissibility of such an action depends largely on whether the bad effect is intended, or merely foreseen and permitted to happen. St. Thomas drew this distinction in discussing whether it is lawful to kill someone in self-defense. There is, he noted, nothing to prevent an act's having two effects, only one of which is intended, while the other is beside the intention. The morality of an act is determined by what is intended, not by what is beside the intention or accidental.[12] It is permissible, then, to ward off an attack, even if that involves killing one's attacker. One's intent is to defend oneself, not to kill. (Later theologians have maintained that killing in self-defense is permissible not by the doctrine of the double effect, but because God in such a case gives permission to the victim to protect himself, if necessary, by a direct slaying of the unjust assailant.)

St. Thomas did not formulate the DDE, but suggested the importance of the distinction on which it turns. Subsequent Catholic moralists elaborated conditions under which the doctrine may be applied. In addition to the requirement that the bad effect may not be directly willed, but only permitted, it must also be the case that:

1. The act itself must be morally good or at least indifferent.
2. The good effect must flow from the action at least as immediately (causally, not necessarily temporally) as the bad effect. That is, the good effect must be produced directly by the action and not by the bad effect, for that would be using a bad means to achieve a good end, which is always forbidden.
3. The good effect must be sufficiently desirable to compensate for the allowing of the bad effect.[13]

The DDE is typically invoked in the following sort of situation. A pregnant woman bearing a nonviable fetus is discovered to have cancer of the uterus. May the doctors perform a hysterectomy in order to save the woman's life? The operation is permissible, according to the DDE, because the resulting death of the fetus is not directly intended or positively willed, but is permitted as an unavoidable evil. By contrast, a woman whose life in endangered by a pregnancy because of a heart condition, kidney disease, or tuberculosis may not abort, according to Catholic law. This would violate the second and possibly the first condition. A hysterectomy is, in itself, morally indifferent, but it is doubtful whether abortion can be seen by Catholics in this way. Secondly, it is the abortion itself that saves the woman and this is seen to violate the second condition. It is the presence of the fetus that threatens her life, and the death of the fetus is the means to saving her life. Since this would be using a bad means to achieve a good end, it is not permissible.

Many people have found the doctrine confusing, and the distinction it attempts to draw between direct and indirect killing fanciful or irrelevant. Why, for example, is the killing of the fetus of the woman with heart disease seen as direct? The relief to the woman, it might be argued, comes directly as a result of having the fetus removed. The death of the fetus is, to be sure, physically necessary, but so is the death of the nonviable fetus when a hysterectomy is performed. In neither case is the death logically necessary. We need to understand better the concept of "means" and "intention." At present, one might ask whether the distinction between direct and indirect killing is sufficiently clear to provide guidance.

Even if the distinction can be made clear, people have wondered why it should carry the moral weight it is thought to have, asking, "If you are permitted to bring about the death of a child, what does it matter how it is done?" In both cases, the result is one dead fetus or one dead woman. The plausibility of the doctrine is important since it is often used by Catholics and others to defend absolutist morality. As we will see in the next section, appeal to the doctrine of the double effect is one approach to the killing/letting die question.

PHILOSOPHICAL APPROACHES

Like lawyers, doctors, and members of the clergy, philosophers who are interested in normative ethics are concerned with the killing/letting die distinction because of the implications it is thought to have in determining what ought to be done in certain situations. But the killing/letting die distinction raises issues for philosophers which go beyond practical problems and has implications for theories of ethics and action.

It has already been stated that whether or not the killing/letting die distinction has moral significance can be seen as a battle between consequentialism and absolutism. In Jonathan Bennett's "Whatever the Consequences," the absolutist regards killing the

innocent as absolutely forbidden, but since there is no such un-
equivocal prohibition against letting die, the distinction between
the two has moral significance for the absolutist. But is this simply
a matter of dogmatic adherence to an absolute principle? Or can
the absolutist's position be rationally defended?

The consequentialist holds that it is the consequences of an
action which are ultimately (and perhaps solely) relevant to its
moral assessment. If a death is brought about, what difference
does it make if it is brought about by killing or letting die? But
those who are unsatisfied with consequentialist ethics argue that
sometimes it makes a great deal of difference. They then are
obliged to try to say why.

In "Whatever the Consequences," Bennett is concerned to
show that there is no intrinsic moral significance in the distinction
between killing and letting die in order to attack "conservatism."
He does this by introducing a particularly poignant example: a
woman in labor will die unless an operation is performed in which
the head of her unborn child is crushed or dissected. If it is not
performed, the child can be delivered, alive, by postmortem
Caesarean section. How is such a situation to be resolved? In
particular, what features are relevant to a moral decision? The
conservative, Bennett says, is concerned with only one feature—
namely, that performing the craniotomy is killing an innocent
human being. Since this is absolutely forbidden, whatever the
consequences of not doing so, the obstetrician is morally required
not to operate and to let the woman die. Bennett's goal is to
show that conservatism cannot be recommended to a normal,
independent, moral conscience. Either it depends on unquestioning obedience to an authority or it is the result of conceptual
confusion. Conservatism is confused, according to Bennett, because it puts great moral stress on the distinction between doing
something and allowing it to happen, of which killing/letting die
is just a special case. Now, very often there is a moral difference
between killing a person and merely letting him/her die, but this
is due to other features, such as the agent's motive or intention,
the inevitability of the upshot, etc. Where these features are absent
or symmetrical, the distinction can still be drawn, but according
to Bennett, it turns on the number of movements open to the
agents. Bennett says, "I do not see how anyone doing his own

moral thinking about the matter could find the least shred of moral significance in *this* difference. . . ."

In "On Killing and Letting Die" Daniel Dinello provides two counterexamples to show that Bennett's analysis will not distinguish killing from letting die. Dinello thinks that the distinction as he draws it may have moral significance, but he does not explain how or why.

Jeffrie Murphy attempts to defend the absolutist's position in "Is Killing the Innocent Absolutely Immoral?", appealing to the Kantian distinction between perfect and imperfect duties. Perfect duties rest on rights, imperfect duties do not. If someone has a right to something, he has a claim against interference. Simply to refuse to be beneficent to him is not an invasion of his rights, according to Murphy, because it is not to interfere with him at all. This is perhaps not the best way of expressing the point, since one can infringe a person's rights without interfering with him— for example, by not providing him with what he has a right to—decent housing or an education. If, on the other hand, it is maintained that to infringe someone's rights *is* to interfere with him, then noninterference cannot be a mark of not infringing his rights. The point that Murphy wants to make is that rights ought to be distinguished from mere beneficence and that rights (as opposed to happiness or utility) are central to morality. The rights of persons must not be infringed, even in order to avoid the misery of others. Therefore, Murphy claims it is absolutely wrong to sacrifice the innocent, who have not forfeited their rights against interference, for the sake of greater general happiness. He thinks that he has shown, against Bennett, that one can accept this principle without necessarily being an authoritarian or a dogmatic moral fanatic.

The question John Harris raises in "The Survival Lottery" is whether refraining from saving cannot be just as much an infringement of a person's rights as killing. Harris offers the following possible institution: a lottery in which healthy people are selected at random to be killed so their organs can be used to save a greater number of lives. Most people would reject the idea of such a lottery, but it not clear that one can consistently object to the practice on consequentialist grounds. A nonconsequentialist is not limited to these grounds, but it is not obvious what nonconsequentialist objection can be forwarded against it. Simply appealing to the rights of the healthy victims (if the lottery is adopted) is not a sufficient objection unless one can show that the rights of those allowed to die (if the lottery is adopted) are not equally infringed. Nor is it enough to invoke the killing/letting die distinction, since the claim is that, in this case, letting die is killing. Harris says, "If the absolutist wishes to maintain his objection he must point to some morally relevant difference between positive and negative killing."

Jonathan Bennett would agree with Harris that it is on this distinction that the absolutist must build his case. In a forthcoming book (titled *The Act Itself*), portions of which Professor Bennett has kindly allowed me to read, Bennett responds to his critics and develops a sophisticated analysis of the distinction between positive and negative instrumentality. He acknowledges that the focus on the distinction between killing and letting die in "Whatever the Consequences" was an error. The crucial distinction is between positively and negatively contributing to an upshot; the error was to think that the distinction between killing and letting die, or, more broadly, between making happen and letting happen, coincides with this distinction.

As in his earlier paper, Bennett is attacking absolutism. The absolutist believes that some kinds of actions are absolutely wrong, so that no instance of them could ever be rendered permissible by the special facts of a particular situation. It would always be wrong to do such actions, even if not doing them, in a particular situation, would have much worse consequences. Thus, a great deal of weight is placed on the distinction between something's happening because of what one *does* and its happening because of what one *does not do*. Bennett terms this the distinction between positive and negative instrumentality.

The analysis of the distinction between positive and negative instrumentality is similar to the earlier analysis of the distinction between killing and letting die, turning on the number of movements open to the agent. A positive contribution to an upshot is one-of-few; a negative contribution is one-of-many. The conclusion is that the difference between positive and negative instrumentality is without moral significance. This conclusion is far stronger than he needs for the case against absolutism. To defeat absolutism, Bennett needs to show simply that even if the positive/negative instrumentality distinction has some moral weight, it can sometimes be outweighed by other features of the situation. In fact, however, Bennett makes the stronger claim that the positive/negative instrumentality distinction has no moral weight at all. Such a view might seem to have extremely counterintuitive results—e.g., that not sending food to starving people in distant lands is as bad as sending them poisoned food. Bennett denies that his view has this implication, since even if there is no moral difference between contributing positively and contributing negatively to an upshot, other features of the situation may make a moral difference. His claim is rather that when there is a moral difference (and, for example, it is morally worse to contribute positively to an upshot than to contribute negatively) the moral difference cannot stem from the bare difference in the two kinds of instrumentality, but always lies elsewhere. Nevertheless, Bennett thinks that his thesis has "substantive and even disturbing moral implications." His new work will be an important contribution to this ongoing controversy.

Another way of defending absolutism is to employ the doctrine of the double effect, which we encountered in the last section. There has been a lot of debate concerning the plausibility of the DDE, particularly concerning how to distinguish direct and indirect intention, between effects that are intended and effects that are foreseen but not intended. The doctrine has been scornfully rejected by a number of philosophers as a ruse to yield consequentialist results without acknowledging consequentialist method. But Philippa Foot, in "The Problem of Abortion and the Doctrine of the Double Effect" says that the doctrine should be taken seriously in spite of the fact that it sounds rather odd, that there are difficulties about the distinction on which it depends and that it sometimes seems to yield sophistical conclusions. For it has seemed that without such a doctrine, we are left with an unsatisfactory consequentialism in which the only morally relevant feature is the nonmoral goodness or badness of the consequences. However, Foot argues that the distinction between direct and oblique intention really plays only a subsidiary role, while the important distinction is between avoiding injury and bringing aid. The first is a negative duty, the second a positive duty, and Foot claims that, in general, negative duties are stricter than positive ones.

In "Saving Life and Taking Life" Richard Trammell tries to show why this should be so, citing three features to explain the moral significance of the distinction between positive and negative duties. However, while Trammell's features might, if correct, show that there is a statistical correlation between transgressing a negative duty and greater moral badness, this does not show that negative duties are more stringent *as such*. Trammell's explanation, then, may be seen as compatible with consequentialism and cannot support a position meant as an alternative to consequentialism.

N. Ann Davis points out problems with Foot's attempt to replace the DDE with another principle, the principle of the priority of avoiding injury. Davis ("The Priority of Avoiding Harm") illustrates some difficulties in distinguishing negative from positive duties and questions whether negative duties always outweigh positive ones. Davis also raises some questions about the possibility of the distinction between doing and allowing providing a basis for drawing a moral distinction between types of actions. She concludes that Foot has not provided a satisfactory alternative to the DDE and that the important questions concern, not a moral difference between doing and allowing (which Foot thinks is the strength of the DDE), but agency, responsibility, and autonomy.

NOTES

1. Michael Wechsler, "A Rationale of the Law of Homicide," *Columbia Law Review*, 37 (1937), 725.

2. See, for example, Jerome Hall, *General Principles of Criminal Law*, 2nd ed. (Indianapolis: Bobbs-Merrill, 1960).

3. According to Norman L. Cantor, however, "courts need not acquiesce in medical practices, particularly in a matter so delicate as the preservation of life. Medical standards will be accepted only if consistent with societal norms as expressed in existing legal doctrines surrounding the physician-patient relationship." Norman L. Cantor, "Law and the Termination of an Incompetent Patient's Life-Preserving Care," in *Dilemmas of Euthanasia*, ed. John Behnke and Sissela Bok (New York: Anchor Books, 1975), p. 76.

4. See Robert M. Byrn, "Compulsory Lifesaving Treatment for the Competent Adult," *Fordham Law Review*, 44 (1975), 1–36.

5. Edward M. Scher, "Legal Aspects of Euthanasia," *Albany Law Review*, 36 (1972), 674.

6. Byrn, "Compulsory Lifesaving Treatment," 14.

7. Cantor, "Law and the Termination," p. 70.

8. John Fletcher, "Abortion, Euthanasia, and the Care of Defective Newborns," *New England Journal of Medicine*, 292 (January 9, 1975), 75–78.

9. Byron L. Sherwin, "Jewish Views on Euthanasia," *Humanist*, 34 (July–August 1974), 20.

10. *Ibid.*

11. Theodore F. Dagi, "The Paradox of Euthanasia," *Judaism*, 24 (Spring 1975), 157–67.

12. *Summa Theologica*, II–II, Q. 64, Art. 7.

13. "Double Effect," *New Catholic Encyclopedia.*

PART I

EUTHANASIA AND THE TERMINATION OF LIFE-PROLONGING TREATMENT

1

70 N.J. 10:
In the Matter of Karen Quinlan, an Alleged Incompetent

Supreme Court of New Jersey

Argued Jan. 26, 1976
Decided March 31, 1976

FATHER SOUGHT to be appointed guardian of person and property of his 21-year-old daughter who was in a persistent vegetative state and sought the express power of authorizing the discontinuance of all extraordinary procedures for sustaining daughter's vital processes. The Superior Court . . . denied authorization for termination of the life-supporting apparatus and withheld letters of guardianship over the person of the incompetent, and father appealed and the Attorney General crossappealed. The Supreme Court, Hughes, C. J., held that a decision by daughter to permit a noncognitive, vegetative existence to terminate by natural forces was a valuable incident of her right to privacy which could be asserted on her behalf by her guardian; that the state of the pertinent medical standards and practices which guided the attending physician who held opinion that removal from the respirator would not conform to medical practices, standards and traditions was not such as would justify court in deeming itself bound or controlled thereby in responding to case for declaratory relief; and that upon the concurrence of guardian and family, should the attending physicians conclude there was no reasonable possibility of daughter's ever emerging from her comatose condition to a

---

In the Matter of Karen Quinlan, An Alleged Incompetent, Supreme Court of New Jersey 355A 2d 647.

cognitive, sapient state and that the life-support apparatus should be discontinued, physicians should consult with hospital ethics committee and if committee should agree with physician's prognosis, the life-support systems may be withdrawn and said action shall be without any civil or criminal liability therefor, on the part of any participant, whether guardian, physician, hospital or others.

Modified and remanded. . . .

The opinion of the Court was delivered by HUGHES, C. J.

The Litigation

The central figure in this tragic case is Karen Ann Quinlan, a New Jersey resident. At the age of 22, she lies in a debilitated and allegedly moribund state at Saint Clare's Hospital in Denville, New Jersey. The litigation has to do, in final analysis, with her life—its continuance or cessation—and the responsibilities, rights and duties, with regard to any fateful decision concerning it, of her family, her guardian, her doctors, the hospital, the State through its law enforcement authorities, and finally the courts of justice.

The issues are before this Court following its direct certification of the action under the rule, R.2:12-1, prior to hearing in the Superior Court, Appellate Division, to which the appellant (hereafter "plaintiff") Joseph Quinlan, Karen's father, had appealed the adverse judgment of the Chancery Division.

Due to extensive physical damage fully described in the able opinion of the trial judge, Judge Muir, supporting that judgment, Karen allegedly was incompetent. Joseph Quinlan sought the adjudication of that incompetency. He wished to be appointed guardian of the person and property of his daughter. It was proposed by him that such letters of guardianship, if granted, should contain an express power to him as guardian to authorize the discontinuance of all extraordinary medical procedures now allegedly sustaining Karen's vital processes and hence her life, since these measures, he asserted, present no hope of her eventual recovery. A guardian *ad litem* was appointed by Judge Muir to represent the interest of the alleged incompetent.

By a supplemental complaint, in view of the extraordinary nature of the relief sought by plaintiff and the involvement therein of their several rights and responsibilities, other parties were added. These included the treating physicians and the hospital, the relief sought being that they be restrained from interfering with the carrying out of any such extraordinary authorization in the event it were to be granted by the court. Joined, as well, was the Prosecutor of Morris County (he being charged with responsibility for enforcement of the criminal law), to enjoin him from interfering with, or projecting a criminal prosecution which otherwise might ensue in the event of, cessation of life in Karen resulting from the exercise of such extraordinary authorization were it to be granted to the guardian.

The Attorney General of New Jersey intervened as of right pursuant to R.4:33-1 on behalf of the State of New Jersey, such intervention being recognized by the court in the pretrial conference order (R.4.25:1 *et seq.*) of September 22, 1975. Its basis, of course, was the interest of the State in the preservation of life, which has an undoubted constitutional foundation.[1]

The matter is of transcendent importance involving questions related to the definition and existence of death, the prolongation of life through artificial means developed by medical technology undreamed of in past generations of the practice of the healing arts;[2] the impact of such durationally indeterminate and artificial life prolongation on the rights of the incompetent, her family and society in general; the bearing of constitutional right and the scope of judicial responsibility, as to the appropriate response of an equity court of justice to the extraordinary prayer for relief of the plaintiff. Involved as well is the right of the plaintiff, Joseph Quinlan, to guardianship of the person of his daughter. . . .

THE FACTUAL BASE

An understanding of the issues in their basic perspective suggests a brief review of the factual base developed in the testimony and documented in greater detail in the opinion of the trial judge. . . .

On the night of April 15, 1975, for reasons still unclear, Karen Quinlan ceased breathing for at least two 15 minute periods. She received some ineffectual mouth-to-mouth resuscitation from friends. She was taken by ambulance to Newton Memorial Hospital. There she had a temperature of 100 degrees, her pupils were unreactive and she was unresponsive even to deep pain. The history at the time of her admission to that hospital was essentially incomplete and uninformative.

Three days later, Dr. Morse examined Karen at the request of the Newton admitting physician, Dr. McGee. He found her comatose with evidence of decortification, a condition relating to derangement of the cortex of the brain causing a physical posture in which the upper extremities are flexed and the lower extremities are extended. She required a respirator to assist her breathing. Dr. Morse was unable to obtain an adequate account of the circumstances and events leading up to Karen's admission to the Newton Hospital. Such initial history or etiology is crucial in neurological diagnosis. Relying as he did upon the Newton Memorial records and his own examination, he concluded that prolonged lack of oxygen in the bloodstream, anoxia, was identified with her condition as he saw it upon first observation. When she was later transferred to Saint Clare's Hospital she was still unconscious, still on a respirator and a tracheotomy had been performed. On her arrival Dr. Morse conducted extensive and detailed examinations. An electroencephalogram (EEG) measuring electrical rhythm of the brain was performed and Dr. Morse characterized the result as "abnormal but it showed some activity and was consistent with her clinical state." Other significant neurological tests, including a brain scan, an angiogram, and a lumbar puncture were normal in result. Dr. Morse testified that Karen had been in a state of coma, lack of consciousness, since he began treating her. He explained that there are basically two types of coma, sleep-like unresponsiveness and awake unresponsiveness. Karen was originally in a sleep-like unresponsive condition but soon developed "sleep-wake" cycles, apparently a normal improvement for comatose patients occurring within three to four weeks. In the wake cycle she blinks, cries out and does things of that sort but is still totally unaware of anyone or anything around her.

Dr. Morse and other expert physicians who examined her characterized Karen as being in a "chronic persistent vegetative state." Dr. Fred Plum, one of such expert witnesses, defined this as a "subject who remains with the capacity to maintain the vegetative parts of neurological function but who . . . no longer has any cognitive function."

Dr. Morse, as well as the several other medical and neurological experts who testified in this case, believed with certainty that Karen Quinlan is not "brain dead." They identified the Ad Hoc Committee of Harvard Medical School report *(infra)* as the ordinary medical standard for determining brain death, and all of them were satisfied that Karen met none of the criteria specified in that report and was therefore not "brain dead" within its contemplation.

In this respect it was indicated by Dr. Plum that the brain works in essentially two ways, the vegetative and the sapient. He testified:

> We have an internal vegetative regulation which controls body temperature, which controls breathing, which controls to a considerable degree blood pressure, which controls to some degree heart rate, which controls chewing, swallowing and which controls sleeping and waking. We have a more highly developed brain which is uniquely human which controls our relation to the outside world, our capacity to talk, to see, to feel, to sing, to think. Brain death necessarily must mean the death of both of these functions of the brain, vegetative and the sapient. Therefore, the presence of any function which is regulated or governed or controlled by the deeper parts of the brain which in laymen's terms might be considered purely vegetative would mean that the brain is not biologically dead.

Because Karen's neurological condition affects her respiratory ability (the respiratory system being a brain stem function) she requires a respirator to assist her breathing. From the time of her admission to Saint Clare's Hospital Karen has been assisted by an MA-1 respirator, a sophisticated machine which delivers a given volume of air at a certain rate and periodically provides a "sigh" volume, a relatively large measured volume of air designed to purge the lungs of excretions. Attempts to "wean" her from the respirator were unsuccessful and have been abandoned.

The experts believe that Karen cannot now survive without the assistance of the respirator; that exactly how long she would live without it is unknown; that the strong likelihood is that death would follow soon after its removal, and that removal would also risk further brain damage and would curtail the assistance the respirator presently provides in warding off infection.

It seemed to be the consensus not only of the treating physicians but also of the qualified experts who testified in the case, that removal from the respirator would not conform to medical practices, standards and traditions.

The further medical consensus was that Karen in addition to being comatose is in a chronic and persistent "vegetative" state, having no awareness of anything or anyone around her and existing at a primitive reflex level. Although she does have some brain stem function (ineffective for respiration) and has other reactions one normally associates with being alive, such as moving, reacting to light, sound and noxious stimuli, blinking her eyes, and the like, the quality of her feeling impulses is unknown. She grimaces, makes stereotyped cries and sounds and has chewing motions. Her blood pressure is normal.

Karen remains in the intensive care unit at Saint Clare's Hospital, receiving 24-hour care by a team of four nurses characterized, as was the medical attention, as "excellent." She is nourished by feeding by way of a nasal-gastro tube and is routinely examined for infection, which under these circumstances is a serious life threat. The result is that her condition is considered remarkable under the unhappy circumstances involved.

Karen is described as emaciated, having suffered a weight loss of at least 40 pounds, and undergoing a continuing deteriorative process. Her posture is described as fetal-like and grotesque; there is extreme flexion-rigidity of the arms, legs and related muscles and her joints are severely rigid and deformed.

From all of this evidence, and including the whole testimonial record, several basic findings in the physical area are mandated. Severe brain and associated damage, albeit of uncertain etiology, has left Karen in a chronic and persistent vegetative state. No form of treatment which can cure or improve that condition is known or available. As nearly as may be determined, considering the guarded area of remote uncertainties characteristic of most medical science predictions, she can *never* be restored to cognitive or sapient life. Even with regard to the vegetative level and improvement therein (if such it may be called) the prognosis is extremely poor and the extent unknown if it should in fact occur.

She is debilitated and moribund and although fairly stable at the time of argument before us (no new information having been filed in the meanwhile in expansion of the record), no physician risked the opinion that she could live more than a year and indeed she may die much earlier. Excellent medical and nursing care so far has been able to ward off the constant threat of infection, to which she is peculiarly susceptible because of the respirator, the tracheal tube and other incidents of care in her vulnerable condition. Her life accordingly is sustained by the respirator and tubal feeding, and removal from the respirator would cause her death soon, although the time cannot be stated with more precision.

The determination of the fact and time of death in past years of medical science was keyed to the action of the heart and blood circulation, in turn dependent upon pulmonary activity, and hence cessation of these functions spelled out the reality of death.[3]

Developments in medical technology have obfuscated the use of the traditional definition of death. Efforts have been made to define irreversible coma as a new criterion for death, such as by the 1968 report of the Ad Hoc Committee of the Harvard Medical School (the Committee comprising ten physicians, an historian, a lawyer and a theologian), which asserted that:

> From ancient times down to the recent past it was clear that, when the respiration and heart stopped, the brain would die in a few minutes; so the obvious criterion of no heart beat as synonymous with death was sufficiently accurate. In those times the heart was considered to be the central organ of the body; it is not surprising that its failure marked the onset of death. This is no longer valid when modern resuscitative and supportive measures are used. These improved activities can now restore "life" as judged by the ancient standards of persistent respiration and continuing heart beat. This can be the case even when there is not the remotest possibility of an individual recovering consciousness following massive brain damage. . . .

The Ad Hoc standards, carefully delineated, included absence of response to pain or other stimuli, pupillary reflexes, corneal, pharyngeal and other reflexes, blood pressure, spontaneous respiration, as well as "flat" or isoelectric electroencephalograms and the like, with all tests repeated "at least 24 hours later with no change." In such circumstances, where all of such criteria have

been met as showing "brain death," the Committee recommends
with regard to the respirator:

> The patient's condition can be determined only by a physician.
> When the patient is hopelessly damaged as defined above, the fam-
> ily and all colleagues who have participated in major decisions con-
> cerning the patient, and all nurses involved, should be so informed.
> Death is to be declared and *then* the respirator turned off. The
> decision to do this and the responsibility for it are to be taken by
> the physician-in-charge, in consultation with one or more physi-
> cians who have been directly involved in the case. It is unsound
> and undesirable to force the family to make the decision. . . .

But, as indicated, it was the consensus of medical testimony in
the instant case that Karen, for all her disability, met none of these
criteria, nor indeed any comparable criteria extant in the medical
world and representing, as does the Ad Hoc Committee report,
according to the testimony in this case, prevailing and accepted
medical standards.

We have adverted to the "brain death" concept and Karen's
disassociation with any of its criteria, to emphasize the basis of
the medical decision made by Dr. Morse. When plaintiff and his
family, finally reconciled to the certainty of Karen's impending
death, requested the withdrawal of life support mechanisms, he
demurred. His refusal was based upon his conception of medical
standards, practice and ethics described in the medical testimony,
such as in the evidence given by another neurologist, Dr. Sidney
Diamond, a witness for the State. Dr. Diamond asserted that no
physician would have failed to provide respirator support at the
outset, and none would interrupt its life-saving course thereafter,
except in the case of cerebral death. In the latter case, he thought
the respirator would in effect be disconnected from one already
dead, entitling the physician under medical standards and, he
thought, legal concepts, to terminate the supportive measures. We
note Dr. Diamond's distinction of major surgical or transfusion
procedures in a terminal case not involving cerebral death, such
as here.

> The subject has lost human qualities. It would be incredible, and
> I think unlikely, that any physician would respond to a sudden
> hemorrhage, massive hemorrhage or a loss of all her defensive

blood cells, by giving her large quantities of blood. I think that
. . . major surgical procedures would be out of the question even
if they were known to be essential for continued physical existence.

This distinction is adverted to also in the testimony of Dr. Julius
Korein, a neurologist called by plaintiff. Dr. Korein described a
medical practice concept of "judicious neglect" under which the
physician will say: "Don't treat this patient anymore, . . . it does
not serve either the patient, the family, or society in any meaning-
ful way to continue treatment with this patient." Dr. Korein also
told of the unwritten and unspoken standard of medical practice
implied in the foreboding initials DNR (do not resuscitate), as
applied to the extraordinary terminal case:

> Cancer, metastatic cancer, involving the lungs, the liver, the brain,
> multiple involvements, the physician may or may not write: Do
> not resuscitate. . . . It could be said to the nurse: if this man stops
> breathing don't resuscitate him. . . . No physician that I know
> personally is going to try and resuscitate a man riddled with cancer
> and in agony and he stops breathing. They are not going to put
> him on a respirator. . . . I think that would be the height of misuse
> of technology.

While the thread of logic in such distinctions may be elusive to
the non-medical lay mind, in relation to the supposed imperative
to sustain life at all costs, they nevertheless relate to medical decisions, such as the decision of Dr. Morse in the present case. We
agree with the trial court that that decision was in accord with
Dr. Morse's conception of medical standards and practice.

We turn to that branch of the factual case pertaining to the
application for guardianship, as distinguished from the nature of
the authorization sought by the applicant. The character and general suitability of Joseph Quinlan as guardian for his daughter, in
ordinary circumstances, could not be doubted. The record be-
speaks the high degree of familial love which pervaded the home
of Joseph Quinlan and reached out fully to embrace Karen, although she was living elsewhere at the time of her collapse. The
proofs showed him to be deeply religious, imbued with a morality
so sensitive that months of tortured indecision preceded his be-
lated conclusion (despite earlier moral judgments reached by the
other family members, but unexpressed to him in order not to

influence him) to seek the termination of life-supportive measures sustaining Karen. A communicant of the Roman Catholic Church, as were other family members, he first sought solace in private prayer looking with confidence, as he says, to the Creator, first for the recovery of Karen and then, if that were not possible, for guidance with respect to the awesome decision confronting him.

[1] To confirm the moral rightness of the decision he was about to make he consulted with his parish priest and later with the Catholic chaplain of Saint Clare's Hospital. He would not, he testified, have sought termination if that act were to be morally wrong or in conflict with the tenets of the religion he so profoundly respects. He was disabused of doubt, however, when the position of the Roman Catholic Church was made known to him as it is reflected in the record in this case. While it is not usual for matters of religious dogma or concepts to enter a civil litigation (except as they may bear upon constitutional right, or sometimes, familial matters; *cf. In re Adoption of E,* 59 N.J. 36, 279 A.2d 785 (1971), they were rightly admitted in evidence here. The judge was bound to measure the character and motivations in all respects of Joseph Quinlan as prospective guardian; and insofar as these religious matters bore upon them, they were properly scrutinized and considered by the court.

Thus germane, we note the position of that Church as illuminated by the record before us. We have no reason to believe that it would be at all discordant with the whole of Judeo–Christian tradition, considering its central respect and reverence for the sanctity of human life. It was in this sense of relevance that we admitted as *amicus curiae* the New Jersey Catholic Conference, essentially the spokesman for the various Catholic bishops of New Jersey, organized to give witness to spiritual values in public affairs in the statewide community. The position statement of Bishop Lawrence B. Casey, reproduced in the *amicus* brief, projects these views:

(a) The verification of the fact of death in a particular case cannot be deduced from any religious or moral principle and, under this aspect, does not fall within the competence of the church; that dependence must be had upon traditional and medical standards, and by these standards Karen Ann Quinlan is assumed to be alive.

(b) The request of plaintiff for authority to terminate a medical procedure characterized as "an extraordinary means of treatment" would not involve euthanasia. This upon the reasoning expressed by Pope Pius XII in his "allocutio" (address) to anesthesiologists on November 24, 1957, when he dealt with the question:

> Does the anesthesiologist have the right, or is he bound, in all cases of deep unconsciousness, even in those that are completely hopeless in the opinion of the competent doctor, to use modern artificial respiration apparatus, even against the will of the family?

His answer made the following points:

1. In ordinary cases the doctor has the right to act in this manner, but is not bound to do so unless this is the only way of fulfilling another certain moral duty.
2. The doctor, however, has no right independent of the patient. He can act only if the patient explicitly or implicitly, directly or indirectly gives him the permission.
3. The treatment as described in the question constitutes extraordinary means of preserving life and so there is no obligation to use them nor to give the doctor permission to use them.
4. The rights and the duties of the family depend on the presumed will of the unconscious patient if he or she is of legal age, and the family, too, is bound to use only ordinary means.
5. This case is not to be considered euthanasia in any way; that would never be licit. The interruption of attempts at resuscitation, even when it causes the arrest of circulation, is not more than an indirect cause of the cessation of life, and we must apply in this case the principle of double effect.

So it was that the Bishop Casey statement validated the decision of Joseph Quinlan:

> Competent medical testimony has established that Karen Ann Quinlan has no reasonable hope of recovery from her comatose state by the use of any available medical procedures. The continuance of mechanical (cardiorespiratory) supportive measures to sustain continuation of her body functions and her life constitute extraordinary means of treatment. *Therefore, the decision of Joseph . . . Quinlan to request the discontinuance of this treatment is, according*

to the teachings of the Catholic Church, a morally correct decision [emphasis in original].

And the mind and purpose of the intending guardian were undoubtedly influenced by factors included in the following reference to the interrelationship of the three disciplines of theology, law and medicine as exposed in the Casey statement:

> The right to a natural death is one outstanding area in which the disciplines of theology, medicine and law overlap; or, to put it another way, it is an area in which these three disciplines convene.
>
> Medicine with its combination of advanced technology and professional ethics is both able and inclined to prolong biological life. Law with its felt obligation to protect the life and freedom of the individual seeks to assure each person's right to live out his human life until its natural and inevitable conclusion. Theology with its acknowledgement of man's dissatisfaction with biological life as the ultimate source of joy . . . defends the sacredness of human life and defends it from all direct attacks.
>
> These disciplines do not conflict with one another, but are necessarily conjoined in the application of their principles in a particular instance such as that of Karen Ann Quinlan. Each must in some way acknowledge the other without denying its own competence. The civil law is not expected to assert a belief in eternal life; nor, on the other hand, is it expected to ignore the right of the individual to profess it, and to form and pursue his conscience in accord with that belief. Medical science is not authorized to directly cause natural death; nor, however, is it expected to prevent it when it is inevitable and all hope of a return to an even partial exercise of human life is irreparably lost. Religion is not expected to define biological death; nor, on its part, is it expected to relinquish its responsibility to assist man in the formation and pursuit of a correct conscience as to the acceptance of natural death when science has confirmed its inevitability beyond any hope other than that of preserving biological life in a merely vegetative state.

And the gap in the law is aptly described in the Bishop Casey statement:

> In the present public discussion of the case of Karen Ann Quinlan it has been brought out that responsible people involved in medical care, patients and families have exercised the freedom to terminate or withhold certain treatments as extraordinary means in cases

judged to be terminal, i.e., cases which hold no realistic hope for some recovery, in accord with the expressed or implied intentions of the patients themselves. To whatever extent this has been happening it has been without sanction in civil law. Those involved in such actions, however, have ethical and theological literature to guide them in their judgments and actions. Furthermore, such actions have not in themselves undermined society's reverence for the lives of sick and dying people.

It is both possible and necessary for society to have laws and ethical standards which provide freedom for decisions, in accord with the expressed or implied intentions of the patient, to terminate or withhold extraordinary treatment in cases which are judged to be hopeless by competent medical authorities, without at the same time leaving an opening for euthanasia. Indeed, to accomplish this, it may simply be required that courts and legislative bodies recognize the present standards and practices of many people engaged in medical care who have been doing what the parents of Karen Ann Quinlan are requesting authorization to have done for their beloved daughter.

Before turning to the legal and constitutional issues involved, we feel it essential to reiterate that the "Catholic view" of religious neutrality in the circumstances of this case is considered by the Court only in the aspect of its impact upon the conscience, motivation and purpose of the intending guardian, Joseph Quinlan, and not as a precedent in terms of the civil law.

If Joseph Quinlan, for instance, were a follower and strongly influenced by the teachings of Buddha, or if, as an agnostic or atheist, his moral judgments were formed without reference to religious feelings, but were nevertheless formed and viable, we would with equal attention and high respect consider these elements, as bearing upon his character, motivations and purposes as relevant to his qualification and suitability as guardian.

It is from this factual base that the Court confronts and responds to three basic issues:

1. Was the trial court correct in denying the specific relief requested by plaintiff, *i.e.,* authorization for termination of the life-supporting apparatus, on the case presented to him? Our determination on that question is in the affirmative.
2. Was the court correct in withholding letters of guardianship

from the plaintiff and appointing in his stead a stranger? On that issue our determination is in the negative.

3. Should this Court, in the light of the foregoing conclusions, grant declaratory relief to the plaintiff? On that question our Court's determination is in the affirmative.

This brings us to a consideration of the constitutional and legal issues underlying the foregoing determinations.

Constitutional and Legal Issues

. . .

III. The Right of Privacy[4]

It is the issue of the constitutional right of privacy that has given us most concern, in the exceptional circumstances of this case. Here a loving parent, *qua* parent and raising the rights of his incompetent and profoundly damaged daughter, probably irreversibly doomed to no more than a biologically vegetative remnant of life, is before the court. He seeks authorization to abandon specialized technological procedures which can only maintain for a time a body having no potential for resumption or continuance of other than a "vegetative" existence.

We have no doubt, in these unhappy circumstances, that if Karen were herself miraculously lucid for an interval (not altering the existing prognosis of the condition to which she would soon return) and perceptive of her irreversible condition, she could effectively decide upon discontinuance of the life-support apparatus, even if it meant the prospect of natural death. To this extent we may distinguish *Heston, supra,* which concerned a severely injured young woman (Delores Heston), whose life depended on surgery and blood transfusion; and who was in such extreme shock that she was unable to express an informed choice (although the Court apparently considered the case as if the patient's own religious decision to resist transfusion were at stake), but most importantly a patient apparently salvable to long life and vibrant health; a situation not at all like the present case.

We have no hesitancy in deciding, in the instant diametrically opposite case, that no external compelling interest of the State could compel Karen to endure the unendurable, only to vegetate a few measurable months with no realistic possibility of returning to any semblance of cognitive or sapient life. We perceive no thread of logic distinguishing between such a choice on Karen's part and a similar choice which, under the evidence in this case, could be made by a competent patient terminally ill, riddled by cancer and suffering great pain; such a patient would not be resuscitated or put on a respirator in the example described by Dr. Korein, and *a fortiori* would not be kept *against his will* on a respirator.

Although the Constitution does not explicitly mention a right of privacy, Supreme Court decisions have recognized that a right of personal privacy exists and that certain areas of privacy are guaranteed under the Constitution. . . . The Court has interdicted judicial intrusion into many aspects of personal decision, sometimes basing this restraint upon the conception of a limitation of judicial interest and responsibility, such as with regard to contraception and its relationship to family life and decision. . . .

The Court in *Griswold* found the unwritten constitutional right of privacy to exist in the penumbra of specific guarantees of the Bill of Rights "formed by emanations from those guarantees that help give them life and substance." . . . Presumably this right is broad enough to encompass a patient's decision to decline medical treatment under certain circumstances, in much the same way as it is broad enough to encompass a woman's decision to terminate pregnancy under certain conditions. . . .

Nor is such right of privacy forgotten in the New Jersey Constitution. . . .

The claimed interests of the State in this case are essentially the preservation and sanctity of human life and defense of the right of the physician to administer medical treatment according to his best judgment. In this case the doctors say that removing Karen from the respirator will conflict with their professional judgment. The plaintiff answers that Karen's present treatment serves only a maintenance function; that the respirator cannot cure or improve her condition but at best can only prolong her inevitable slow deterioration and death; and that the interests of the patient, as seen by her surrogate, the guardian, must be evaluated by the court as predominant, even in the face of an opinion *contra* by the present attending physicians. Plaintiff's distinction is significant. The nature of Karen's care and the realistic chances of her recovery are quite unlike those of the patients discussed in many of the cases where treatments were ordered. In many of those cases the medical procedure required (usually a transfusion) constituted a minimal bodily invasion and the chances of recovery and return to functioning life were very good. We think that the State's interest *contra* weakens and the individual's right to privacy grows as the degree of bodily invasion increases and the prognosis dims. Ultimately there comes a point at which the individual's rights overcome the State interest. It is for that reason that we believe Karen's choice, if she were competent to make it, would be vindicated by the law. Her prognosis is extremely poor—she will never resume cognitive life. And the bodily invasion is very great—she requires 24-hour intensive nursing care, antibiotics, the assistance of a respirator, a catheter and feeding tube.

. . . Our affirmation of Karen's independent right of choice, however, would ordinarily be based upon her competency to assert it. The sad truth, however, is that she is grossly incompetent and we cannot discern her supposed choice based on the testimony of her previous conversations with friends, where such testimony is without sufficient probative weight. . . . Nevertheless we have concluded that Karen's right of privacy may be asserted on her behalf by her guardian under the peculiar circumstances here present.

If a putative decision by Karen to permit this noncognitive, vegetative existence to terminate by natural forces is regarded as a valuable incident of her right of privacy, as we believe it to be, then it should not be discarded solely on the basis that her condition prevents her conscious exercise of the choice. The only practical way to prevent destruction of the right is to permit the guardian and family of Karen to render their best judgment, subject to the qualifications hereinafter stated, as to whether she would exercise it in these circumstances. If their conclusion is in the affirmative this decision should be accepted by a society the overwhelming majority of whose members would, we think, in similar circumstances, exercise such a choice in the same way for themselves or for those closest to them. It is for this reason that we determine that Karen's right of privacy may be asserted in her behalf, in this respect, by her guardian and family under the particular circumstances presented in this record. . . .

IV. The Medical Factor

Having declared the substantive legal basis upon which plaintiff's rights as representative of Karen must be deemed predicated, we face and respond to the assertion on behalf of defendants that our premise unwarrantably offends prevailing medical standards. We thus turn to consideration of the medical decision supporting the determination made below, conscious of the paucity of pre-existing legislative and judicial guidance as to the rights and liabilities therein involved.

A significant problem in any discussion of sensitive medical-legal issues is the marked, perhaps unconscious, tendency of many to distort what the law is, in pursuit of an exposition of what they would like the law to be. Nowhere is this barrier to the intelligent resolution of legal controversies more obstructive than in the debate over patient rights at the end of life. Judicial refusals to order lifesaving treatment in the face of contrary claims of bodily self-determination or free religious exercise are too often cited in support of a preconceived "right to die," even though the patients, wanting to live, have claimed no such right. Conversely, the assertion of a religious or other objection to lifesaving treatment is at times condemned as attempted suicide, even though suicide means something quite different in the law [Byrn, "Compulsory Lifesaving Treatment for the Competent Adult," *Fordham L. Rev.*, 44, no. 1 (1975)].

Perhaps the confusion there adverted to stems from mention by some courts of statutory or common law condemnation of suicide as demonstrating the state's interest in the preservation of life. We would see, however, a real distinction between the self-infliction of deadly harm and a self-determination against artificial life support or radical surgery, for instance, in the face of irreversible, painful and certain imminent death. The contrasting situations mentioned are analogous to those continually faced by the medical profession. When does the institution of life-sustaining procedures, ordinarily mandatory, become the subject of medical discretion in the context of administration to persons *in extremis*? And when does the withdrawal of such procedures, from such persons already supported by them, come within the orbit of medical discretion? When does a determination as to either of the foregoing contingencies court the hazard of civil or criminal liability on the part of the physician or institution involved?

The existence and nature of the medical dilemma need hardly be discussed at length, portrayed as it is in the present case and complicated as it has recently come to be in view of the dramatic advance of medical technology. The dilemma is there, it is real, it is constantly resolved in accepted medical practice without attention in the courts, it pervades the issues in the very case we here examine. The branch of the dilemma involving the doctor's responsibility and the relationship of the court's duty was thus conceived by Judge Muir:

> Doctors . . . to treat a patient, must deal with medical tradition and past case histories. They must be guided by what they do know. The extent of their training, their experience, consultation with other physicians, must guide their decision-making processes in providing care to their patient. The nature, extent and duration of care by societal standards is the responsibility of a physician. The morality and conscience of our society places this responsibility in the hands of the physician. What justification is there to remove it from the control of the medical profession and place it in the hands of the courts? . . .

Such notions as to the distribution of responsibility, heretofore generally entertained, should however neither impede this Court in deciding matters clearly justiciable nor preclude a re-examination by the Court as to underlying human values and rights. Determinations as to these must, in the ultimate, be responsive not only to the concepts of medicine but also to the common moral judgment of the community at large. In the latter respect the Court has a nondelegable judicial responsibility.

Put in another way, the law, equity and justice must not themselves quail and be helpless in the face of modern technological marvels presenting questions hitherto unthought of. Where a Karen Quinlan, or a parent, or a doctor, or a hospital, or a State seeks the process and response of a court, it must answer with its most informed conception of justice in the previously unexplored circumstances presented to it. That is its obligation and we are here fulfilling it, for the actors and those having an interest in the matter should not go without remedy.

Courts in the exercise of their *parens patriae* responsibility to protect those under disability have sometimes implemented medical decisions and authorized their carrying out under the doctrine of "substituted judgment." . . . For as Judge Muir pointed out:

> As part of the inherent power of equity, a Court of Equity has full and complete jurisdiction over the persons of those who labor under any legal disability. . . . The Court's action in such a case is not limited by any narrow bounds, but it is empowered to stretch forth its arm in whatever direction its aid and protection may be needed. While this in indeed a special exercise of equity jurisdiction, it is beyond question that by virtue thereof the Court may pass upon purely personal rights. . . .

But insofar as a court, having no inherent medical expertise, is called upon to overrule a professional decision made according to prevailing medical practice and standards, a different question is presented. As mentioned below, a doctor is required

> "to exercise in the treatment of his patient the degree of care, knowledge and skill ordinarily possessed and exercised in similar situations by the average member of the profession practicing in his field." . . . If he is a specialist he "must employ not merely the skill of a general practitioner, but also that special degree of skill normally possessed by the average physician who devotes special study and attention to the particular organ or disease or injury involved, having regard to the present state of scientific knowledge." . . . This is the duty that establishes his legal obligations to his patients.

The medical obligation is related to standards and practice prevailing in the profession. The physicians in charge of the case, as noted above, declined to withdraw the respirator. That decision was consistent with the proofs below as to the then existing medical standards and practices.

Under the law as it then stood, Judge Muir was correct in declining to authorize withdrawal of the respirator.

However, in relation to the matter of the declaratory relief sought by plaintiff as representative of Karen's interests, we are required to re-evaluate the applicability of the medical standards projected in the court below. The question is whether there is such internal consistency and rationality in the application of such standards as should warrant their constituting an ineluctable bar to the effectuation of substantive relief for plaintiff at the hands of the court. We have concluded not.

In regard to the foregoing it is pertinent that we consider the impact on the standards both of the civil and criminal law as to medical liability and the new technological means of sustaining life irreversibly damaged.

The modern proliferation of substantial malpractice litigation and the less but even more unnerving possibility of criminal sanctions would seem, for it is beyond human nature to suppose otherwise, to have bearing on the practice and standards as they exist. The brooding presence of such possible liability, it was testified here, had no part in the decision of the treating physicians. As did Judge Muir, we afford this testimony full credence. But we cannot believe that the stated factor has not had a strong influence on the standards, as the literature on the subject plainly reveals. Moreover our attention is drawn not so much to the recognition by Drs. Morse and Javed of the extant practice and standards but to the widening ambiguity of those standards themselves in their application to the medical problems we are discussing.

The agitation of the medical community in the face of modern life prolongation technology and its search for definitive policy are demonstrated in the large volume of relevant professional commentary.[5]

The wide debate thus reflected contrasts with the relative paucity of legislative and judicial guides and standards in the same field. The medical profession has sought to devise guidelines such as the "brain death" concept of the Harvard Ad Hoc Committee mentioned above. But it is perfectly apparent from the testimony we have quoted of Dr. Korein, and indeed so clear as almost to be judicially noticeable, that humane decisions against resuscitative or maintenance therapy are frequently a recognized *de facto* response in the medical world to the irreversible, terminal, pain-ridden patient, especially with familial consent. And these cases, of course, are far short of "brain death."

We glean from the record here that physicians distinguish between curing the ill and comforting and easing the dying; that they refuse to treat the curable as if they were dying or ought to die, and they have sometimes refused to treat the hopeless and dying as if they were curable. In this sense, as we were reminded by the testimony of Drs. Korein and Diamond, many of them have refused to inflict an undesired prolongation of the process of dying on a patient in irreversible condition when it is clear that such "therapy" offers neither human nor humane benefit. We think these attitudes represent a balanced implementation of a profoundly realistic perspective on the meaning of life and death and that they respect the whole Judeo-Christian tradition of regard for human life. No less would they seem consistent with the moral matrix of medicine, "to heal," very much in the sense of the endless mission of the law, "to do justice."

Yet this balance, we feel, is particularly difficult to perceive and apply in the context of the development by advanced technology of sophisticated and artificial life-sustaining devices. For those possibly curable, such devices are of great value, and, as ordinary medical procedures, are essential. Consequently, as pointed out by Dr. Diamond, they are necessary because of the ethic of medical practice. But in the light of the situation in the present case (while the record here is somewhat hazy in distinguishing between "ordinary" and "extraordinary" measures), one would have to think that the use of the same respirator or like support could be considered "ordinary" in the context of the possibly curable patient but "extraordinary" in the context of the forced sustaining by cardio-respiratory processes of an irreversibly doomed patient. And this dilemma is sharpened in the face of the malpractice and criminal action threat which we have mentioned.

We would hesitate, in this imperfect world, to propose as to physicians that type of immunity which from the early common law has surrounded judges and grand jurors . . . so that they might without fear of personal retaliation perform their judicial duties with independent objectivity. In *Bradley v. Fisher* . . . the Supreme Court held:

It is a general principle of the highest importance to the proper administration of justice that a judicial officer, in exercising the authority vested in him, shall be free to act upon his own convictions, without apprehension of personal consequences to himself.

Lord Coke said of judges that "they are only to make an account to God and the King [the State]." . . .

Nevertheless, there must be a way to free physicians, in the pursuit of their healing vocation, from possible contamination by self-interest or self-protection concerns which would inhibit their independent medical judgments for the well-being of their dying patients. We would hope that this opinion might be serviceable to some degree in ameliorating the professional problems under discussion.

A technique aimed at the underlying difficulty (though in a somewhat broader context) is described by Dr. Karen Teel, a pediatrician and a director of Pediatric Education, who writes in the *Baylor Law Review* under the title "The Physician's Dilemma: A Doctor's View: What The Law Should Be." Dr. Teel recalls:

> Physicians, by virtue of their responsibility for medical judgments are, partly by choice and partly by default, charged with the responsibility of making ethical judgments which we are sometimes ill-equipped to make. We are not always morally and legally authorized to make them. The physician is thereby assuming a civil and criminal liability that, as often as not, he does not even realize as a factor in his decision. There is little or no dialogue in this whole process. The physician assumes that his judgment is called for and, in good faith, he acts. Someone must and it has been the physician who has assumed the responsibility and the risk.
>
> I suggest that it would be more appropriate to provide a regular forum for more input and dialogue in individual situations and to allow the responsibility of these judgments to be shared. Many hospitals have established an Ethics Committee composed of physicians, social workers, attorneys, and theologians, . . . which serves to review the individual circumstances of ethical dilemma and which has provided much in the way of assistance and safeguards for patients and their medical caretakers. Generally, the authority of these committees is primarily restricted to the hospital setting and their official status is more that of an advisory body than of an enforcing body.
>
> The concept of an Ethics Committee which has this kind of organization and is readily accessible to those persons rendering medical care to patients, would be, I think, the most promising

direction for further study at this point. . . . [This would allow] some much needed dialogue regarding these issues and [force] the point of exploring all of the options for a particular patient. It diffuses the responsibility for making these judgments. Many physicians, in many circumstances, would welcome this sharing of responsibility. I believe that such an entity could lend itself well to an assumption of a legal status which would allow courses of action not now undertaken because of the concern for liability [27 Baylor L Rev, 6, 8-9 (1975)].

V. Alleged Criminal Liability

. . . Having concluded that there is a right of privacy that might permit termination of treatment in the circumstances of this case, we turn to consider the relationship of the exercise of that right to the criminal law. We are aware that such termination of treatment would accelerate Karen's death. The County Prosecutor and the Attorney General maintain that there would be criminal liability for such acceleration. Under the statutes of this State, the unlawful killing of another human being is criminal homicide. . . . We conclude that there would be no criminal homicide in the circumstances of this case. We believe, first, that the ensuing death would not be homicide but rather expiration from existing natural causes. Secondly, even if it were to be regarded as homicide, it would not be unlawful.

These conclusions rest upon definitional and constitutional bases. The termination of treatment pursuant to the right of privacy is, within the limitations of this case *ipso facto* lawful. Thus, a death resulting from such an act would not come within the scope of the homicide statutes proscribing only the unlawful killing of another. There is a real and in this case determinative distinction between the unlawful taking of the life of another and the ending of artificial life-support systems as a matter of self-determination.

. . . Furthermore, the exercise of a constitutional right such as we have here found is protected from criminal prosecution. . . . We do not question the State's undoubted power to punish the taking of human life, but that power does not encompass individuals terminating medical treatment pursuant to their right of privacy. . . . The constitutional protection extends to third parties whose action is necessary to effectuate the exercise of that right where the individuals themselves would not be subject to prosecution or the third parties are charged as accessories to an act which could not be a crime. . . . And, under the circumstances of this case, these same principles would apply to and negate a valid prosecution for attempted suicide were there still such a crime in this State.[6]

VI. The Guardianship of the Person

. . . The trial judge bifurcated the guardianship, as we have noted, refusing to appoint Joseph Quinlan to be guardian to the person and limiting his guardianship to that of the property of his daughter. Such occasional division of guardianship, as between responsibility for the person and the property of an incompetent person, has roots deep in the common law and was well within the jurisdictional capacity of the trial judge. . . .

The statute creates an initial presumption of entitlement to guardianship in the next of kin, for it provides:

> In any case where a guardian is to be appointed, letters of guardianship shall be granted . . . to the next of kin, or if . . . it is proven to the court that no appointment from among them will be to the best interest of the incompetent or his estate, then to such other proper person as will accept the same. . . .

The trial court was apparently convinced of the high character of Joseph Quinlan and his general suitability as guardian under other circumstances, describing him as "very sincere, moral, ethical and religious." The court felt, however, that the obligation to concur in the medical care and treatment of his daughter would be a source of anguish to him and would distort his "decision-making processes." We disagree, for we sense from the whole record before us that while Mr. Quinlan feels a natural grief, and understandably sorrows because of the tragedy which has befallen his daughter, his strength of purpose and character far outweighs these sentiments and qualifies him eminently for guardianship of the person as well as the property of his daughter. Hence we discern no valid reason to overrule the statutory intendment of preference to the next of kin.

Declaratory Relief

. . . We thus arrive at the formulation of the declaratory relief which we have concluded is appropriate to this case. Some time has passed since Karen's physical and mental condition was described to the Court. At that time her continuing deterioration was plainly projected. Since the record has not been expanded we assume that she is now even more fragile and nearer to death than she was then. Since her present treating physicians may give reconsideration to her present posture in the light of this opinion, and since we are transferring to the plaintiff as guardian the choice of the attending physician and therefore other physicians may be in charge of the case who may take a different view from that of the present attending physicians, we herewith declare the following affirmative relief on behalf of the plaintiff. Upon the concurrence of the guardian and family of Karen, should the responsible attending physicians conclude that there is no reasonable possibility of Karen's ever emerging from her present comatose condition to a cognitive, sapient state and that the life-support apparatus now being administered to Karen should be discontinued, they shall consult with the hospital "Ethics Committee" or like body of the institution in which Karen is then hospitalized. If that consultative body agrees that there is no reasonable possibility of Karen's ever emerging from her present comatose condition to a cognitive, sapient state, the present life-support system may be withdrawn and said action shall be without any civil or criminal liability therefor on the part of any participant, whether guardian, physician, hospital or others.[7] We herewith specifically so hold.

Conclusion

We therefore remand this record to the trial court to implement (without further testimonial hearing) the following decisions:

    1. To discharge, with the thanks of the Court for his service,

the present guardian of the person of Karen Quinlan, Thomas R. Curtin, Esquire, a member of the Bar and an officer of the court.

2. To appoint Joseph Quinlan as guardian of the person of Karen Quinlan with full power to make decisions with regard to the identity of her treating physicians.

We repeat for the sake of emphasis and clarity that upon the concurrence of the guardian and family of Karen, should the responsible attending physicians conclude that there is no reasonable possibility of Karen's ever emerging from her present comatose condition to a cognitive, sapient state and that the life-support apparatus now being administered to Karen should be discontinued, they shall consult with the hospital "Ethics Committee" or like body of the institution in which Karen is then hospitalized. If that consultative body agrees that there is no reasonable possibility of Karen's ever emerging from her present comatose condition to a cognitive, sapient state, the present life-support system may be withdrawn and said action shall be without any civil or criminal liability therefor on the part of any participant, whether guardian, physician, hospital or others.

By the above ruling we do not intend to be understood as implying that a proceeding for judicial declaratory relief is necessarily required for the implementation of comparable decisions in the field of medical practice.

Modified and remanded.

For modification and remandment: Chief Justice HUGHES, Justices MOUNTAIN, SULLIVAN, PASHMAN, CLIFFORD and SCHREIBER and Judge CONFORD–7.

Opposed: None.

NOTES

1. The importance of the preservation of life is memorialized in various organic documents. The Declaration of Independence states as self-evident truths "that all men . . . are endowed by their Creator with certain unalienable Rights, that among these are Life, Liberty and the pursuit of Happiness." This ideal is inherent in the Constitution of the United States. It is explicitly recognized in our Constitution of 1947 which provides for "certain natural and unalienable rights, among which

are those of enjoying and defending life. . . . N.J. Const. (1947), Art.
I, par. 1. Our State government is established to protect such rights,
N.J. Const. (1947), Art. I, par. 2, and acting through the Attorney
General (N.J.S.A. 52:17A-4(h)), it enforces them.

    2. Dr. Julius Korein, a neurologist, testified:

> A. . . . you've got a set of possible lesions that prior to the era of advanced
> technology and advances in medicine were no problem inasmuch as the
> patient would expire. They could do nothing for themselves and even
> external care was limited. It was—I don't know how many years ago
> they couldn't keep a person alive with intravenous feedings because they
> couldn't give enough calories. Now they have these high caloric tube
> feedings that can keep people in excellent nutrition for years so what's
> happened is these things have occurred all along but the technology has
> now reached a point where you can in fact start to replace anything outside
> of the brain to maintain something that is irreversibly damaged.
> Q. Doctor, can the art of medicine repair the cerebral damage that was
> sustained by Karen?
> A. In my opinion, no. . . .
> Q. Doctor, in your opinion is there any course of treatment that will lead
> to the improvement of Karen's condition?
> A. No.

    3. Death. The cessation of life; the ceasing to exist; defined by physi-
cians as a total stoppage of the circulation of the blood, and a cessation
of the animal and vital functions consequent thereon, such as respiration,
pulsation, etc. *Black's Law Dictionary* 488 (rev. 4th ed. 1968).

    4. The right we here discuss is included within the class of what have
been called rights of "personality." *See* Pound, "Equitable Relief against
Defamation and Injuries to Personality," *Harv.L.Rev.*, 29, 640 (1916),
668-76. Equitable jurisdiction with respect to the recognition and enforcement of such rights has long been recognized in New Jersey. See,
e.g., *Vanderbilt v. Mitchel*, 72 N.J. Eq. 910, 919-20, 67 A. 97 (E. &
A. 1907).

    5. See, e.g., Downing, *Euthanasia and the Right to Die* (1969); St. John-
Stevas, *Life, Death, and the Law* (1961); Williams, *The Sanctity of Human
Life and the Criminal Law* (1957); Appel, "Ethical and Legal Questions
Posed by Recent Advances in Medicine," *J.A.M.A.* 205, 513 (1968);
Cantor, "A Patient's Decision to Decline Life-Saving Medical Treatment:
Bodily Integrity Versus the Preservation of Life," 26 *Rutgers L.Rev.*, 228
(1973); Claypool, "The Family Deals with Death," *Baylor L.Rev.*, 27
34 (1975); Elkington, "The Dying Patient, the Doctor and the Law,"
Vill.L.Rev. 13 740 (1968); Fletcher, "Legal Aspects of the Decision Not
to Prolong Life," *J.A.M.A.*, 203 65 (1968); Foreman, "The Physician's

Criminal Liability for the Practice of Euthanasia," *Baylor L.Rev.,* 27, 54 (1975); Gurney, "Is There a Right to Die?—A Study of the Law of Euthanasia," *Cumb.-Sam.L.Rev.,* 3, 235 (1972); Mannes, "Euthanasia vs. the Right to Life," *Baylor L.Rev.,* 27, 68 (1975); Sharp & Crofts, "Death with Dignity and The Physician's Civil Liability," *Baylor L.Rev.,* 27, 86 (1975); Sharpe & Hargest, "Lifesaving Treatment for Unwilling Patients," *Fordham L.Rev.,* 36, 695 (1968); Skegg, "Irreversibly Comatose Individuals: 'Alive' or 'Dead'?" *Camb.L.J.,* 33, 130 (1974); Comment, "The Right to Die," *Houston L.Rev.,* 7, 654 (1970); Note, "The Time of Death—A Legal, Ethical and Medical Dilemma," *Catholic Law,* 18, 243 (1972); Note, "Compulsory Medical Treatment; The State's Interest Re-evaluated," *Minn.L.Rev.,* 51, 293 (1966).

6. An attempt to commit suicide was an indictable offense at common law and as such was indictable in this State as a common law misdemeanor. 1 *Schlosser, Criminal Laws of New Jersey* § 12.5 (3d ed. 1970); *see* N.J.S.A. 2A:85-1. The legislature downgraded the offense in 1957 to the status of a disorderly persons offense, which is not a "crime" under our law. N.J.S.A. 2A:170-25.6. And in 1971, the legislature repealed all criminal sanctions for attempted suicide. N.J.S.A. 2A:85-5.1. Provision is now made for temporary hospitalization of persons making such an attempt. N.J.S.A. 30:4-26.3a. We note that under the proposed New Jersey Penal Code (Oct. 1971) there is no provision for criminal punishment of attempted suicide. *See* Commentary, § 2C:11-6. There is, however, an independent offense of "aiding suicide." § 2C:11-6b. This provision, if enacted, would not be incriminatory in circumstances similar to those presented in this case.

7. The declaratory relief we here award is not intended to imply that the principles enunciated in this case might not be applicable in divers other types of terminal medical situations such as those described by Drs. Korein and Diamond, *supra,* not necessarily involving the hopeless loss of cognitive or sapient life.

2

Majority Opinion in
Cruzan v. Director
Missouri Department of Health
Justice William H. Rehnquist

This case developed when the parents of Nancy Beth Cruzan—a woman existing in a persistent vegetative state subsequent to an automobile accident suffered at the age of twenty-five—sought authorization from a Missouri trial court to terminate their daughter's artificial nutrition and hydration. The trial court authorized termination of treatment, but the Supreme Court of Missouri reversed the decision of the court trial. The United States Supreme Court upheld the judgment of the Missouri Supreme Court.

Writing the majority opinion in a five-to-four decision, Justice Rehnquist acknowledges that a competent *person has a constitutionally protected right to refuse lifesaving nutrition and hydration. However, in the case of an* incompetent *person, he argues, it is not unconstitutional for Missouri to insist that nutrition and hydration can be terminated only if there is "clear and convincing evidence" that termination of treatment is what the person would have wanted. Since this standard of proof has presumably not been satisfied in the case of Nancy Beth Cruzan, he concludes, the judgment of the Missouri Supreme Court is affirmed. (In subsequent developments, a Missouri court considered new evidence presented by Cruzan's parents and concluded that there was "clear and convincing evidence" that she would have chosen to terminate treatment. Nutrition and hydration were subsequently withheld and Nancy Cruzan died in December of 1990).*

PETITIONER NANCY BETH CRUZAN was rendered incompetent as a

United States Supreme Court. 110 S. Ct. 2841 (1990)

result of severe injuries sustained during an automobile accident. Co-petitioners Lester and Joyce Cruzan, Nancy's parents and co-guardians, sought a court order directing the withdrawal of their daughter's artificial feeding and hydration equipment after it became apparent that she had virtually no chance of recovering her cognitive faculties. The Supreme Court of Missouri held that because there was no clear and convincing evidence of Nancy's desire to have life-sustaining treatment withdrawn under such circumstances, her parents lacked authority to effectuate such a request. We . . . now affirm.

On the night of January 11, 1983, Nancy Cruzan lost control of her car as she traveled down Elm Road in Jasper County, Missouri. The vehicle overturned, and Cruzan was discovered lying face down in a ditch without detectable respiratory or cardiac function. Paramedics were able to restore her breathing and heartbeat at the accident site, and she was transported to a hospital in an unconscious state. An attending neurosurgeon diagnosed her as having sustained probable cerebral contusions compounded by significant anoxia (lack of oxygen). The Missouri trial court in this case found that permanent brain damage generally results after 6 minutes in an anoxic state; it was estimated that Cruzan was deprived of oxygen from 12 to 14 minutes. She remained in a coma for approximately three weeks and then progressed to an unconscious state in which she was able to orally ingest some nutrition. In order to ease feeding and further the recovery, surgeons implanted a gastrostomy feeding and hydration tube in Cruzan with the consent of her then husband. Subsequent rehabilitative efforts proved unavailing. She now lies in a Missouri state hospital in what is commonly referred to as a persistent vegetative state: generally, a condition in which a person exhibits motor reflexes but evinces no indications of significant cognitive function.[1] The State of Missouri is bearing the cost of her care.

After it had become apparent that Nancy Cruzan had virtually no chance of regaining her mental faculties her parents asked hospital employees to terminate the artificial nutrition and hydration procedures. All agree that such a removal would cause her death. The employees refused to honor the request without court approval. The parents then sought and received authorization from the state trial court for termination. The court found that a person in Nancy's condition had a fundamental right under the State and Federal Constitutions to refuse or direct the withdrawal of "death prolonging procedures." The court also found that Nancy's "expressed thoughts at age twenty-five in somewhat serious conversation with a housemate friend that if sick or injured she would not wish to continue her life unless she could live at least halfway normally suggests that given her present condition she would not wish to continue on with her nutrition and hydration."

The Supreme Court of Missouri reversed by a divided vote. The court recognized a right to refuse treatment embodied in the common-law doctrine of informed consent, but expressed skepticism about the application of that doctrine in the circumstances of this case. The court also declined to read a broad right of privacy into the State Constitution which would "support the right of a person to refuse medical treatment in every circumstance," and expressed doubt as to whether such a right existed under the United States Constitution. It then decided that the Missouri Living Will statute (1986) embodied a state policy strongly favoring the preservation of life. The court found that Cruzan's statements to her roommate regarding her desire to live or die under certain conditions were "unreliable for the purpose of determining her intent," "and thus insufficient to support the co-guardians' claim to exercise substituted judgment on Nancy's behalf." It rejected the argument that Cruzan's parents were entitled to order the termination of her medical treatment, concluding that "no person can assume that choice for an incompetent in the absence of the formalities required under Missouri's Living Will statutes or the clear and convincing, inherently reliable evidence absent here." . . .

We granted certiorari to consider the question of whether Cruzan has a right under the United States Constitution which would require the hospital to withdraw life-sustaining treatment from her under the circumstances.

At common law, even the touching of one person by another without consent and without legal justification was a battery. Before the turn of the century, this Court observed that "[n]o right is held more sacred, or is more carefully guarded, by the common law, than the right of every individual to the possession and control of his own person, free from all restraint or interference of others, unless by clear and unquestionable authority of law." This notion of bodily integrity has been embodied in the requirement that informed consent is generally required for medical treatment. Justice Cardozo, while on the Court of Appeals of New York, aptly described this doctrine: "Every human being of adult years and sound mind has a right to determine what shall be done with his own body; and a surgeon who performs an operation without his patient's consent commits an assault, for which he is liable in damages." The informed consent doctrine has become firmly entrenched in American tort law.

The logical corollary of the doctrine of informed consent is that the patient generally possesses the right not to consent, that is, to refuse treatment. Until about 15 years ago and the seminal decision [of the New Jersey Supreme Court] in *In re Quinlan* (1976), the number of right-to-refuse-treatment decisions were relatively few. Most of the earlier cases involved patients who refused medical treatment forbidden by their religious beliefs, thus implicating First Amendment rights as well as common law rights of self-determination. More recently, however, with the advance of medical technology capable of sustaining life well past the point where natural forces would have brought certain death in earlier times, cases involving the right to refuse life-sustaining treatment have burgeoned.

In the Quinlan case, young Karen Quinlan suffered severe brain damage as the result of anoxia, and entered a persistent vegetative state. Karen's father sought judicial approval to disconnect his daughter's respirator. The New Jersey Supreme Court granted the relief, holding that Karen had a right of privacy grounded in the Federal Constitution to terminate treatment. Recognizing that this right was not absolute, however, the court balanced it against asserted state interests. Noting that the State's interest "weakens and the individual's right to privacy grows as the degree of bodily invasion increases and the prognosis dims," the court concluded that the state interests had to give way in that case. The court also concluded that the "only practical way" to prevent the loss of Karen's privacy right due to her incompetence was to allow her guardian and family to decide "whether she would exercise it in these circumstances."

After *Quinlan*, however, most courts have based a right to refuse treatment either solely on the common-law right to informed consent or on both the common law right and a constitutional right . . .

. . . State courts have available to them for decision a number of sources—state constitutions, statutes, and common law—which are not available to us. In this Court, the question is simply and starkly whether the United States Constitution prohibits Missouri from choosing the rule of decision which it did. This is the first case in which we have been squarely presented with the issue of whether the United States Constitution grants what is in common parlance referred to as a "right to die." We follow the judicious counsel . . . that in deciding "a question of such magnitude and importance . . . it is the [better] part of wisdom not to attempt, by any general statement, to cover every possible phase of the subject."

The Fourteenth Amendment provides that no State shall "deprive any person of life, liberty, or property, without due process of law." The principle that a competent person has a constitutionally protected liberty interest in refusing unwanted medical treatment may be inferred from our prior decisions. In *Jacobson v. Massachusetts* (1905), for instance, the Court balanced an individual's liberty interest in declining an unwanted smallpox vaccine against the State's interest in preventing disease . . .

Just this Term, in the course of holding that a State's procedures for administering antipsychotic medication to prisoners were sufficient to satisfy due process concerns, we recognized that prisoners possess "a significant liberty interest in avoiding the unwanted administration of antipsychotic drugs under the Due Process Clause of the Fourteenth Amendment." Still other cases support the recognition of a general liberty interest in refusing medical treatment.

But determining that a person has a "liberty interest" under the Due Process Clause does not end the inquiry;[2] "whether respondent's constitutional rights have been violated must be determined by balancing his liberty interests against the relevant state interests."

Petitioners insist that under the general holdings our cases, the forced administration of life-sustaining medical treatment, and even of artificially delivered food and water essential to life, would implicate a competent person's liberty interest. Although we think the logic of the cases [referred to] above would embrace such a liberty interest, the dramatic consequences involved in refusal of such treatment would inform the inquiry as to whether the deprivation of that interest is constitutionally permissible. But for purposes of this case, we assume that the United States Constitution would grant a competent person a constitutionally protected right to refuse lifesaving hydration and nutrition.

Petitioners go on to assert that an incompetent person should possess the same right in this respect as is possessed by a competent person . . .

The difficulty with petitioners' claims is that in a sense it begs the question: an incompetent person is not able to make an informed and voluntary choice to exercise a hypothetical right to refuse treatment or any other right. Such a "right" must be exercised for her, if at all, by some sort of surrogate. Here, Missouri has in effect recognized that under certain circumstances a surrogate may act for the patient in electing to have hydration and nutrition withdrawn in such a way as to cause death, but it has established a procedural safeguard to assure that the action of the surrogate conforms as best it may to the wishes expressed by the patient while competent. Missouri requires that evidence of the incompetent's wishes as to the withdrawal of treatment be proved by clear and convincing evidence. The question, then, is whether the United States Constitution forbids the establishment of this procedural requirement by the State. We hold that it does not.

Whether or not Missouri's clear and convincing evidence requirement comports with the United States Constitution depends in part on what interests the State may properly seek to protect in this situation. Missouri relies on its interest in the protection and preservation of human life, and there can be no gainsaying this interest. As a general matter, the States—indeed, all civilized nations—demonstrate their commitment to life by treating homicide as serious crime. Moreover, the majority of States in this country have laws imposing criminal penalties on one who assists another to commit suicide. We do think a State is required to remain neutral in the face of an informed and voluntary decision by a physically able adult to starve to death.

But in the context presented here, a State has more particular interests at stake. The choice between life and death is a deeply personal decision of obvious and overwhelming finality. We believe Missouri may legitimately seek to safeguard the personal element of this choice through the imposition of heightened evidentiary requirements. It cannot be disputed that the Due Process Clause protects an interest in life as well as an interest in refusing life-sustaining medical treatment. Not all incompetent patients will have loved ones available to serve as surrogate decisionmakers. And even where family members are present, "[t]here will, of course, be some unfortunate situations in which family members will not act to protect a patient." A State is entitled to guard against potential abuses in such situations. Similarly, a State is entitled to consider that a judicial proceeding to make a determination regarding an incompetent's wishes may very well not be an adversarial one, with the added guarantee of accurate factfinding that the adversary process brings with it. Finally, we think a State may properly decline to make judgments about the "quality" of life that a particular individual may enjoy, and simply assert an unqualified interest in the preservation of human life to be weighed against the constitutionally protected interests of the individual.

In our view, Missouri has permissibly sought to advance these interests through the adoption of a "clear and convincing" standard of proof to govern such proceedings. "The function of a standard of proof, as that concept is embodied in the Due Process Clause and in the realm of factfinding, is to 'instruct the factfinder concerning the degree of confidence our society thinks he should have in the correctness of factual conclusions for a particular type of adjudication.'" . . .

We think it self-evident that the interests at stake in the instant proceedings are more substantial, both on an individual and societal level, than those involved in a run-of-the-mine civil dispute. But not only does the standard of proof reflect the importance of a particular adjudication, it also serves as "a societal judgment about how the risk of error should be distributed between the litigants." The more stringent the burden of proof a party must bear, the more that party bears the risk of an erroneous decision. We believe that Missouri may permissibly place an increased risk of an erroneous decision on those seeking to terminate an incom-

petent individual's life-sustaining treatment. An erroneous decision not to terminate results in a maintenance of the status quo;
the possibility of subsequent developments such as advancements
in medical science, the discovery of new evidence regarding the
patient's intent, changes in the law, or simply the unexpected
death of the patient despite the administration of life-sustaining
treatment, at least create the potential that a wrong decision will
eventually be corrected or its impact mitigated. An erroneous
decision to withdraw life-sustaining treatment, however, is not
susceptible of correction . . .

In sum, we conclude that a State may apply a clear and convincing evidence standard in proceedings where a guardian seeks to
discontinue nutrition and hydration of a person diagnosed to be
in a persistent vegetative state. . . .

The Supreme Court of Missouri held that in this case the testimony adduced at trial did not amount to clear and convincing
proof of the patient's desire to have hydration and nutrition withdrawn. In so doing, it reversed a decision of the Missouri trial
court which had found that the evidence "suggest[ed]" Nancy
Cruzan would not have desired to continue such measures, but
which had not adopted the standard of "clear and convincing evidence" enunciated by the Supreme Court. The testimony adduced
at trial consisted primarily of Nancy Cruzan's statements made
to a house-mate about a year before her accident that she would
not want to live should she face life as a "vegetable," and other
observations to the same effect. The observations did not deal in
terms with withdrawal of medical treatment or of hydration and
nutrition. We cannot say that the Supreme Court of Missouri
committed constitutional error in reaching the conclusion that
it did.[3]

Petitioners alternatively contend that Missouri must accept the
"substituted judgment" of close family members even in the absence of substantial proof that their views reflect the views of the
patient. . . .

No doubt is engendered by anything in this record but that
Nancy Cruzan's mother and father are loving and caring parents.
If the State were required by the United States Constitution to
repose a right of "substituted judgment" with anyone, the Cru-
zans would surely qualify. But we do not think the Due Process

Clause requires the State to repose judgment on these matters with anyone but the patient herself. Close family members may have a strong feeling—a feeling not at all ignoble or unworthy, but not entirely disinterested, either—that they do not wish to witness the continuation of the life of a loved one which they regard as hopeless, meaningless, and even degrading. But there is not automatic assurance that the view of close family members will necessarily be the same as the patient's would have been had she been confronted with the prospect of her situation while competent. All of the reasons previously discussed for allowing Missouri to require clear and convincing evidence of the patient's wishes lead us to conclude that the State may choose to defer only to those wishes, rather than confide the decision to close family members.

The judgment of the Supreme Court of Missouri is *Affirmed*.

NOTES

1. The State Supreme Court, adopting much of the trial court's findings, described Nancy Cruzan's medical condition as follows: " . . . In sum, Nancy is diagnosed as in a persistent vegetative state. She is not dead. She is not terminally ill. Medical experts testified that she could live another thirty years."

2. Although many state courts have held that a right to refuse treatment is encompassed by a generalized constitutional right of privacy, we have never so held. We believe this issue is more properly analyzed in terms of a Fourteenth Amendment liberty interest. See *Bowers v. Hardwick* (1986).

3. The clear and convincing standard of proof has been variously defined in this context as "proof sufficient to persuade the trier of fact that the patient held a firm and settled commitment to the termination of life supports under the circumstances like those presented," and as evidence which "produces in the mind of the trier of fact a firm belief or conviction as to the truth of the allegations sought to be established, evidence so clear, direct and weighty and convincing as to enable [the factfinder] to come to a clear conviction, without hesitancy, of the truth of the precise facts in issue."

3

Prolonging Life:
Some Legal Considerations

George P. Fletcher

I

NEW MEDICAL TECHNIQUES for prolonging life force both the legal and medical professions to re-examine their traditional attitudes towards life and death. New problems emerge from the following recurrent situation: a comatose patient shows no signs of brain activity; according to the best medical judgment, he has an infinitesimal chance of recovery; yet he can be sustained by a mechanical respirator. How long should his physician so keep him alive? And in making his decision, how much weight should the physician give to the wishes and resources of the family, and to the prospect that his time might be profitably used in caring for patients with a better chance of recovery?

According to one line of thought, the physician's leeway in caring for terminal patients is limited indeed. He may turn off the respirator, but only at a risk of prosecution and conviction for murder. The insensitive logic of the law of homicide, disregarding as it does the context of the purpose of the physician's effort, would prompt some to equate the physician's turning off the respirator with a hired gunman's killing in cold blood. The acts of both result in death; the actors intend that death should follow; and in neither case is the killing provoked, excused or justified. Thus like the gunman, the physician is guilty of murder.

The approach of equating the physician's turning off a mechanical respirator with the gunman's killing for hire is, to say the least,

George P. Fletcher, "Prolonging Life: Some Legal Considerations," *42 Wash. L. Rev.*, pp. 999–1016 (1967). Reprinted by permission of the publisher.

askew with reality. It totally misses the demands of the medical mission. It means that physicians must use modern devices for sustaining life with trepidation; they must proceed haltingly, unsure of the legal consequences of discontinuing therapy. It is of little solace to the medical practitioner that institutional facts check the cold rigor of the common law. True, his decisions in the operating room are minimally visible; not even the patient's family need learn whether death came "naturally" or upon the disruption of therapy. And even if it should become known to the family and the community that the physician's decision shortened the lifespan of the patient, it is unlikely that the physician should suffer. Common law courts have never convicted a medical practitioner either for shortening the life of a suffering, terminal patient or for refusing to render life-sustaining aid. Yet men of goodwill wish to proceed not by predictions of what will befall them but by perceiving and conforming to their legal and moral obligations.

The apparent rigidity of the common law of homicide has evoked demands for reform. The proposals for vesting physicians with greater flexibility in caring for terminal patients are of two strands. The first is a movement towards instituting voluntary euthanasia, which would permit the medically supervised killing of patients who consent to death. These proposals warrant continued discussion and criticism, but they apply only in cases of patients still conscious and able to consent to their own demise. Separate problems adhere to the cases of doomed, unconscious patients who may be kept alive by mechanical means. In the latter area, the movement for reform has stimulated the pursuit of a definition of death that would permit physicians to do what they will with the bodies of hopeless, "legally dead" patients. In France and Sweden, as well as in the United States, proponents of reform have urged the cessation of brain activity—as evidenced by a flat electroencephalograph (EEG) reading—as the criterion of death. Setting the moment of legal death prior to the stilling of the heart is critical to those pressing for greater legal flexibility in transplanting vital organs from doomed patients to those with greater hopes of recovery. Waiting until the heart fails makes transplanting difficult, if not impossible. At stake in the pursuit of a legal definition of death is the prospect of a vast increase in the supply of kidneys and, some day, of livers, hearts and ovaries for the purpose of transplanting. The reliance on the concept of death, however, is a verbal detour. The reformers are concerned about two practical decisions: (1) when can a physician legally discontinue aid to a patient with an infinitesimal chance of recovery; and (2) when can a physician legally remove organs from a terminal patient. To resolve these problems, one need not construct a concept of legal death. Concern for the moment of death presupposes: (1) that both of these decisions should depend on the same criteria; and (2) that the controlling criteria should be medical facts, rather than the host of criteria relating to the patient's family condition and to the importance of the physician's time and of the machinery used in sustaining life.

Rather than promote either the movement for voluntary euthanasia or the search for a new definition of death, this essay proposes a third approach to the legal situation. We can furnish practising physicians at least some flexibility in the operating room by invoking a more sensitive interpretation of the law as it now stands. To loosen the legal vise of the law of homicide, we need only take a closer look at its pinions. We need to question each of the steps leading to the view that the physician's turning off a respirator or a kidney machine is an act subjecting him to tort and criminal liability for homicide.

There are only a few points at which the structure can give. Consider the applicable elements of common law murder: (1) an act resulting in death, (2) a intent to inflict death, (3) malice aforethought, (4) absence of defences. Beginning at the end of the list, one is hard pressed to justify or excuse the killing by invoking a recognized defence. If the common law courts were more amenable to a general defence of necessity in homicide cases, one could argue that if another patient had a superior likelihood of recovery using the machine, the attending physician would be warranted in removing a patient from the machine who was then dependent upon it for his life. A defence of this sort could serve as a welcome guide to those concerned about the legal limits of allocating the use of kidney machines. The appropriate foothold for the defence would be a physician's common law prerogative to abort a foetus when necessary to save the life of the mother. Yet that defence is premised on the judgment that the life of the mother represents a more worthy interest than that of the unborn child; when it comes to a choice between the two, the mother has a superior right to live. One is advisedly wary of the analogical claim that the patient with the greater likelihood of recovery has a superior right to live. We have lived too long with the notion that all human beings have an equal claim to life.

If the prospects of a defence are questionable, forays on the issues of intent and malice seem hopeless. The aim of the physician's behaviour may not be to kill, yet he knows that death is certain to follow if he interrupts therapy to free the respirator for another patient. And knowledge that death is certain to follow is enough to say, at least according to the dictionary of the law, that he "intends" death to result from his conduct. Also, it is too late in the evolution of the common law to make the concept of malice mean what it purports to mean, namely ill-will, base motives and the like. Surely, the man on the street would not say that a physician is malicious in breaking off his care of a fated patient? Indeed, in the interest of saving the family from financial ruin or directing his efforts more profitably, it might be the humane thing to do. Yet the common law long ago betrayed the ordinary English background of its rule that a man must kill "maliciously" to be guilty of murder. The rigours of distinguishing good motives from bad and the elusiveness of motive as an object of prosecutorial proof gave way nearly four centuries ago to the concept of implied malice as a tool for drawing important distinctions in the law of homicide.

It appears that there is only one stage in the structure that might readily yield under analysis. That is the initial claim that the turning off of a mechanical respirator is an act resulting in death. The alternative would be to regard the flipping of the switch as an omission, a forbearance—a classification that would lead to a wholly different track of legal analysis. It seems novel to suggest that flipping a switch should count as an omission or forbearance to act. For like the act of the gunman in pulling a trigger, flipping a switch represents an exertion of the will. It is bodily movement, and for many, that would be enough to say that the behaviour constitutes an act, not an omission. Yet as I shall argue in this essay, the turning off of a mechanical respirator should be classified as omission. It should be regarded on a par with the passivity of that infamous passer-by who gleefully watches a stranded child drown in a swimming-pool. As we shall see, this view of the problem has vast implications for advising physicians of their legal leeway in rendering therapy to terminal patients.

Much of what follows is an exercise of conceptual analysis. It is an effort to devise a test for determining which of two competitive schemes—that for acts or that for omissions—should apply in analysing a given question of responsibility for the death of another. It is significant inquiry, if only to add a word to the discussion of the ponderous legal quandaries of physicians who care for terminal patients. The problem is also of wider significance for the theory of tort and criminal liability. The area of liability for omissions bristles with moral, analytic and institutional puzzles. In the course of this inquiry, we shall confront some of those problems; others we shall catalogue in passing.

II

The question is posed: Is the physician's discontinuing aid to a terminal patient an act or omission? To be sure, the choice of legal track does not yield radically different results. For some omissions, physicians are liable in much the same way as they are for unpermitted operations and negligent treatment. One need only consider the following turn of events. Dr. Brown is the family doctor of the Smith family and has been for several years. Tim Smith falls ill with pneumonia. Brown sees him once or twice at the family home and administers the necessary therapy. One evening, upon receiving a telephone call from the Smith family that Tim is in a critical condition, Dr. Brown decides that he should prefer to remain at his bridge game than to visit the sick child. Brown fails to render aid to the child; it is clear that Brown would be liable criminally and civilly if death should ensue. That he has merely omitted to act, rather than asserted himself intentionally to end life, is immaterial in assessing his criminal and civil liability. Of course, the doctor would not be under an obligation to respond to the call of a stranger who said that he needed help. But there is a difference between a stranger and someone who has placed himself in the care of a physician. The factor of reliance and reasonable expectation that the doctor will render aid means that the doctor is legally obligated to do so. His failure to do so is then tantamount to an intentional infliction of harm. As his motive, be it for good or ill, is irrelevant in analysing his liability for assertive killing, his motive is also irrelevant in analysing his liability for omitting to render aid when he is obligated to do so.

Thus, it makes no difference whether a doctor omits to render aid because he prefers to continue playing bridge, or if he does so in the hope that the patient's misery will come quickly to a natural end. A doctor may be criminally and civilly liable either for intentionally taking life or for omitting to act and thus permitting death to occur. However, the sources of these two legal proscriptions are different. And this difference in the source of the law may provide the key for the analysis of the doctor's liability in failing to prolong life in the case discussed at the outset of this essay. That a doctor may not actively kill is an application of the general principle that no man may actively kill a fellow human being. In contrast, the principle that a doctor may not omit to render aid to a patient justifiably relying upon him is a function of the special relationship that exists between doctor and patient. Thus, in analysing the doctor's legal duty to his patient, one must take into consideration whether the question involved is an act or an omission. If it is an act, the relationship between the doctor and patient is irrelevant. If it is an omission, the relationship is all-controlling.

With these points in mind, we may turn to an analysis of specific aspects of the medical decision not to prolong life. The first problem is to isolate the relevant medical activity. The recurrent pattern includes: stopping cardiac resuscitation, turning off a respirator, a pacemaker or a kidney machine, and removing the tubes and devices used with these life-sustaining machines. The initial decision of classification determines the subsequent legal analysis of the case. If turning off the respirator is an "act" under the law, then it is unequivocally forbidden: it is on a par with injecting air into the patient's veins. If, on the other hand, it is classified as an "omission," the analysis proceeds more flexibly. Whether it would be forbidden as an omission would depend on the demands imposed by the relationship between doctor and patient.

There are gaps in the law; and we are confronted with one of them. There is simply no way of focusing the legal authorities so as to determine whether the process of turning off the respirator is an act or an omission. That turning off the respirator takes physical movement need not be controlling. There might be "acts" without physical movement, as, for example, if one should sit motionless in the driver's seat as one's car heads towards an intended victim. Surely that would be an act causing death; it would be murder regardless of the relationship between the victim and his assassin. Similarly, there might be cases of omissions involving physical exertion, perhaps even the effort required to turn off the respirator. The problem is not whether there is or there is not physical movement; there must be another test.

That other test, I should propose, is whether on all the facts we should be inclined to speak of the activity as one that causes harm or one merely that permits harm to occur. The usage of the verbs "causing" and "permitting" corresponds to the distinction in the clear cases between acts and omissions. If a doctor injects air into the veins of a suffering patient, he causes harm. On the other hand, if the doctor fails to stop on the highway to aid a stranger injured in a motor-car accident, he surely permits harm to occur, and he might be morally blameworthy for that; but as the verb "cause" is ordinarily used, his failing to stop is not the cause of the harm.

As native speakers of English, we are equipped with linguistic sensitivity for the distinction between causing harm and permitting harm to occur. That sensitivity reflects a common-sense perception of reality; and we should employ it in classifying the hard cases arising in discussions of the prolongation of life. Is turning off the respirator an instance of causing death or permitting death to occur? If the patient is beyond recovery and on the verge of death, one balks at saying that the activity causes death. It is far more natural to speak of the case as one of permitting death to occur. It is significant that we are inclined to refer to the respirator as a means for prolonging life; we would not speak of insulin shots for a diabetic in the same way. The use of the term "prolongation of life" builds on the same perception of reality that prompts us to say that turning off the respirator is an activity permitting death to occur, rather than causing death. And that basic perception is that using the respirator interferes artificially in the pattern of events. Of course, the perception of the natural and of the artificial is a function of time and culture. What may seem artificial today, may be a matter of course in ten years. Nonetheless, one *does* perceive many uses of the respirator today as artificial prolongations of life. And that perception of artificiality should be enough to determine the legal classification of the case. Because we are prompted to refer to the activity of turning off the respirator as activity permitting death to occur, rather than causing death, we may classify the case as an omission, rather than as an act.

To clarify our approach, we might consider the following possible case. A pedestrian D. notices that a nearby car, parked with apparently inadequate brakes, is about to roll downhill. P.'s house is parked directly in its path. D. rushes to the front of the car and with effort manages to arrest its movement for a few minutes. Though he feels able to hold back the car for several more minutes (time enough perhaps to give warning of the danger), he decides that he has had enough; and he steps to one side, knowing full well that the car will roll squarely into P.'s front-yard. That is precisely what it does. What are P.'s rights against D.? Again, the problem is whether the defendant's behaviour should be treated as an act or as an omission. If it is an act, he is liable for trespass against P.'s property. If it is an omission, the law of trespass is inapplicable; and the problem devolves into a search for a relationship between P. and D. that would impose on D. the duty to prevent this form of damage to P.'s property. Initially, one is inclined to regard D.'s behaviour as an act bringing on harm. Like the physician's turning off a respirator, his stepping aside represents physical exertion. Yet, as in the physician's case, we are led to the opposite result by asking whether in the circumstances D. caused the harm or merely permitted it to occur. Surely, a newspaper account would employ the latter description; D. let the car go, he permitted it to roll on, but he is no more a causal factor that if he had not initially intervened to halt its forward motion. We deny D.'s causal contribution for reasons akin to those in the physician's case. In both instances, other factors are sufficient in themselves to bring on the harmful result. As the car's brakes were inadequate to hold it on the hill, so the patient's hopeless condition brought on his death. With sufficient causal factors present, we can imagine the harm's occurring without the physician's or the pedestrian's contribution. And thus we are inclined to think of the behaviour of each as something less than a causal force.

One might agree that, as a matter of common sense, we can distinguish between causing harm and permitting harm to occur and yet balk at referring to the way people ordinarily describe phenomena in order to solve hard problems of legal policy. After all, what if people happen to describe things differently? Would that mean that we would have to devise different answers to the same legal problems? To vindicate a resort to common-sense notions and linguistic usage as a touchstone for separating acts from omissions, we must clarify the interlacing of these three planes of the problem: (1) the distinction between acts and omissions, (2) the ordinary usage of the terms "causing" and "permitting," and (3) resorting in cases of omissions, but not in cases of acts, to the relationship between the agent and his victim in setting the scope of the agent's duties. The ultimate claim is that perceiving an activity as one permitting rather than causing harm is a sufficient condition for classifying it as an omission. Admittedly, the path of demonstration is roundabout. We turn first to the proposition that the relationship between the parties is an indispensable factor in the just evaluation of liability for permitting harm; and second to the conclusion that, to permit recourse to the relationship of the parties, cases of permitting harm should be classified as legal omissions. The former proposition is one of policy and fairness; the latter is one of the demands of the legal tradition. To make the policy claim, we need a clear understanding of the function of causal judgments in legal analysis. It is only then that we may perceive why the relationship of the parties is critical when the actor does not cause, but merely permits, harm to occur.

In the ascription of tort and criminal liability, causal judgments function to isolate from the mass of society those individuals whose liability may be left to turn on an examination of personal fault. Those who have caused harm are, in this sense, candidates for liability. They possess a minimal connection with the harm that has occurred. From this class of candidates for liability, the apt rules of law function to determine who should be held liable and who should be excused from liability.

The one area of the law where one has difficulty in isolating candidates for liability is the area of omissions. When others have stood by and permitted harm to occur, we either have too many candidates for liability or we have none at all. A helpless old woman succumbs to starvation. Many people knew of her condition and did nothing: the postman, her hired nurse, her daughter, the bill collector, the telephone operator—each of them allowed her to die. Could we say, on analogy to causing death, that permitting the death to occur should serve as the criterion for selecting these people as candidates for liability? If we say that all of them are candidates for liability, then the burden falls to the criteria of fault to decide which of them, if any, should be liable for wrongful death and criminal homicide. The problem is whether the criteria of fault are sufficiently sensitive to resolve the question of liability. What kinds of questions should we ask in assessing fault? Did each voluntarily omit to render aid? Did any of them face a particular hazard in doing so? Were any of them in a particularly favourable position to avert the risk of death? If these are the questions we must ask in assessing fault and affixing liability, we are at a loss to discriminate among the candidates for liability. Each acted voluntarily with knowledge of the peril; none faced personal hazard in offering assistance; and their capacities to avert the risk were equal. Thus the criteria of fault are useless (at least in the type of case sketched here) for discriminating among the candidates.

Affixing liability fairly in cases of omission requires a more sensitive filtering mechanism prior to the application of the traditional criteria of personal fault. The concept of permitting harm sweeps too wide; and the criteria of personal fault tend to be of little avail in narrowing the field. Thus one can understand the role of the relationship between the parties as a touchstone of liability. Legal systems, both common law and continental, have resorted to the relationship between the parties as a device for narrowing the field to those individuals whose liability may be left to depend on personal fault. According to the conventional rules, the old woman's nurse and daughter are candidates potentially liable for permitting death to occur. Liability would rest on personal fault, primarily on the voluntariness of each in omitting to render aid. Thus the conventional rules as to when one has a duty to render aid fulfill the same function as the causal inquiry in its domain: these rules, like the predication of causation, isolate individuals whose behaviour is then scrutinized for the marks of negligent and intentional wrongdoing.

By demonstrating the parallel between the causal concept in cases of acts and the relationship between the parties in cases of omission, we have come a long way in support of our thesis. We have shown that in cases of permitting harm to occur, one is required to resort to the relationship between the parties in order fairly to select those parties whose liability should turn on criteria of personal fault. In the absence of a causal judgment, with its attendant assignment of differentiated responsibility for the risk of harm, one can proceed only by asking: Is this the kind of relationship—for example, parent-child, doctor-patient—in which one person ought to help another? And on grounds ranging from common decency to contract, one derives individual duties to render aid when needed.

One step of the argument remains: the conclusion that cases of permitting harm are instances of omissions, not of acts. This is a step that turns not so much on policy and analysis as on acceptance of the received premises of the law of homicide. One of these premises is that acting intentionally to cause death is unconditionally prohibited: the relationship between the defendant and his victim is irrelevant. One may resort to the relationship between the parties only in cases of omissions indirectly resulting in harm.[1] With these two choices and no others, the logic of classification is ineluctable. Cases of permitting harm, where one must have recourse to the relationship between the parties, cannot be classified as cases of acts: to do so would preclude excusing the harm on the ground that the relationship between the parties did not require its avoidance. Thus, to permit recourse to relationship of the parties, one must treat cases of permitting harm as cases of omissions.

To complete our inquiry, we need attend to an asymmetry in the analysis of causing and permitting. As Professors Hart and Honoré have shown, some omissions may be the causes of harm.[2] And thus, the category of causing harm includes some cases of omitting, as well as all cases of acting, to bring on harm. Suppose, for example, that an epileptic regularly takes pills to avert a seizure. Yet on one occasion he omits to take the pills in the hope that he is no longer required to do so. He has a seizure. The cause of his seizure is clear: he omitted to take the prescribed pill. In the same way, a physician failing to give a diabetic patient a routine shot of insulin would be the cause of harm that might ensue. The taking of the pill and the giving of the shot are the expected state of affairs. They represent normality, and their omission, abnormality. Because we anticipate the opposite, the omission explains what went wrong, why our expectations were not realized. In contrast, if pills to avert epileptic seizures had just been devised, we would not say, as to someone who had never taken the pills, that his failure to do so had brought on his attack. In that case, our expectations would be different, the omission to take pills would not represent an abnormality, and the anticipated omission would not be a satisfying causal explanation of the attack.[3]

A doctor's failure to give his diabetic patient an insulin shot is a case warranting some attention. By contemporary standards, insulin shots, unlike mechanical respirators, do not interfere artificially in the course of nature; because the use of insulin is standard medical practice, we would not describe its effect as one of prolonging life. We would not say that withholding the shot permits death; it is a case of an omission causing harm. With the prohibition against causing death, one should not have to refer to the doctor-patient relationship to determine the criminality of the doctor's omission. Yet, in fact, common law courts would ground a conviction for omitting to give the shot on the doctor's duty to render aid to his patient—a duty derived from the doctor-patient relationship. Thus we encounter an apparent inconsistency: a case of causing in which one resorts to the relationship of the parties to determine criminality. We can reconcile the case with our thesis by noting that cases of omissions causing harm possess the criteria—regularity of performance and reliance—that give rise to duties of care. The doctor is clearly under a duty to provide his patient with an insulin shot if the situation demands it. And the duty is so clear, precisely because one expects an average doctor . . . to use insulin when necessary; this is the same expectation that prompts us to say that his failure to give the shot would be the cause of his patient's death.

That an omission can on occasion be the cause of harm prompts us, to some extent, to reformulate our thesis. We cannot say that causing harm may serve as the criterion for an act, as opposed to an omission, because some instances of causation are omissions. But we may claim with undiminished force that permitting harm to occur should be sufficient for classification as an omission. Upon analysis, we find that our thesis for distinguishing acts from omissions survives only in part; it works for some omissions, but not for all. Yet, so far as the stimulus of this investigation is concerned, the problem of physicians' permitting death to come to their terminal patients, the thesis continues to hold: permitting a patient to die is a case in which one appropriately refers to the relationship of the parties to set the scope of the physician's legal duty to his patient; in this sense it functions as an omission in legal analysis.

III

By permitting recourse to the doctor-patient relationship in fixing the scope of the doctor's duties to his patient, we have at least fashioned the concepts of the common law to respond more sensitively to the problems of the day. We have circumvented the extravagant legal conclusion that a physician's turning off a kidney machine or a respirator is tantamount to murder. Yet one critical inquiry remains. How does shunting the analysis into the track of legal omission actually affect the physician's flexibility in the operating room? We say that his duties are determined by his relationship with his patient; specifically, it is the consensual aspect of the relationship that is supposed to control the leeway of the physician. Yet there is some question as to where the control actually resides.

To take a clear case, let us suppose that prior to the onset of a terminal illness, the patient demands that his physician do everything to keep him alive and breathing as long as possible. And the physician responds, "Even if you have a flat EEG reading and there is no chance of recovery?" "Yes," the patient replies. If the doctor agrees to this bizarre demand, he becomes obligated to keep the respirator going indefinitely. Happily, cases of this type do not occur in day-to-day medical practice. In the average case, the patient has not given a thought to the problem; and his physician is not likely to alert him to it. The problem then is whether there is an implicit understanding between physician and patient as to how the physician should proceed in the last stages of a terminal illness. But would there be an implicit understanding about what the physician should do if the patient is in a coma and dependent on a mechanical respirator? This is not the kind of eventuality the average man anticipates or expects. And if he did, his would be expectations based on the customary practices of the time. If he had heard about a number of cases in which patients had been sustained for long periods of time on respirators, he might (at least prior to going into the coma) expect that he would be similarly sustained.

Thus, the analysis leads us along the following path. The doctor's duty to prolong life is a function of his relationship with his patient; and in the typical case, that relationship devolves into the patient's expectations of the treatment he will receive. Those expectations, in turn, are a function of the practices prevailing in the community at the time; and practices in the use of respirators to prolong life are no more and no less than what doctors actually do in the time and place. Thus, we have come full circle. We began the inquiry by asking: Is it legally permissible for doctors to turn off respirators used to prolong the life of doomed patients? And the answer after our tortuous journey is simply: It all depends on what doctors customarily do. The law is sometimes no more precise than that.

The conclusion of our circular journey is that doctors are in a position to fashion their own law to deal with cases of prolongation of life. By establishing customary standards, they may determine the expectations of their patients and thus regulate the understanding and the relationship between doctor and patient. And by regulating that relationship, they may control their legal obligations to render aid to doomed patients.

Thus the medical profession confronts the challenge of developing humane and sensitive customary standards of guiding decisions to prolong the lives of terminal patients. This is not a challenge that the profession may shirk. For the doctor's legal duties to render aid derive from his relationship with the patient.

George P. Fletcher

That relationship, along with the expectations implicit in it, is the responsibility of the individual doctor and the individual patient. With respect to problems not commonly discussed by the doctor with his patient, particularly the problems of prolonging life, the responsibility for the patient's expectations lies with the medical profession as a whole.

NOTES

1. For example, *Rex v. Smith,* 2 Car. and p. 448, 172 E. R. 203 (Gloucester Assizes, 1826). The analysis of criminality of D., for failing to care for an idiot brother, turns on whether keeping the brother locked up was an act or an omission. Finding the latter, the court held that the defendant bore no duty to aid his brother and directed an acquittal.

2. H. L. A. Hart and A. M. Honoré, *Causation in the Law* IX (Oxford: Oxford University Press, 1959) pp. 35–36.

3. The relationship between expectations and causation is developed more fully in Hart and Honoré, *ibid.,* Chapter 2.

4

An Irrelevant Consideration: Killing Versus Letting Die

Michael Tooley

MANY PEOPLE HOLD that there is an important moral distinction between passive euthanasia and active euthanasia. Thus, while the AMA [American Medical Association] maintains that people have a right "to die with dignity," so that it is morally permissible for a doctor to allow someone to die if that person wants to and is suffering from an incurable illness causing pain that cannot be sufficiently alleviated, the AMA is unwilling to countenance active euthanasia for a person who is in similar straits, but who has the misfortune not to be suffering from an illness that will result in a speedy death.

A similar distinction with respect to infanticide has become a commonplace of medical thinking and practice. If an infant is a mongoloid, or a microcephalic, and happens also to have some other defect requiring corrective surgery if the infant is to live, many doctors and hospitals believe that the parents have the right to decide whether the surgery will be performed, and thus whether the infant will survive. But if the child does not have any other defect, it is believed that the parents do not have the right to terminate its life.[1]

The rationale underlying these distinctions between active and passive euthanasia, and between active and passive infanticide, is the same: the idea that there is a crucial moral difference between intentionally killing and intentionally letting die. This idea is admittedly very common. But I believe that it can be shown to reflect either confused thinking or a moral point of view unrelated to the interests of individuals.

Two sons are looking forward to the death of their nasty but very wealthy father. Tired of waiting, they decide, independently of one another, to kill their father. The one puts some poison in his father's whiskey, and is discovered doing so by his brother, who was just about to do the same thing. The latter then allows his father to imbibe the deadly drink, and refrains from administering an antidote which he happens to have. The one son killed his father. The other merely allowed him to die. Did the former do something significantly more wrong than the latter?

My own view is that the actions are morally equivalent, since I think that the following general principle—which may be referred to as the moral symmetry principle—is sound:[2]

> Let C be a causal process that normally leads to an outcome E. Let A be an action that initiates process C, and B be an action that stops process C before outcome E occurs. Assume further that actions A and B do not have any other morally significant consequences, and that E is the only part or outcome of C which is morally significant in itself. Then there is no moral difference between performing action A, and intentionally refraining from performing action B, assuming identical motivation in the two cases.

This principle implies that, other things being equal, it is just as wrong intentionally to refrain from administering an antidote to someone who is dying of poisoning as it is to administer the poison, provided that the same motive is operative in both cases. And, more generally, it follows that the distinction between killing and intentionally letting die is not in itself a morally significant one.

Some people find this hard to accept. However, it has been my experience that those who are inclined to reject the moral symmetry principle often do so because of a failure to understand exactly what it does and does not imply. Let me begin by considering an objection which, though badly confused, helps to clarify the principle.[3] The criticism in question claims that the moral symmetry principle can be shown to be mistaken by the following counterexample. It involves considering these two actions:

Action M: An individual refrains from giving information to the enemy even though he knows that the enemy will torture a child as long as he refuses to divulge the information.

Action N: An individual tortures a child in order to induce the enemy to give him information.

The contention is that it is "surely monstrous" to view these two actions as morally equivalent. The intuitive appeal of this position is obvious. Whether it will stand up under critical reflection is quite another matter. The crucial point, however, is that this example is just not relevant to the moral symmetry principle. That principle states, very roughly, that it is as wrong intentionally to refrain from interfering with a causal process leading to some morally significant result as it is to initiate the process. It does *not* assert that it is as wrong to refrain from *preventing someone else* from initiating a causal process as it is to initiate it oneself. So it does not imply that actions M and N are morally equivalent.

One might try to argue that although the moral symmetry principle does not imply that actions such as M and N are morally equivalent, one can formulate a generalized moral symmetry principle which does have this implication, and which ought to be accepted by anyone who is willing to accept the original principle. One can certainly formulate such a principle. The difficulty is to justify the claim that anyone who accepts the original principle ought to accept the generalization of it. For it would seem that if intentionally refraining from preventing someone else from doing something and doing it oneself are morally equivalent actions, then preventing someone else from doing something and intentionally refraining from doing it oneself are also morally equivalent actions.[4] But the intuitive feeling of most people would surely be that the mere fact that when one prevents someone else from doing something one is interfering with someone's action, whereas when one merely refrains from doing something oneself one is not, is a morally relevant difference. Thus there is a *prima facie* case against any extension of the moral symmetry principle that would have the consequence that intentionally refraining from preventing someone else from doing something is morally equivalent to doing it oneself. I certainly do not wish to assert that this *prima facie* case cannot be overcome. However, any argument that succeeded in overthrowing it would *ipso facto* give one reason to reject the contention that it is "monstrous" to treat actions M and N as morally equivalent.

What the objection to the moral symmetry principle has in effect done is to confuse that principle with *consequentialism* in ethics. If consequentialism is true, then so is the moral symmetry principle. But the converse is emphatically not the case. It is very important to realize that one can accept the moral symmetry principle without committing oneself to a consequentialist position.[5]

In order to reinforce my contention that any moral difference between actions M and N, rather than counting against the moral symmetry principle, merely reflects the fact that one's obligation to prevent others from doing something may not be as great as one's obligation to refrain from doing it oneself, consider actions that are similar to M and N except that the relevant effects are achieved *directly* rather than by influencing someone else's action:

Action M*:   One is confronted with a machine that contains a child and a military secret. The machine is so constructed that unless one pushes a button, the child will be tortured and the secret will be destroyed. If one pushes the button, the child will emerge unharmed, but the secret will be transmitted to the enemy. One refrains from pushing the button.

Action N*:   One is confronted with a similar machine. This time, however, it is so constructed that unless one pushes a button, a secret will be transmitted to the enemy, while a child will emerge unharmed. If one pushes the button, the secret will be destroyed, but the child will be tortured. One pushes the button.

Although the moral symmetry principle does not quite entail that actions M* and N* are morally equivalent, I believe that anyone who accepts that principle would agree that there is no moral difference between M* and N*. Doubtless there are *some* philosophers who would also characterize this view as "monstrous." And some philosophers have tried to argue that there is, at least, significant moral difference between acting and refraining from acting; however, all the arguments that I have seen in support of this contention seem to me to be either unsound or else not relevant to the claim that the distinction is significant *in itself.*[6]

But what is one to say about the feeling—which is admittedly fairly widespread—that there is a morally significant difference between acting and refraining from acting? I do not want simply to dismiss this feeling, even though I would maintain that appeal to such "moral intuitions" does not constitute a good way of arriving at sound moral principles. What I want to do is to try to show how the feelings in question may rest upon certain confusions.

The place to begin is by distinguishing the following two questions:

1. Is the distinction between killing and intentionally letting die morally significant *in itself?*
2. Are there *other factors* which make it *generally* the case that killing someone is more seriously wrong than intentionally letting someone die?

The answer to the second question is surely yes. In the first place, the *motive* of a person who kills someone is generally more evil than the motive of a person who merely lets someone die. A person may let someone die out of laziness or apathy, and though I would insist that such inaction is seriously wrong, it is surely not as seriously wrong as the action of a person who kills someone else because he *wants* him dead. Secondly, the alternative to letting someone die—saving his life—may involve considerable risk to the agent, or a very large expenditure of society's resources. This will rarely be true of refraining from killing someone. Thirdly, if one performs an action that normally results in the death of a person, there is little likelihood that the person will survive. While if one merely refrains from saving someone's life, there is often a substantial chance that he will survive in some other way.

These three factors—motive, cost to the agent and/or society, and the probability that death will result from one's action or inaction—all tend to make it the case that an attempt to kill someone will generally be more seriously wrong than intentionally refraining from saving someone's life. It is these factors that make the difference, rather than the difference between killing and letting die. People are right in thinking that killing is generally morally worse than merely letting someone die. Where they go wrong is in failing to notice that there are factors involved that can explain this difference in a perfectly satisfactory fashion. And, as a result, they mistakenly conclude that the difference between killing and letting die must be morally significant *in itself.*

Let me conclude my case against the distinction by mentioning an example which isolates the interfering variables, and thus raises in a vivid way the issue of whether there really is any significant moral difference between acting and intentionally refraining from acting. Imagine a machine containing two children, John and Mary. If one pushes a button, John will be killed, but Mary will emerge unharmed. If one does not push the button, John will emerge unharmed, but Mary will be killed. In the first case one kills John, while in the second case one merely lets Mary die. Does one really wish to say that the action of intentionally refraining from pushing the button is morally preferable to the action of pushing it, even though exactly one person perishes in either case? The best action, it would seem to me, would be to flip a coin to decide which action to perform, thus giving each person an equal chance of surviving. But if that isn't possible, it seems to me a matter of indifference whether one pushes the button or not.

If there is no intrinsic difference between killing and intentionally letting die, where does this leave the distinction between active and passive euthanasia? There are two possibilities that need to be considered. The first is that even if neither active nor passive euthanasia is wrong is itself, it may be that legalizing the former would have undesirable consequences, as Yale Kamisar and others have contended.[7] I do not think that this line of argument is sound; however it is certainly one that deserves very serious consideration.

The second possibility is one that arises if one holds both that there is no intrinsic difference between active and passive euthanasia and that euthanasia is, nevertheless, wrong in itself, on the grounds, say, that a person does not have a right to kill even himself in order to put an end to unbearable suffering. Such a view would be compatible with the acceptance of passive euthanasia in some cases, though not in all. For while one would be committed to holding that passive euthanasia, like active euthanasia, was wrong in itself, there might be circumstances in which the former was morally justified. The cost of keeping a person alive, for example, might be so great that allowing him to die would be the lesser of evils.

My response to this second attempt to ascribe at least limited moral significance, albeit of a derived variety, to the distinction between active and passive euthanasia, is to reject the view that active euthanasia is wrong in itself. What I should argue, ultimately, is that there must surely be some justification for the institution of morality, some reason for society to accept moral rules. And what reason more plausible than that the acceptance of a certain set of moral rules accords better with the interests of people than the acceptance of some other set of moral rules, or none at all? But some moral rules that people accept, or have accepted, are clearly such as do not serve the interests of individuals—e.g., various sexual prohibitions, such as that against masturbation. The prohibition of active euthanasia seems to be another case of a moral point of view which does not further the interests of individuals living together in society. Why, then, has this moral point of view been accepted? The answer here, as in the case of the traditional sexual outlook of Western society, is found in the powerful influence of the Christian churches.[8] This historical point deserves to be kept firmly in view when one is reflecting upon the morality of euthanasia. Many otherwise thoughtful people somehow lose sight of the fact that what they refer to as "moral intuitions" regarding euthanasia sprang originally from a certain theological outlook, one that is no longer taken seriously by most people who have taken the trouble to examine its credentials carefully and impartially.

In conclusion, then, it is far from clear that the commonly accepted distinction between active and passive euthanasia is morally significant. This has been, admittedly, a very brief survey of the relevant issues. In some cases I have been able to do little more than touch upon them in passing. However, I have tried to argue, in some detail, that the distinction between killing and letting die is not morally significant in itself. If this is right, then the reason that is most commonly offered for holding that there is a morally significant difference between active and passive euthanasia is in fact unsound.

NOTES

This essay is a slightly revised version of part of a lecture on moral issues involved in medical decisions to terminate life, which was given at a conference on medical ethics held at Brown University, February 15–16, 1974. A number of articles have subsequently appeared, some of which are contained in the present volume, which raise objections to some of the contentions advanced here. In a forthcoming book on abortion, infanticide, and euthanasia I argue that the objections are mistaken, and the central contentions sound.

1. See, for example, Raymond S. Duff and A. G. M. Campbell, "Moral and Ethical Dilemmas in the Special-Care Nursery," *The New England Journal of Medicine*, 289 (October 25, 1973), 890–94, and Anthony Shaw, "Dilemmas of 'Informed Consent' in Children," *The New England Journal of Medicine*, 289 (October 25, 1973), p. 886.

2. I appealed to a closely related principle in my papers discussing abortion and infanticide. See pages 58–60 of "Abortion and Infanticide" *Philosophy and Public Affairs*, 2 (Fall 1972), 37–65, and pages 84–86 of "A Defense of Abortion and Infanticide" in *The Problem of Abortion*, ed. J. Feinberg (Belmont, Cal.: Wadsworth, 1973), 51–92, for some remarks that are relevant to the present principle as well. My view is that when actions A and B are related in the way indicated, it is true both that performing A is morally equivalent to intentionally refraining from performing B, and that performing B is morally equivalent to intentionally refraining from performing A, assuming the same motivation in both cases.

3. This objection was advanced by Philip E. Devine in his paper "Tooley on Infanticide," read at the Eastern Meeting of the American Philosophical Association in Atlanta, December 1973.

4. This is surely very reasonable. But if justification is wanted, one can argue that (1) if actions Q and R are morally equivalent, then so are the actions of intentionally refraining from Q and intentionally refraining from R, and that (2) the action of intentionally refraining from performing some action Q is equivalent to performing action Q.

5. There is some relevant discussion by Bernard Williams in *Utilitarianism: For and Against*, by J. J. C. Smart and Bernard Williams (Cambridge: Cambridge University Press, 1973), pp. 82–100.

6. The argument offered by Daniel Dinello in his article "On Killing and Letting Die" (this volume, chapter 11) seems simply unsound. The argument advanced by P. J. Fitzgerald, on the other hand, in his article "Acting and Refraining" (*Analysis*, 27 [1967], 133–39) appears irrelevant to the contention that the distinction is morally significant in itself. For a vigorous defense of the view that the distinction is not in itself morally significant, see Jonathan Bennett's paper "Whatever the Consequences," (*Analysis*, 26, no. 23 [1966], 83–102; this volume, chapter 10). Bennett's

article is slightly marred by an inadequate analysis of the distinction between acting and refraining, but this does not affect his central contentions.

7. Yale Kamisar, "Euthanasia Legislation: Some Non-Religious Objections," in *Euthanasia and the Right to Death,* ed. A. B. Downing (Los Angeles: Nash, 1969).

8. For a discussion that helps to bring out the extent to which contemporary Western aversion to voluntary euthanasia reflects the influence of the Christian church, see Raanan Gillon's article, "Suicide and Voluntary Euthanasia: Historical Perspective," in *Euthanasia and the Right to Death,* ed. A. B. Downing (Los Angeles: Nash, 1969). Also very helpful in this regard is the discussion by Glanville Williams in *The Sanctity of Life and the Criminal Law* (New York: Knopf, 1957), chapter 8.

5

Active and Passive Euthanasia

James Rachels

The traditional distinction between active and passive euthanasia requires critical analysis. The conventional doctrine is that there is such an important moral difference between the two that, although the latter is sometimes permissible, the former is always forbidden. This doctrine may be challenged for several reasons. First of all, active euthanasia is in many cases more humane than passive euthanasia. Secondly, the conventional doctrine leads to decisions concerning life and death on irrelevant grounds. Thirdly, the doctrine rests on a distinction between killing and letting die that itself has no moral importance. Fourthly, the most common arguments in favor of the doctrine are invalid. I therefore suggest that the American Medical Association policy statement that endorses this doctrine is unsound.

THE DISTINCTION between active and passive euthanasia is thought to be crucial for medical ethics. The idea is that it is permissible, at least in some cases, to withhold treatment and allow a patient to die, but it is never permissible to take any direct action designed to kill the patient. This doctrine seems to be accepted by most doctors, and it is endorsed in a statement adopted by the House of Delegates of the American Medical Association on December 4, 1973:

> The intentional termination of the life of one human being by another—mercy killing—is contrary to that for which the medical profession stands and is contrary to the policy of the American Medical Association.
>
> The cessation of the employment of extraordinary means to prolong the life of the body when there is irrefutable evidence that

---

Printed by permission from the *New England Journal of Medicine*, 292 (January 9, 1975), 78–80.

biological death is imminent is the decision of the patient and/or his immediate family. The advice and judgment of the physician should be freely available to the patient and/or his immediate family.

However, a strong case can be made against this doctrine. In what follows I will set out some of the relevant arguments, and urge doctors to reconsider their views on this matter.

To begin with a familiar type of situation, a patient who is dying of incurable cancer of the throat is in terrible pain, which can no longer be satisfactorily alleviated. He is certain to die within a few days, even if present treatment is continued, but he does not want to go on living for those days since the pain is unbearable. So he asks the doctor for an end to it, and his family joins in the request.

Suppose the doctor agrees to withhold treatment, as the conventional doctrine says he may. The justification for his doing so is that the patient is in terrible agony, and since he is going to die anyway, it would be wrong to prolong his suffering needlessly. But now notice this. If one simply withholds treatment, it may take the patient longer to die, and so he may suffer more than he would if more direct action were taken and a lethal injection given. This fact provides strong reason for thinking that, once the initial decision not to prolong his agony has been made, active euthanasia is actually preferable to passive euthanasia, rather than the reverse. To say otherwise is to endorse the option that leads to more suffering rather than less, and is contrary to the humanitarian impulse that prompts the decision not to prolong his life in the first place.

Part of my point is that the process of being "allowed to die" can be relatively slow and painful, whereas being given a lethal injection is relatively quick and painless. Let me give a different sort of example. In the United States about one in 600 babies is born with Down's syndrome. Most of these babies are otherwise healthy—that is, with only the usual pediatric care, they will proceed to an otherwise normal infancy. Some, however, are born with congenital defects such as intestinal obstructions that require operations if they are to live. Sometimes, the parents and the doctor will decide not to operate, and let the infant die. Anthony Shaw describes what happens then:

. . . When surgery is denied [the doctor] must try to keep the infant from suffering while natural forces sap the baby's life away. As a surgeon whose natural inclination is to use the scalpel to fight off death, standing by and watching a salvageable baby die is the most emotionally exhausting experience I know. It is easy at a conference, in a theoretical discussion, to decide that such infants should be allowed to die. It is altogether different to stand by in the nursery and watch as dehydration and infection wither a tiny being over hours and days. This is a terrible ordeal for me and the hospital staff—much more so than for the parents who never set foot in the nursery.[1]

I can understand why some people are opposed to all euthanasia, and insist that such infants must be allowed to live. I think I can also understand why other people favor destroying these babies quickly and painlessly. But why should anyone favor letting "dehydration and infection wither a tiny being over hours and days"? The doctrine that says that a baby may be allowed to dehydrate and wither, but may not be given an injection that would end its life without suffering, seems so patently cruel as to require no further refutation. The strong language is not intended to offend, but only to put the point in the clearest possible way.

My second argument is that the conventional doctrine leads to decisions concerning life and death made on irrelevant grounds.

Consider again the case of the infants with Down's syndrome who need operations for congenital defects unrelated to the syndrome to live. Sometimes, there is no operation, and the baby dies, but when there is no such defect, the baby lives on. Now, an operation such as that to remove an intestinal obstruction is not prohibitively difficult. The reason why such operations are not performed in these cases is, clearly, that the child has Down's syndrome and the parents and the doctor judge that because of that fact it is better for the child to die.

But notice that this situation is absurd, no matter what view one takes of the lives and potentials of such babies. If the life of such an infant is worth preserving, what does it matter if it needs a simple operation? Or, if one thinks it better that such a baby should not live on, what difference does it make that it happens to have an unobstructed intestinal tract? In either case, the matter of life and death is being decided on irrelevant grounds. It is the

Down's syndrome, and not the intestines, that is the issue. The matter should be decided, if at all, on that basis, and not be allowed to depend on the essentially irrelevant question of whether the intestinal tract is blocked.

What makes this situation possible, of course, is the idea that when there is an intestinal blockage, one can "let the baby die," but when there is no such defect there is nothing that can be done, for one must not "kill" it. The fact that this idea leads to such results as deciding life or death on irrelevant grounds is another good reason why the doctrine should be rejected.

One reason why so many people think that there is an important moral difference between active and passive euthanasia is that they think killing someone is morally worse than letting someone die. But is it? Is killing, in itself, worse than letting die? To investigate this issue, two cases may be considered that are exactly alike except that one involves killing whereas the other involves letting someone die. Then, it can be asked whether this difference makes any difference to the moral assessments. It is important that the cases be exactly alike, except for this one difference, since otherwise one cannot be confident that it is this difference and not some other that accounts for any variation in the assessments of the two cases. So, let us consider this pair of cases:

In the first, Smith stands to gain a large inheritance if anything should happen to his six-year-old cousin. One evening while the child is taking his bath, Smith sneaks into the bathroom and drowns the child, and then arranges things so that it will look like an accident.

In the second, Jones also stands to gain if anything should happen to his six-year-old cousin. Like Smith, Jones sneaks in planning to drown the child in his bath. However, just as he enters the bathroom Jones sees the child slip and hit his head, and fall face down in the water. Jones is delighted; he stands by, ready to push the child's head back under if it is necessary, but it is not necessary. With only a little thrashing about, the child drowns all by himself, "accidentally," as Jones watches and does nothing.

Now Smith killed the child, whereas Jones "merely" let the child die. That is the only difference between them. Did either man behave better, from a moral point of view? If the difference between killing and letting die were in itself a morally important matter, one should say that Jones's behavior was less reprehensible than Smith's. But does one really want to say that? I think not. In the first place, both men acted from the same motive, personal gain, and both had exactly the same end in view when they acted. It may be inferred from Smith's conduct that he is a bad man, although that judgment may be withdrawn or modified if certain further facts are learned about him—for example, that he is mentally deranged. But would not the very same thing be inferred about Jones from his conduct? And would not the same further considerations also be relevant to any modification of this judgment? Moreover, suppose Jones pleaded, in his own defense, "After all, I didn't do anything except just stand there and watch the child drown. I didn't kill him; I only let him die." Again, if letting die were in itself less bad than killing, this defense should have at least some weight. But it does not. Such a "defense" can only be regarded as a grotesque perversion of moral reasoning. Morally speaking, it is no defense at all.

Now, it may be pointed out, quite properly, that the cases of euthanasia with which doctors are concerned are not like this at all. They do not involve personal gain or the destruction of normal healthy children. Doctors are concerned only with cases in which the patient's life is of no further use of him, or in which the patient's life has become or will soon become a terrible burden. However, the point is the same in these cases: the bare difference between killing and letting die does not, in itself, make a moral difference. If a doctor lets a patient die, for humane reasons, he is in the same moral position as if he had given the patient a lethal injection for humane reasons. If his decision was wrong—if, for example, the patient's illness was in fact curable—the decision would be equally regrettable no matter which method was used to carry it out. And if the doctor's decision was the right one, the method used is not in itself important.

The AMA policy statement isolates the crucial issue very well: the crucial issue is "the intentional termination of the life of one human being by another." But after identifying this issue, and forbidding "mercy killing," the statement goes on to deny that the cessation of treatment is the intentional termination of a life. This is where the mistake comes in, for what is the cessation of treatment, in these circumstances, if it is not "the intentional termination of the life of one human being by another"? Of course it is exactly that, and if it were not, there would be no point to it. Many people will find this judgment hard to accept. One reason, I think, is that it is very easy to conflate the question of whether killing is, in itself, worse than letting die, with the very different question of whether most actual cases of killing are more reprehensible than most actual cases of letting die. Most actual cases of killing are clearly terrible (think, for example, of all the murders reported in the newspapers), and one hears of such cases every day. On the other hand, one hardly ever hears of a case of letting die, except for the actions of doctors who are motivated by humanitarian reasons. So one learns to think of killing in a much worse light than of letting die. But this does not mean that there is something about killing that makes it in itself worse than letting die, for it is not the bare difference between killing and letting die that makes the difference in these cases. Rather, the other factors—the murderer's motive of personal gain, for example, contrasted with the doctor's humanitarian motivation—account for different reactions to the different cases.

I have argued that killing is not in itself any worse than letting die; if my contention is right, it follows that active euthanasia is not any worse than passive euthanasia. What arguments can be given on the other side? The most common, I believe, is the following:

> The important difference between active and passive euthanasia is that, in passive euthanasia, the doctor does not do anything to bring about the patient's death. The doctor does nothing, and the patient dies of whatever ills already afflict him. In active euthanasia, however, the doctor does something to bring about the patient's death: he kills him. The doctor who gives the patient with cancer a lethal injection has himself caused his patient's death; whereas if he merely ceases treatment, the cancer is the cause of the death.

A number of points need to be made here. The first is that it is not exactly correct to say that in passive euthanasia the doctor does nothing, for he does do one thing that is very important: he lets the patient die. "Letting someone die" is certainly different, in some respects, from other types of action—mainly in that it is a kind of action that one may perform by way of not performing certain other actions. For example, one may let a patient die by way of not giving medication, just as one may insult someone by way of not shaking his hand. But for any purpose of moral assessment, it is a type of action nonetheless. The decision to let a patient die is subject to moral appraisal in the same way that a decision to kill him would be subject to moral appraisal: it may be assessed as wise or unwise, compassionate or sadistic, right or wrong. If a doctor deliberately let a patient die who was suffering from a routinely curable illness, the doctor would certainly be to blame for what he had done, just as he would be to blame if he had needlessly killed the patient. Charges against him would then be appropriate. If so, it would be no defense at all for him to insist that he didn't "do anything." He would have done something very serious indeed, for he let his patient die.

Fixing the cause of death may be very important from a legal point of view, for it may determine whether criminal charges are brought against the doctor. But I do not think that this notion can be used to show a moral difference between active and passive euthanasia. The reason why it is considered bad to be the cause of someone's death is that death is regarded as a great evil—and so it is. However, if it has been decided that euthanasia—even passive euthanasia—is desirable in a given case, it has also been decided that in this instance death is no greater an evil than the patient's continued existence. And if this is true, the usual reason for not wanting to be the cause of someone's death simply does not apply.

Finally, doctors may think that all of this is only of academic interest—the sort of thing that philosophers may worry about but that has no practical bearing on their own work. After all, doctors must be concerned about the legal consequences of what they do, and active euthanasia is clearly forbidden by the law. But even so, doctors should also be concerned with the fact that the law is forcing upon them a moral doctrine that may well be indefensible, and has a considerable effect on their practices. Of course, most doctors are not now in the position of being coerced in this matter, for they do not regard themselves as merely going along with what the law requires. Rather, in statements such as the AMA policy statement that I have quoted, they are endorsing this doctrine as a central point of medical ethics. In that statement, active euthanasia is condemned not merely as illegal but as "contrary to that for which the medical profession stands," whereas passive euthanasia is approved. However, the preceding considerations suggest that there is really no moral difference between the two, considered in themselves (there may be important moral differences in some cases in their *consequences,* but, as I pointed out, these differences may make active euthanasia, and not passive euthanasia, the morally preferable option). So, whereas doctors may have to discriminate between active and passive euthanasia to satisfy the law, they should not do any more than that. In particular, they should not give the distinction any added authority and weight by writing it into official statements of medical ethics.

NOTE

1. A. Shaw, "Doctor, Do We Have a Choice?" *The New York Times Magazine,* January 30, 1972, p. 54.

6

The Intentional Termination Of Life

Bonnie Steinbock

ACCORDING TO James Rachels and Michael Tooley, whose articles immediately precede this, a common mistake in medical ethics is the belief that there is a moral difference between active and passive euthanasia. This is a mistake, they argue, because the rationale underlying the distinction between active and passive euthanasia is the idea that there is a significant moral difference between intentionally killing and intentionally letting die. "This idea," Tooley says, "is admittedly very common. But I believe that it can be shown to reflect either confused thinking or a moral point of view unrelated to the interests of individuals." Whether or not the belief that there is a significant moral difference is mistaken is not my concern here. For it is far from clear that this distinction *is* the basis of the doctrine of the American Medical Association which Rachels attacks. And if the killing/letting die distinction is not the basis of the AMA doctrine, then arguments showing that the distinction has no moral force do not, in themselves, reveal in the doctrine's adherents either "confused thinking" or "a moral point of view unrelated to the interests of individuals." Indeed, as we examine the AMA doctrine, I think it will become clear that it appeals to and makes use of a number of overlapping distinctions, which may have moral significance in particular cases, such as the distinction between intending and foreseeing, or between ordinary and extraordinary care. Let us then turn to the 1973 statement, from the House of Delegates of the American Medical Association, which Rachels cites:

"The Intentional Termination of Life" appeared in *Ethics in Science and Medicine*, Vol. 6, No. 1, 1979, pp. 59–64.

The intentional termination of the life of one human being by another—mercy killing—is contrary to that for which the medical profession stands and is contrary to the policy of the American Medical Association.

The cessation of the employment of extraordinary means to prolong the life of the body when there is irrefutable evidence that biological death is imminent is the decision of the patient and/or his immediate family. The advice and judgment of the physician should be freely available to the patient and/or his immediate family.

Rachels attacks this statement because he believes that it contains a moral distinction between active and passive euthanasia. Tooley also believes this to be the position of the AMA, saying:

Many people hold that there is an important moral distinction between passive euthanasia and active euthanasia. Thus, while the AMA maintains that people have a right "to die with dignity," so that it is morally permissible for a doctor to allow someone to die if that person wants to and is suffering from an incurable illness causing pain that cannot be sufficiently alleviated, the AMA is unwilling to countenance active euthanasia for a person who is in similar straits, but who has the misfortune not to be suffering from an illness that will result in a speedy death.

Both men, then, take the AMA position to prohibit active euthanasia, while allowing, under certain conditions, passive euthanasia.

I intend to show that the AMA statement does not imply support of the active/passive euthanasia distinction. In forbidding the intentional termination of life, the statement rejects both active and passive euthanasia. It does allow for "the cessation of the employment of extraordinary means" to prolong life. The mistake Rachels and Tooley make is in identifying the cessation of life-prolonging treatment with passive euthanasia, or intentionally letting die. If it were right to equate the two, then the AMA statement would be self-contradictory, for it would begin by condemning, and end by allowing, the intentional termination of life. But if the cessation of life-prolonging treatment is not always or necessarily passive euthanasia, then there is no confusion and no contradiction.

Why does Rachels think that the cessation of life-prolonging treatment is the intentional termination of life? He says:

> The AMA policy statement isolates the crucial issue very well: the crucial issue is "the intentional termination of the life of one human being by another." But after identifying this issue, and forbidding "mercy killing," the statement goes on to deny that the cessation of treatment is the intentional termination of a life. This is where the mistake comes in, for what is the cessation of treatment, in these circumstances, if it is not "the intentional termination of the life of one human being of another"? Of course it is exactly that, and if it were not, there would be no point to it.

However, there *can* be a point (to the cessation of life-prolonging treatment) other than an endeavor to bring about the patient's death, and so the blanket identification of cessation of treatment with the intentional termination of a life is inaccurate. There are at least two situations in which the termination of life-prolonging treatment cannot be identified with the intentional termination of the life of one human being by another.

The first situation concerns the patient's right to refuse treatment. Both Tooley and Rachels give the example of a patient dying of an incurable disease, accompanied by unrelievable pain, who wants to end the treatment which cannot cure him but can only prolong his miserable existence. Why, they ask, may a doctor accede to the patient's request to stop treatment, but not provide a patient in a similar situation with a lethal dose? The answer lies in the patient's right to refuse treatment. In general, a competent adult has the right to refuse treatment, even where such treatment is necessary to prolong life. Indeed, the right to refuse treatment has been upheld even when the patient's reason for refusing treatment is generally agreed to be inadequate.[1] This right can be over-ridden (if, for example, the patient has dependent children) but, in general, no one may legally compel you to undergo treatment to which you have not consented. "Historically, surgical intrusion has always been considered a technical battery upon the person and one to be excused or justified by consent of the patient or justified by necessity created by the circumstances of the moment. . . ."[2]

At this point, an objection might be raised that if one has the right to refuse life-prolonging treatment, then consistency demands that one have the right to decide to end his or her life, and to obtain help in doing so. The idea is that the right to refuse treatment somehow implies a right to voluntary euthanasia, and we need to see why someone might think this. The right to refuse treatment has been considered by legal writers as an example of the right to privacy or, better, the right to bodily self-determination. You have the right to decide what happens to your own body, and the right to refuse treatment is an instance of that right. But if you have the right to determine what happens to your own body, then should you not have the right to choose to end your life, and even a right to get help in doing so?

However, it is important to see that the right to refuse treatment is not the same as, nor does it entail, a right to voluntary euthanasia, even if both can be derived from the right to bodily self-determination. The right to refuse treatment is not itself a "right to die"; that one may choose to exercise this right even at the risk of death, or even *in order to die,* is irrelevant. The purpose of the right to refuse medical treatment is not to give persons a right to decide whether to live or die, but to protect them from the unwanted interferences of others. Perhaps we ought to interpret the right to bodily self-determination more broadly, so as to include a right to die; but this would be a substantial extension of our present understanding of the right to bodily self-determination, and not a consequence of it. If we were to recognize a right to voluntary euthanasia, we would have to agree that people have the right not merely to be left alone but also the right to be killed. I leave to one side that substantive moral issue. My claim is simply that there can be a reason for terminating life-prolonging treatment other than "to bring about the patient's death."

The second case in which termination of treatment cannot be identified with intentional termination of life is where continued treatment has little chance of improving the patient's condition and brings greater discomfort than relief.

The question here is what treatment is appropriate to the particular case. A cancer specialist describes it in this way:

My general rule is to administer therapy as long as a patient responds well and has the potential for a reasonably good quality of

life. But when all feasible therapies have been administered and a
patient shows signs of rapid deterioration, the continuation of therapy can cause more discomfort than the cancer. From that time I
recommend surgery, radiotherapy, or chemotherapy only as a
means of relieving pain. But if a patient's condition should once
again stabilize after the withdrawal of active therapy and if it should
appear that he could still gain some good time, I would immediately reinstitute active therapy. The decision to cease anticancer
treatment is never irrevocable, and often the desire to live will push
a patient to try for another remission, or even a few more days
of life.[3]

The decision here to cease anticancer treatment cannot be construed as a decision that the patient die, or as the intentional termination of life. It is a decision to provide the most appropriate
treatment for that patient at that time. Rachels suggests that the
point of the cessation of treatment is the intentional termination
of life. But here the point of discontinuing treatment is not to
bring about the patient's death but to avoid treatment that will
cause more discomfort than the cancer and has little hope of benefiting the patient. Treatment that meets this description is often
called "extraordinary."[4] The concept is flexible, and what might
be considered "extraordinary" in one situation might be ordinary
in another. The use of a respirator to sustain a patient through a
severe bout with a respiratory disease would be considered ordinary; its use to sustain the life of a severely brain-damaged person
in an irreversible coma would be considered extraordinary.

Contrasted with extraordinary treatment is ordinary treatment,
the care a doctor would normally be expected to provide. Failure
to provide ordinary care constitutes neglect, and can even be construed as the intentional infliction of harm, where there is a legal
obligation to provide care. The importance of the ordinary/ex-
traordinary care distinction lies partly in its connection to the
doctor's intention. The withholding of extraordinary care should
be seen as a decision not to inflict painful treatment on a patient
without reasonable hope of success. The withholding of ordinary
care, by contrast, must be seen as neglect. Thus, one doctor says,
"We have to draw a distinction between ordinary and extraordinary means. We never withdraw what's needed to make a baby
comfortable, we would never withdraw the care a parent would

provide. We never kill a baby. . . . But we may decide certain heroic intervention is not worthwhile."[5]

We should keep in mind the ordinary/extraordinary care distinction when considering an example given by both Tooley and Rachels to show the irrationality of the active/passive distinction with regard to infanticide. The example is this: a child is born with Down's syndrome and also has an intestinal obstruction that requires corrective surgery. If the surgery is not performed, the infant will starve to death, since it cannot take food orally. This may take days or even weeks, as dehydration and infection set in. Commenting on this situation in his article in this book, Rachels says:

> I can understand why some people are opposed to all euthanasia, and insist that such infants must be allowed to live. I think I can also understand why other people favor destroying these babies quickly and painlessly. But why should anyone favor letting "dehydration and infection wither a tiny being over hours and days"? The doctrine that says that a baby may be allowed to dehydrate and wither, but may not be given an injection that would end its life without suffering, seems so patently cruel as to require no further refutation.

Such a doctrine perhaps does not need further refutation; but this is not the AMA doctrine. The AMA statement criticized by Rachels allows only for the cessation of extraordinary means to prolong life when death is imminent. Neither of these conditions is satisfied in this example. Death is not imminent in this situation, any more than it would be if a normal child had an attack of appendicitis. Neither the corrective surgery to remove the intestinal obstruction nor the intravenous feeding required to keep the infant alive until such surgery is performed can be regarded as extraordinary means, for neither is particularly expensive, nor does either place an overwhelming burden on the patient or others. (The continued existence of the child might be thought to place an overwhelming burden on its parents, but that has nothing to do with the characterization of the means to prolong its life as extraordinary. If it had, then *feeding* a severely defective child who required a great deal of care could be regarded as extraordinary.) The chances of success if the operation is undertaken are quite good, though there is always a risk in operating on infants.

Though the Down's syndrome will not be alleviated, the child will proceed to an otherwise normal infancy.

It cannot be argued that the treatment is withheld for the infant's sake, unless one is prepared to argue that all mentally retarded babies are better off dead. This is particularly implausible in the case of Down's syndrome babies, who generally do not suffer and are capable of giving and receiving love, of learning and playing, to varying degrees.

In a film on this subject entitled "Who Should Survive?" a doctor defended a decision not to operate, saying that since the parents did not consent to the operation, the doctors' hands were tied. As we have seen, surgical intrusion requires consent, and in the case of infants, consent would normally come from the parents. But, as legal guardians, parents are required to provide medical care for their children, and failure to do so can constitute criminal neglect or even homicide. In general, courts have been understandably reluctant to recognize a parental right to terminate life-prolonging treatment.[6] Although prosecution is unlikely, physicians who comply with invalid instructions from the parents and permit the infant's death could be liable for aiding and abetting, failure to report child neglect, or even homicide. So it is not true that, in this situation, doctors are legally bound to do as the parents wish.

To sum up, I think that Rachels is right to regard the decision not to operate in the Down's syndrome example as the intentional termination of life. But there is no reason to believe that either the law or the AMA would regard it otherwise. Certainly the decision to withhold treatment is not justified by the AMA statement. That such infants have been allowed to die cannot be denied; but this, I think, is the result of doctors misunderstanding the law and the AMA position.

Withholding treatment in this case is the intentional termination of life because the infant is deliberately allowed to die; that is the point of not operating. But there are other cases in which that is not the point. If the point is to avoid inflicting painful treatment on a patient with little or no reasonable hope of success, this is not the intentional termination of life. The permissibility of such withholding of treatment, then, would have no implications for the permissibility of euthanasia, active or passive.

The decision whether or not to operate, or to institute vigorous treatment, is particularly agonizing in the case of children born with spina bifida, an opening in the base of the spine usually accompanied by hydrocephalus and mental retardation. If left unoperated, these children usually die of meningitis or kidney failure within the first few years of life. Even if they survive, all affected children face a lifetime of illness, operations, and varying degrees of disability. The policy used to be to save as many as possible, but the trend now is toward selective treatment, based on the physician's estimate of the chances of success. If operating is not likely to improve significantly the child's condition, parents and doctors may agree not to operate. This is not the intentional termination of life, for again the purpose is not the termination of the child's life but the avoidance of painful and pointless treatment. Thus, the fact that withholding treatment is justified does not imply that killing the child would be equally justified.

Throughout the discussion, I have claimed that intentionally ceasing life-prolonging treatment is not the intentional termination of life unless the doctor has, as his or her purpose in stopping treatment, the patient's death.

It may be objected that I have incorrectly characterized the conditions for the intentional termination of life. Perhaps it is enough that the doctor intentionally ceases treatment, foreseeing that the patient will die.

In many cases, if one acts intentionally, foreseeing that a particular result will occur, one can be said to have brought about that result intentionally. Indeed, this is the general legal rule. Why, then, am I not willing to call the cessation of life-prolonging treatment, in compliance with the patient's right to refuse treatment, the intentional termination of life? It is not because such an *identification* is necessarily opprobrious; for we could go on to *discuss* whether such cessation of treatment is a *justifiable* intentional termination of life. Even in the law, some cases of homicide are justifiable; e.g., homicide in self-defense.

However, the cessation of life-prolonging treatment, in the cases which I have discussed, is not regarded in law as being justifiable homicide, because it is not homicide at all. Why is this? Is it because the doctor "doesn't do anything," and so cannot be guilty of homicide? Surely not, since, as I have indicated, the law sometimes treats an omission as the cause of death. A better explanation, I think, has to do with the fact that in the context of the patient's right to refuse treatment, a doctor is not at liberty to continue treatment. It seems a necessary ingredient of intentionally letting die that one could have done something to prevent the death. In this situation, of course the doctor can physically prevent the patient's death, but since we do not regard the doctor as *free* to continue treatment, we say that there is "nothing he can do." Therefore he does not intentionally let the patient die.

To discuss this suggestion fully, I would need to present a full-scale theory of intentional action. However, at least I have shown, through the discussion of the above examples, that such a theory will be very complex, and that one of the complexities concerns the agent's reason for acting. The reason why an agent acted (or failed to act) may affect the characterization of what he did intentionally. The mere fact that he did *something* intentionally, foreseeing a certain result, does not necessarily mean that he brought about that *result* intentionally.

In order to show that the cessation of life-prolonging treatment, in the cases I've discussed, is the intentional termination of life, one would either have to show that treatment was stopped in order to bring about the patient's death, or provide a theory of intentional action according to which the reason for ceasing treatment is irrelevant to its characterization as the intentional termination of life. I find this suggestion implausible, but am willing to consider arguments for it. Rachels has provided no such arguments: indeed, he apparently shares my view about the intentional termination of life. For when he claims that the cessation of life-prolonging treatment *is* the intentional termination of life, his reason for making the claim is that "if it were not, there would be no point to it." Rachels believes that the point of ceasing treatment, "in these cases," is to bring about the patient's death. If that were not the point, he suggests, why would the doctor cease treatment? I have shown, however, that there can be a point to ceasing treatment which is not the death of the patient. In showing this, I have refuted Rachels' reason for identifying the cessation of life-prolonging treatment with the intentional termination of life, and thus his argument against the AMA doctrine.

Here someone might say: Even if the withholding of treatment is not the intentional termination of life, does that make a difference, morally speaking? If life-prolonging treatment may be withheld, for the sake of the child, may not an easy death be provided, for the sake of the child, as well? The unoperated child with spina bifida may take months or even years to die. Distressed by the spectacle of children "lying around, waiting to die," one doctor has written, "It is time that society and medicine stopped perpetuating the fiction that withholding treatment is ethically different from terminating a life. It is time that society began to discuss mechanisms by which we can alleviate the pain and suffering for those individuals whom we cannot help."[7]

I do not deny that there may be cases in which death is in the best interests of the patient. In such cases, a quick and painless death may be the best thing. However, I do not think that, once active or vigorous treatment is stopped, a quick death is always preferable to a lingering one. We must be cautious about attributing to defective children *our* distress at seeing them linger. Waiting for them to die may be tough on parents, doctors, and nurses— it isn't necessarily tough on the child. The decision not to operate need not mean a decision to neglect, and it may be possible to make the remaining months of the child's life comfortable, pleasant, and filled with love. If this alternative is possible, surely it is more decent and humane than killing the child. In such a situation, withholding treatment, foreseeing the child's death, is not ethically equivalent to killing the child, and we cannot move from the permissibility of the former to that of the latter. I am worried that there will be a tendency to do precisely that if active euthanasia is regarded as morally equivalent to the withholding of life-prolonging treatment.

CONCLUSION

The AMA statement does not make the distinction Rachels and Tooley wish to attack, that between active and passive euthanasia. Instead, the statement draws a distinction between the intentional termination of life, on the one hand, and the cessation of the employment of extraordinary means to prolong life, on the other. Nothing said by Rachels and Tooley shows that this distinction is confused. It may be that doctors have misinterpreted the AMA statement, and that this has led, for example, to decisions to allow defective infants to starve slowly to death. I quite agree with Rachels and Tooley that the decisions to which they allude were cruel and made on irrelevant grounds. Certainly it is worth pointing out that allowing someone to die *can* be the intentional termination of life, and that it can be just as bad as, or worse than, killing someone. However, the withholding of life-prolonging treatment is not necessarily the intentional termination of life, so that if it is permissible to withhold life-prolonging treatment it does not follow that, other things being equal, it is permissible to kill. Furthermore, most of the time, other things are not equal. In many of the cases in which it would be right to cease treatment, I do not think that it would also be right to kill.

NOTES

I would like to express my thanks to Jonathan Bennett, Josiah Gould, Deborah Johnson, David Pratt, Bruce Russell, and David Zimmerman, all of whom provided helpful criticism and suggestions for this article.

1. For example, *In re Yetter,* 62 Pa. D. & C. 2d 619 (C.P., Northampton County Ct. 1974).

2. David W. Meyers, "Legal Aspects of Voluntary Euthanasia," in *Dilemmas of Euthanasia,* ed. John Behnke and Sissela Bok (New York: Anchor Books, 1975), p. 56.

3. Ernest H. Rosenbaum, M.D., *Living With Cancer* (New York: Praeger, 1975), p. 27.

4. See Tristram Engelhardt, Jr., "Ethical Issues in Aiding the Death of Young Children," in *Beneficent Euthanasia,* ed. Marvin Kohl (Buffalo: Prometheus Books, 1975).

5. B. D. Colen, *Karen Ann Quinlan: Living and Dying in the Age of Eternal Life* (Los Angeles: Nash, 1976), p. 115.

6. See Norman L. Cantor, "Law and the Termination of an Incompetent Patient's Life-Preserving Care," in *Dilemmas of Euthanasia,* ed. John Behnke and Sissela Bok (New York: Anchor Books, 1975), pp. 69–105.

7. John Freeman, "Is There a Right to Die—Quickly?" *Journal of Pediatrics,* 80, no. 5 (1972), 904–905.

7

Active and Passive Euthanasia: An Impertinent Distinction?

Thomas D. Sullivan

BECAUSE OF RECENT ADVANCES in medical technology, it is today possible to save or prolong the lives of many persons who in an earlier era would have quickly perished. Unhappily, however, it often is impossible to do so without committing the patient and his or her family to a future filled with sorrows. Modern methods of neurosurgery can successfully close the opening at the base of the spine of a baby born with severe myelomeningocoele, but do nothing to relieve the paralysis that afflicts it from the waist down or to remedy the patient's incontinence of stool and urine. Antibiotics and skin grafts can spare the life of a victim of severe and massive burns, but fail to eliminate the immobilizing contractions of arms and legs, the extreme pain, and the hideous disfigurement of the face. It is not surprising, therefore, that physicians and moralists in increasing number recommend that assistance should not be given to such patients, and that some have even begun to advocate the deliberate hastening of death by medical means, provided informed consent has been given by the appropriate parties.

The latter recommendation consciously and directly conflicts with what might be called the "traditional" view of the physician's role. The traditional view, as articulated, for example, by the House of Delegates of the American Medical Association in 1973, declared:

From *Human Life Review,* vol. III, no. 3 (Summer 1977), pp. 40–46. Reprinted with permission of the publisher (The Human Life Foundation, Inc., 150 East 35th Street, New York, NY 10016).

The intentional termination of the life of one human being by another—mercy killing—is contrary to that for which the medical profession stands and is contrary to the policy of the American Medical Association.

The cessation of the employment of extra-ordinary means to prolong the life of the body when there is irrefutable evidence that biological death is imminent is the decision of the patient and/or his immediate family. The advice and judgment of the physician should be freely available to the patient and/or his immediate family.

Basically this view involves two points: (1) that it is impermissible for the doctor or anyone else to terminate intentionally the life of a patient, but (2) that it is permissible in some cases to cease the employment of "extraordinary means" of preserving life, even though the death of the patient is a foreseeable consequence.

Does this position really make sense? Recent criticism charges that it does not. The heart of the complaint is that the traditional view arbitrarily rules out all cases of intentionally acting to terminate life, but permits what is in fact the moral equivalent, letting patients die. This accusation has been clearly articulated by James Rachels in a widely read article that appeared in a recent issue of the *New England Journal of Medicine,* entitled "Active and Passive Euthanasia."[1] By "active euthanasia" Rachels seems to mean *doing something* to bring about a patient's death, and by "passive euthanasia," not doing anything, i.e., just letting the patient die. Referring to the A.M.A. statement, Rachels sees the traditional position as always forbidding active euthanasia, but permitting passive euthanasia. Yet, he argues, passive euthanasia may be in some cases morally indistinguishable from active euthanasia, and in other cases even worse. To make his point he asks his readers to consider the case of a Down's syndrome baby with an intestinal obstruction that easily could be remedied through routine surgery. Rachels comments:

> I can understand why some people are opposed to all euthanasia, and insist that such infants must be allowed to live. I think I can also understand why other people favor destroying these babies quickly and painlessly. But why should anyone favor letting "dehydration and infection wither a tiny being over hours and days"? The doctrine that says that a baby may be allowed to dehydrate

and wither, but may not be given an injection that would end its life without suffering, seems so patently cruel as to require no further refutation.[2]

Rachels' point is that decisions such as the one he describes as "patently cruel" arise out of a misconceived moral distinction between active and passive euthanasia, which in turn rests upon a distinction between killing and letting die that itself has no moral importance.

> One reason why so many people think that there is an important moral difference between active and passive euthanasia is that they think killing someone is morally worse than letting someone die. But is it? . . . To investigate this issue, two cases may be considered that are exactly alike except that one involves killing whereas the other involves letting someone die. Then, it can be asked whether this difference makes any difference to the moral assessments. . . .
>
> In the first, Smith stands to gain a large inheritance if anything should happen to his six-year-old cousin. One evening while the child is taking his bath, Smith sneaks into the bathroom and drowns the child, and then arranges things so that it will look like an accident.
>
> In the second, Jones also stands to gain if anything should happen to his six-year-old cousin. Like Smith, Jones sneaks in planning to drown the child in his bath. However, just as he enters the bathroom Jones sees the child slip and hit his head, and fall face down in the water. Jones is delighted; he stands by, ready to push the child's head back under if it is necessary, but it is not necessary. With only a little thrashing about the child drowns all by himself, "accidentally," as Jones watches and does nothing.[3]

Rachels observes that Smith killed the child, whereas Jones "merely" let the child die. If there's an important moral distinction between killing and letting die, then, we should say that Jones' behavior from a moral point of view is less reprehensible than Smith's. But while the law might draw some distinctions here, it seems clear that the acts of Jones and Smith are not different in any important way, or, if there is a difference, Jones's action is even worse.

In essence, then, the objection to the position adopted by the A.M.A. of Rachels and those who argue like him is that it endorses a highly questionable moral distinction between killing and

letting die, which, if accepted, leads to indefensible medical decisions. Nowhere does Rachels quite come out and say that he fa-
vors active euthanasia in some cases, but the implication is clear.
Nearly everyone holds that it is sometimes pointless to prolong
the process of dying and that in those cases it is morally permissible to let a patient die even though a few hours or days could
be salvaged by procedures that would also increase the agonies of
the dying. But if it is impossible to defend a general distinction
between letting people die and acting to terminate their lives directly, then it would seem that active euthanasia also may be morally permissible.

Now what shall we make of all this? It *is* cruel to stand by
and watch a Down's baby die an agonizing death when a simple
operation would remove the intestinal obstruction, but to offer
the excuse that in failing to operate we didn't *do* anything to bring
about death is an example of moral evasiveness comparable to the
excuse Jones would offer for his action of "merely" letting his
cousin die. Furthermore, it is true that if someone is trying to
bring about the death of another human being, then it makes little
difference from the moral point of view if his purpose is achieved
by action or by malevolent omission, as in the cases of Jones
and Smith.

But if we acknowledge this, are we obliged to give up the
traditional view expressed by the A.M.A. statement? Of course
not. To begin with, we are hardly obliged to assume the Jones-
like role Rachels assigns the defender of the traditional view. We
have the option of operating on the Down's baby and saving its
life. Rachels mentions that possibility only to hurry past it as if
that is not what his opposition would do. But, of course, that is
precisely the course of action most defenders of the traditional
position would choose.

Secondly, while it may be that the reason some rather confused
people give for upholding the traditional view is that they think
killing someone is always worse than letting them die, nobody
who gives the matter much thought puts it that way. Rather they
say that killing someone is clearly morally worse than not killing
them, and killing them can be done by acting to bring about their
death or by refusing ordinary means to keep them alive in order
to bring about the same goal.

What I am suggesting is that Rachels' objections leave the position he sets out to criticize untouched. It is worth noting that the jargon of active and passive euthanasia—and it is jargon—does not appear in the resolution. Nor does the resolution state or imply the distinction Rachels attacks, a distinction that puts a moral premium on overt behavior—moving or not moving one's parts—while totally ignoring the intentions of the agent. That no distinction is being drawn seems clear from the fact that the A.M.A. resolution speaks approvingly of ceasing to use extraordinary means in certain cases, and such withdrawals might easily involve bodily movement, for example unplugging an oxygen machine.

In addition to saddling his opposition with an indefensible distinction it doesn't make, Rachels proceeds to ignore one that it does make—one that is crucial to a just interpretation of the view. Recall the A.M.A. allows the withdrawal of what it calls extraordinary means of preserving life; clearly the contrast here is with ordinary means. Though in its short statement those expressions are not defined, the definition Paul Ramsey refers to as standard in his book *The Patient as Person* seems to fit.

> Ordinary means of preserving life are all medicines, treatments, and operations, which offer a reasonable hope of benefit for the patient and which can be obtained and used without excessive expense, pain, and other inconveniences.
>
> Extra-ordinary means of preserving life are all those medicines, treatments, and operations which cannot be obtained without excessive expense, pain, or other inconvenience, or which, if used, would not offer a reasonable hope of benefit.[4]

Now with this distinction in mind, we can see how the traditional view differs from the position Rachels mistakes for it. The traditional view is that the intentional termination of human life is impermissible, irrespective of whether this goal is brought about by action or inaction. Is the action or refraining *aimed* at producing a death? Is the termination of life *sought, chosen or planned*? Is the intention deadly? If so, the act or omission is wrong.

But we all know it is entirely possible that the unwillingness of a physician to use extraordinary means for preserving life may be prompted not by a determination to bring about death, but by other motives. For example, he may realize that further treatment may offer little hope of reversing the dying process and/or be excruciating, as in the case when a massively necrotic bowel condition in a neonate is out of control. The doctor who does what he can to comfort the infant but does not submit it to further treatment or surgery may foresee that the decision will hasten death, but it certainly doesn't follow from that fact that he intends to bring about its death. It is, after all, entirely possible to foresee that something will come about as a result of one's conduct without intending the consequence or side effect. If I drive downtown, I can foresee that I'll wear out my tires a little, but I don't drive downtown with the intention of wearing out my tires. And if I choose to forego my exercises for a few days, I may think that as a result my physical condition will deteriorate a little, but I don't omit my exercise with a view to running myself down. And if you have to fill a position and select Green, who is better qualified for the post than her rival Brown, you needn't appoint Mrs. Green with the intention of hurting Mr. Brown, though you may foresee that Mr. Brown will feel hurt. And if a country extends it general education programs to its illiterate masses, it is predictable the suicide rate will go up, but even if the public officials are aware of this fact, it doesn't follow that they initiate the program with a view to making the suicide rate go up. In general, then, it is not the case that all the foreseeable consequences and side effects of our conduct are necessarily intended. And it is because the physician's withdrawal of extra-ordinary means can be otherwise motivated than by a desire to bring about the predictable death of the patient that such action cannot categorically be ruled out as wrong.

But the refusal to use ordinary means is an altogether different matter. After all, what is the point of refusing assistance which offers reasonable hope of benefit to the patient without involving excessive pain or other inconvenience? How could it be plausibly maintained that the refusal is not motivated by a desire to bring about the death of the patient? The traditional position, therefore, rules out not only direct actions to bring about death, such as giving a patient a lethal injection, but malevolent omissions as well, such as not providing minimum care for the newborn.

The reason the A.M.A. position sounds so silly when one listens to arguments such as Rachels' is that he slights the distinction between ordinary and extra-ordinary means and then drums on cases where *ordinary* means are refused. The impression is thereby conveyed that the traditional doctrine sanctions omissions that are morally indistinguishable in a substantive way from direct killings, but then incomprehensibly refuses to permit quick and painless termination of life. If the traditional doctrine would approve of Jones's standing by with a grin on his face while his young cousin drowned in a tub, or letting a Down's baby wither and die when ordinary means are available to preserve its life, it would indeed be difficult to see how anyone could defend it. But so to conceive the traditional doctrine is simply to misunderstand it. It is not a doctrine that rests on some supposed distinction between "active" and "passive euthanasia," whatever those words are supposed to mean, or on a distinction between moving and not moving our bodies. It is simply a prohibition against intentional killing, which includes both direct actions and malevolent omissions.

To summarize—the traditional position represented by the A.M.A. statement is not incoherent. It acknowledges or, more accurately, insists upon the fact that withholding ordinary means to sustain life may be tantamount to killing. The traditional position can be made to appear incoherent only by imposing upon it a crude idea of killing held by none of its more articulate advocates.

Thus the criticism of Rachels and other reformers, misapprehending its target, leaves the traditional position untouched. That position is simply a prohibition of murder. And it is good to remember, as C. S. Lewis once pointed out:

No man, perhaps, ever at first described to himself the act he was about to do as Murder, or Adultery, or Fraud, or Treachery. . . . And when he hears it so described by other men he is (in a way) sincerely shocked and surprised. Those others "don't understand." If they knew what it had really been like for him, they would not use those crude "stock" names. With a wink or a titter, or a cloud of muddy emotion, the thing has slipped into his will as something not very extraordinary, something of which, rightly understood in all of his peculiar circumstances, he may even feel proud.[5]

I fully realize that there are times when those who have the noble duty to tend the sick and the dying are deeply moved by the sufferings of their patients, especially of the very young and the very old, and desperately wish they could do more than comfort and companion them. Then, perhaps, it seems that universal moral principles are mere abstractions having little to do with the agony of the dying. But of course we do not see best when our eyes are filled with tears.

NOTES

1. *The New England Journal of Medicine*, 292 (January 9, 1975), pp. 78–80; this volume, chapter 5.

2. *Ibid.*, pp. 78–79; this volume, p. 114.

3. *Ibid.*, p. 79; this volume, p. 115.

4. Paul Ramsey, *The Patient As Person* (New Haven and London: Yale University Press, 1970), p. 122. Ramsey abbreviates the definition first given by Gerald Kelly, s.j., *Medico-Moral Problems* (St. Louis, Mo.: The Catholic Hospital Association, 1958), p. 129.

5. C. S. Lewis, *A Preface to Paradise Lost* (London and New York: Oxford University Press, 1970), p. 126.

8

More Impertinent Distinctions and a Defense of Active Euthanasia

James Rachels

MANY THINKERS, including almost all orthodox Catholics, believe that euthanasia is immoral. They oppose killing patients in any circumstances whatever. However, they think it is all right, in some special circumstances, to allow patients to die by withholding treatment. The American Medical Association's policy statement on mercy killing supports this traditional view. In my paper "Active and Passive Euthanasia"[1] I argued, against the traditional view, that there is in fact no moral difference between killing and letting die—if one is permissible, then so is the other.

Professor Sullivan[2] does not dispute my argument; instead he dismisses it as irrelevant. The traditional doctrine, he says, does not appeal to or depend on the distinction between killing and letting die. Therefore, arguments against that distinction "leave the traditional position untouched."

Is my argument really irrelevant? I don't see how it can be. As Sullivan himself points out,

> Nearly everyone holds that it is sometimes pointless to prolong the process of dying and that in those cases it is morally permissible to let a patient die even though a few hours or days could be salvaged by procedures that would also increase the agonies of the dying. But if it is impossible to defend a general distinction between letting people die and acting to terminate their lives directly,

From Thomas A. Mappes and Jane S. Zembaty, eds., *Biomedical Ethics* (New York: McGraw Hill, 1981), pp. 355–359. Copyright © 1978 by James Rachels. Reprinted by permission of the author.

then it would seem that active euthanasia also may be morally permissible [p. 134].

But traditionalists like Professor Sullivan hold that active euthanasia—the direct killing of patients—is *not* morally permissible; so, if my argument is sound, their view must be mistaken. I cannot agree, then, that my argument "leaves the traditional position untouched."

However, I shall not press this point. Instead I shall present some further arguments against the traditional position, concentrating on those elements of the position which Professor Sullivan himself thinks most important. According to him, what is important is, first, that we should never *intentionally* terminate the life of a patient, either by action or omission, and second, that we may cease or omit treatment of a patient, knowing that this will result in death, only if the means of treatment involved are *extraordinary*.

INTENTIONAL AND NONINTENTIONAL TERMINATION OF LIFE

We can, of course, distinguish between what a person does and the intention with which he does it. But what is the significance of this distinction for ethics?

> The traditional view [says Sullivan] is that the intentional termination of human life is impermissible, irrespective of whether this goal is brought about by action or inaction. Is the action or refraining *aimed at* producing a death? Is the termination of life *sought, chosen or planned*? Is the intention deadly? Is so, the act or omission is wrong [p. 135].

Thus on the traditional view there is a very definite sort of moral relation between act and intention. An act which is otherwise permissible may become impermissible if it is accompanied by a bad intention. The intention makes the act wrong.

There is reason to think that this view of the relation between act and intention is mistaken. Consider the following example. Jack visits his sick and lonely grandmother, and entertains her for the afternoon. He loves her and his only intention is to cheer her up. Jill also visits the grandmother, and provides an afternoon's cheer. But Jill's concern is that the old lady will soon be making her will; Jill wants to be included among the heirs. Jack also knows that his visit might influence the making of the will, in his favor, but that is no part of his plan. Thus Jack and Jill do the very same thing—they both spend an afternoon cheering up their sick grandmother—and what they do may lead to the same consequences, namely influencing the will. But their intentions are quite different.

Jack's intention was honorable and Jill's was not. Could we say on that account that what Jack did was right, but what Jill did was wrong? No; for Jack and Jill did the very same thing, and if they did the same thing, we cannot say that one acted rightly and the other wrongly.[3] Consistency requires that we assess similar actions similarly. Thus if we are trying to evaluate their *actions,* we must say about one what we say about the other.

However, if we are trying to assess Jack's *character,* or Jill's, things are very different. Even though their actions were similar, Jack seems admirable for what he did, while Jill does not. What Jill did—comforting an elderly sick relative—was a morally good thing, but we would not think well of her for it since she was only scheming after the old lady's money. Jack, on the other hand, did a good thing *and* he did it with an admirable intention. Thus we think well, not only of what Jack did, but of Jack.

The traditional view, as presented by Professor Sullivan, says that the intention with which an act is done is relevant to determining whether the act is right. The example of Jack and Jill suggests that, on the contrary, the intention is not relevant to deciding whether the *act* is right or wrong, but instead it is relevant to assessing the character of the person who does the act, which is very different.

Now let us turn to an example that concerns more important matters of life and death. This example is adapted from one used by Sullivan himself (p. 135–36). A massively necrotic bowel condition in a neonate is out of control. Dr. White realizes that further treatment offers little hope of reversing the dying process and will only increase the suffering; so, he does not submit the infant to further treatment—even though he knows that this decision will hasten death. However, Dr. White does not seek, choose, or plan that death, so it is not part of his intention that the baby dies.

Dr. Black is faced with a similar case. A massively necrotic bowel condition in a neonate is out of control. He realizes that further treatment offers little hope of saving the baby and will only increase its suffering. He decides that it is better for the baby to die a bit sooner than to go on suffering pointlessly; so, with the intention of letting the baby die, he ceases treatment.

According to the traditional position, Dr. White's action was acceptable, but Dr. Black acted wrongly. However, this assessment faces the same problem we encountered before. Dr. White and Dr. Black did *the very same thing*: their handling of the cases was identical. Both doctors ceased treatment, knowing that the baby would die sooner, and both did so because they regarded continued treatment as pointless, given the infants' prospects. So how could one's action be acceptable and the other's not? There was, of course, a subtle difference in their *attitudes* toward what they did. Dr. Black said to himself, "I want this baby to die now, rather than later, so that it won't suffer more; so I won't continue the treatment." A defender of the traditional view might choose to condemn Dr. Black for this, and say that his character is defective (although I would not say that); but the traditionalist should not say that Dr. Black's *action* was wrong on that account, at least not if he wants to go on saying that Dr. White's action was right. A pure heart cannot make a wrong act right; neither can an impure heart make a right act wrong. As in the case of Jack and Jill, the intention is relevant, not to determining the rightness of actions, but to assessing the character of the people who act.

There is a general lesson to be learned here. The rightness or wrongness of an act is determined by the reasons for or against it. Suppose you are trying to decide, in this example, whether treatment should be continued. What are the reasons for and against this course of action? On the one hand, if treatment is ceased the baby will die very soon. On the other hand, the baby will die eventually anyway, even if treatment is continued. It has no chance of growing up. Moreover, if its life is prolonged, its suffering will be prolonged as well, and the medical resources used will be unavailable to others who would have a better chance of a satisfactory cure. In light of all this, you may well decide against continued treatment. But notice that there is no mention here of anybody's intentions. The intention you would have, if you decide to cease treatment, is not one of the things you need to consider. It is not among the reasons either for or against the action. That is why it is irrelevant to determining whether the action is right.

In short, a person's intention is relevant to an assessment of his character. The fact that a person intended so-and-so by his action may be a reason for thinking him a good or a bad person. But the intention is not relevant to determining whether the act itself is morally right. The rightness of the act must be decided on the basis of the objective reasons for or against it. It is permissible to let the baby die, in Sullivan's example, because of the facts about the baby's condition and its prospects—not because of anything having to do with anyone's intentions. Thus the traditional view is mistaken on this point.

Ordinary and Extraordinary Means of Treatment

The American Medical Association policy statement says that life-sustaining treatment may sometimes be stopped if the means of treatment are "extraordinary"; the implication is that "ordinary" means of treatment may not be withheld. The distinction between ordinary and extraordinary treatments is crucial to orthodox Catholic thought in this area, and Professor Sullivan re-emphasizes its importance: he says that, while a physician may sometimes rightly refuse to use extraordinary means to prolong life, "the refusal to use ordinary means is an altogether different matter" (p. 136).

However, upon reflection it is clear that it is sometimes permissible to omit even very ordinary sorts of treatments.

> Suppose that a diabetic patient long accustomed to self-administration of insulin falls victim to terminal cancer, or suppose that a terminal cancer patient suddenly develops diabetes. Is he in the first case obliged to continue, and in the second case obliged to begin, insulin treatment and die painfully of cancer, or in either or both cases may the patient choose rather to pass into diabetic coma and an earlier death? . . . What of the conscious patient suffering from painful incurable disease who suddenly gets pneumonia? Or an old man slowly deteriorating who from simply being

inactive and recumbent gets pneumonia: Are we to use antibiotics in a likely successful attack upon this disease which from time immemorial has been called "the old man's friend"?[4]

These examples are provided by Paul Ramsey, a leading theological ethicist. Even so conservative a thinker as Ramsey is sympathetic with the idea that, in such cases, life-prolonging treatment is not mandatory: the insulin and the antibiotics need not be used. Yet surely insulin and antibiotics are "ordinary" treatments by today's medical standards. They are common, easily administered, and cheap. There is nothing exotic about them. So it appears that the distinction between ordinary and extraordinary means does not have the significance traditionally attributed to it.

But what of the *definitions* of "ordinary" and "extraordinary" means which Sullivan provides? Quoting Ramsey, he says that

Ordinary means of preserving life are all medicines, treatments, and operations, which offer a reasonable hope of benefit for the patient and which can be obtained and used without excessive expense, pain, and other inconveniences.

Extra-ordinary means of preserving life are all those medicines, treatments, and operations which cannot be obtained without excessive expense, pain, or other inconvenience, or which, if used, would not offer a reasonable hope of benefit [p. 135].

Do these definitions provide us with a useful distinction—one that can be used in determining when a treatment is mandatory and when it is not?

The first thing to notice is the way the word "excessive" functions in these definitions. It is said that a treatment is extraordinary if it cannot be obtained without *excessive* expense or pain. But when is an expense "excessive"? Is a cost of $10,000 excessive? If it would save the life of a young woman and restore her to perfect health, $10,000 does not seem excessive. But if it would only prolong the life of Ramsey's cancer-stricken diabetic a short while, perhaps $10,000 is excessive. The point is not merely that what is excessive changes from case to case. The point is that what is excessive *depends* on whether it would be a good thing for the life in question to be prolonged.

Second, we should notice the use of the word "benefit" in the definitions. It is said that ordinary treatments offer a reasonable hope of *benefit* for the patient; and that treatments are extraordinary if they will not benefit the patient. But how do we tell if a treatment will benefit the patient? Remember that we are talking about life-prolonging treatments; the "benefit," if any, is the continuation of life. Whether continued life is a benefit depends on the details of the particular case. For a person with a painful terminal illness, a temporarily continued life may not be a benefit. For a person in irreversible coma, such as Karen Quinlan, continued biological existence is almost certainly not a benefit. On the other hand, for a person who can be cured and resume a normal life, life-sustaining treatment definitely is a benefit. Again, the point is that in order to decide whether life-sustaining treatment is a benefit we must *first* decide whether it would be a good thing for the life in question to be prolonged.

Therefore, these definitions do not mark out a distinction that can be used to help us decide when treatment may be omitted. We cannot by using the definitions identify which treatments are extraordinary, and then use that information to determine whether the treatment may be omitted. For the definitions require that we must *already* have decided the moral questions of life and death *before* we can answer the question of which treatments are extraordinary!

We are brought, then, to this conclusion about the distinction between ordinary and extraordinary means. If we apply the distinction in a straightforward, commonsense way, the traditional doctrine is false, for it is clear that it is sometimes permissible to omit ordinary treatments. On the other hand, if we define the terms as suggested by Ramsey and Sullivan, the distinction is useless in practical decision-making. In either case, the distinction provides no help in formulating an acceptable ethic of letting die.

To summarize what has been said so far: the distinction between killing and letting die has no moral importance; on that Professor Sullivan and I agree. He, however, contends that the distinctions between intentional and nonintentional termination of life, and ordinary and extraordinary means, must be at the heart of a correct moral view. I believe that the arguments given above refute this view. Those distinctions are no better than the first one. The traditional view is mistaken.

In my original paper I did not argue in favor of active euthanasia. I merely argued that active and passive euthanasia are equivalent: *if* one is acceptable, so is the other. However, Professor Sullivan correctly inferred that I do endorse active euthanasia. I believe that it is morally justified in some instances and that at least two strong arguments support this position. The first is the argument from mercy; the second is the argument from the golden rule.

THE ARGUMENT FROM MERCY

Preliminary Statement of the Argument

The single most powerful argument in support of euthanasia is the argument from mercy. It is also an exceptionally simple argument, at least in its main idea, which makes one uncomplicated point. Terminal patients sometimes suffer pain so horrible that it is beyond the comprehension of those who have not actually experienced it. Their suffering can be so terrible that we do not like even to read about it or think about it; we recoil even from the descriptions of such agony. The argument from mercy says: Euthanasia is justified because it provides an end to *that.*

The great Irish satirist Jonathan Swift took eight years to die, while, in the words of Joseph Fletcher, "His mind crumbled to pieces."[5] At times the pain in his blinded eyes was so intense he had to be restrained from tearing them out with his own hands. Knives and other potential instruments of suicide had to be kept from him. For the last three years of his life, he could do nothing but sit and drool; and when he finally died it was only after convulsions that lasted thirty-six hours.

Swift died in 1745. Since then, doctors have learned how to eliminate much of the pain that accompanies terminal illness, but the victory has been far from complete. So, here is a more modern example.

Steward Alsop was a respected journalist who died in 1975 of a rare form of cancer. Before he died, he wrote movingly of his experiences as a terminal patient. Although he had not thought much about euthanasia before, he came to approve of it after rooming briefly with someone he called Jack:

The third night that I roomed with Jack in our tiny double room in the solid-tumor ward of the cancer clinic of the National Institutes of Health in Bethesda, Md., a terrible thought occurred to me.

Jack had a melanoma in his belly, a malignant solid tumor that the doctors guessed was about the size of a softball. The cancer had started a few months before with a small tumor in his left shoulder, and there had been several operations since. The doctors planned to remove the softball-sized tumor, but they knew Jack would soon die. The cancer had metastasized—it had spread beyond control.

Jack was good-looking, about 28, and brave. He was in constant pain, and his doctor had prescribed an intravenous shot of a synthetic opiate—a pain-killer, or analgesic—every four hours. His wife spent many of the daylight hours with him, and she would sit or lie on his bed and pat him all over, as one pats a child, only more methodically, and this seemed to help control the pain. But at night, when his pretty wife had left (wives cannot stay overnight at the NIH clinic) and darkness fell, the pain would attack without pity.

At the prescribed hour, a nurse would give Jack a shot of the synthetic analgesic, and this would control the pain for perhaps two hours or a bit more. Then he would begin to moan, or whimper, very low, as though he didn't want to wake me. Then he would begin to howl, like a dog.

When this happened, either he or I would ring for a nurse, and ask for a pain-killer. She would give him some codeine or the like by mouth, but it never did any real good—it affected him no more than half an aspirin might affect a man who had just broken his arm. Always the nurse would explain as encouragingly as she could that there was not long to go before the next intravenous shot— "Only about 50 minutes now." And always poor Jack's whimpers and howls would become more loud and frequent until at last the blessed relief came.

The third night of this routine, the terrible thought occurred to me: "If Jack were a dog," I thought, "what would be done with him?" The answer was obvious: the pound, and chloroform. No human being with a spark of pity could let a living thing suffer so, to no good end.[6]

The NIH clinic is, of course, one of the most modern and best-equipped hospitals we have. Jack's suffering was not the result of poor treatment in some backward rural facility; it was the inevitable product of his disease, which medical science was powerless to prevent.

I have quoted Alsop at length not for the sake of indulging in gory details but to give a clear idea of the kind of suffering we are talking about. We should not gloss over these facts with euphemistic language, or squeamishly avert our eyes from them. For only by keeping them firmly and vividly in mind can we appreciate the full force of the argument from mercy: If a person prefers—and even begs for—death as the only alternative to lingering on *in this kind of torment,* only to die anyway after a while, then surely it is not immoral to help this person die sooner. As Alsop put it, "No human being with a spark of pity could let a living thing suffer so, to no good end."

The Utilitarian Version of the Argument

In connection with this argument, the utilitarians should be mentioned. They argue that actions and social policies should be judged right or wrong *exclusively* according to whether they cause happiness or misery; and they argue that when judged by this standard, euthanasia turns out to be morally acceptable. The utilitarian argument may be elaborated as follows:

1. Any action or social policy is morally right if it serves to increase the amount of happiness in the world or to decrease the amount of misery. Conversely, an action or social policy is morally wrong if it serves to decrease happiness or to increase misery.
2. The policy of killing, at their own request, hopelessly ill patients who are suffering great pain would decrease the amount of misery in the world. (An example could be Alsop's friend Jack.)
3. Therefore, such a policy would be morally right.

The first premise of this argument, (1), states the Principle of Utility, which is the basic utilitarian assumption. Today most philosophers think that this principle is wrong, because they think that the promotion of happiness and the avoidance of misery are not the *only* morally important things. Happiness, they say, is only one among many values that should be promoted: freedom, justice, and a respect for people's rights are also important. To take one example: People *might* be happier if there were no freedom of religion; for, if everyone adhered to the same religious beliefs, there would be greater harmony among people. There would be no unhappiness caused within families by Jewish girls marrying Catholic boys, and so forth. Moreover, if people were brainwashed well enough, no one would mind not having freedom of choice. Thus happiness would be increased. But, the argument continues, even if happiness *could* be increased this way, it would not be right to deny people freedom of religion, because people have a right to make their own choices. Therefore, the first premise of the utilitarian argument is unacceptable.

There is a related difficulty for utilitarianism, which connects more directly with the topic of euthanasia. Suppose a person is leading a miserable life—full of more unhappiness than happiness—but does *not* want to die. This person thinks that a miserable life is better than none at all. Now I assume that we would all agree that the person should not be killed; that would be plain, unjustifiable murder. Yet it *would* decrease the amount of misery in the world if we killed this person—it would lead to an increase in the balance of happiness over unhappiness—and so it is hard to see how, on strictly utilitarian grounds, it could be wrong. Again, the Principle of Utility seems to be an inadequate guide for determining right and wrong. So we are on shaky ground if we rely on *this* version of the argument from mercy for a defense of euthanasia.

Doing What Is in Everyone's Best Interests

Although the foregoing utilitarian argument is faulty, it is nevertheless based on a sound idea. For even if the promotion of happiness and avoidance of misery are not the *only* morally important things, they are still very important. So, when an action or a social policy would decrease misery, that is *a* very strong reason in its favor. In the cases of voluntary euthanasia we are now considering, great suffering is eliminated, and since the patient requests it, there is no question of violating individual rights. That is why, regardless of the difficulties of the Principle of Utility, the utilitarian version of the argument still retains considerable force.

I want now to present a somewhat different version of the argument from mercy, which is inspired by utilitarianism but which avoids the difficulties of the foregoing version by not making the Principle of Utility a premise of the argument. I believe that the following argument is sound and proves that active euthanasia *can* be justified:

1. If an action promotes the best interests of *everyone* concerned, and violates *no one's* rights, then that action is morally acceptable.
2. In at least some cases, active euthanasia promotes the best interests of everyone concerned and violates no one's rights.
3. Therefore, in at least some cases active euthanasia is morally acceptable.

It would have been in everyone's best interests if active euthanasia had been employed in the case of Stewart Alsop's friend, Jack. First, and most important, it would have been in Jack's own interests, since it would have provided him with an easier, better death, without pain. (Who among us would choose Jack's death, if we had a choice, rather than a quick painless death?) Second, it would have been in the best interests of Jack's wife. Her misery, helplessly watching him suffer, must have been almost equal to his. Third, the hospital staff's best interests would have been served, since if Jack's dying had not been prolonged, they could have turned their attention to other patients whom they could have helped. Fourth, other patients would have benefited since medical resources would no longer have been used in the sad, pointless maintenance of Jack's physical existence. Finally, if Jack himself requested to be killed, the act would not have violated his rights. Considering all this, how can active euthanasia in this case be wrong? How can it be wrong to do an action that is merciful, that benefits everyone concerned, and that violates no one's rights?

THE ARGUMENT FROM THE GOLDEN RULE

"Do unto others as you would have them do unto you" is one of the oldest and most familiar moral maxims. Stated in just that way, it is not a very good maxim: Suppose a sexual pervert started treating others as he would like to be treated himself; we might not be happy with the results. Nevertheless, the basic idea behind the golden rule is a good one. The basic idea is that moral rules apply impartially to everyone alike; therefore, you cannot say that you are justified in treating someone else in a certain way unless you are willing to admit that that person would also be justified in treating *you* in that way if your positions were reversed.

Kant and the Golden Rule

The great German philosopher Immanuel Kant (1724–1804) incorporated the basic idea of the Golden Rule into his system of ethics. Kant argued that we should act only on rules that we are willing to have applied universally; that is, we should behave as we would be willing to have *everyone* behave. He held that there is one supreme principle of morality, which he called "the Categorical Imperative." The Categorical Imperative says:

> Act only according to that maxim by which you can at the same time will that it should become a universal law.[7]

Let us discuss what this means. When we are trying to decide whether we ought to do a certain action, we must first ask what general rule or principle we would be following if we did it. Then, we ask whether we would be willing for everyone to follow that rule, in similar circumstances. (This determines whether "the maxim of the act"—the rule we would be following—can be "willed" to be "a universal law") If we would not be willing for the rule to be followed universally, then we should not follow it ourselves. Thus, if we are not willing for others to apply the rule to *us,* we ought not apply it to *them.*

In the eighteenth chapter of St. Matthew's gospel there is a story that perfectly illustrates this point. A man is owed money by another, who cannot pay, and so he has the debtor thrown into prison. But he himself owes money to the king and begs that *his* debt be forgiven. At first the king forgives the debt. However, when the king hears how this man has treated the one who owed him, he changes his mind and "delivers him unto the tormentors" until he can pay. The moral is clear: If you do not think that others should apply the rule "Don't forgive debts!" to *you,* then you should not apply it to others.

The application of all this to the question of euthanasia is fairly obvious. Each of us is going to die someday, although most of us do not know when or how. But suppose you were told that you would die in one of two ways, and you were asked to choose between them. First, you could die quietly, and without pain, from a fatal injection. Or second, you could choose to die of an affliction so painful that for several days before death you would be reduced to howling like a dog, with your family standing by helplessly, trying to comfort you, but going through its own psychological hell. It is hard to believe that any sane person, when confronted by these possibilities, would choose to have a rule applied that would force upon him or her the second option. And if we would not want such a rule, which excludes euthanasia, applied to us, then we should not apply such a rule to others.

Implications for Christians

There is a considerable irony here. Kant [himself] was personally opposed to active euthanasia, yet his own Categorical Imperative seems to sanction it. The larger irony, however, is for those in the Christian Church who have for centuries opposed active euthanasia. According to the New Testament accounts, Jesus himself promulgated the Golden Rule as the supreme moral principle— "This is the Law and the Prophets," he said. But if this is the supreme principle of morality, then how can active euthanasia be always wrong? If I would have it done to me, how can it be wrong for me to do likewise to others?

R. M. Hare has made this point with great force. A Christian as well as a leading contemporary moral philosopher, Hare has long argued that "universalizability" is one of the central characteristics of moral judgment. ('Universalizability' is the name he gives to the basic idea embodied in both the Golden Rule and the Categorical Imperative. It means that a moral judgment must conform to universal principles, which apply to everyone alike, if it is to be acceptable.) In an article called "Euthanasia: A Christian View," Hare argues that Christians, if they took Christ's teachings about the Golden Rule seriously, would not think that euthanasia is always wrong. He gives this (true) example:

> The driver of a petrol lorry [i.e., a gas truck] was in an accident in which his tanker overturned and immediately caught fire. He

himself was trapped in the cab and could not be freed. He therefore besought the bystanders to kill him by hitting him on the head, so that he would not roast to death. I think that somebody did this, but I do not know what happened in court afterwards.

Now will you please all ask yourselves, as I have many times asked myself, what you wish that men should do to you if you were in the situation of that driver. I cannot believe that anybody who considered the matter seriously, as if he himself were going to be in that situation and had now to give instructions as to what rule the bystanders should follow, would say that the rule should be one ruling out euthanasia absolutely.[8]

We might note that *active* euthanasia is the only option here; the concept of passive euthanasia, in these circumstances, has no application. . . .

Professor Sullivan finds my position pernicious. In his penultimate paragraph he says that the traditional doctrine "is simply a prohibition of murder," and that those of us who think otherwise are confused, teary-eyed sentimentalists. But the traditional doctrine is not that. It is a muddle of indefensible claims, backed by tradition but not by reason.

Notes

1. "Active and Passive Euthanasia," *The New England Journal of Medicine*, 292 (January 9, 1975), pp. 78–80; this volume, chapter 5.

2. "Active and Passive Euthanasia: An Impertinent Distinction?" *The Human Life Review*, 3 (1977), pp. 40–46. Parenthetical references in the text are to this article (as reprinted in this volume, chapter 7).

3. It might be objected that they did not "do the same thing," for Jill manipulated and deceived her grandmother, while Jack did not. If their actions are described in this way, then it may seem that "what Jill did" was wrong, while "what Jack did" was not. However, this description of what Jill did incorporates her intention into the description of the act. In the present context we must keep the act and the intention separate, in order to discuss the relation between them. If they *cannot* be held separate, then the traditional view makes no sense.

4. *The Patient as Person* (New Haven: Yale University Press, 1970), pp. 115–116.

5. *Morals and Medicine* (Boston: Beacon Press, 1960), p. 174.

6. "The Right to Die with Dignity," *Good Housekeeping,* August 1974, pp. 69, 130.

7. *Foundations of the Metaphysics of Morals,* p. 422.

8. *Philosophic Exchange* (Brockport, New York), 2, no. 1 (Summer 1975), p. 45.

9

Coming to Terms:
A Response to Rachels

Thomas D. Sullivan

WE HAVE MADE some progress. The issues stand out more clearly than they did at the outset of this exchange. We can safely put to one side the key contention of Professor Rachels' "Active and Passive Euthanasia" that traditional medical ethics allows such atrocities as letting a Down's syndrome infant wither and die when a simple surgery would save its life. This charge is clearly mistaken. The American Medical Association statement that Rachels targets allows the withholding of only *extraordinary* means. The entire argument of "Active and Passive Euthanasia" depends on the mistaken assumption that traditional medical ethics sanctions the withholding of *ordinary* means. In his reply to me, "More Impertinent Distinctions," Rachels does not deny that "Active and Passive Euthanasia" misconstrued the traditional position. Rather, he starts over, making two new and more accurately focused charges. Traditional teaching on euthanasia is confused about intentions and about ordinary and extraordinary means. As a result, the traditional teaching is worthless.

Let us take a closer look.

INTENTIONAL AND NONINTENTIONAL TERMINATION OF LIFE

The traditional position forbids acting or refraining from acting with the intent thereby of bringing about a patient's death. It recognizes the legitimacy, however, of withholding treatment in some cases even though death predictably will ensue. In these cases, the medication or procedure may be too painful or too costly. But it is one thing not to help in such circumstances, quite another to act (or refrain from acting) with the deliberate intention of killing the patient. Intentionally killing patients, traditional medical ethics maintains, is always wrong. It is for this reason that intentions matter.

Professor Rachels believes otherwise. For him, the difference between foreseeing and intending is morally insignificant.[1] Intentions do not count *at all* when it comes to evaluating an act, but only when evaluating someone's moral state. "The example of Jack and Jill suggests that, on the contrary, the intention is not relevant to deciding whether the *act* is right or wrong, but instead it is relevant to assessing the character of the person who does the act, which is very different" (p. 141).

The claim that no intention is ever relevant to the evaluation of acts is exceedingly strong, but nothing less will serve Rachels' purposes. For if only some intentions are irrelevant, then it is by no means obvious or even plausible that deadly intentions are among those irrelevant to the evaluation of deadly acts. So, as Rachels appears to recognize, he has to say intentions are *never* relevant. But can this be true?

It is hard to see how it can be. To begin with, the paradigm cases of acts we evaluate as morally right or wrong are intentional. Feeding the downtrodden, comforting the sick, visiting the lonely—these good acts are all intentional. And so are the wicked acts of embezzlement, murder, and rape. We certainly do not begin by thinking that the fact that an action is intentional has nothing whatever to do with its rightness or wrongness. Typically, acts we subject to moral evaluation are chosen acts, and there are no intentionless choices. Further reflection supports the initial judgment that intentions are relevant to the morality of an action. If we draw out of an act *all* the motivating intention, the residue seems not to be the same act, if it is, properly speaking, any act at all. If we drain a lie of its intention to assert falsely, what remains is not a lie. If we further drain the act of the intention to communicate and drain from it all other intentions, what remains is no more a human act susceptible of moral evaluation than talk in a coma. Furthermore, establishing intent is crucial to the prosecution of criminal acts in courts of law. That intent should nonetheless be utterly irrelevant to the morality of an act seems, to say the least, hard to swallow.

Nor is it easy to see how Rachels' examples overturn the initial assumption that intentions are relevant to evaluating at least some deeds. We are not asked to consider a situation in which Jack and Jill *accidentally* wind up in the same room with Grandmother. We are rather asked to consider their visiting, entertaining, cheering up—all *intentional* actions. Drained of their intentionality, the acts vanish. The residues are insusceptible of moral evaluation: "Your body's being in a room at the same time as another person's body is in the room—right or wrong?" The question is senseless.

What, then, do Rachels' examples show if not that intentions are irrelevant to the morality of an act? Perhaps they show that *not every* intention is relevant to the evaluation of a particular act. We can distinguish between Jill's intention to visit her Grandmother and her *further* manipulative intention to work her way into Grandmother's will. Then, abstracting from this *further* manipulative intention we can ask whether she did the right thing by visiting Grandmother. This *may* show that *some* intentions are entirely irrelevant to the evaluation of *some* moral acts. But it certainly does not demonstrate the point at issue, for it does not show that *all* intentions are irrelevant to *all* acts. Let it be stipulated for the sake of argument that Jill performs the same act as Jack, though with a different *further* intention.[2] It does not follow from the fact that "the [*further*] intention is not relevant to deciding whether the *act* is right or wrong" (p. 141) that *no* intention is relevant. For the *prior* intention to visit Grandmother is certainly germane to seeing (as does Rachels) Jill's act as "a morally good thing" (p. 141).[3]

The same, *mutatis mutandis*, holds for the example of Dr. Black and Dr. White. As depicted, each does something intentionally— each withholds treatment. Again, if we draw the intention out of the act, there is nothing left to evaluate. We are not asked to consider a doctor *accidentally* pulling the plug of a life-support system by, say, tripping over a badly positioned wire laid by someone else. Such incidents give us nothing to discuss from a moral standpoint. And so, even if it should be allowed that the *further intentions* of Dr. Black and Dr. White play no role in identifying the acts they perform, and hence no role in the evaluation of their acts, that would not in the least serve to show that *all* their intentions are irrelevant to the evaluation of their acts. For whatever else they intend, they intend not to treat; in the absence of intention there would be nothing properly depictable as a human act and nothing left to evaluate.[4]

Thus we have good reason to believe and as yet no reason to doubt that at least some intentions are relevant to the evaluation of a moral act.[5] If so, and if deadly intent can initiate and guide an action, why must such deadly intent always and everywhere be irrelevant to the evaluation of a deadly deed?

Ordinary and Extraordinary Means of Treatment

Rachels further contends that the distinction between ordinary and extraordinary means is worthless because it cannot be used without circularity.[6]

> We cannot by using the definitions identify which treatments are extraordinary, and then use that information to determine whether the treatment may be omitted. For the definitions require that we must *already* have decided the moral questions of life and death *before* we can answer the question of which treatments are extraordinary [p. 145]!

Really? Recall *ordinary* means are medicines, treatments, and operations that offer a reasonable hope of benefit to the patient and which can be obtained without excessive expense, pain, or other inconvenience. Extraordinary are those medicines, treatments, and operations that fail to meet these criteria.[7] Now suppose you can live for three more days if you submit to a treatment which for those three days will burn like white-hot fire. It seems fairly clear that the good achieved is not worth the personal cost. The treatment in the traditional language (though the *terms* are unimportant) is extraordinary. And *so*, you reason, you need not go through the treatment. Why should anyone assume that you must *first* ascertain whether you are obliged to go through the ordeal *before* you can figure out whether the gain is greater than the loss? It quite clearly seems to be the other way around.

Rachels' summary statement of his reason for thinking that the concepts cannot be applied without circularity is this:

Again, the point is that in order to decide whether life-sustaining treatment is a benefit we must *first* decide whether it would be a good thing for the life in question to be prolonged [p. 145].

But note the ambiguity the passive voice introduces. What is it *precisely* that we must decide first? On one reading, (A), it is the value of *the life* (prolonged). Is such a *life* worth living? On another reading, (B), it is the value of *the act of prolonging*, the act of providing assistance. Is the *prolonging* good? Granted, to begin reasoning this way we have to do somewhat as (A) specifies, that is, determine the value of life lived under the envisioned conditions. Once we do, we can then go on to do as (B) specifies, evaluate the act of prolonging a life to be lived in those conditions. But we need not do what (B) prescribes before we do what (A) prescribes.

With the distinction between (A) and (B) in mind, let us consider the case just mentioned of the possible use of extraordinary means.

In accord with (A), we first judge:

(1) The life lived in these conditions for three days is of very slight or no value to the one living it.

We infer:

(2) The treatment is of slight or no benefit to the patient (The treatment is extraordinary).

And add the consideration that:

(3) If a treatment is of slight or no benefit to the patient (if it is extraordinary), then it is not obligatory.

And infer (B):

(4) The treatment is not obligatory.

Where is the circularity? If we keep distinct the (A) and (B) readings of the phrase "decide whether it would be a good thing for the life in question to be prolonged," why can't we decide (1) before (4)?

Consider now a case involving ordinary means. A dying girl's life can be quickly restored to perfect health by using an inexpensive and painless remedy.

Again, in accord with (A), we first determine that:

(1) The life lived in the expected condition is certainly a good life for the one living it.

From which we infer:

(2) The treatment is a great benefit to the patient.

And we further note:

(3) The treatment imposes no heavy burdens on others.

And, invoking the principle:

(4) If a treatment is a great benefit to the patient and imposes no heavy burdens on others (if the treatment involves only ordinary means), then the doctor should treat this patient.

Thus we arrive in accord with (B) at:

(5) The doctor should treat this patient.

Again, where is the alleged circularity? Why should we think that we must determine whether (5) is true, that the obligation is in place, before determining the truth of the premises that state the benefits and burdens? How *could* we possibly do this? How could we determine the factual questions about the effectiveness and cost of a remedy by first determining what a doctor ought to do?

Of course, sometimes it will be hard to say whether a treatment offers much of a benefit or whether providing it imposes disproportionate burdens on the patient or on others. But just as the existence of twilight does not prove there is no difference between night and day, so the existence of borderline cases does not show that there is no difference between ordinary and extraordinary means.

For these reasons I find nothing in Rachels' criticisms, either in his celebrated "Active and Passive Euthanasia" or in his reply to me, to weaken confidence in the age-old precept of benevolence:

The intentional termination of the life of an innocent human being, whether by action or omission, is wrong.

NOTES

1. Rachels does not claim, as some do, that it is impossible to believe your intended act will bring with it some consequence without intending the consequence as well. For an argument against that idea see Joseph Boyle, Jr., and Thomas D. Sullivan, "The Diffusiveness of Intention Principle: A Counter Example," *Philosophical Studies* (Holland), 31 (1977), 357–60. Gary Atkinson and I elaborate the connection between the psychological and the intentional in "Malum Vitandum: The Role of Intentions in First-Order Morality," *International Journal of Philosophical Studies*, 1 (1993), 99–110.

2. In other words, Rachels appears to argue: (1) Jack and Jill perform the same act; (2) The acts should be evaluated the same way; (3) They have different intentions; (4) If all the preceding are true, then intentions are irrelevant to the evaluation of the act. So, (5) intentions are irrelevant to the evaluation of an act.

My criticism in the text amounts to observing that an ambiguity in (3) wrecks the argument. For (3) is ambiguous between: (3a) All their intentions are different, and (3b) Some of their intentions are different. Only (3b) is true, since they both intend to visit Grandmother. But (4) is true only on (3a).

I might add that proposition (1) is also doubtful. As Rachels himself notes, "Jill manipulated and deceived her grandmother, while Jack did not." Rachels objects that this incorporates Jill's intention into the act. "In the present context," he continues, we must keep the act and the intention separate. If they cannot be held separate, the traditional view makes no sense" (p.153n3). It is true enough that the tradition requires distinguishing between the physical movement and the motivating act, but it certainly does not require identifying the human act, the act subject to evaluation, with mere physical movement. As stressed in the body of this article, all intention absent, a human act has nothing left to evaluate.

3. Nor does it follow that there is no act to which Jill's manipulative intention is relevant. For as hypothesized, Jill manipulates her grandmother. To manipulate is to do something intentionally. So, there is an intentional act of manipulation. Why can't this act be evaluated and, especially, in light of its manipulative intent? Although it is always possible to limit the description of the intentions informing a concrete moral act to a single selected intention, and to assess the residuum from a moral

standpoint, it is futile to pretend that by waving the wand of abstraction over the reality a feature of it disappears. Jill manipulates. This act wrong. So far as I can see, it is important to say why without referring at all to her intentions, for it is impossible to say what she does without referring to her intentions.

4. In this connection it is worth noting that the proponent of the traditional position is not committed to saying Dr. White did the right thing; Dr. Black, the wrong thing. For they both intentionally withhold only extraordinary means, and this is allowable. Dr. Black, whom Rachels supposes the tradition must condemn, has, according to Rachels' own account, an intention only of "letting the patient die." He shares with Dr. White the conviction that "further treatment offers little hope of saving the baby and will only increase its suffering" (p. 142). Given these convictions and intents, he too does the right thing. To get the picture in focus, consider Dr. Green in a new scenario. He mistakenly thinks the treatment will help, but because he hates the baby's parents, he withholds treatment. Shall we say he too does the right thing by withholding treatment? And if not, how do we explain why without reference to intentions?

5. Several possible replies to the arguments we have made in this section come to mind, none successful.

a. Rachels picked unfortunate examples. There are examples of unintentional doings or failings that are susceptible of moral evaluation, e.g., forgetting an important appointment, incautiously giving someone the wrong medicine, and the like.

Even if true, however, this hardly shows that intentions are always and necessarily irrelevant to the worth of an act, any more than the fact that one can win or lose a baseball game without a run being scored (by forfeit) shows scoring runs is never relevant to winning or losing a baseball game.

b. While intentional acts are subject to moral evaluation, they are never so in virtue of their being intentional, but only in virtue of their results.

But why should anyone think so? The claim seems to be on a par with the claim which no one dreams of making that while illuminated objects are visible, being illuminated has nothing whatever to do with being visible. If actions are right or wrong *solely* in virtue of their effects, and not in virtue of the effects being incorporated into a plan or intention, then volcanic eruptions, which do plenty of damage, are morally bad deeds.

c. It is not because intentional actions are intentional that they can be evaluated morally, but because, necessarily, intentional acts are conscious acts, and it is in virtue of our being conscious of the effects our acts will likely produce that the acts are right or wrong. Consciousness, not intentionality, marks the distinction between our acts and acts such as volcanic eruptions.

It is true that we are morally responsible for the effects of our actions even if the effects are not incorporated into our intentions. The arsonist who burns down a building for the insurance money without intending to kill its occupants is certainly guilty of their deaths. But it does not follow that intentions are irrelevant to the arsonist's act. For the arsonist chooses to do something, namely, *to burn down the building*. And there are no intentionless choices. It is in virtue of this conscious *choice* to proceed with reckless disregard for their lives that he is guilty of their deaths. Mere knowledge of what will eventuate from some happening to which you are subject does not necessarily result in a human action that can be evaluated morally. If you trip at the head of the stairs and foresee as you tumble down that you will bowl over Grandmother, it does not follow that your action is wrong. In fact, it hardly seems to count as an action at all. What we primarily evaluate are choices, and there are no intentionless choices.

6. Rachels remarks the distinctions are "crucial to orthodox Catholic thought." Why is this supposed to be pertinent? Rachels targets the American Medical Association statement. The AMA is not to my knowledge renowned for promoting orthodox Catholicism. The definitions of "ordinary" and "extraordinary" means I invoke for the purpose of defending the AMA statement are taken from a medical ethics textbook by Paul Ramsey, a Protestant.

7. Paul Ramsey, *The Patient as Person* (New Haven and London: Yale University Press, 1970), p. 122. Part of Rachels' trouble may be that he understands as "ordinary means" those means that we are obliged to use. But this is not the stated definition. The definition does not refer to an obligation to use the means.

PART II

PHILOSOPHICAL
PROBLEMS

10

Whatever the Consequences
Jonathan Bennett

THE FOLLOWING KIND of thing can occur.[1] A woman in labour will certainly die unless an operation is performed in which the head of her unborn child is crushed or dissected; while if it is not performed the child can be delivered, alive, by post-mortem Caesarean section. This presents a straight choice between the woman's life and the child's.

In a particular instance of this kind, some people would argue for securing the woman's survival on the basis of the special facts of the case: the woman's terror, or her place in an established network of affections and dependences, or the child's physical defects, and so on. For them, the argument could go the other way in another instance, even if only in a very special one—e.g., where the child is well formed and the woman has cancer which will kill her within a month anyway.

Others would favour the woman's survival in any instance of the kind presented in my opening paragraph, on the grounds that women are human while unborn children are not. This dubious argument does not need to be attacked here, and I shall ignore it.

Others again would say, just on the facts as stated in my first paragraph, that the *child* must be allowed to survive. Their objection to any operation in which an unborn child's head is crushed, whatever the special features of the case, goes like this:

To do the operation would be to kill the child, while to refrain from doing it would not be to kill the woman but merely to conduct oneself in such a way that—as a foreseen but unwanted consequence—the woman died. The question we should ask is not: "The woman's life or the child's?," but rather: "To kill, or not to kill,

From *Analysis*, Vol. 26, no. 23 (1966). Reprinted by permission of the publisher, Basil Blackwell & Mott, Ltd., and the author.

an innocent human?" The answer to *that* is that it is always absolutely wrong to kill an innocent human, even in such dismal circumstances as these.

This line of thought needs to be attacked. Some able people find
it acceptable; it is presupposed by the Principle of Double Effect[2]
which permeates Roman Catholic writing on morals; and I cannot
find any published statement of the extremely strong philosophical case for its rejection.

I shall state that case as best I can. My presentation of it owes
much to certain allies and opponents who have commented on
earlier drafts. I gratefully acknowledge my debt to Miss G. E. M.
Anscombe, A. G. N. Flew, A. Kenney and T. J. Smiley; and to a
number of Cambridge research students, especially D. F. Wallace.

THE PLAN OF ATTACK

There is no way of disproving the principle: "It would always be
wrong to kill an innocent human, whatever the consequences of
not doing so." The principle is consistent and reasonably clear; it
can be fed into moral syllogisms to yield practical conclusions; and
although its application to borderline cases may raise disturbing
problems, this is true of any moral principle. Someone who thinks
that the principle is laid down by a moral authority whose deliver-
ances are to be accepted without question, without *any* testing
against the dictates of the individual conscience, is vulnerable only
to arguments about the credentials of his alleged authority; and
these are not my present concern. So I have no reply to make to
anyone who is prepared to say: "I shall obey God's command
never to kill an innocent human. I shall make no independent
moral assessment of this command—whether to test the reasonableness of obeying it, or to test my belief that it *is* God's command, or for any other purpose." My concern is solely with those
who accept the principle: "It would always be wrong to kill an
innocent human, whatever the consequences of not doing so,"
not just because it occurs in some received list of moral principles
but also because they think that it can in some degree be recommended to the normal conscience. Against this, I shall argue that
a normal person who accepts the principle must either have failed

to see what it involves or be passively and unquestionably obedient to an authority.

I do not equate "the normal conscience" with "the 'liberal' conscience." Of course, the principle *is* rejected by the "liberal" majority; but I shall argue for the stronger and less obvious thesis that the principle is in the last resort on a par with "It would always be wrong to shout, whatever the consequences of not doing so," or "It would always be wrong to leave a bucket in a hallway, whatever etc." It is sometimes said that we "should not understand" someone who claimed to accept such wild eccentricities as these as fundamental moral truths—that he would be making a logical mistake, perhaps about what it is for something to be a "moral" principle. I need not claim so much. It is enough to say that such a person, if he was sincere and in his right mind, could safely be assumed to have delivered himself over to a moral authority and to have opted out of moral thinking altogether. The same could be said of anyone who accepted and *really understood* the principle: "It would always be wrong to kill an innocent human, whatever the consequences of not doing so." This principle is accepted by reasonable people who, though many of them give weight to some moral authority, have not abdicated from independent moral thinking. Clearly, they regard the principle as one which others might be led to accept, or at least to take seriously, on grounds other than subservience to an authority. From this fact, together with the thesis for which I shall argue, it follows that those who accept the principle (like others who at least treat it with respect) have not thought it through, have not seen what it comes to in concrete cases where it yields a different practical conclusion from that yielded by "It is wrong to kill an innocent human unless there are very powerful reasons for doing so." I aim to show what the principle comes to in these cases, and so to expose it for what it is.

My arguments will tell equally against any principle of the form "It would always be wrong to . . . , whatever the consequences of not doing so"; but I shall concentrate on the one principle about killing, and indeed on its application to the kind of obstetrical situation described in my opening paragraph.

I need a label for someone who accepts principles of the form: "It would always be wrong to . . . , whatever the consequences of not doing so." "Roman Catholic" is at once too wide, and too narrow; "intrinsicalist" is nasty; "absolutist" is misleading; "deontologist" means too many other things as well. Reluctantly, I settle for "conservative." This use has precedents, but I offer it as a stipulative definition—an expository convenience and not a claim about "conservatism" in any ordinary sense.

Well then: When the conservative condemns the operation described in my opening paragraph, he does so *partly* because the operation involves the death of an innocent human. So does its non-performance; but for the conservative the dilemma is asymmetrical because the two alternatives involve human deaths in different ways: in one case the death is part of a killing, in the other there is no killing and a death occurs only as a consequence of what is done. From the premiss that operating would be killing an innocent human, together with the principle: "It would always be wrong to kill an innocent human, whatever etc.," it does follow that it would be wrong to operate. But the usual conservative—the one I plan to attack—thinks that his principle has *some* measure of acceptability on grounds other than unquestioning obedience to an authority. He must therefore think that the premiss: "In this case, operating would be killing an innocent human while not-operating would involve the death of an innocent human only as a consequence" gives some reason for the conclusion: "In this case, operating would be wrong." I shall argue that it gives no reason at all: once the muddles have been cleared away, it is just not humanly possible to see the premiss as supporting the conclusion, however weakly, except by accepting the principle "It would always be wrong etc." as an unquestionable donnée.

THE ACTION/CONSEQUENCE DISTINCTION

When James killed Henry, what happened was this: James contracted his fingers round the handle of a knife, and moved his hand in such a way that the knife penetrated Henry's body and severed an artery; blood escaped from the wound, the rate of oxygen-transfer to Henry's body-cells fell drastically, and Henry died. In general, someone's performing a physical action includes

his moving some part or parts of his body. (The difference between "He moved his hand" and "His hand moved" is not in
question here: I am referring to movements which he *makes*.) He
does this in a physical environment, and other things happen in
consequence. A description of what he *did* will ordinarily entail
something not only about his movements but also, *inter alia*, about
some of their upshots. Other upshots will not ordinarily be covered by any description of "what he did," but will be counted
amongst "the consequences of what he did." There are various
criteria for drawing the line between what someone did and the
consequences of what he did; and there can be several proper ways
of drawing it in a given case.

This last point notwithstanding, there are wrong ways of dividing a set of happenings into action and consequences. Even where
it is not positively wrong to give a very parsimonious account of
"what he did," it may be preferable to be more inclusive. If in
my chosen example the obstetrician does the operation, it is true
that he crushes the child's head with the consequence that the
child dies, but a better account, perhaps, would say that he *kills*
the child by crushing his head. There can certainly be outright
wrongness at the other end of the scale: we cannot be as inclusive
as we like in our account of "what he did." If at the last time
when the operation could save the woman's life the obstetrician
is resignedly writing up his notes, it is just not true that, as he
sits at his desk, he is killing the woman; nor, indeed, is he killing
her at any other time.

The use of the action/consequence distinction in the conservative premiss is, therefore, perfectly correct. Operating *is* killing;
not-operating is not. What are we saying when we say this? By
what criteria is the action/consequence distinction drawn in the
present case? I shall try, by answering this, to show that in this
case one cannot attach moral significance to the fact that the line
drawn by the distinction falls where it does. Briefly, the criteria
for the action/consequence distinction fall into two groups: those
which could support a moral conclusion but which do not apply
to every instance of the obstetrical example; and those which do
apply to the example but which it would be wildly eccentric to

think relevant to the moral assessment of courses of action. There is no overlap between the two groups.

Some differences which tend to go with the action/consequence distinction, and are perhaps to be counted amongst the criteria for it, clearly do have moral significance. None of them, however, is generally present in the obstetrical example.

Given a question about whether some particular upshot of a movement I made is to be covered by the description of what I did:

(a) The answer may depend in part upon whether in making the movement I was entirely confident that that upshot would ensue; and this could reasonably be thought relevant to the moral assessment of my conduct. This aspect of the action/consequence distinction, however, is absent from most instances of the obstetrical example. The classification of not-operating as something other than killing does not imply that the obstetrician rates the woman's chance of survival (if the operation is not performed) higher than the child's chance of survival (if it is performed). If it did imply this then, by contraposition, not-operating would in many such cases have to be classified as killing after all.

(b) The answer may depend in part upon how certain or inevitable it was that that upshot would ensue from my movement, or upon how confidently I ought to have expected it to ensue; and that too may have a strong bearing on the moral assessment of my conduct. But it gets no grip on the obstetrical example, for in many cases of that kind there is moral certainty on both sides of the dilemma. If the conservative says that the action/consequence distinction, when correctly drawn, is always associated with morally significant differences in the inevitability of upshots of movements, then he is vulnerable to an argument by contraposition like the one in (a). He is vulnerable in other ways as well, which I shall discuss in my next section.

(c) The answer may depend in part upon whether I made the movement partly or wholly for the sake of achieving that upshot; and this is a morally significant matter. But the obstetrical example is symmetrical in that respect also: if the obstetrician crushes the child's head he does so not because this will lead to the child's death or because it constitutes killing the child, but because that is his only way of removing the child's body from the woman's.

To summarize: moral conclusions may be supported by facts (a) about what is expected, but in the example each upshot is confidently expected; (b) about what is inevitable, but in the example each upshot is inevitable; or (c) about what is ultimately aimed at, but in the example neither upshot is aimed at.

An Aside: Degrees of Inevitability

I have suggested that a conservative might say: "The action/consequence distinction is always associated with a morally significant difference in the degree to which upshots are certain or inevitable." This is false; but let us grant it in order to see whether it can help the conservative on the obstetrical example. I concede, for purposes of argument, that if the operation is not performed the woman will pretty certainly die, while if it is performed the child will even more certainly die.

What use can the conservative make of this concession? Will he say that the practical decision is to be based on a weighing of the comparative desirability of upshots against the comparative certainty of their achievement? If so, then he must allow that there *could* be a case in which it was right to kill the child—perhaps a case where a healthy young widow with four children is bearing a hydrocephalic child, and where her chance of survival if the operation is not performed is *nearly* as bad as the child's chance of survival if it is performed. If a professed "conservative" allows that there could, however improbably, be such a case, then he is not a conservative but a consequentialist; he does after all base his final judgment on the special features of the case; and he has misrepresented his position by using the language of action and consequence to express his implausible views about the comparative inevitability of upshots. On the other hand, if the conservative still absolutely rules out the killing of the child, whatever the details of the particular case, then what could be his point in claiming that there is a difference in degree of inevitability? The moral significance of this supposed difference would, at best, have to be conceded to be an obscure one which threw no light on why anyone should adopt the conservative view.

A certain conservative tactic is at issue here. Miss G. E. M. Anscombe has said: "If someone really thinks, *in advance,* that it is open to question whether such an action as procuring the judicial execution of the innocent should be quite excluded from consideration—I do not want to argue with him; he shows a corrupt mind."[3] The phrase "quite excluded from consideration" clearly places Miss Anscombe as what I am calling a "conservative." (The phrase "a corrupt mind," incidentally, tends to confirm my view that conservatives think their position can stand the light of day, i.e., that they do not see it as tenable only by those who passively obey some moral authority.) Now, in the course of a footnote to this passage Miss Anscombe remarks:

> In discussion when this paper was read, as was perhaps to be expected, this case was produced: a government is required to have an innocent man tried, sentenced and executed under threat of a "hydrogen bomb war." It would seem strange to me to have much hope of averting a war threatened by such men as made this demand. But the most important thing about the way in which cases like this are invented in discussions is the assumption that only two courses are open: here, compliance and open defiance. No one can say in advance of such a situation what the possibilities are going to be—e.g., that there is none of stalling by a feigned willingness to comply, accompanied by a skilfully arranged "escape" of the victim.

This makes two points about the case as described: there might be nothing we could do which would have a good chance of averting a war; and if there were one such thing we could do there might be several. The consequentialist might meet this by trying yet again to describe a case in which judicially executing an innocent man is the only thing we could do which would have a good chance of averting a war. When he had added the details which block off the other alternatives, his invented case may well be far removed from present political likelihood; it may even be quite fantastic. Still, what does the conservative say about it?

Here is Miss Anscombe, at her most gamesome, on the subject of "fantastic" examples:

A point of method I would recommend to the corrupter of the youth would be this: concentrate on examples which are either banal: you have promised to return a book, but . . . and so on, or fantastic: what you ought to do if you have to move forward, and stepping with your right foot meant killing twenty-five young men, while stepping with your left foot would kill fifty drooling old ones. (Obviously the right thing to do would be to jump and polish off the lot.)[4]

The cards are now well stacked; but this is a game in which a conservative should not be taking a hand at all. Someone may say (i): "In no situation could it be right to procure the judicial execution of the innocent: political probability aside, the judicial execution of the innocent is absolutely impermissible in any possible circumstances." Or some may say (ii): "It is never right to procure the judicial execution of the innocent: a situation in which this would be right has never arisen, isn't going to arise, and cannot even be described without entering into the realm of political fantasy." These are different. The former is conservatism, according to which "the judicial execution of the innocent should be quite excluded from consideration." The latter is not conservatism: according to it, the judicial execution of the innocent is taken into consideration, assessed in the light of the political probabilities of the world we live in, and excluded on that basis. The former is Miss Anscombe's large type; the latter, apparently, is her footnote. The difference between (i) "In no situation could it be right . . ." and (ii) "No situation is even remotely likely to occur in which it would be right . . ." can be masked by dismissing what is relevant but unlikely as "fantastic" and therefore negligible. But the difference between the two positions is crucial even if in the first instance it can be brought out only by considering "fantastic" possibilities. The two may yield the same real-life practical conclusions, but (ii) can be understood and argued with in a way in which (i) cannot. If someone accepts (ii), and is not afraid to discuss a "fantastic" but possible situation in which he would approve the judicial execution of an innocent man, he can be challenged to square this with his contrary judgment in regard to some less fantastic situation. Whether he could meet the challenge would depend on the details of his moral position and of the situations in question. The point is that we should know where we stood with him: for example, we should know that it was *relevant* to adduce evidence about how good the chances would be of averting war in this way in this situation, or in that way in that. It is just this sort of thing which the unwavering conservative must regard as irrelevant; and that is what is wrong with his position. Miss Anscombe says: "No one can say in advance of such a situation what the possibilities are going to be"; but the central objection to conservatism is, precisely, that it says in advance that for the judging of the proposed course of action *it does not matter* what the possibilities are going to be. Why, then, go on about them—if not to disguise conservatism as something else when the going gets tough?

I have based this paper on the obstetrical example in the hope that, without being jeered at for having "invented" an example which is "fantastic," I could present a kind of case in which a conservative principle would yield a practical conclusion different from any likely to be arrived at by consequentialist arguments. The claim that in these cases there would always be a morally significant difference between the woman's chance of survival and the child's could only be another attempt to get the spotlight off conservatism altogether—to get the consequentialist to accept the conservative's conclusion and forget about his principle. In the obstetrical example, the attempt is pretty desperate (though, with the aid of judiciously selected statistics, it is made often enough); with other kinds of examples, used to examine this or other conservative principles, it might be easier for the conservative to make a show of insisting on the addition of details which render the examples "fantastic." But this does not mean that the case against conservatism is stronger here than elsewhere. It means only that the obstetrical example gives less scope than most for the "there-might-be-another-way-out" move, or protective-coloration gambit, which some conservatives sometimes use when they shelter their position by giving the impression that it does not really exist.

A conservative might invoke inevitability, without comparing degrees of it in the consequentialist manner, by saying that if the operation is not performed the woman still has *some* chance of survival while if it is performed the child has *none*. Barring miracles, this is wrong about the woman; not barring miracles, it is wrong about the child. It could seem plausible only to someone who did not bar miracles but took a peculiar view of how they operate. Some people do attach importance in this regard to the fact that if the operation is not performed the woman may take some time to die: they seem to think—perhaps encouraged by an eccentric view of God as powerful but *slow*—that the longer an upshot is delayed the more room there is for a miraculous intervention. This belief, whatever the assumptions which underlie it, gives no help to the conservative position. For suppose the obstetrician decides to try, after operating and delivering the child, to repair its head by microsurgery. The woman's supposed "some chance" of survival if the child's head is not crushed is of the same kind as the obstetrician's "some chance" of saving the child after crushing its head: in each case there is what the well-informed plain man would call "no chance," but in each case it will take a little time for the matter to be finally settled by the events themselves—for the woman to die or the obstetrician to admit failure. Would the conservative say that the obstetrician's intention to try to save the child in this way, though hopeless, completely alters the shape of the problem and perhaps makes it all right for the obstetrician to crush the child's head? If so, then what we have here is a morality of gestures and poses.

ASPECTS OF THE DISTINCTION: SECOND GROUP

I return to the main thread of my argument. Of the remaining three aspects of the action/consequence distinction, it was not quite true to say that all are present in (every instance of) the obstetrical example; for the first of them has not even that merit. The main point, however, is that even if it were always present it would not help the conservative—though it might help us to diagnose his trouble.

(d) Someone's decision whether an upshot of a movement of mine is to be covered by his description of what I *did* may depend partly on his moral assessment of my role in the total situation. Your condemnation of me, or perhaps your approval, may be reflected in your putting on the "Action" side of the line an upshot which an indifferent onlooker would count as merely a "consequence." This aspect of the action/consequence distinction—if indeed it is one independently of those already discussed—cannot help the conservative who believes that a premiss using the distinction tends to *support* a moral conclusion. That belief demands a relevance relation which scopes the other way.

There seem to be just two remaining aspects of the action/consequence distinction. Certainly, there are only two which do appear in all instances of the obstetrical example. These two must be the sole justification for saying that operating would be killing while not-operating would not be killing; and so they must bear the whole weight of any conservative but non-authoritarian case against killing the child.

(e) Operating is killing-the-child because if the obstetrician operates there is a high degree of *immediacy* between what he does with his hands and the child's dying. This immediacy consists in the brevity or absence of time-lag, spatial nearness, simplicity of causal connexions, and paucity of intervening physical objects. The relations amongst these are complex; but they are severally relevant to the action/consequence distinction, and in the obstetrical example they all pull together, creating an overwhelming case for calling the performance of the operation the *killing* of the child.

(f) Not-operating is not killing-the-woman because it is not *doing* anything at all but is merely *refraining* from doing something.

Since (e) and (f) are so central to the action/consequence distinction generally, it is appropriate that they should sometimes bear its whole weight, as they do in the conservative's (correct) application of the distinction to the obstetrical example. But if (e) and (f) are all there is to the premiss: "In this case, operating would be killing an innocent human while not-operating would involve the death of an innocent human only as a consequence," then this premiss offers no support at all to the conclusion: "In this case, operating would be wrong."

The matters which I group under "immediacy" in (e) may borrow moral significance from their loose association with facts about whether and in what degree upshots are (a) expected, (b) inevitable or (c) aimed at. In none of these respects, however, is there a relevant asymmetry in the obstetrical example. The question is: why should a difference in degree of immediacy, unaccompanied by other relevant differences, be taken to support a moral discrimination? I cannot think of a remotely plausible answer which does not consist solely in an appeal to an authority.[5]

Suggestions come to mind about "not getting one's hands dirty"; and the notion of what I call "immediacy" does help to show how the literal and the metaphorical are mingled in some uses of that phrase. In so doing, however, it exposes the desire to "keep one's hands clean," in cases like the obstetrical example, as a symptom of muddle or primness or, worst of all, a moral egoism like Pilate's. (To be fair: I do not think that many conservatives would answer in this way. If they used similar words it would probably not be to express the nasty sentiment I have mentioned but rather to say something like: "I must obey God's law; and the rest is up to God." Because this suggests a purely authoritarian basis, and because it certainly has nothing to do with immediacy, it lies beyond my present scope.)

Similarly with the action/refraining distinction in (f). I shall argue in my next section that our criteria for this distinction do not invest it with any moral significance whatever—except when the distinction is drawn on the basis of independently formed moral judgments, and then it cannot help the conservative case for the reason given in (d). And if neither (e) immediacy or (f) acting/refraining separately has moral significance, then clearly they cannot acquire any by being taken together.

Acting and Refraining

Suppose the obstetrician does not operate, and the woman dies. He does not kill her, but he *lets her die.* The approach suggested by these words is just an unavoidable nuisance, and I shall not argue from it. When I say "he lets her die," I mean only that he knowingly refrains from preventing her death which he alone could prevent, and he cannot say that her survival is in a general way "none of my business" or "not [even *prima facie*] my concern." If my arguments so far are correct, then this one fact—the fact that the non-operating obstetrician *lets the woman die* but does not *kill her*—is the only remaining feature of the situation which the conservative can hope to adduce as supporting his judgment about what ought to be done in every instance of the obstetrical example.[6] Let us examine the difference between "X killed Y" and "X let Y die."

Some cases of letting-die are also cases of killing. If on a dark night X knows that Y's next step will take him over the edge of a high cliff, and he refrains from uttering a simple word of warning because he doesn't care or because he wants Y dead, then it is natural to say not only that X lets Y die but also that he kills him—even if it was not X who suggested the route, removed the fence from the cliff-top, etc. Cases like this, where a failure-to-prevent is described as a doing partly *because* it is judged to be wicked or indefensible, are beside my present point; for I want to see what difference there is between killing and letting-die which might be a *basis for* a moral judgment. Anyway, the letting-die which is also killing must involve malice or wanton indifference, and there is nothing like that in the obstetrical example. In short, to count these cases as relevant to the obstetrical example would be to suggest that not-operating would after all be killing the woman—a plainly false suggestion which I have disavowed. I wish to criticise the conservative's argument, not to deny his premiss. So from now on I shall ignore cases of letting-die which are also cases of killing; and it will make for brevity to pretend that they do not exist. For example, I shall say that killing involved moving one's body—which is false of some of these cases, but true of all others.

One more preliminary point: the purposes of the present enquiry do not demand that a full analysis be given either of "X killed Y" or of "X let Y die." We can ignore any implications either may have about what X (a) expected, (b) should have expected, or (c) was aiming at; for the obstetrical example is symmetrical in all those respects. We can also ignore the fact that "X killed Y" loosely implies something about (e) immediacy which is not implied by "X let Y die," for immediacy in itself has no moral significance.

Consider the statement that *Joe killed the calf*. A certain aspect of the analysis of this will help us to see how it relates to *Joe let the calf die*. To say that Joe killed the calf is to say that

(1) Joe moved his body

and

(2) the calf died;

but it is also to say something about how Joe's moving was connected with the calf's dying—something to the effect that

(3) if Joe had not moved as he did, the calf would not have died.

How is (3) to be interpreted? We might take it, rather strictly, as saying

(3'): If Joe had moved in *any* other way, the calf would not have died.

This, however, is too strong to be a necessary condition of Joe's having killed the calf. Joe may have killed the calf even if he could have moved in other ways which would equally have involved the calf's dying. Suppose that Joe cut the calf's throat, but could have shot it instead: in that case he clearly killed it; but (3') denies that he killed it, because the calf might still have died even if Joe had moved in just the way he did.

We might adopt a weaker reading of (3), namely as saying

(3''): Joe could have moved in *some* other way without the calf's dying.

But where (3') was too strong to be necessary, (3'') is too weak to express a sufficient connexion between Joe's moving and the calf's dying. It counts Joe as having killed the calf not only in cases where we should ordinarily say that he killed it but also in cases where the most we should say is that he let it die.

The truth lies somewhere between (3'), which is appropriate to "Joe killed the calf in the only way open to him," and (3''), which is appropriate to "Joe killed the calf or let it die." Specifically, the connexion between Joe's moving and the calf's dying which is appropriate to "Joe killed calf" but not to "Joe let the calf die" is expressed by

(3'''): Of all the other ways in which Joe might have moved, *relatively* few satisfy the condition: if Joe had moved like that, the calf would have died.

And the connexion which is appropriate to "Joe let the calf die" but not to "Joe killed the calf" is expressed by

(4): Of all the other ways in which Joe might have moved, *almost all* satisfy the condition: if Joe had moved like that, the calf would have died.

This brings me to the main thesis of the present section: apart from the factors I have excluded as already dealt with, the difference between "X killed Y" and "X let Y die" *is* the difference between (3′′′) and (4). When the killing/letting-die distinction is stripped of its implications regarding immediacy, intention etc.— which lack moral significance or don't apply to the example—all that remains is a distinction having to do with where a set of movements lies on the scale which has "the only set of movements which would have produced that upshot" at one end and "movements other than the only set which would have produced that upshot" at the other.

This, then, is the conservative's residual basis for a moral discrimination between operating and not-operating. Operating would be killing: if the obstetrician makes movements which constitute operating, then the child will die; and there are very few other movements he could make which would also involve the child's dying. Not-operating would only be letting-die: if throughout the time when he could be operating the obstetrician makes movements which constitute not-operating, then the woman will die; but in a vast majority of alternative movements he could make during that time would equally involve the woman's dying. I do not see how anyone doing his own moral thinking about the matter could find the least shred of moral significance in *this* difference between operating and not-operating.

Suppose you are told that X killed Y in the only way possible in the circumstances; and this, perhaps together with certain other details of the case, leads you to judge X's conduct adversely. Then you are told: "You have been misled: there is another way in which X could have killed Y." Then a third informant says: "That is wrong too: there are two other ways . . . etc." Then a fourth: "No: there are three other ways . . . etc." Clearly, these successive corrections put no pressure at all on your original judgment: you will not think it relevant to your judgment on X's killing of Y that it could have been carried out in any one of n different ways.

But the move from "X killed Y in the only possible way" to "X killed Y in one of the only five possible ways" is of the same *kind* as the move from "X killed Y" to "X let Y die" (except for the latter's implications about immediacy); and the moral insignificance of the former move is evidence for the moral insignificance of the latter move also.

The difference between "X killed Y" and "X let Y die" is the sum-total of a vast number of differences such as that between "X killed Y in one of the only n possible ways" and "X killed Y in one of the only n + 1 possible ways." If the difference between ". . . n . . ." and ". . . n + 1 . . ." were morally insignificant only because it was too *small* for any moral discrimination to be based upon it, then the sum-total of millions of such differences might still have moral significance. But in fact the differences in question, whatever their size, are of the *wrong kind* for any moral discrimination to be based upon them. Suppose you have judged X adversely, on the basis of the misinformation: "X killed Y in the only way possible in the circumstances"; and this is then replaced, in one swoop, by the true report: "X did not kill Y at all, though he did knowingly let Y die." Other things being equal, would this give you the slightest reason to retract your adverse judgment? Not a bit of it! It would be perfectly reasonable for you to reply: "The fact remains that X chose to conduct himself in a way which he knew would involve Y's death. At first I thought his choice could encompass Y's death only by being the choice of some rather specific course of conduct; whereas the revised report shows me that X's choice could have encompassed Y's death while committing X to very little. At first I thought it had to be a choice to act; I now realize that it could have been a choice to refrain. What of it?"

There are several things a conservative is likely to say at this point—all equivalent. "When we know that the crucial choice could have been a choice to refrain from something, we can begin to allow for the possibility that it may have been a choice to refrain from doing something wrong, such as killing an innocent human." Or: "You say 'other things being equal,' but in the obstetrical example they aren't equal. By representing letting-die as a kind of wide-optioned killing you suppress the fact that the alternative to letting the woman die is killing the child."

Replies like these are available to the conservative only if he does not need them and can break through at some other point; for they assume the very point which is at issue, namely that in every instance of the obstetrical example it would be wrong to kill the child. I think that in some cases it would indeed be wrong—(I do not press for a blanket judgment on all instances of the example—quite the contrary); and in such a case the obstetrician, if he rightly let the woman die, could defend his doing so on the basis of the details of the particular case. Furthermore, he might wish to begin his defence by explaining: "I let the woman die, but I did not kill her"; for letting-die is in general likely to be more defensible than killing. My analysis incidentally shows one reason why: the alternatives to killing are always very numerous, and the odds are that at least one of them provides an acceptable way out of the impasse; whereas the alternative to letting-die is always some fairly specific course of conduct, and if there are conclusive objections to *that* then there's an end of the matter. All this, though, is a matter of likelihoods. It is no help in the rare case where the alternatives to killing, numerous as they are, do *not* include an acceptable way out of the impasse because they all involve something of the same order of gravity as a killing, namely a letting-die. The conservative may say: "Where innocent humans are in question, letting-die is not of the same order of gravity as killing: for one of them is not, and the other is, absolutely wrong in all possible circumstances." But this, like the rejoinders out of which this paragraph grew, assumes the very point which is at issue. All these conservative moves come down to just one thing: "At this point your argument fails; for the wrongness of killing the child, in any instance of the obstetrical example, *can* be defended on the basis of your own analysis of the acting/refraining distinction—plus the extra premiss that it would always be wrong to kill the child."

THE STRESS ON THE SPECIFIC

My argument is finished; but its strategy might be thought to be open to a certain criticism which I want to discuss.

The obstetrical example is a *kind* of situation, on every instance of which the conservative makes a certain judgment. I have argued that this judgment, as applied to many instances of the example, cannot be defended except by the unquestioning invocation of authority. This would have been damaging to the conservative position even if I had appealed only to "fantastic" kinds of instance such as seldom or never occur; but in fact my claims have been true of many real-life instances of the obstetrical example. Still, a conservative might resist my drive towards the relatively specific, my insistence upon asking: "What is there about *this* kind of instance which justifies your judgment upon it?" He might claim that even my opening paragraph presents so special a kind of situation that he cannot fairly be asked to find in *it* something which supports his judgment other than by a blanket appeal to his general principle that it would always be wrong to kill an innocent human. There are two ways in which he might defend this stand: they look alike, but their fatal defects are very different.

The first is by the use of sub-Wittgensteinian argument from the nature of language. Although I have never encountered it, it is a possible and plausible objection to my strategy of argument. The conservative might say: "Granted that facts about (a) expectation, (b) inevitability and (c) intention are irrelevant to the way the action/consequence distinction applies to the obstetrical example; it does not follow that when we apply the distinction to the example *all* we are doing—apart from (d) reflecting our already-formed moral judgments—is to report facts about (e) immediacy and (f) acting/refraining. Language and thought don't work like this. When we say: 'Operating would be killing; not-operating would not be killing though it would have death as a consequence' we are not *just* talking about immediacy and specificity of options. We are using words which, *qua* words in the language, are laden with associations having to do with (a)–(d); and these associations of the words cannot simply be ignored or forgotten in a particular case. Language is not atomic in that way, and it would be at best a clumsy instrument if it were."

I agree that we often do, and perhaps must sometimes, decide our conduct in one situation partly through verbal carry-overs from others in which similar conduct could be justified more directly. But I think that everyone will agree that the more serious a practical problem is, the greater is our obligation to resist such verbal carry-overs and scrutinize the particular problem in order to see what there is about *it* which would justify this or that solution to it. A practical problem in which human lives are at stake is a deeply serious one, and it would be an abdication from all moral seriousness to settle it by verbal carry-overs. I am not saying: "Take pity on the poor woman, and never mind what the correct description of the situation is." I am opposing someone who says: "This is the correct description of the situation—never mind what its force is in this particular case."

The second objection to my stress on the particular case, or the specific kind of case, is one which conservatives do sometimes use; and it connects with a muddle which is not special to conservatives. It goes like this: "We must have rules. If every practical problem had to be solved on the spot, on the basis of the fine details of the particular case, the results would be disastrous. Take a situation which falls under some rule which I know to be justi-fied in most situations. There may not be time or means for me to learn much more about the present situation than just that it does fall under the rule; the details of the case, even if I can dis-cover them, may be too complex for me to handle; my handling of them, even if intellectually efficient, may without my knowing it be self-interested or corrupt; by deciding, however uncorruptly, not to follow the rule on this occasion, I may weaken its hold on me in other situations where it clearly ought to be followed; and even if I could be sure that I was in no such danger, I might help others into it by publicly breaking the rule."[7]

This is all true, but it does not help the conservative. Notice first that it tells against undue attention to individual cases rather than against undue attention to limited kinds of cases: its target is not the specific but the particular. Still, it could be developed into an attack on over-stressing very specifically detailed kinds of case: its opening words would then have to be replaced by: "We must have rather general rules." This is true too, but it is still no help to the conservative.

This argument for our bringing practical problems under rather general rules is based on the consequences of our not doing so: it points to the dangers attendant on suspending a general rule and considering whether one's practical problem might be better re-solved by applying a less general one. But sometimes these dangers will be far too slight to justify doing what a given general rule enjoins in a particular situation. If the thesis under discussion is to have any practical upshot which is not ludicrous ("Never break any general rule which would enjoin the right action in more cases than not"), or vague to the point of vacuity ("Always apply some fairly general rule"), or merely question-begging ("Never break a rule forbidding an action which really is absolutely impermissible"), then it must allow us to raise questions of the form: "Need we be deterred by the dangers attendant on suspending *this* rule in favour of *this* more specific rule in *this* kind of situation?" The answer will depend upon what the challenged general rule is, what the proposed substitute for it is, the intelligence and character of the agent, and the likelihood that his breaking the rule (if it comes to that) would become generally known and, if known, demoralizing to others. These matters need not be so complex as to defeat finite intelligence, or so primrose-strewn that fallen man dare not venture among them. Furthermore, they can themselves be embodied in rules carefully formulated in advance—meta-rules about the kinds of situation in which this or that ground-level general rule may be suspended in favour of this or that more specific one.

Here is a possible case. A certain obstetrician accepts the rule, "Do not kill innocent humans," as applicable in every kind of situation he has thought of except the kind described in my opening paragraph. He wants a rule for this kind too, as a shield against the confusions, temptations and pressures of the concrete situation; and after reflection he adopts the following: "If the child is not hydrocephalic it is not to be killed. If it is hydrocephalic it is to be killed unless either (a) the woman is bound to die within a month anyway, or (b) the woman has no other children under eighteen and she is known to be a chronic acute depressive. If (a) or (b) or both are true, the child is not to be killed."

By preferring this rule to the more general one for instances of the obstetrical example, the obstetrician is not rendering it likely that in some situations he will flounder around not knowing what rule about killing to apply. For he has a clear enough meta-rule: "If the only way to save a woman's life is to kill the child she is bearing, apply this rule: . . . ; otherwise apply the rule: Do not kill innocent humans."

The obstetrician is not satisfied with his ground-level rule for instances of the obstetrical example, and he hopes to be able to improve it. Still, he is resigned to his rule's ignoring various matters which, though they are relevant to what the ideally right action would be, would involve him in the dangers of over-specificity mentioned above. "Is the woman a potential murderess or the child a mongol?"—the answers are probably unobtainable. "In what ways would the woman's death represent a real loss to others?"—the answer, even if discoverable, could be so complex as to elude any manageable rule. "Would either course of action bring the medical profession into undeserved but seriously damaging disrepute?"—it would be too easy for that to be unconsciously conflated with the question of which course would best further the obstetrician's own career. "'Would the child, if delivered alive, be especially helpful to students of hydrocephalus?"— asking that could be the first step on a downward path: by allowing one woman to die partly because her child will be medically interesting if alive, even an uncorrupt man may ease the way towards allowing some other woman to die partly because *she* will be medically interesting when dead.

Although he pays heed—neurotically pays far too much heed— to the conservative's warnings against over-specificity, this obstetrician arrives at a conclusion quite different from the conservative's. That is the crux. The conservative who warns against the dangers of overspecifying is trying to find a consequentialist basis for his whole position. Unlike the "protective-coloration gambit" discussed earlier, this is legitimate enough in itself; but it simply does not yield the conservative position on the matter under discussion. For it to do so, the conservative would have to show that our obstetrician's more specific rule is *too* dangerous in the ways mentioned above; and he would have to do this without applying danger-inflating standards which would commit him also to condemning as too dangerous the suspension of the general rule: "Never leave a bucket in a hall-way." He may object: "Buckets in hall-ways are not important enough to provide a fair analogy. Where something as grave as killing is in question, we should be especially sensitive to the dangers of suspending a general rule." But then when something as grave as letting someone die is involved in applying the rule, we should be especially reluctant to accept, without good empirical evidence, popular clichés about the dangers of suspending general rules. The two points cancel out.

Of course, there are these dangers, and we should guard against them. To assess them at all precisely, though, would require more than we know of sociology, psychology and the philosophy of mind; and so our guarding against them can consist only in our keeping the urge towards specificity under some restraint, our remembering that in this matter it is not always true that the sky is the limit. The conservative who hopes to secure his position by pointing out these dangers must claim that he *can* assess them, and can discover in them a simple, sweeping pattern which picks out a certain list of general rules as the ones which ought never to be suspended by anyone in any circumstances. No-one would explicitly make so preposterous a claim.

"So you do at any rate retreat from act- to rule-utilitarianism?" No. Rule-utilitarianism can be presented (1) as a quasi-mystical doctrine about the importance of rule following *"per se,"* or (2) as a doctrine about the importance of rule-following because of what rule-following empirically *is,* because of what happens when people follow rules and what happens when they don't. In version (1), rule-utilitarianism is a distinct doctrine which has nothing to recommend it. In version (2), it is just part of a thorough act-utilitarianism. (In most actual presentations, there is a cloudy attempt to combine (2)'s reasonableness with (1)'s rejection of act-utilitarianism.) In this section I have been discussing what the consequences might be, for myself or others, of my suspending or breaking a given general rule. These are among, not additional to, the consequential factors whose relevance I have been urging all through the paper. There has been no retreat.

Conclusion

Principles of the form: "It would always be wrong to . . . , whatever the consequences of not doing so" seem defensible because the action/consequence distinction does not often have a certain kind of moral significance. But in proportion as a situation gives real work to the rider ". . . whatever the consequences of not doing so," in proportion as it puts pressure on this rider, in proportion as the "consequences of not doing so" give some moral reason for "doing so"—to that extent the action/consequence distinction lacks moral significance in that situation. The obstetrical example is just an extreme case: there the rider serves to dismiss the entire moral case against applying the principle; and, proportionately, the action/consequence distinction carries no moral weight at all.

The phenomenon of conservatism, then, can be explained as follows. The conservative naturally thinks that the action/consequence distinction has great moral significance because of its frequent connexion with differences concerning (a) expectation, (b) inevitability, (c) intention and (d) independently formed moral judgments. He then encounters cases like the obstetrical example, where (a)–(d) are irrelevant but where the distinction can still be applied because of facts about (e) immediacy and (f) acting/refraining. Failing to see that in these cases the distinction has lost absolutely all its moral bite, and perhaps encouraged by a mistake about "rule-following *per se,*" he still applies his principle in the usual way. Those who do not follow him in this he finds lax or opportunist or corrupt; and many of them half agree, by conceding to his position a certain hard and unfeeling uprightness. Both are wrong. Conservatism, when it is not mere obedience, is mere muddle.

Notes

1. J. K. Feeney and A. P. Barry, "The Specialties in General Practice," *Journal of Obstetrics and Gynaecology of the British Empire* (1954), 61; *The Specialties of General Practice,* eds. R. L. Cecil and H. F. Conn (Philadelphia, 1957), p. 410.

2. See G. Kelly, *Medico-Moral Problems* (Dublin, 1955), p. 20; C. J. McFadden, *Medical Ethics* (London, 1962), pp. 27–33; T. J. O'Donnell, *Morals in Medicine* (London, 1959), pp. 39–44; N. St. John-Stevas, *The Right to Life* (London, 1963), p. 71.

3. G. E. M. Anscombe, "Modern Moral Philosophy," *Philosophy,* 33 (1958), 17.

4. G. E. M. Anscombe, "Does Oxford Moral Philosophy Corrupt the Youth?" *The Listener,* February 14, 1957, p. 267. See also the corre-

spondence in ensuing numbers, and Michael Tanner, "Examples in Moral Philosophy," *Proceedings of the Aristotelian Society,* 65 (1964–65).

5. Conservatives use words like "direct" to cover a jumble of factors of which immediacy is the most prominent. Pius XII has said that a pain-killing, life-shortening drug may be used "if there exists no direct causal link, either through the will of interested parties or by the nature of things, between the induced consciousness [*sic*] and the shortening of life . . ." (Quoted in St. John-Stevas, *The Right to Life,* p. 61).

6. In a case where the child cannot survive anyway: "It is a question of the *direct taking* of one innocent life or merely *permitting* two deaths. In other words, there is question of one *murder* against two deaths . . ." (Kelly, *Medico-Moral Problems,* p. 181).

7. For a gesture in this direction, see St. John-Stevas, *The Right to Life,* pp. 14–16. See also McFadden, *Medical Ethics,* p. 133.

11

On Killing and Letting Die

Daniel Dinello

JONATHAN BENNETT in his paper "Whatever the Consequences" attempts to refute what he refers to as the conservative position on the following problem:

> A woman in labour will certainly die unless an operation is performed in which the head of her unborn child is crushed or dissected; while if it is not performed the child can be delivered, alive, by post-mortem Caesarean section. This presents a straight choice between the woman's life and the child's.

The conservative position is as follows: The child's death is part of a killing; but, in the case of the mother, there is no killing and death occurs only as a consequence of what is done. Therefore, the principle, "It would always be wrong to kill an innocent human being whatever the consequences," when added to the premise, "operating involves the killing of an innocent human being," yields the conclusion: "it would be wrong to operate."

Part I of this paper is a brief exposition of Bennett's attempt to refute the conservative position; Part II consists of two counter-examples to Bennett's position; and Part III is my analysis of the issue.

I

Bennett states correctly that, without an appeal to authority as ground for the principle, the conservative must argue that the premise: "In this case, operating would be killing an innocent

From *Analysis*, Vol. 31 (1971). Reprinted by permission of the publisher, Basil Blackwell & Mott, Ltd., and the author.

human while not-operating would involve the death of an innocent human only as a consequence" gives some reason for the conclusion. The conservatives have drawn the action/consequence distinction correctly, namely, operating is killing while not-operating is not. The questions are: By what criteria is the distinction drawn and are the criteria morally significant in this case?

Bennett argues correctly that a number of criteria could support a moral conclusion, but are irrelevant in this case. One criterion remains, namely, not-operating is not killing-the-woman because it is not doing anything at all, but is merely refraining from doing something. This is the conservative's final support. The question now is: Is there any moral significance in the acting/refraining (*i.e.*, killing/letting die) distinction?

Bennett suggests that the conditions for distinguishing between "x killed y" and "x let y die" are the following:

(1) x kills y if
    (a) x moved his body
    (b) y died
    (c) there are relatively few other ways x could have moved which satisfy the condition: if x moved like that, y would have died.
(2) x lets y die if
    (a) x moved his body
    (b) y died
    (c) almost all the ways x could have moved satisfy the conditions: if x moved like that, y would have died.

Bennett concludes that since the conservative position rests on there being a morally significant difference between killing and letting die, and since there is no moral significance in the distinction based on the number of moves the agent can make, the conservative position has absolutely no moral bite.

II

The following two counter-examples show that Bennett's conditions for drawing the "killing/letting die" distinction are incorrect.

Case I:

Jones and Smith are watching television. Jones intentionally swallows a quantity of poison sufficient to kill himself. Smith, who knows the antidote, pulls out a pistol, shoots, and *kills* Smith. But, according to Bennett's criteria, this would be a case of "letting die" since almost all the moves Jones could make (*i.e.,* moves other than, *e.g.,* forcing the antidote down Smith's throat) would satisfy the condition "if Jones moved like that, y would have died."

Case II:

Jones and Smith are spies who have been captured by the enemy. They have been wired to each other such that a movement by one would electrocute the other. Jones moves and kills Smith. But, according to Bennett's criteria, this too would be a case of "letting die" since almost all the moves Jones could make, *etc.*

Bennett's conditions for drawing the distinction are clearly wrong, but it remains to be seen whether his conclusion ("the conservative position has no moral bite") is correct.

III

The following are what I take to be the conditions which distinguish "x killed y" from "x let y die":

(A) x killed y if x caused y's death by performing movements which affect y's body such that y dies as a result of these movements.

(B) x let y die if

(a) there are conditions affecting y, such that if they are not altered, y will die.

(b) x has reason to believe that the performance of certain movements will alter conditions affecting y, such that y will not die.

(c) x is in a position to perform such movements.

(d) x fails to perform these movements.

The following are clarification and justification of these conditions:

(1) Part (b) is necessary, in that we would not want to say that a person who knew no way of altering conditions that are affecting y had let y die. For example, suppose y is dying of an incurable

disease and a doctor, x, has no choice, but to watch y die. It would not be true that x let y die.

(2) (c) is necessary because the other conditions could be fulfilled, and if x were incapable of performing the movements, we would not say that he had let y die. For example: y is dying. X knows what movements would alter the conditions affecting y, but he has been securely tied to a chair.

The "killing/letting die" distinction drawn in terms of the number of moves the agent could make clearly can have no moral significance. It is not obvious, though, that the distinction as I have now drawn it could have no moral significance. Consider the following example: Jones and Smith are in a hospital. Jones cannot live longer than two hours unless he gets a heart transplant. Smith, who had had one kidney removed, is dying of an infection in the other kidney. If he does not get a kidney transplant, he will die in about four hours. When Jones dies, his one good kidney can be transplanted to Smith, or Smith could be killed and his heart transplanted to Jones. Circumstances are such that there are no other hearts or kidneys available within the time necessary to save either one. Further, the consequences of either alternative are approximately equivalent, that is, heart transplants have been perfected, both have a wife and no children, *etc.* On Bennett's analysis, there is no morally significant difference between letting Jones die and killing Smith: the consequences of either alternative are equivalent and there is no moral distinction between killing and letting die. But, it seems clear that it would, in fact, be wrong to kill Smith and save Jones, rather than letting Jones die and saving Smith.

Further, suppose that Jones and Smith are in the same situation, but there is one difference between them: Jones has a wife and Smith does not. Bennett would have to say that since killing and letting die are morally distinguishable only by reference to the consequences of each alternative, the doctor ought to kill Smith and save Jones (Jones' death would sadden his wife, but Smith has no wife and other things are equal). But, this also seems to be wrong.

Bennett argued that the conservative has absolutely no morally relevant factor to which he could appeal, *i.e.,* the "killing/letting die" distinction is not morally significant. The preceding two examples show this conclusion to be false: There are cases where consequences are equivalent and cases where the consequences of killing are preferable, yet still wrong to kill. The distinction as I have drawn it has some moral bite: it seems intuitively clear that causing a death is morally somewhat more reprehensible than knowingly refraining from altering conditions which are causing a death. Bennett has not refuted the conservative position because the question of whether an act is one of killing or letting die *is* relevant in determining the morality of the act. The conservative, though, gives this factor absolute status. In order to refute this position it must be shown that in many cases other factors outweigh this one. In other words, the question is not whether the conservative position has moral bite, but rather how much moral bite it has.

NOTE

I am indebted to David Blumenfeld (University of Illinois, Chicago Circle) for earlier criticisms of this paper.

12

Is Killing the Innocent Absolutely Immoral?

Jeffrie G. Murphy

. . . That is, is killing the innocent a prima facie immorality that can be overridden by other, more weighty, moral requirements or is it absolutely immoral, i.e., incapable of being overridden by any other moral requirements? Miss Anscombe[1] holds that the prohibition against killing the innocent is absolute in this sense. And one would suspect that she would echo Kant's sentiments that we should do no injustice though the heavens fall. Unfortunately, she tends simply to assert her position rather than argue for it and so fails to come to terms with the worry that might bother anti-Kantians—namely, does it not matter upon whom the heavens fall? I agree with Miss Anscombe that no argument can be given to demonstrate that there is *something* wrong with killing babies, but it does not follow from this alone that this "something" is not capable of being overridden by another "something"—saving the lives of even more babies, perhaps.

Now in trying to come to grips with this issue, I propose to start with the case of killing babies as a clear example of killing creatures innocent in every possible sense. If a case can be made out that it is sometimes right to kill them, then I assume it will follow a fortiori that it is sometimes right to kill those who may be innocent in a less rich sense, e.g. merely noncombatant. Of course if it is *not* ever right to kill babies, this will not in itself show that it is not ever right to kill noncombatants; for it may be the special kind of innocence found in babies (but not necessarily in noncombatants) which protects them.

Reprinted from *The Monist*, vol. 57, no. 4, 1973 with the permission of the author and the publisher.

First of all, we need to ask ourselves the question "What is it deliberately to kill a baby?" I am certain that Miss Anscombe does not mean the following: that one deliberately kills a baby whenever one pursues a policy that one knows will result in the deaths of some babies. If anyone meant this, then that person would have to regard the construction of highways as absolutely immoral. For it is a statistical fact that on every completed highway a certain number of babies meet their deaths in accidents. Yet normally we do not regard this as a moral case against highways or as a moral proof that highway engineers are murderers. What is done is to weigh the social value of a highway against the knowledge that some deaths will occur and judge that the former outweighs the latter. (If we did not make this judgment, and if this judgment was not reasonable, then we *would* be acting immorally. For example: Suppose we let people blast with dynamite whenever and wherever they felt like it—conduct with little or no social value—in spite of our knowledge that this would result in many children dying.) Of course, situations comparable to the highway example arise in war. For example, consider the pinpoint bombing of a military installation in a war reasonably believed to be necessary and just coupled with the knowledge that bombs will occasionally go off target and that occasionally a wife, with baby in arms, may be visiting her husband on the base.

The natural way to interpret Miss Anscombe's view is as follows: One kills a baby deliberately either when one (a) brings about the death of a baby as one's final purpose or (b) brings about the death of a baby as a *means* to one's final purpose.[2] Since war is hardly to be regarded as motivated by fetishistic infanticide, it is (b) which is crucial. And (b) lets off the highway engineer. For the highway engineer, whom we do not want to regard as a murderer, will not be a murderer on (b). The deaths of babies in highway accidents are in no sense *means* to the socially useful goal of good transportation but are rather accidental byproducts. That is, highway transportation is not furthered by these deaths but is, if anything, hindered by them. And so it is unreasonable to suppose that highway engineers desire the deaths of these babies because they want to use their deaths as a means to their goal of transportation. Similarly with the accidental deaths of babies resulting from a pinpoint bombing raid on a military installation.

But consider the following kind of case: One knows that one is fighting a war in defense of civilization itself. (It was not unreasonable to regard the war against Hitler in such terms.[3]) Suppose also that one knows that the only way (causally) to bring a power like Hitler's to a collapse is to undercut his support among the German people by achieving their total demoralization. Further suppose that one knows that the only way to do this is by the obliteration terror bombing of civilian centers (e.g., Dresden) so that, by killing many German babies among others, one can create a desire on the part of the German people to abandon the venture. I am not suggesting that we could ever in fact know these things (they might be false) or that we should ever even let ourselves believe such things.[4] But my worry here is one of principle— namely, assuming the factual situation is as described, would it be wrong *on principle* to initiate a campaign of antimorale obliteration bombing? Here I take it that Miss Anscombe will say that, even in such circumstances, those making a decision to initiate such a campaign are murderers. For they will be deliberately killing the innocent as a means to their goal and that (no matter how good the goal) is absolutely wrong.

But why? Miss Anscombe fails to bring fully into the open a latent issue that is absolutely crucial here—namely, are we as morally responsible for our omissions (e.g., failing to save lives) as for our commissions (e.g., killing people)? Of course there are differences between the two expressions, but are they *morally relevant* differences? If our basic value here is the sanctity of life, or the sanctity of innocents, or the sanctity of babies, then—as Jonathan Bennett has pointed out[5]—it is hard to see their moral difference. For consider the following kind of case: Suppose we know that a victory by Hitler would mean the extermination of all or a great many non-Aryan babies. And further suppose that these babies far outnumber the German babies to be killed in an obliteration bombing campaign.[6] Now, given this knowledge, what would a man who really values the lives of babies do? Is the moral case to rest upon the different descriptions "killing babies" and "letting babies die"? If so, *why?* If the argument is that by not positively killing we will at least be preserving our own moral purity, then it is important to note that this argument, in addition to being rather selfish, is question-begging. For to assume that one remains morally pure if one does nothing is to beg the question of whether we are as responsible for omissive as for commissive conduct. If moral purity means never choosing anything which one will have to regard as in some sense wrong and regret for all one's days, then moral purity may be impossible in a complex world. Albert Camus based his theory of rebellion on this kind of claim—a theory which Howard Zinn summarizes as follows:

> Camus spoke in *The Rebel* of the absurdities in which we are trapped, where the very acts with which we seek to do good cannot escape the imperfections of the world we are trying to change. And so the rebel's "only virtue will lie in never yielding to the impulse to be engulfed in the shadows that surround him, and in obstinately dragging the chains of evil, with which he is bound, toward the good."[7]

The issue here is not over whether we should ever allow ourselves to be persuaded by any argument that killing the innocent is *in fact* necessary; and I am certainly not suggesting that I find plausible such arguments as have actually been given in the past. For a practical maxim I am much in favor of the slogan "Never trade a certain evil for a possible good." However, this does not solve the issue of principle. If the good (e.g., saving the lives of scores of babies) *is certain* and not just possible, is it anything more than dogmatism to assert that it would never be right to bring about this good through evil means? The maxim "Never trade a certain evil for a certain good" is by no means self-evidently true and, indeed, does not even seem plausible to many people. Thus I do not think that it has yet been shown that it is always absolutely wrong, whatever the consequences, to kill innocent babies. And thus it has not yet been shown that it is absolutely wrong to kill those innocent in a less rich sense of the term, i.e. noncombatants. Of course we may *feel* differently about actually killing innocents and simply letting innocents die; but I do not think that this phenomenological evidence in itself proves anything. Bomber pilots no doubt feel differently about dropping bombs on babies from thirty thousand feet than they would about shooting a baby face to face, but surely this does not show that the acts differ in moral quality.

Feelings do not prove anything in morality; but they sometimes *point* to something. And it is at least possible that we have not yet captured the worry which motivates the responses of people like Kant, Miss Anscombe, and those who want to defend some version of the doctrine of the Double Effect. If what they really value is the lives of babies and other innocents *simpliciter*, then— as Bennett argues—it does not seem that the distinction between "killing babies" and "letting babies die" will help them to save their principle. But perhaps this is to conceive their position too teleologically. That is, we have so far (with Bennett) been assuming that the person who says "never kill babies" says this because he sees the maxim as instrumental to *something else* that he values— namely, the lives of babies. But it is at least possible that he does not hold this principle to be instrumentally right (in which case he would be subject to Bennett's refutation) but intrinsically right, i.e., right in itself or from its very description. The problem is to explicate this notion of intrinsic rightness in such a way that it does not involve either of the two following pitfalls noted by Bennett:

(a) *Authoritarianism*, e.g., "God commands not killing babies."
(b) *Dogmatism*, e.g., "It is just absolutely wrong to kill babies; and, if you do not see this, you are just too corrupt to talk to."

Now the reason why (a) is a bad move is obvious—namely, it is an appeal to authority rather than reason and thus has no place in a philosophical discussion of moral questions. But (b) is more problematical. For I have said that I am willing to accept such a move if made in the name of there being *something* wrong with killing babies. Why will I not accept such a move in favor of its being *absolutely* wrong to kill babies?

Roughly, I should argue as follows: That there is something wrong with killing babies (i.e., that "*A* is a case of killing a baby" *must* count as a moral reason against *A*) explicates, in part, what may be called "the moral point of view." To be worried about moral issues just is, among other things, to be worried about killing innocents. But the judgment "Never kill babies under any circumstances" does not explicate the moral point of view but is, rather, a controversial moral judgment—or, if you prefer, explicates *a* moral point of view rather than *the* moral point of view. And so, to build *it* into the moral point of view is to beg a controversial question of moral substance—something which presumably metaethics should not do. Someone who said "I see nothing at all wrong with killing babies so let's bomb Dresden" would be an *a*moral monster—one with whom it would be senseless to conduct a moral argument. But one who sincerely said "Of course it is terrible to kill babies but I believe, to save more lives, we must regretfully do it in this case" is not such a monster. He is one with whom, if we think him wrong (*im*moral), we should hope to be able to argue.[8] Since, among war supporters, there are (one would hope) few of the former sort but many of the latter sort, being able to argue with and persuade the latter has some practical importance. It will hardly do simply to say to them "But I can just see the absolute wrongness of what you contemplate and, if you do not, I refuse to discuss the matter with you." We know, alas, what will then happen.

Now I am not going to pretend that I can give anything resembling a *proof* that it is absolutely wrong to kill the innocent (though not to allow them to die), but I hope at least to be able to elaborate a way of thinking which (a) does give some sense to such a prohibition and (b) cannot be condemned as simple dogmatism or authoritarianism, i.e. is a way of *thinking*.[9]

The way of thinking I want to elaborate is one in which the notion of people's having *rights* plays a predominate role. (Kant's ethical theory, in broad outline, is one such way of thinking.) And an ethical outlook in which the notion of rights looms large will want to draw a distinction between the following two claims:

(1) Doing *A* to Jones would be to violate one of his rights.
(2) It would be bad to do *A* to Jones.

To use Kant's own examples:[10] If I have made a promise to Jones, he has a *right* to expect me to keep it, can properly regard me as having *wronged* him if I do not keep it, and could properly expect that others (the state) should *coerce* me into keeping it. Kant's opaque way of putting this is to say that keeping a promise is a *perfect* duty. A quite different situation is the following: If Jones is in distress (assuming I have not put him there) and I could help him out without extraordinary sacrifice, he would certainly want me to help him and I would be doing something bad if I did not help him. But he does not have a *right* to expect my help, is not *wronged* if I fail to help him, and it would be unreasonable to expect the state or anyone else to *coerce* me into helping him. Helping him is beneficence and (unlike justice) is a comparatively weak moral demand. Kant's opaque way of putting this is to say that the duty to help others in distress is *imperfect*.

When a man has a right, he has a claim against interference. Simply to refuse to be beneficent to him is not an invasion of his rights because it is not to interfere with him at all. When a person uses his freedom to invade the rights of others, he forfeits certain of his own rights and renders interference by others legitimate. (Kant calls this a moral title or authorization—*Befugnis*—to place "obstacles to obstacles to freedom."[11]) Thus if I have an imperfect duty to help others, I may interfere with those trying to harm those others because, by such an attempt, they have forfeited their right against interference. Here I have the imperfect duty; and, since those attacking have by the attack forfeited certain of their rights, I violate no perfect duty in interfering with them. Thus there is no conflict here. However, if the only way I could save someone from harm would be by interfering with an innocent person (i.e., one who has not forfeited his rights by initiating attack against others) then I must not save the person, for this would be to violate a perfect duty. And, in cases of conflict, perfect duties override imperfect duties.

Suppose that Jones is being attacked by Smith. In such a case it is certainly true to say that Jones's *rights* to liberty, security, etc. are being threatened and that Smith, therefore, is acting wrongly and thereby forfeits his right to be left free from interference. Thus I would not be acting wrongly (i.e., against Smith's rights) if I attacked him to prevent his attack on Jones. Similarly, Jones would not be acting wrongly if he defended himself. However, it does not follow from any of this that I have a *duty* to help Jones or even that Jones has a *duty* to defend himself. Defense, though permissible, is not obligatory. This being so, it does not follow that Jones has a *right to be saved* by me. Thus, since it is far from obvious that Jones has a right to be saved even from an attack by the guilty, it is even more implausible to assert that he has a right to be saved if so doing would involve killing the innocent. (Consider the following: We are all, at this very moment, sitting and talking philosophy and are thus omitting to save the lives of countless people we might save throughout the world. Are we acting wrongly in so doing? If we are, is this because all these people have a *right* to be saved by us?)

Now what sort of a moral view could one hold that make one accept the principle that perfect duties, resting on rights, override imperfect duties, not resting on rights? I think it is this: a view which makes primary the status of persons as free or choosing beings who, out of respect for that status, are to be regarded as having the right to be left alone to work out their own lives—for better or worse. This is a basic right that one has just because one is a person. Respecting it is what Kant calls respecting the dignity of humanity by not treating people as *means* only. Part of respecting them in this sense is not to use them as a means in one's calculations of what would be good for others. It is fine (indeed admirable) for a person to sacrifice himself for others by his own choice; but it is presumptuous (because lacking in respect for his choices) if *I* choose to sacrifice him. This is his business and not mine. I may only interfere with the person who, by his own evil actions, has forfeited his right against interference. Innocent persons by definition have not done this. And therefore it is absolutely wrong to sacrifice the innocent, though not to kill aggressors. On this view there is something terribly perverse in arguing, as many do, that a defense of freedom requires a sacrifice of those who in no way give their free consent to the sacrifice.[12]

Of course babies are not yet, in the full sense, free or choosing beings who clearly have rights. They are, perhaps, only potential or dispositional persons and enjoyers of rights. But if one accepts the maxim "Innocent until proven otherwise" they may be regarded as equally protected in the above way of thinking. For they certainly cannot be described in the only way which, on this view, makes harmful interference permissible—namely described as having, through their own deliberate acts of aggression, forfeited their right to be left in peace.

Now this view that what is central in morality involves notions like rights, dignity, freedom, and choice (rather than notions like maximizing the general utility) cannot be proven. But it is a plausible view which may lie behind the maxim "Never kill the innocent" and is a view which would be sacrificed (at least greatly compromised) by the maxim "Kill the innocent to save the innocent." I am myself deeply sympathetic to this way of thinking and would make neither the compromise nor the sacrifice. But I cannot *prove* that one ought not make it. Neither, of course, can my teleological opponent prove his case either. For we lie here at the boundaries of moral discourse where candidates for ultimate principles conflict; and it is part of the logical character of an ultimate principle that it cannot be assessed by some yet higher ("more ultimate"?) principle.[13] You pays your money and you takes your choice. It is simply my hope that many people, if they could see clearly what price they have to pay (i.e., the kind of moral outlook they have to give up and what they have to put in its place), would make the choice against killing the innocent.

Consider the following example: Suppose that thousands of babies could be saved from a fatal infant disease if some few babies were taken by the state and given over to a team of medical researchers for a series of experiments which, though killing the babies, would yield a cure for the disease. In what way except degree (i.e., numbers of babies killed) does this situation differ from the rationale behind antimorale obliteration bombing raids, i.e., is there not a disturbing parallel between Allied raids on Dresden and Tokyo and Nazi "medicine"? With respect to either suggestion, when we really think about it, do we not want to say with the poet James Dickey

> Holding onto another man's walls
> My hat should crawl on my head
> In streetcars, thinking of it,
> The fat on my body should pale.[14]

How can any such thing be in the interest of humanity when its practice would change the very meaning of "humanity" and prevent us from unpacking from it, as we now do, notions like rights, dignity, and respect? No matter how good the consequences, is there not some point in saying that we simply do not have the *right* to do it? For there is, I think, an insight of secular value in the religious observation that men are the "children of God." For this means, among other things, that other people do not *belong* to me. They are not *mine* to be manipulated as resources in my projects. It is hard to imagine all that we might lose if we abandoned this way of thinking about ourselves and others.

My appeal here, of course, is in a sense emotive. But this in my judgment is not an objection. Emotive appeals may rightly be condemned if they are masquerading as proofs. But here I am attempting to prove nothing but only to say—"Here, look, see what you are doing and what way of thinking your doing it involves you in." If one sees all this and still goes forth to do it anyway, we have transcended the bounds of what can be *said* in the matter.

What about noncombatants? Though they are not necessarily innocent in all the senses in which babies are, they clearly are innocent in the sense I have elaborated above—namely, they have not performed actions which forfeit their right to be free from execution (or, better: it is not *reasonable* for the enemy to believe this of them). Thus, in a very tentative conclusion, I suggest the following: I have not been able to prove that we should never kill noncombatants or innocents (I do not think this could be proven in any ordinary sense of proof); but I do think that I have elaborated a way of thinking which gives sense to the acceptance of such an absolute prohibition. Thus, against Bennett, I have at least shown that one can accept the principle "Never kill the innocent" without thereby necessarily being an authoritarian or a dogmatic moral fanatic.

NOTES

1. G. E. M. Anscombe, "Modern Moral Philosophy," *Philosophy*, 33 (1958).

2. Another factor, relevant both to war and to the highway example, is the following: acting with the knowledge that deaths could be prevented by taking reasonable precautions and yet not taking those precautions. Such grossly negligent or reckless behavior, while perhaps not "deliberate" in the strict sense, is surely immoral in either context.

3. See Michael Walzer, "World War II: Why Was This War Different?" *Philosophy and Public Affairs*, 1, no. 1 (Fall 1971).

4. As the citizens of London and Hanoi have illustrated, for example, terror bombing has a tendency to backfire. Rather than demoralizing the enemy, it sometimes strengthens their courage and will to resist.

5. Jonathan Bennett, "Whatever the Consequences," *Analysis*, 26, no. 3 (January 1966), 83–102; in this volume, chapter 10.

6. I take it that, from a moral point of view, their being *German* babies is irrelevant. As Howard Zinn has argued, we should accept the principle that "all victims are created equal" (*Disobedience and Democracy: Nine Fallacies on Law and Order* [New York: Random House, 1968], p. 50).

7. *Ibid.*, p. 40.

8. One important metaethical inquiry that has been conducted in recent years concerns the nature of moral judgments and the moral point of view or "language game." The task here is to distinguish the moral from the *non*moral or *a*moral. Normative ethics, on the other hand, is concerned to distinguish the moral from the *im*moral. This is too large a dispute to enter here, but I can at least make my own commitments clear. Unlike the so-called "formalists" (e.g., R. M. Hare, *The Language of Morals* [Oxford University Press, 1952]), I am inclined to believe that the moral point of view must be defined, in part, in terms of the *content* of the judgments it contains. Here I am siding, if I understand them correctly, with such writers as H. L. A. Hart (*The Concept of Law* [Oxford: Oxford University Press, 1961]), and G. J. Warnock (*The Object of Morality* [London: Methuen, 1971]). Someone who does not see that "*A* is a case of killing an innocent" is a relevant reason against doing *A,* does not understand what moral discourse is all about, what it is *necessarily* concerned with. And this is so no matter how much he is prepared to universalize and regard as overriding his own idiosyncratic imperatives. If this is true, then the gulf between metaethics and normative ethics is not quite as wide as many have supposed, since the relevance of certain substantive judgments is now going to be regarded as part of the *meaning* of morality as a point of view, language game, or form of life. There still is some gulf between metaethics and normative ethics, however, since I should argue that only the *relevance,* and not the *decisiveness,* of certain substantive judgments (e.g., do not kill the innocent) can be regarded as a defining feature of the moral point of view. Normative ethics, however, is primarily interested in which of the relevant moral considerations are, in certain circumstances, decisive. (I am grateful to Ronald Milo for discussing these matters with me. He is totally responsible for whatever clarity is to be found in my views.)

9. Though I shall not explore it here, I think that the religious acceptance of the principle could be elaborated as a way of thinking and so distinguished from the authoritarianism and dogmatism that Bennett so rightly condemns. The view I shall develop also has implications (though I shall not draw them out here) for the abortion issue. For more on this, see Philippa Foot's "The Problem of Abortion and the Doctrine of the Double Effect," *Oxford Review,* 5 (1967), chapter 16 in this vol-

ume. This has been reprinted in *Moral Problems: A Collection of Philosophical Essays,* ed. James Rachels (New York: Harper & Row, 1971), and in my *An Introduction to Moral and Social Philosophy: Basic Readings in Theory and Practice* (Belmont, Calif.: Wadsworth, 1973). She sees the doctrine of the Double Effect as groping in a confused way toward an insight of moral importance: "There is worked into our moral system a distinction between what we owe people in the form of aid and what we owe them in the way of non-interference."

10. These well-known examples are drawn from Kant's *Foundations of the Metaphysics of Morals,* trans. Lewis White Beck (Indianapolis: Bobbs-Merrill, 1959), pp. 39ff.; pp. 421ff. of the Academy edition of Kant's works. Kant distinguishes perfect duties (duties of respect) and imperfect duties (duties of love) in many places. See, for example, *The Doctrine of Virtue,* trans. Mary J. Gregor (New York: Harper & Row, 1964), pp. 134–35; p. 463 of the Academy edition.

11. Kant, *Metaphysical Elements of Justice,* trans. John Ladd (Indianapolis: Bobbs-Merrill, 1965), pp. 35ff.; pp. 230ff. of the Academy edition. See also pp. 94ff. and 107–109 of my *Kant: The Philosophy of Right* (New York: St. Martin's, 1970).

12. Someone (e.g., Jan Narveson in his "Pacifism: A Philosophical Analysis," *Ethics,* 75 [1965]) might say the following: If what you value are the *rights* of people, does this not entail (as a part of what it means to say that one values something) that you would recognize an obligation to take steps to secure those rights against interference? Perhaps. But "take steps" does not have to mean "do whatever is causally necessary." Such an obligation will presumably be limited by (a) what I can reasonably be expected to do or sacrifice and (b) my moral judgment about the permissibility of the *means* employed. It does seem perverse for a person to say "I value the rights of people above all else but I do not propose to do anything to secure those rights." However, it by no means seems to me equally perverse to say the following: "I deplore interferences with human rights above all else and I will do everything in my power to prevent such interferences—everything, of course, short of being guilty of such interferences myself."

13. See Brian Barry, "Justice and the Common Good," *Analysis,* 21–22 (1960–61). Though the existentialists tend to overdo this sort of claim, there is truth in their claim that there are certain moral problems that are in principle *undecidable* by any rational decision procedure. Such cases are not perhaps as numerous as the existentialists would have us believe, but they do arise, e.g., when candidates for ultimate moral principles conflict. In such cases, we find it impossible to nail down with solid arguments those principles which matter to us the most. Perhaps

this even deserves to be called "absurd." In his article "The Absurd" (*Journal of Philosophy*, 68, no. 20 [October 21, 1971]), Thomas Nagel suggests that absurdity in human life is found in "the collision between the seriousness with which we take our lives and the perpetual possibility of regarding everything about which we are serious as arbitrary, or open to doubt." It is here that talk about faith or commitment seems to have some life.

14. James Dickey, "The Firebombing," in *Poems 1957–1967* (Middletown, Conn.: Wesleyan University Press, 1967), p. 185. Reprinted with the permission of the publisher.

13

The Moral Equivalence
of Action and Omission

Judith Lichtenberg

Is DOING NOTHING sometimes as bad as doing something bad? In
this or some less naive form the question I address in this paper
is an old one that has been asked not only by philosophers and
religious thinkers but also by ordinary people in their more reflec-
tive moments. We have recently seen its relevance to such issues
as abortion, euthanasia, and the legitimate conduct of war. Active
euthanasia is distinguished from passive, aiming to kill from killing as an unintended effect of one's aims, bringing about harm
from letting it happen. The Catholic doctrine of the double effect
endorses the moral distinction between what one positively does
and what one allows to occur.

The significance of the action/omission distinction also has crucial implications for central political issues, though this has not
been adequately recognized. Libertarian views like Nozick's, according to which political coercion is limited to the classical night-
watchman functions of protection from force, fraud, theft and
enforcement of contract, depend on the assumption of a necessary
moral difference between action and omission. This is expressed
in terms of individuals' rights and obligations: people have uncontracted negative rights and obligations but not uncontracted positive ones, and it is such fundamental rights and obligations that
legitimize coercion.[1] The action/omission distinction is also at the
heart of the controversy over negative and positive freedom.

Here I maintain that the fact of a strand of behavior's involving
an action or an omission is per se morally irrelevant. In the first

Reprinted from *Canadian Journal of Philosophy*, supplementary vol. 8 (1982), 19–
36 with the permission of the author and the publisher.

part I distinguish the various ways action and omission might be or are different—conceptually and morally, necessarily and practically—and consider some problems that result when these are confused. In II two ideal cases are presented which I believe reveal the equivalence of action and omission. In III–V I consider objections to this view, apparent counterexamples and their supporting arguments. Looking closely at the examples offered by both sides brings into focus the considerations proper to an agent deciding what to do. Morally relevant features fall under two general headings: (1) certainty or probability of the connection between an act or omission and the harm to be avoided; and (2) sacrifice or cost to the agent in having to forbear or to act. The idea that there is a moral difference between action and omission comes from comparing cases that are asymmetrical with respect to these features; when comparable cases are compared, the gulf disappears. This becomes especially clear as we break away from the paradigm of harmful behavior which has come to obscure our thinking—actions which result directly and immediately in harm—and attend to behavior along the continuum whose harmful effects are increasingly less direct and immediate, both in space and in time.[2]

I

It is often said that a person's behavior can't be neatly divided into what he does and does not do. Yet unless action and omission can be distinguished, the question of their moral equivalence or difference isn't intelligible: there aren't two distinguishable things to be compared. Doubt about their distinctness arises from the realization that one has access to a strand of behavior only via some description of it, and that the same strand can often be described alternatively in terms of something the agent did, or in terms of something he didn't do. So, e.g., if a parent doesn't feed his child and the child dies, one might say any of the following: he didn't feed his child; he starved his child; he let his child die; he caused his child's death. It would seem, then, that strands of behavior are not per se actions or omissions.

The puzzle here can on further reflection be dispelled. In the first place, it is clear that not every active verb corresponds to a positive action.[3] In saying the parent starved his child one does not say or imply that the parent performed physical actions that resulted in the child's death—on the contrary. The use of 'starve' emphasizes the significance of the parent's omission, as perceived by the speaker.

But the description of the parent as starving his child is not just an injection of the speaker's moral beliefs into his description. Compare the parent's behavior with another case. If a stranger doesn't give food to a beggar and the beggar dies, we will say that the stranger didn't feed the beggar, but not that he starved the beggar.[4] Yet the same strand of behavior—no physical actions relevant to the starving person's death—is involved in both cases. What warrants the different descriptions is that the parent has undertaken to care for his child, but the stranger has not undertaken to care for the beggar. Agreeing or undertaking to do something not only establishes a moral obligation; it also legitimizes certain otherwise inappropriate descriptions. Specifically, it legitimizes descriptions expanded in scope to include more than the bare omission. For the omission is, in light of the undertaking, no longer bare; it is not what I shall call a genuine or ex nihilo omission. The apparent similarity of the parent's and the stranger's behavior is illusory. Although both 'didn't feed,' the parent in addition *did certain things* (e.g. brought a child into the world) which warrant picking up the train of behavior at an earlier stage.

For a large class of omissions—those that occur in the context of a prior agreement or undertaking of some kind—one has discretion to describe what happens either negatively or positively. Positive descriptions cover a longer strand of behavior of which the omission is only a part. By attending to such omissions one may be led to think there is no conceptual difference between action and omission.[5] For about a given segment of behavior it is not usually hard to distinguish physical movements from their absence. The question under consideration is whether one can be obligated to perform physical movements without having performed earlier physical movements—as, it is generally thought, one can be obligated *not* to perform physical movements without having performed earlier physical movements. (Nozick, for example, believes there is an uncontracted obligation not to commit aggression but no such obligation to give aid; and accordingly the state may coerce people not to commit aggression but not to aid others.)

Given the conceptual distinctness of action and omission, the question arises whether they are morally different or not. A person is committed to a moral difference between them if, given a pair of cases parallel in every respect except that one requires positive action and the other requires forbearance, he thinks the latter more morally binding than the former. Just what 'more morally binding' means will vary according to the particular moral theory and as the moral difference between action and omission is thought to be more or less significant. At the least one will have to say that given a pair of otherwise parallel cases, 'acting badly' is worse than 'omitting badly.'

It should be noted, however, that a moral difference of this kind will not do the work for which it is generally needed. To distinguish generically between, e.g., negative and positive rights, as Nozick does, action/omission must be not just one morally relevant feature among others but one which overrides others, which by itself generates a qualitative difference between cases requiring action and those requiring forbearance. It is not clear how one would argue for the stronger claim; since I deny even a weak difference, I leave this problem to those who need to solve it.

Necessary differences (both weak and strong) between action and omission are to be contrasted with practical differences. The latter might, in practice, be as significant as necessary ones: one might reach very different conclusions about cases because some morally relevant characteristic(s) were contingently connected— highly correlated—with the action/omission distinction. If, e.g., refraining ordinarily does not involve significant cost to the agent while positive action does, then this ought to be reflected in conclusions about most cases. But this question is different in kind from the question of a necessary difference; and the answers are not to be found in the same ways.

The distinction between a necessary difference between action and omission and a practical one would seem to be quite clear. Yet the claim that negative duties are more stringent than positive ones is sometimes ambiguous:

> It is an empirical fact that in most cases it is possible for a person
> not to inflict serious physical injury on any other person. It is also
> an empirical fact that in no case is it possible for a person to aid
> everyone who needs help. . . . In short, the negative duty of not
> killing can be discharged completely . . . But the positive duty of
> saving can never be discharged completely.[6]

Since it isn't possible for a person to aid everyone who needs help,
obviously one cannot be obligated to do so. But it in no way
follows that one's obligations to aid some particular person in
specific circumstances isn't as stringent as one's duty not to inflict
physical injury. Trammell's general point about dischargeability
depends on this confusion of the general and the particular. For a
particular obligation to save this individual now *can* be discharged
completely: save him and it is discharged. And since there is no
obligation to save all who need saving, there is no obligation
which can't be discharged. The concept of dischargeability doesn't
apply to the particular case, because a particular obligation is always an obligation to do what can be done. With respect to the
general, talk of dischargeability is a misleading way of asserting
the universality or exceptionlessness of a right or obligation. The
duty not to kill can be completely discharged in the sense that it
is possible *never* to kill (but not in the sense that one 'finishes' not
killing all those one is obligated not to kill). But though it is
possible, few people believe the duty not to kill is exceptionless.
And, furthermore, the extreme case of killing is misleading as
exemplar of the general problem of harming. It is not clear that
the duty not to cause harm is so much more easily discharged
than the duty to prevent it. So Trammell's point shows at most
a difference in degree between negative and positive duties, not a
difference in kind.

Imagine the following situation. A person is stranded on a desert island, far from other land and human life. The island provides
no source of sustenance, and provisions are almost gone. Just as
he is about to give up hope, the stranded man sights a vessel. It
lands, and a sailor comes ashore. The ship contains plenty of
supplies, as well as providing a way back to the human world.

Now consider two possible scenarios that follow. In the first,
the sailor won't share his provisions with the stranded man, and
won't take him aboard the ship. He is ready to leave as he has

come. In the second, the sailor attempts to kill the man he finds on the island.

I believe that in these circumstances, the sailor's failure to share his provisions or his ship with the stranded man is morally equivalent to his killing him.[7] Is this a judgment of the sailor's conduct or of his character, or both? So far no mention has been made of any motives, intentions or the like. But although it is important to distinguish the evaluation of conduct from that of agents, here we want to ensure that no differences but action/omission operate, even if only implicitly, to affect our judgment. Harmful actions and omissions resulting in harm are often asymmetrical in terms of motives and intentions. This is because a sane person doesn't ordinarily attack someone unless he has some sort of a reason; but a reason isn't needed to explain why someone doesn't act except in certain circumstances.[8] But the present case provides such circumstances. Intuitively, the sailor's refusal to take the stranded man aboard cries out for an explanation as much as his killing him does. It is no less plausible that he wants him dead if he leaves him alone than if he kills him. Looked at the other way, the idea that the sailor kills for no reason seems no more absurd than that he leaves for no reason. So the assumption of parallel internal states isn't artificial here.

What is it about these circumstances that makes the sailor's failure to aid as wrong as killing? One condition is that no significant sacrifice of any kind is required for him to help, just as none is required for him to refrain from killing. But what is most important is that there is a probability bordering on certainty that if he leaves the stranded man he will die. It is not just that he can save him, but that no one else can. (So the case is unlike many of the examples that come up in discussions of these issues: only the solitary bystander can be so sure that his omission is sufficient for death to occur.)

This morally crucial factor—the certainty of the connection between conduct and harmful consequence—explains the prohibition against physical aggression. For physical aggression greatly increases the chances that harm will ensue. Of course, if what a person does is described as killing someone—a description incorporating both physical movements and their consequences—then the connection between action and consequence is not just morally certain but logically necessary. But a description of what someone does not do can also be given which connects the omission necessarily with a certain upshot.[9] Here it is enough to say that, given descriptions that do not incorporate the death, the (contingent) connection between certain physical movements of the sailor and the other's death is not more probable than the connection between his leaving the stranded man alone without provisions and the latter's death. We can be quite certain that he will die in either case.

A pair of cases whose description is entirely upshot-free reveals the equivalence of action and omission more clearly. Suppose a person finds himself in a room before a set of controls. In the first scenario, he is told that if he pushes a certain button, someone in another room will die. In the second, he is told that if he does not push a certain button, that person will die.[10] Here it seems incontrovertible that the agent's duty to refrain from pushing the button in the first case is equal to his duty to push it in the second. Why? As far as the agent has any reason to believe, the probability that acting will result in death in the first case is equal to the probability that not acting will result in death in the second. (And it is clear that no other variables distinguish the cases: e.g., the 'effort' required to push the button is no greater than the 'effort' required to refrain.)

A way of further testing one's judgment is to ask what follows upon aggression or failure to aid in terms of the rights and obligations of the involved parties. To return to the desert island example, it is clear that if the sailor tries to kill the stranded man, the latter has the right to defend himself. But it seems also that if the sailor refuses to share what he has (when he can, with no loss to himself), the stranded man may do what he must to preserve himself. If he must steal, then he may steal; if he must kill, then he may kill. But this right of the stranded man is not sufficient to show that the sailor is obligated to save him. A Hobbesian, e.g., would acknowledge an absolute right of self-preservation without positing a corresponding obligation on the part of another. (Non-Hobbesians can test their judgment of the stranded man's right by comparing it to their judgment of the right of a murderer to preserve himself.) More telling is one's judgment of the sailor who has tried to kill or failed to aid, and has suffered the consequences. If the stranded man kills him in self-defense, no moral imbalance has been created; no injustice has been done. Similarly, if in the struggle to get what he needs to survive the stranded man can't avoid killing the sailor, no injustice has been done either, and for the same reason: the sailor has brought his troubles on himself. This situation can be contrasted with one where a person kills someone who threatens his life through no fault of his own (what Nozick calls an 'innocent threat'); i.e. the agent kills in self-defense. Even though we may justify the killing, such situations are morally problematic precisely because the innocent threat does not choose to endanger others' lives, and could not avoid it. But the case of the sailor poses no such moral dilemma, because the sailor is not innocent. He has chosen to act the way he does, when he could easily have acted otherwise. So our attitude toward his death is the same whether he actually tries to kill or just fails to aid.

III

There are, I think, two main lines of argument that underlie opposition to the equivalence thesis. One has to do with the extent to which sacrifice or difficulty is involved in fulfilling negative and positive duties; the other concerns the attribution of responsibility for the plight of those harmed or left unaided. I shall take these up in turn.

The sacrifice question has been touched on above, in the discussion of dischargeability and the confusion of necessary and practical differences between action and omission. It is raised by this example of Trammell's:

> If someone threatened to steal $1000 from a person if he did not take a gun and shoot a stranger between the eyes, it would be very wrong for him to kill the stranger to save his $1000. But if someone asked from that person $1000 to save a stranger, it would seem that his obligation to grant this request would not be as great as his obligation to refuse the first demand—even if he had good reason for believing that without his $1000 the stranger would certainly die.[11]

In general, Trammell argues that negative duties are stricter than positive ones (in part) because they are easier to fulfil and don't involve great sacrifices.[12] This is perfectly consistent with the equivalence of action and omission; and indeed it would seem to follow that when a negative duty did involve great sacrifice, this would diminish its stringency. But now Trammell says that morally we require people to make greater sacrifices to fulfill negative duties than positive ones, implying that their greater stringency is independent of how much sacrifice is involved. One may suspect that insensitivity to the distinctions between what is true in general and what is true of any particular case, and between necessary and practical differences, has led Trammell to impose his view of what is true in general on the case which is supposed to test for what is necessarily true. This kind of 'spillover effect' is no doubt common in ordinary thinking and partly accounts for the prevalence of the view that negative duties are stricter than positive.

To test the hypothesis that morally we require greater sacrifices in the fulfilment of negative than positive duties, we need two cases in which the sacrifice involved in fulfilling the duty is approximately equivalent *and* significant (since similar assessment for cases where the sacrifice is equivalent but minimal is, Trammell thinks, inconclusive), and where other morally relevant factors are parallel. But the problem is that it is very difficult to construct such cases. For what is needed is a case to compare with the one where I am required to give something very significant— say, my life's savings—to save someone, and where only I can save him. For it is Trammell's feeling that one would not be morally bound to do *this* that leads him to say that greater sacrifices are required in the fulfilment of negative than positive duties.

It's easy to think of cases where significant sacrifices have to be made to avoid harming or even killing people, where those harmed or killed are unspecified, and the harm is indirect. Such situations form the substance of many legal and political problems, involving such issues as pollution and civil liberties. Here it seems clear that the question of how much sacrifice is involved for people to refrain from doing something operates in a straightforward way to determine judgments about whether the actions ought to be permitted. This tells in favor of the view that the cost involved in acting or not acting is a determinant of obligation, rather than being determined by it.

But in the special cases needed to compare with those direct omissions where great sacrifice is involved to aid someone, it is hard to imagine the appropriate circumstances. For why, after all, when one is about to pull the trigger or plunge the knife into his heart, can't one simply refrain, just like that? How *could* a great sacrifice be involved? That it is so hard to imagine a comparable situation is in itself reason to be suspicious, for the sense that action and omission aren't equivalent is strongest where parallel cases are not available. Where they are it is often easier to see how other factors intrude.

One conclusion we may draw is that direct physical violence is the paradigm of prohibited behavior precisely because it exemplifies the extreme of the two morally relevant factors: certainty that one's action will result in harm, and minimal sacrifice needed to refrain. If it happened that people had to give up something significant to avoid directly harming or killing people, this would be relevant, just as it is in the less extreme cases. Thus, in the only comparable instances of the extreme cases that are plausible, where one might have to risk life or limb to avoid harming someone—situations of extreme scarcity, or freak occurrences (having to drive over a cliff to avoid running someone over)—having to make such a sacrifice crucially enters into our judgment. Many would say that the usual duties are in such circumstances inapplicable.[13] So all the ways we reason about these questions support the view that if, or rather when, negative duties are more stringent than positive ones, it is because they involve less sacrifice and are therefore easier to fulfil.[14]

IV

The question of responsibility is raised by another of Trammell's examples:

(1) Jones sees that Smith will be killed [by a bomb] unless he warns him. But Jones is apathetic. So Smith is killed by the bomb even though Jones could have warned him. (2) Jones is practicing shooting his gun. Smith accidentally walks in the path and Jones sees

Smith; but Jones's reaction is apathy. Jones pulls the trigger and Smith is killed.

This example supports the 'plausibility of the distinction between action and inaction,' Trammell thinks, because

> In Case 2, if Jones had not pulled the trigger, Smith would not have been killed. But in Case 1, Smith might still have been killed by the bomb even if Jones had never existed. The link between action and responsibility does not seem accidental, since the more directly and clearly a person is responsible for another person needing to be saved, the more likely we are to say that the first person is killing the second.[15]

What Trammell means to say is that there is a significant moral difference between killing (or, more generally, doing positive harm) and not saving (more generally, not aiding), because no matter how otherwise unlike the circumstances, in the former case one has caused or brought into existence the harm, while in the latter one has not. Whether morally significant or not, this difference is necessary in the sense that it distinguishes all actions from all (genuine, or ex nihilo) omissions. Instead of asking whether action and omission are morally equivalent, we could ask if (other things being equal) not preventing harm is as bad as causing it; or if making someone worse off is necessarily worse than not making him better off.

The idea that bringing a harm into existence (what I call being causally responsible for it) is morally of a different order than failing to prevent or alleviate it goes deep in our thinking about moral responsibility. This is odd, on reflection. For moral responsibility can be ascribed only (as far as we now know) to human beings, while causal responsibility can be ascribed to almost everything in nature. This ought to lead one to ask what it is about human beings that makes their causal agency morally significant.

What distinguishes the causal role of a human being from that of an object or nonhuman animal is that ordinarily, at least, the human being can choose to act in one way or another; and he can choose on the basis of his knowledge of various things. If this were not so, causal agency would be as morally irrelevant for humans as it is for everything else in nature. And, indeed, when a person could not have chosen not to be a causal agent in a process that results in someone's harm, he is absolved of moral responsibility. Morally his conduct is on a par with floods and earthquakes: unfortunate but not morally ascribable to anyone.

Normally, however, a person is *able to choose not to act in a way that he foresees will cause harm* to someone.[16] It is this that gives causal agency moral significance. But this condition equally warrants (other things being equal) holding a person morally responsible when he is *able to choose to act in a way that he foresees will prevent harm* to someone. For it is the ability to choose now to act, in light of knowledge, that distinguishes human beings from the rest of nature and legitimizes holding them (and nothing else) morally responsible—for what they do and for what they do not do. With respect to adult humans, causal responsibility is merely a sign, usually though not always reliable, of moral responsibility. That moral responsibility ultimately has nothing to do with causal responsibility is revealed in the case of one who knows that someone will die if he does/does not (in the alternative scenes) push a button. There it seems incontrovertible that one is equally obligated in both cases. And it is clear that the only difference between the cases (unlike the complicated examples given by Trammell and others which do not clearly isolate the feature under consideration) is that in the one case one must choose to perform a minimal physical movement to avoid someone's death and in the other one must choose not to perform it.

If still it seems somehow unfair or wrong that we can be held morally responsible in situations we do not create, the defect would seem to be in the nature of things—something, therefore, that must be taken for granted. We can be held morally responsible because within certain constraints we can choose how to act; but it is just a fact that we can't, beyond a certain point, choose the circumstances from which we must choose. But this applies equally to acting and refraining. It's true that if someone falls into the water and starts to drown, it's not the passerby's fault. But likewise if a person finds himself inclined to kill someone, it may not be his fault that he is so inclined. Just as we think the latter is morally required to refrain if he can, so also the passerby may be required to act if he can. Confronted with circumstances, we have to choose and can't choose not to choose.

If there is no moral difference between causing harm and failing to prevent it, then, if Trammell's cases are indeed parallel in every other respect, Jones's failure to warn Smith of the bomb is morally equivalent to his shooting him. The inclination to think otherwise comes from the natural assumption that other asymmetries are embedded in the cases. Simply avowing that they are parallel is not enough to ensure that such assumptions won't intrude, though not necessarily explicitly or consciously. So, e.g., in the first case it is natural to imagine that someone else might be able to warn Smith of the bomb; that Jones might be in some danger himself if he warned Smith; that the urgency of the situation might cause Jones to lose his head, thereby making his inaction partially excusable.[17]

One might be reluctant to accept the equivalence thesis because it is thought to imply that a person causally responsible for a harm is no more obligated to alleviate it than one not causally responsible for it. But what follows is just that one who is *merely* causally responsible is no more obligated than one who is not; and this is not difficult to accept. When the person who has caused harm could have *not* caused it (had he chosen to), then his causal agency implies moral responsibility. However obligated to give aid a person with no causal responsibility might be, one who has non-accidentally or negligently caused harm is bound by that obligation plus the duty arising from having caused the harm.

If, e.g., a person accidentally and non-negligently trips a non-swimmer who then falls into the lake, the former is causally responsible for the latter's predicament. This agent is as obligated (no more and no less) to try to save the non-swimmer as anyone else similarly situated. For

> To call the act accidental and non-negligent is to imply that the relevant person is completely absolved of moral responsibility for the resulting situation. If the person has no moral responsibility for the situation, there would seem to be no grounds for assigning him a greater duty for changing it than others similarly situated.[18]

But the situation is very different when someone deliberately pushes a non-swimmer into the lake. Such a person is morally responsible for the resulting predicament because he could have chosen not to do what he did. His action is morally comparable to that of someone who willingly allows a non-swimmer to fall into the lake when he could easily prevent his falling in—e.g., by holding out his hand. This action and this omission are related in the same way to the non-swimmer's trouble: he wouldn't be in trouble if the first person hadn't pushed him, or if the second had held out his hand.

The question then arises what a person's obligation is given the existence of the harm—when the non-swimmer is flailing about in the water. On the view I have argued for, if for some reason everyone else (including any guilty parties) has disappeared from the scene, the failure to save of the sole remaining individual (where no sacrifice is required, etc.) is morally equivalent to his killing the drowning man; for his omission is sufficient for the death to occur. But if we are asking which of a number of individuals is obligated (or how obligated) to remedy the situation, someone's having non-accidentally or negligently caused the harm is morally relevant, for it is his action that has vastly increased the probability of harm in the first place. (Similarly, other things being equal, for one who at the critical moment chose not to hold out his hand.) Of course, in the situation described, *any* person's failure to try to save would be blameworthy, to say the least. But considering the whole episode, one who could have chosen to behave in such a way that the harm would not have occurred is morally responsible for not so choosing, as well as being bound in the way anyone finding himself able to save would be.

Thus, the equivalence of action and omission is consistent with the commonsense belief that (normally) one who has caused a person harm owes him more in the way of assistance than one who has not.

V

Commonly taken as counterexamples to the equivalence thesis are those cases where one must choose, e.g., between killing a person in order to save others, and not killing him with the result that these others die. Though all agree that more deaths are worse than fewer, almost no one believes that it is permissible to kill people 'in the interests of cancer research or to obtain, let us say, spare parts for grafting on to those who need them.'[19]

A similar problem is posed by this familiar example, described by Philippa Foot:

> Suppose that a judge or magistrate is faced with rioters demanding that a culprit be found for a certain crime and threatening otherwise to take their own bloody revenge on a particular section of the community. The real culprit being unknown, the judge sees himself as able to prevent the bloodshed only by framing some innocent person and having him executed.[20]

Foot's explanation of the belief that it is not permissible for the judge to frame an innocent person, and that, more generally, one may not kill a person in order to save others, is that 'even where the strictest duty of positive aid exists, this still does not weigh as if a negative duty were involved.'[21]

One thing to be noticed about these cases, in contrast to those presented earlier, is that they all involve a choice between two evils and between the interests of different individuals. More than this, they all involve a decision about whether to sacrifice one person for another—something so repellent we are reluctant to allow it no matter what the cost. But whatever it is about sacrificing a person or his interests that is objectionable, it has no necessary connection with the action/omission distinction. This is demonstrated nicely by Russell's twist on the case described by Foot: here the judge's charge is a diabetic.[22] So to stop the rioters the judge needn't kill his charge; he need only refrain from giving him his insulin, and let him die. It is clear that if it is wrong for the judge to execute his prisoner, it is equally wrong for him to let him die in this way. For in either case he sacrifices the person, and it is this that is objectionable. Similar variations can be introduced in the medical cases to show that what is wrong with killing people for their parts has nothing per se to do with the greater stringency of negative duties. (Instead of killing the patient for his heart or liver, the nurse watches as he chokes on his dinner.)

What is common to these cases is that the death or injury of one person is needed for some purpose. The most common way to achieve someone's death is to kill him; and this makes it look as if it is the action of killing per se that is wrong. But cases where death can be achieved by refraining from performing a simple action that would prevent it reveals that it is achieving the death, and not achieving it through action, that is objectionable.[23] In both the negative and positive case, one chooses to act in a way that one knows will result in someone's death; and one chooses to act in that way *because* one knows it will result in a death. This doesn't explain everything important about the issue of sacrificing people, nor does it follow that it is never permissible to do so. But it shows that the problem these cases present is not that of the significance of the action/omission distinction. One can sacrifice a person by killing him, or by letting him die.

I conclude that there is no moral difference between action and omission. The tendency to think otherwise results from the commission of various errors and fallacies, which can be briefly summarized as follows: (a) Comparing cases that are asymmetrical with respect to features other than action/omission. (This is almost inevitable if one compares an omission with physical violence.) (b) Not distinguishing clearly between necessary and practical differences, so that what is at most a practical difference is generalized to operate as a necessary one. (c) Mistaking what is morally significant about a case or a class of cases. (E.g., taking causal agency per se to be morally significant; or thinking that what is wrong with sacrificing a person is that it involves killing.) (d) Mistakenly thinking that the equivalence of action and omission has unacceptable consequences. (E.g., that one who causes harm is under no greater obligation to alleviate it than one who does not; or that nothing short of total devotion to the well-being of others is morally possible.[24])

The moral equivalence of action and omission is supported at one level by its consistency with a coherent and persuasive view of what an agent deciding how to act ought to take into account: the connection between his conduct and a certain consequence, and the amount of sacrifice required of him to fulfill a would-be obligation. At a deeper level, the idea that action and omission are equivalent is strengthened by its connection with the very condition of moral responsibility: the possibility of choosing, given a set of circumstances, how to act.

NOTES

I am grateful to Bernard Baumrin, Gertrude Ezorsky, Virginia Held and J. B. Schneewind for helpful conversations and criticisms of an earlier version of this paper.

1. Robert Nozick, *Anarchy, State, and Utopia* (New York: Basic Books, 1974); e.g., pp. ix, 7, 32. For an extended argument for the claims made in this paragraph, see my *On Being Obligated to Give Aid: Moral and Political Arguments*, unpublished doctoral dissertation (City University of New York 1978), Chapter 3.

2. For such a treatment, see *ibid.*, Chapter 5.

3. I.e., a physical occurrence. If actions are physical occurrences, then, contrary to the schoolbook view, verbs are not necessarily action words. But we may operate under the influence of the simpler picture: we may think that sacrificing a person, or treating him as a means, necessarily involves doing something rather than not doing. Nozick, e.g., assumes that one can satisfy the Kantian injunction not to treat a person as a means simply by forbearance. But whether one sacrifices someone or treats him as a means depends on the reasons for one's conduct. See p. 224.

4. In other cases it would be odd to say of someone that he didn't *x*, even when he *didn't x*. One doesn't say 'He didn't feed x' unless there is some reason to think he would have, could have, should have, might have fed x. See Eric D'Arcy, *Human Acts* (Oxford: Clarendon Press 1963), p. 41ff.

5. See Graham Hughes, "Criminal Omissions," *Yale Law Journal*, 67 (1958), 598; Orvill C. Snyder, "Liability for Negative Conduct," *Virginia Law Review*, 35 (1949).

6. Richard Trammell, "Saving Life and Taking Life," *Journal of Philosophy*, 72 (1975), 133; this volume, p. 292. For further evidence of Trammell's confusion of the general and the particular and of practical and necessary differences, see pp. 217–19.

7. Certain features of this case are worth noting. The sailor's failure to aid doesn't make the stranded man worse off than he would have been had the sailor not appeared at all; the sailor has had no causal role in bringing about the plight of the other. So this situation is unlike that where someone owns the only waterhole in the desert. It is comparable to Nozick's case of the medical researcher who 'synthesizes a new substance that effectively treats a certain disease and who refuses to sell except on his terms.' The substance is easily available, and so the researcher's appropriation of it doesn't make others worse off than they would have been had he not appropriated it. On Nozick's view, the researcher is within his rights in refusing to sell (Nozick, *Anarchy, State, and Utopia*, pp. 179–81).

8. This doesn't mean that a reason couldn't be given why someone doesn't do something, should the question arise. But clearly one doesn't

have a reason for not doing all the many things one isn't doing at any given time.

9. E.g. the description 'letting die.' One could specify more or less stringent conditions under which it was legitimate to describe someone as letting another person die. See Jonathan Bennett, "Whatever the Consequences," *Analysis*, 26 (1966), 83–102; this volume, Chapter 10; Bruce Russell, "On the Relative Strictness of Negative and Positive Duties," *American Philosophical Quarterly*, 14 (1977), 87.

10. Michael Tooley gives a similar example, but in his two people's lives are involved. This introduces obscuring factors having to do with sacrificing one person to save another. See below, pp. 224n25 (Tooley, "Abortion and Infanticide Revisited," quoted in Trammell, "Saving Life and Taking Life"; see below, p. 292n2).

11. Trammell, "Saving Life and Taking Life," p. 290. A hazard of such complicated and artificial examples is that irrelevant factors intrude to influence our judgment. Notice here, e.g., that the person in the first case is being threatened. For it is not just that one is expected not to kill under such threats; it is questionable whether one ought to alter any of one's behavior in response to threats. Certainly if I wouldn't kill to avoid the threatened loss of my money, I wouldn't fail to save someone for that reason either. But there is no threat in Trammell's second case, and so the two cases are not parallel.

Part of the reason we oppose giving in to threats is that it is hard to be sure the threat will be carried out if one doesn't comply. As I am less sure, I am less inclined to cooperate, especially if what is demanded is irrevocable. On the other hand, how disposed I am to give up a lot to save someone depends on how certainly the death will follow upon my failure to act and on how immediate the need is. If I thought 'Unless I hand over the money right now, he'll die on the spot,' I would be more inclined to do it than if there were time to make up my mind, time in which something or someone else might intervene. Depending on how we fill in these particulars or how our imaginations complete the story Trammell leaves untold, our assessment of the relative moral status of the cases changes or becomes explainable on grounds other than action/omission.

12. *Ibid.*, pp. 292–94; see also above, pp. 216–17.

13. See, e.g., Hobbes, *Leviathan*, pt. 1, ch. 14; Hume, *Enquiry Concerning the Principles of Morals*, sec. 3, pt. 1.

14. I have benefitted from discussion of these issues with Frances Myrna Kamm.

A related argument sometimes made to support a necessary difference between action and omission is that action requires an output of energy or effort not involved when a person doesn't act. The argument presupposes a machine-like conception of human beings. For a machine, energy is required for the performance of operations, not for nonperformance: machines do not forbear. But if a person wants to do something, not acting may involve as much or more effort than is required to act when one does not want or wants not to act. (Think of trying to break a habit, or keeping to a diet.) To demand that a person not act is not to demand nothing.

15. Richard Trammell, "Tooley's Moral Symmetry Principle," *Philosophy and Public Affairs*, 5 (1975–76), 308. Trammell is obviously talking about some kind of nonmoral (e.g. causal) responsibility, since it is moral responsibility we are trying to determine. But his manner of expression obscures the crucial issue. For the question is not whether we would describe a particular failure to save as a killing, but whether in a given set of circumstances these are morally equivalent.

16. Sometimes we hold people responsible for causing harm when they didn't foresee the consequences of their actions, because we think they ought to have foreseen them. But this is warranted only on the assumption that the person is responsible for his ignorance, i.e., that he could have chosen not to put himself in a position where he would be ignorant. As Aristotle says about drunkenness, 'the moving principle is in the man himself, since he had the power of not getting drunk and his getting drunk was the cause of his ignorance' (*Nicomachean Ethics*, 1113b30).

17. The cases then resemble the desert island example. But the test used there to confirm the equivalent evaluations won't work here. The sailor's refusal to aid warrants the stranded man in doing what he must to preserve himself; and the sailor, having chosen not to cooperate, can't claim an injustice. But in this case what Smith needs (the information that there is a bomb) is something he doesn't know he needs; and of course if he did know he needed it, he wouldn't need it—he would have it. There is nothing for Smith to wrest from Jones, and nothing for Jones to lose to Smith.

18. Russell, "On the Relative Strictness of Negative and Positive Duties," 92. Any inclination to think otherwise can probably be explained by a kind of spillover of guilt from the typical case of causal responsibility that is not accidental or non-negligent, as well as doubt (implanted by Freud, among others) as to the accidentalness of so-called accidents.

19. Philippa Foot, "The Problem of Abortion and the Doctrine of the Double Effect," *Oxford Review*, 5 (1967); reprinted in James Rachels, ed., *Moral Problems*, 2d ed. (New York: Harper & Row 1975) 64; this volume, p. 271.

20. *Ibid.*, pp. 269–70.

21. *Ibid.*, p. 274.

22. Russell, "On the Relative Strictures of Negative and Positive Duties," 90.

23. So Regina in Lillian Hellman's play *The Little Foxes,* who waits to get her husband's medicine until it is too late, is the moral equivalent of a murderer. See n. 3 above.

24. Concerning the latter question, nothing at all follows from the equivalence thesis. If changes need to be made in our way of life (as I believe they do), these will follow from practical differences.

14

Negation and Abstention: Two Theories of Allowing

Jonathan Bennett

I. Introduction

THE TREE FELL, in consequence of your behavior: whether it fell or not depended on how you acted. There are two ways for that to be so. You could have felled the tree, made it fall, caused it to fall; or you could have allowed it to fall, not prevented or saved it from falling. This difference between *making* and *allowing* looms large in moral philosophy, with many urgent problems depending upon it. We need a clear understanding of what distinction it is. Here are some of the locutions through which we express it:

she fells the tree	she lets the tree fall
she causes it to fall, or makes it fall	she permits or allows it to be the case that the tree falls
it falls because of something she does	it falls because of something she doesn't do
it falls because she intervenes in the course of nature	it falls because she allows nature to take its course

Those will do to go on with; there are others. The consequential states of affairs are endless: she cures the patient (lets him recover), she spoils the cheese (lets it deteriorate), she compacts the earth (lets it settle), and so on. On the allowing side of the line the consequential state of affairs is always explicitly declared—either in a whole nested sentence ("allows it to be the case that *the tree falls*") or in a noun-infinitive transform of that ("allows *the tree to*

Reprinted from *Ethics*, 104 (October 1993), 75–96, with permission of the author and the publisher. ©1993 by The University of Chicago. All rights reserved.

fall" or "lets *the tree fall*"). In reports on makings, we can also explicitly state the consequential state of affairs, but in practice we usually do not. By far the most common form of "making" report is with an active verb phrase that has the consequential state of affairs buried in its meaning: she fells the tree, they rescued him, you ruined me, we amused them, and so on.

My guess is that these two lists of expressions are separated by a single distinction which I call "making/allowing." I do not mean to give a privilege to the words "make" and "allow": we shan't get to the bottom of this distinction by tracing out the precise meanings of any pair of verbs. In trying to analyze the making/allowing distinction I shall be looking for the longest clean, hard thread running through my two lists of locutions.

The important question for moral theory is whether the distinction between making and allowing has basic moral significance. That is to ask:

If someone's behavior has a bad state of affairs as a consequence, is the morality of his conduct affected by whether he *made* the consequence obtain or only *allowed* it to do so?

The answer "no" means that the difference between making and allowing is morally neutral; I shall call this "the neutrality thesis." The question arises in first-and second-order morality (I here borrow Donagan's terminology); it concerns which sort of conduct is worse and which justifies the greater moral indignation.

Some moral philosophers have argued for the neutrality thesis, and others have argued against it, by comparing pairs of cases and inviting us to agree with their moral intuitions about them. There are reasons for doubting whether that approach will get us far,[1] and this paper will concern a different one, namely, trying to get clear about the moral significance of making/allowing by first getting deeply clear about what distinction it is.

Discontent with an analysis which I offered in 1966 triggered a spate of attempts to do better.[2] Two analyses, in my opinion, show more promise than all the rest. Indeed, the others look best when they are seen as attempts to formulate one of those two. One is my old one, which I do not concede is discredited by the single argument that is always brought against it; the other is an analysis presented in Alan Donagan's *The Theory of Morality*. I shall present and compare Donagan's and my attempts to analyze the making/allowing distinction.

II. Positive/Negative

I need these two short stories, in each of which a vehicle stands on ground that slopes down to a cliff top:

Push: The vehicle stands, unbraked, on the slope; Agent pushes it, and it rolls to its destruction.

Stayback: The vehicle is already rolling; Agent could but does not interpose a rock which could stop it, and the vehicle rolls to its destruction.

In each case we have a person, a time, and a vehicle's smashing at the foot of a cliff. It is uncontroversial that in Push the relevance of conduct to upshot belongs on the left (positive, active-verb, "making") side of the line, and that in Stayback it belongs on the right (negative, passive, "allowing") side. An analysis of making/allowing should at least get these two right and make clear how it does so.

My analysis identifies making/allowing with something I call the positive/negative distinction. This does not distinguish two kinds of action: there are no negative actions. I use "negative" primarily in the phrase "negative proposition" and thus also in "negative fact" (facts are true propositions). In Stayback, for instance, Agent moves his fingers, he makes a daisy chain, he smiles; also, he does not resign his job, he does not stand on his head, he does not interpose the rock; three positive facts about how he behaved and three negative ones.

Given "positive" and "negative" as predicates of facts or propositions, we can define the relations "is positively relevant to" and "is negatively relevant to" between behavior and upshots. These definitions are the first of the three stages in my analysis. In giving it, I use "T_1" to name the moment when Agent pushes the vehicle in Push, and the last moment when he could usefully have interposed the rock in Stayback.

1. Suppose we want a full T_1-dated explanation of the vehicle's fate in Stayback—that is, facts about how the world is at T_1 from

which it will follow causally that the vehicle is destroyed at T_2. Let E be the environmental portion of this material: it is the proposition about Agent's environment that is needed for the causal explanation that we seek. What must we add to E to complete the explanation? That is, what is the weakest proposition A about Agent's conduct at T_1 such that E & A causally imply that the vehicle is destroyed at T_2? The answer is that we need $A = $ the negative fact that Agent does not interpose the rock. There are positive facts about how he behaves at T_1, but none fits the description "weakest fact that, when added to E, yields a complete causal explanation of the disaster." The fact that Agent smiled at T_1 does not yield a complete causal explanation; the fact that he turned and walked away does yield one, but it is not the weakest fact that does so. The negative fact that Agent does not interpose the rock is exactly what is needed: it is just strong enough to complete the explanation.

Now look for a T_1-dated explanation for the disaster in Push. Here there are countless negative facts about how Agent behaves at T_1, but none is strong enough to complete the explanation. For that we need the positive fact that he pushes the vehicle hard enough to start it moving.

In short: Agent's behavior in Push is *positively relevant to* the destruction of the vehicle. That is, the weakest fact about his conduct that suffices to complete a causal explanation of the vehicle's being destroyed is positive. Agent's conduct in Stayback is *negatively relevant to* the disaster. That is, the weakest fact about the conduct that suffices to complete a causal explanation of the vehicle's being destroyed is negative.

2. What is it for a fact or proposition to be negative? We can call a *sentence* "negative" if it contains an odd number of negating expressions, but that is not useful. The "negative *proposition*" problem is hard, and Frege suspected that it cannot be solved.[3] I know of only two lines of solution that have been tried: one is due to Chisholm, and I don't accept it because it assumes that a negative proposition, like a negative sentence, contains a negating part and a negated part, and I don't believe this.[4] The other has occurred to philosophers as disparate as Berkeley, Kant, and Ayer—and I shall work with it.

I shall present it through Venn diagrams. Let all the ways Agent could move at time *T*—including staying still—be represented by a square. Each point on the square represents a proposition attributing to him some absolutely specific way of moving. A region of the square represents the disjunction of the propositions represented by the points in the region. Start, for example, with the proposition that *He walks fairly slowly northwards*. Take every point proposition—every absolutely specific way of moving—that would make it true that Agent walks fairly slowly northwards; identify the points that represent those; then the region of the square that represents our original proposition is the region that contains just exactly those points.

A line across this square represents a pair of propositions which are complementary within the square. They are not strictly contradictories because each entails the existence of Agent at that time. I offer to define propositional negativeness only with respect to that framework.

I propose this: A proposition about how Agent moves at *T* is negative if it is fit to be represented by a region that covers nearly the whole of the space of possibilities for him at that time. That is, a proposition and its complement are positive and negative, respectively, if they divide the relevant space extremely unevenly; the highly informative one is positive, and its almost empty complement is negative. This is the idea that is at work in Kant's account of why the judgment "The soul is non-mortal," which has the positive form "S is P," is negative in content. Its predicate "non-mortal" is negative, Kant says, because it picks out only "the unlimited sphere of non-mortal beings":

> Nothing more is said by [this] proposition than that the soul is one of the infinitely many things which remain when I take away all that is mortal. The infinite sphere of all that is possible is thereby limited only to the extent that the mortal is excluded from it, and that the soul is located in the remaining part of its space. But, even allowing for such exclusion, this space still remains infinite, and several more parts of it may be taken away without the concept of the soul being thereby . . . determined in an affirmative manner.[5]

This explains the familiar fact that negative commands are in general easier to obey than positive ones, negative plans easier to execute, and negative hope easier to realize. To obey a positive command or execute a positive plan (become a teacher, go to Sri Lanka), you have to actualize some one of a relatively small range of possibilities, and it may be that each is in some way costly—or that most are and it would be hard to identify any that are not. On the other hand, to execute a negative plan (don't become a teacher, keep out of Sri Lanka), one need only behave in a way that actualizes one of an enormous range of possibilities, a range so large that the odds are that there are easily findable costless ones among them.

III. A Metric for the Possibility Space

We need a metric for the relevant space of possibilities—a basis for saying that one proposition is consistent with more possible states of affairs than another. This is easy when one entails the other, but otherwise it is hard. I need a basis for saying, of two complementary propositions, that they divide up their total space of possibilities unevenly, and for saying which corresponds to the larger subspace. We cannot do this by counting the number of points in each, for there will usually be infinitely many points on each side of the line—for example, infinitely many ways of walking fairly slowly northwards and infinitely many ways of not doing so. Or so it seems. One might stave off this threat of infinity, but I prefer to acknowledge the threat and steer around it.

Here is how. Two propositions about how Agent moves at a particular time are to be accorded the same amount of the possibility space if they are equally specific. This will not work with every determinable, for example, with colors, because for them we have no agreed objective measure of specificity; but we have such measures for space and time, and thus for movement and for specificity of propositions about movement. This puts us in a position to say that a given complementary pair divides the possibilities very unevenly, so that one is positive and the other negative. For example, *He walks northwards* and *He does not walk northwards* are positive and negative, respectively, because the former is much more informative, much more specific, than the latter. The fact that one is and the other is not expressed with help from the word "not" has nothing to do with it.

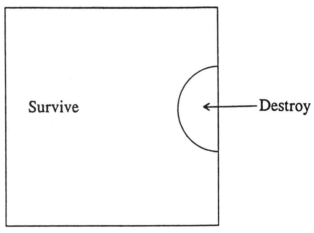

FIG. 1

I do not claim that any two propositions about how Agent moves at a time can be compared for specificity. If P_1 describes with great precision the trajectory of his right hand, while P_2 gives a somewhat vague account of how he moves his whole body, there is no determinate answer to the question of which is the more specific. However, as I explain how the parts of my analysis fit together, it will be seen that this does not matter.

If someone's behavior is (in my sense) relevant to upshot U, the space of his possible ways of moving can be divided into those that satisfy:

If he moved like that, U would obtain,

and those that satisfy:

If he moved like that, U would not obtain.

The line between these is what I call "the U-line." For example, the disaster line through Agent's space of possible conduct has all the vehicle-smashes movements on one side and all the vehicle-survives ones on the other. (For simplicity's sake, I am pretending determinism, so as to get rid of probabilities between 0 and 1.) Now, what makes Agent's conduct *positively* relevant to the disaster in Push is the fact that the disaster line separating his vehicle-is-destroyed options from his vehicle-survives one is like that in figure 1. That is, of all the ways in which he could have moved,

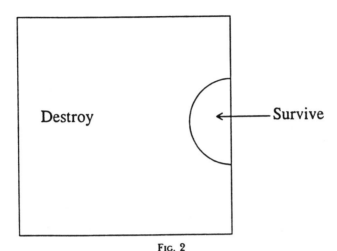

FIG. 2

only a tiny proportion were such as to lead to the vehicle's destruction; virtually all would have had its survival as a consequence. In Stayback, on the other hand, Agent's conduct is relevant to the disaster in a *negative* way, represented by figure 2. To see why this is right about Stayback, consider the proposition that Agent interposes the rock, and think about the different physical ways he could have done this: a few dozen pairwise contrary propositions would pretty well cover the possibilities, each identifying one fairly specific sort of movement which would get the rock into the vehicle's path. Thus, Survive in figure 2 can be divided up into a few dozen smaller regions, each representing some kind of push or kick or the like. Now, each of those can be paired off with an "echo" of it in Destroy—that is, with a proposition which has the same amount of content as it and is indeed very like it except that its truth would not rescue the vehicle. For instance, if Survive contains a proposition attributing to Agent a certain kind of movement with his left foot, let its "echo" attribute to him a similar movement of that foot but with the direction differing so that the foot misses the rock. In general, for each little proposition in Survive, let its echo be one whose truth would make it look as though Agent were trying but failing to interpose the rock. (The "echo" propositions must be pairwise contraries so that their regions don't overlap.) The general idea is given by

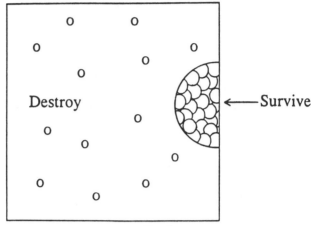

FIG. 3

figure 3. The pockmarks in Destroy represent the echoes. My "degree of specificity" criterion secures that their combined area is the same as that of Survive; and clearly they take up only a tiny proportion of Destroy. I do not base that on how the circles are drawn, but on considerations of specificity. Each of the little propositions in Survive has many echoes in Destroy; we assign just one echo to each, and all the remaining echoes take up further space in Destroy. That region also contains countless propositions that do not echo anything in Survive—that is, countless ways in which Agent could move without looking as though he was trying to interpose the rock—and millions of those will also be comparable for specificity with the echoes. The result is that, according to my criterion, the space of vehicle-rescuing movements that Agent might have made in Stayback is enormously much smaller than the space of vehicle-is-destroyed movements that he could have made; which is to say that figure 2 is correct for Stayback except that it understates the disparity in size between the two regions. A similar line of thought, mutatis mutandis, can be applied to Push and figure 1.

That is why Agent's conduct in Push is positively relevant to the vehicle's being destroyed, and why in Stayback it is negatively relevant to this. In Stayback, the truth of any proposition in Destroy would suffice to complete the causal explanation for the disaster, but relevance is defined in terms of the weakest proposition that would suffice for this; that is the disjunction of all the propositions that would suffice, that is, the proposition represented by the whole of Destroy. I hope it is clear that occurrences of the word "not" play no part in this line of thought.

IV. The Immobility Objection

My account implies that *He moves* is negative and that *He does not move* is positive. In the latter claim I have Locke on my side. He was opposed in this by Leibniz but only with a bad argument.[6] The question does not matter enough to discuss here. I call the distinction that I am presenting "positive/negative," I freely use those words in expounding it, and I think this is reasonable. If not, and that is the only trouble I am in, I shall drop those two words and retain the distinction. What really matters is whether the line I have drawn is plausible as an analysis of the making/allowing distinction which is common property.

The status of *He moves* comes into that question too, but not through a sterile debate about whether it is a negative proposition. To see how, consider the following story:

> Henry is in a sealed room where there is fine metallic dust suspended in the air. If he keeps stock still for two minutes, some dust will settle in such a way as to close a tiny electric circuit which will lead to some notable upshot *U*. Thus, any movement from Henry, and *U* will not obtain; perfect immobility, and we shall get *U*.

My analysis says that if Henry keeps still he *makes U* obtain, whereas if he moves he *allows U* not to obtain. This story is my version of a kind of example that has repeatedly been brought against my analysis, by people who are sure that in this situation if Henry keeps still the relation of his conduct to the upshot *U* is of the allowing rather than the making kind—belongs on the right rather than the left of the line we are inquiring into.

I do not dispute that if Henry keeps still he *allows* the dust to fall; but that is an example of how the detailed meaning of the word "allow" is a poor guide in our present problem area. It would lead us astray about Henry as it would over the following variant on my vehicle stories:

Kick: In the path of the moving vehicle there is a rock which could bring it to a halt; Agent kicks the rock away, and the vehicle rolls to its destruction.

In Kick the relation of conduct to upshot obviously belongs on the left of the line: this is a positive, active, making. Yet it is proper and normal to say that by kicking the rock away Agent *allows* the vehicle to roll on down the slope. In our present context, the niceties of the meaning of "allow" are an ignis fatuus.

If that is not what lies behind the immobility objection, then what does? What else would make people so sure that if Henry keeps still his conduct relates to upshot *U* in a right-of-the-line or allowing way? Here is a guess about that. In most actual situations, relative to most values of *U*, immobility *would* belong on the roomy side of the *U* line. When in Stayback Agent does not interpose the rock, he may do something else instead, but his staying still would have had the same effect on the vehicle's fate. It takes work to rig up a situation where stillness is almost the only route to some interesting upshot. Perhaps that is why, when people confront a result that is produced by Agent's immobility, they immediately and invalidly infer that this is a case of allowing.

To evoke intuitions on my side, suppose that it is almost impossible for Henry to be still for long, and he sweats and strains to do so because he wants *U* to obtain. If he succeeds, doesn't this feel like a "making"? If he fails—gives up trying because the effort is too great, relaxes, and lets his body shift a little—doesn't that feel like an "allowing"?

"What would it take for you to accept defeat?" someone asked me once. He could have continued like this: "Hardly anybody agrees with you that if Henry keeps still he makes *U* obtain; you can try to talk them around, but even if you succeed that will be by changing how people think about making and allowing. Considered as an analysis of the making/allowing distinction that we actually have, yours is wrong. It would be more graceful if you were to admit it." This deserves an answer.

How people use the words "make" and "allow" is a pointer to my concerns, but it does not define them. Let us distinguish three ways things might stand. (1) The ordinary uses of "make" and "allow," and of the other expressions in the two lists at the start of this paper, reflect an underlying jumble with no systematic core. (2) People use those locutions to express a single clean, systematic distinction, and I have failed to describe it. (3) In their uses of the locutions in question, people are guided by a clean, deep concept, but only imperfectly, because they sometimes drift away from it and use the terminology of making/allowing in ways that have no solid conceptual support.

If 1 is true, then there is no such thing as "the making/allowing distinction," and my project is doomed. I cannot prove that this is wrong, but it is implausible, and I have seen no strong case for it. The friends of the immobility objection do not say, "You purport to describe a distinction that doesn't exist"; rather, they hold that the distinction exists and that I have misdescribed it. That is to assert 2. I cannot prove that it is wrong either, but I have seen no convincing evidence that it is right; an intuition that goes against my analysis is not the same as a rival to it. Of the rivals that have been produced, by far the most considerable is Donagan's, which I shall discuss shortly. It conspicuously does not make a big issue of immobility as such, so that it sides with me rather than with those who bring the immobility objection. I conclude that the facts fit best with 3: our thought and talk about how conduct relates to its upshots do reflect a decently grounded making/allowing distinction, from which we sometimes drift away. It is in that spirit that I stand my ground in face of dissent about the case of Henry.

V. Doubts About the Metric

If my analysis is wrong in some matter of detail, I think I know what that must be. The use of "negative fact" to define "negatively relevant" seems secure, as does the explanation of negativeness of facts or propositions in terms of an uneven division of a possibility space. My way of measuring that space is vulnerable, however: I could be using the wrong ruler.

Of two ways of criticizing it, the more radical says that "degree of specificity" has no place in this story. Alternatives to it suggest themselves. One is that the amount of space a proposition occupies is inversely proportional to its probability; another—better looking—would make it inversely proportional to how difficult it would be to make that proposition true. I have not been able to make either of those work out satisfactorily.

The truth may involve a mixture of metrics. When we classify facts about behavior as positive or negative, we may be steering by something that involves specificity and probability and difficulty, and who knows what else. Or perhaps no one metric is right, and we carve up the space varyingly according to context. If that is so, it might be that the making/allowing distinction has moral significance sometimes but not always. All of this is idle speculation at point; I cannot find any way of making it real.

The less radical criticism allows that specificity is crucial but rejects the framework within which I use it. It may seem perverse to define the metric for a space of possible ways of behaving in terms of propositions about ways of moving. That is indeed a defect, because an item of behavior might basically or intrinsically consist not in moving but rather in directing one's thought in a certain way. In practice this matters little, because such nonmovement behavior plays such a small part in our lives; but this gap in the account is theoretically bad; and I do not know how to fill it.

My metric does cover all the rest of human behavior, but not in the terms that interest us: it attends to hand gestures, arm swings, foot shoves, and vibrations of the larynx rather than to kinds of behavior that make up the stuff of the moral life: giving up, betraying him, keeping the faith with her, sharing, hoarding, and so on. These, I repeat, *are* all covered. To say that he kept the faith with her is to attribute a certain relational property to how he moved; similarly with "He gave up the project" and "She shared her food with them" and all the rest. Still, it's a suspicious fact about the metric that it does not *use* any of the relational concepts that give importance to human conduct.

There may be a good deal hanging on this. The positive/negative distinction that I have defined *obviously* has no basic moral significance: if someone moves in a way that causes or makes probable some bad upshot, the moral status of his conduct *obviously* cannot depend on how many other movements by him would have done the same. The obviousness of that, though, depends on the metric I have chosen; if we switched to a different way of measuring the possibility space, the claim might be less compelling.

There are various loose, intuitive ways of revising the metric. Consider these three stories:

Suit: An African village is in need. I launch a lawsuit that deprives them of a thousand dollars they would otherwise have had.

Cancel: Same village, same everything, but this time I learn that my accountant thinks he is supposed to sign away a thousand of my dollars to the village, and I tell him not to.

Nohelp: Same village, etc. This time I could but do not give the villages a thousand dollars.

My positive/negative line has Suit and Cancel on the left and Nohelp on the right. One might hope for a distinction that would put Suit on the left and bracket Cancel with Nohelp on the right: Cancel and Nohelp, one might think, are just two ways of *not giving money to the village,* and it does not matter that one does and the other does not require a fairly specific kind of movement. This presupposes a possibility space that represents not *ways I could move* but rather *things I could do with my money,* with these (perhaps) dividing into such equal-sized kinds as investing it in bonds, giving it to my children, spending it on a swimming pool for myself, and giving it to that African village. That sounds natural, but it is tailored to fit this trio of cases; it is no use until we can generalize it, and I cannot see how to do that.

That brings me to the end of what I have to say about the positive/negative distinction, except in comparing it with Donagan's distinction, to which I now turn.

VI. Agency and "the Course of Nature"

A person's agency can relate to a state of affairs in any of three ways. *Quiescence:* Agency is not involved. Her head moved because a brick hit it. *Intervention:* The person exercises her agency so as to make a difference to what happens. Her head moved because she nodded. *Abstention:* The person exercises her agency so as to make *no* difference to what happens. Her head moved because, feeling the onset of a suppressible sneeze, she decided to let it happen.

These can be described using Donagan's phrase "the course of nature." In the first there is no agency, so the course of nature is followed. In the second, agency makes a difference, so the course of nature is not followed. In the third, the person exercises her agency in such a way that the course of nature is followed. Underlying all this is the principle:

> A train of events occurs in the course of nature if (and only if) it would have occurred if human agency had not been at work.

So the course of nature may be followed because of the person's quiescence or her abstention (from intervening). Here is part of what Donagan says about all this:

> Should she be deprived of all power of action, the situation, including her own bodily and mental states, would change according to the laws of nature. Her deeds as an agent are either interventions in that natural process or abstentions from interventions. When she intervenes, she [causes] whatever would not have occurred had she abstained; and when she abstains, [she allows] to happen whatever would not have happened had she intervened. Hence, from the point of view of action, the situation is conceived as passive, and the agent, *qua* agent, as external to it. She is like a *deus ex machina* whose interventions make a difference to what otherwise would naturally come about without them.[7]

There are some signs that Donagan regarded human agency as unnatural, for example, as able to defeat the laws of nature. Few of us would accept that, and perhaps Donagan didn't either. I choose to interpret him not as advancing any substantive thesis about some kind of antithesis between agency and nature but, rather, as defining "the course of nature" or "what naturally happens" as something like "what happens independently of human agency."

Independently of all human agency? If we say that what happens in the course of nature is what comes about without any human agency anywhere in its causal history, we shall have a basis for a possible moral idea, namely, piety about what is "natural" in this strong sense—the world untouched by man. We would have to soften it, perhaps turning it into a matter of degree, because most significant aspects of our planet already bear the marks of human intervention. I shan't follow this up here; it is not a promising approach.

We'll do better if we attend to human agency during a certain interval, and it is easy to see what one it should be. We are relating behavior to an upshot, so we should attend to human agency during the interval bounded by that conduct and that upshot. So the "course of nature," relative to a given conduct-upshot pair, is what comes about unaffected by agency during that interval.

Whose agency? That of the person whose conduct is in question, of course; but what about others? Suppose that you start a fire and that I could have stopped you. Clearly I did not *make* the fire start. Donagan says that I did not *allow* it to start either, because it didn't come about in the course of nature (pp. 50–51). For him, the course of nature is what is unaffected by any human agency during the conduct-to-upshot interval.

For a reason that I do not have space for here, it is not absurd or arbitrary to handle "allowing" in this way; but I shan't follow Donagan in it, because it runs together two questions that are better taken separately:

i) *U* comes about through my intervening, or *U* would have happened even if I had abstained. Does it morally matter which?

ii) When *U* comes about because I do not intervene and stop it, it does so either through someone else's intervention or through processes not involving agency. Does it morally matter which?

I am inclined to answer no and no; Donagan, I think, would answer yes and yes. The questions are different, though, and it is better not to run them together as Donagan does. His answer to i is "Yes: if *U* came about because you intervened, it is not something you allowed to happen." His answer to ii is "Yes: if *U* came about through the agency of someone else, it is not something you allowed to happen." It is better to address these questions separately, not letting "allow" suggest that they have something real in common.

I therefore choose to understand Donagan's distinction like this: What happens in the course of nature relative to Agent is what would have happened if *he* had not intervened. When I speak of "Donagan's distinction," I always mean this one that I have developed out of his materials.

Donagan sometimes seems to imply that what you allow to happen is what happens because you abstain from intervening in the course of nature (p. 50). That cannot be right, because we allow countless things to happen whereas abstaining from intervening is a strange and rare performance: exercising one's agency so that the rest of the world runs just as it would have done if one had been asleep or on autopilot. In Stayback, for example, where Agent allows the vehicle to go over the cliff, he is probably shuffling his feet or waving his arms or making a daisy chain or somehow intervening in the course of nature.

Donagan presumably made that mistake because he slid into thinking that the crucial question is a monadic one about the nature of the person's conduct: Did he abstain from intervening in the course of nature? Really, it is a dyadic one about how the conduct relates to a specific upshot: Would U have come about if he had abstained from intervening in the course of nature? That points us to the best way to understand the analysis. A person allows U to obtain if (i) the person could have behaved so that U didn't obtain and (ii) U would have obtained if the person had abstained, which will be true just in case U would have obtained if the person's agency had not been exercised at all. The analysis, in short, divides the consequences of a person's behavior according to whether they came about because of some difference that the person's agency made to the course of events. This involves counterfactuals about what would have happened if the person's agency had not been at work, and these are sometimes problematic: some problems beset virtually all counterfactuals, and others come from our imperfect grasp of the concept of agency. Still, we can apply Donagan's active/passive distinction (as I call it) in enough cases to be able to assess it and compare it with my positive/negative one.

VII. How Far Do the Two Distinctions Coincide?

Construct again the possibility space for Agent at T, and draw the U line through it, dividing it into the U region, each of whose points satisfies this:

If he had behaved in that way, U *would* have ensued,

and the non-U region, each of whose points satisfies this:

If he had behaved in that way, U *would not* have ensued.

My positive/negative distinction asks: Is the U region vastly larger than the non-U one? Donagan's asks instead: Does the U region contain the abstention point? That is to ask: Would U have ensued even if Agent had abstained from intervening in the course of nature?

So there is a single structure, with one question being asked about it by the positive/negative distinction and another by Donagan's active/passive distinction. Different as they are, however, the questions usually have the same answer because it is usually the case that if U would have occurred even if the person's agency had not been exercised, then also whatever the person did (with a few exceptions), U would have occurred, and vice versa. Still, it isn't hard to devise cases where the two come apart, and I shall present some shortly, starting with cases that involve the vexed matter of immobility.

Donagan's active/passive distinction makes no more of immobility or unchangingness than mine does. In most possibility spaces, relative to most upshots, the immobility point will be in the region that contains the abstention point, and thus also in the larger of the two regions; which is why, in most cases where U would have ensued if the person had remained still, his conduct's relevance to U will be on the right of Donagan's line and of mine. But neither line employs the concept of stasis: neither asks what would have happened if the person had remained still. Donagan is explicit about this. In the natural course of events, he says in the passage I quoted early in Section VI above, the person's "bodily and mental states *change* according to the laws of nature"—and the changes could include movements. Thus, two considerable analytic treatments of our topic are silent about immobility. If they are both wrong, and immobility deserves a special emphasis, I would like to hear the reasons for this.

We encountered the immobility objection in a case where U will occur if Henry moves and not otherwise. Now consider two ways the story could unfold:

i) Henry sits completely still, *slack and comfortable*; U ensues and would not have done so if Henry had moved.

ii) Henry sits completely still, *heroically enduring a terrible itch*; U ensues and would not have done so if Henry had moved.

The positive/negative distinction ignores the emphasized phrases and classifies Henry's conduct as positively relevant to U both times. But if Henry's itch means that in the course of nature he would move, so that his stillness is an intervention, then Donagan's analysis counts Henry's behavior as relevant passively in i and actively in ii. Case ii is the one I appealed to when I first introduced Henry: I was trying to shift your intuitions about immobility my way, by bringing them up against a case where *both* analyses were against them. Mine without Donagan's is less powerful than are both together.

This situation is symmetrical, however: against the immobility intuition, Donagan's approach has less power on its own than when associated with mine. To see this, consider the following version of the Stayback scenario: At the time when he could be interposing the rock, Agent remains motionless; to do this, he has to suppress a muscular spasm which, if unchecked, would make his leg move in such a way as to shove the rock into the vehicle's path. This *is* still Stayback, so the relation of conduct to upshot is on the right or allowing side of my line; but it is on the left of Donagan's—for him this is a case of making the vehicle go to its destruction—because if Agent had not exercised his agency at all his leg would have jerked out, the rock would have been interposed, and the vehicle would have been safe. In this case, I think, those who are impressed with immobility will side with me rather than Donagan. So, as I said, the two analyses together exert more force against the immobility intuition than does either on its own.

This does not matter much, because the immobility intuition is significant only as a matter of epidemiology: *There's a lot of it about*. There are people out there who have strong, confident ideas about the import of someone's keeping still; but I have offered two ways of explaining these ideas away, and nobody has said anything in their defense. Until that situation changes, I don't think the immobility intuition deserves much respect.

VIII. The Two Distinctions as Collaborators

Still, the symmetry that I have just uncovered goes further. Right across the board, it seems to me, one is happier applying the making/allowing distinction to cases on which active/passive and positive/negative give the same answer. For a case where they do not, and where immobility is not involved, try a variant on Push. I described that as a case where a fairly specific kind of movement by Agent—call it a "shove"—is needed to get the vehicle moving. Now add this detail: Agent feels the onset of an involuntary muscular spasm which, if not checked, will result in his body's making a shove. He could quell this spasm, but he chooses not to and his body does produce the shove which starts the vehicle rolling. For Donagan this is a case of allowing the vehicle to roll: the relevance of conduct to upshot is on the right of his line. It remains on the left of mine. If you are perfectly content to classify this as a case of allowing the vehicle to be destroyed, then for you Donagan's distinction is correct. I suspect, however, that few people will be comfortable describing the case in that way; and that, I believe, is part of a general pattern—we confidently apply the notion of allowing only when the negativeness thought and the abstention thought both favor our doing so.

It is a trivial exercise to modify Stayback in a similar way, so that Donagan puts it on the left while I still have it on the right. I have indeed given one such modification, but now I am talking about one that does not involve immobility. Here again, I think that most people's intuitions about the case will be unsteady.

(Trying to resolve a crucial problem about how we understand ourselves, I have ended up talking about twitches and spasms! This may seem grotesque; but I had to, if I was to consider cases where the two distinctions diverge. If a particular conduct–upshot relation is to fall on the left of my line it must involve some fairly specific kind of movement; for it to fall on the right of Donagan's line, the movement must be one which would occur in the course of nature. Put the two together and you get a fairly specific kind of movement which would occur in the course of nature; which is why I bring in twitches and spasms. And since the behavior in question must involve agency, the twitches and spasms must be suppressible ones. Of course the "kind of movement" could include complete stillness, but I have explained why we ought not to conduct the entire discussion in terms of that.)

I conclude that Donagan and I are both right. When people use the locutions that express the making/allowing distinction, they may be guided by the abstention thought or by the negativeness thought or by both at once, with neither being always uppermost. In the form in which most people have it, the making/allowing distinction does not equip them to deal with the odd cases where only one of those thoughts is available. In short, the two analyses somehow share the truth between them.

IX. Formal Contrasts Between the Two

This is an odder result than it might at first seem. The two distinctions are so unalike in their formal aspects that one would hardly expect them to collaborate, or to operate interchangeably, in our thinking. I shall sketch that contrast, which is (to me, anyway) too interesting to pass up. Assume throughout that a person behaves in a certain way which is relevant to an upshot U. We have the person's possibility space, with the U line drawn through it.

1. Active/passive identifies one particular point on the person's possibility square, namely, the abstention point; positive/negative does not in that way pick out any one absolutely specific way of behaving.

2. Active/passive identifies that particular way of behaving by means of a monadic predicate: . . . *is an abstention from intervening in the course of nature*. All the other possible ways of behaving fall under another monadic description: . . . *is an intervention in the course of nature*. Positive/negative uses no monadic descriptions of items of behavior.

3. Active/passive's central question about the U line is, On which side of it does the abstention point lie? Active/passive does not ask about the relative sizes of the two regions, and the question it does ask must have an answer (vagueness apart). Positive/negative's question about the regions that are marked off by the U line is, Which, if either, is by far the larger? Positive/negative does not ask what movements each region contains, only how many. Also, if neither region is much larger than the other, positive/negative's question has no answer.

4. Given that the person's behavior was relevant to U, active/passive can classify the relevance on the basis of information about either one of the regions that are separated by the U line. If active/passive is told that the U region contains the abstention point, or

that it does not, or that the non-U region contains it, or that it does not, it can draw its conclusion. Not so with positive/negative. Even when it knows the whole truth about one of the regions, it cannot definitely classify the relevance until it looks at the other. One region, taken on its own, might be so limited as to suggest that it is the smaller of the two; but the person might be physically disabled so that the movements represented in that small region are nearly his whole repertoire. Or one region might be large enough to represent virtually the whole repertoire of a normal person, strongly suggesting that it is the larger of the two; but it is theoretically possible that the person's extraordinary powers give him a repertoire of which the possible behaviors we have considered are only a small fraction.

5. I explained in Section II above why it is apt to be easier to pursue a plan or obey a command if it is negative than if it is positive. That explanation depended on the size difference between two subregions of the possibility space, so it was special to positive/negative and could not work for active/passive. One might think: "Active/passive has another route to the same conclusion. Whatever its size, the subregion in which the person allows U to happen always contains the abstention point, which represents a costless way of behaving. It can't be much trouble to the person to slump into inactivity for a while, thus refraining from intervening in the course of nature in *any* way." This implies that the two distinctions share a certain feature but for different reasons. That would be enjoyable, but it isn't right. Granted that it is physically easy to slump, abstaining altogether from intervening in nature's course, an abstention might be costly in other ways: painful, morally repugnant, mentally demanding, and— perhaps above all—a damaging departure from whatever project the person is currently engaged in. It is true that active/passive tends to resemble positive/negative in respect of cost, but the only reason I can find for that is that the two coincide along most of their length. That is, for most significant upshots U, U is reachable through abstention only if it is reachable through most things that the agent might do; so usually the negative (= larger) region marked off by the U line is also the one containing the abstention point; so usually the two distinctions coincide. To the extent that

they do, active/passive can borrow a cost difference from positive/negative.

X. Other Attempted Analyses

In working through other attempts to analyze the making/
allowing distinction, I have been struck by how many of them,
when pressed for clarity and depth, do best by turning themselves
into versions of Donagan's active/passive distinction. I shall give
three examples; there are others.

It has been proposed that you allow P to obtain if (i) you could
have acted so that P did not obtain and (ii) P would have obtained
even if you had been absent from the scene. This does not draw
the line in the right place, because sometimes the person's being
absent would have altered the whole structure of the situation.
For example, it might be that the fool who started the car rolling
in Stayback did so only because he saw Agent standing there; if
Agent had been absent, the car would not have rolled to its destruction. Still, we can rescue this account by making it speak of
what would have happened if the person had been absent *qua*
agent, that is, if he had not exercised his agency; and that brings
in Donagan's active/passive distinction.

The same idea may lie some distance behind Bentham's definition of "negative acts" as "such as consist in forbearing to move
or exert oneself."[8] The immobility aspect of this is indefensible,
I have argued, but "forbearing to exert oneself" is better. It might
be a gesture toward this: negatively relevant conduct is behavior
that bears on the given upshot in the same way as would the
person's not exerting himself, that is, his agency's not being
exercised.

Again, when philosophers offer to explain our distinction—as
the late Warren Quinn did—in terms of "the distinction between
action and inaction," they have clearly gone wrong.[9] A person
who allows something to happen need not be in any reasonable
sense "inactive" at the time. Perhaps these philosophers meant to
be talking about what would have happened *if the person had been*
inactive; in which case we again have rescue through reinterpreta-
tion and Donagan.

Some of the informal locutions that express making/allowing—
and some of the analytic assaults on it—use the language of the
contrast between positive and negative or between "did" and
"didn't." One of these, too, occurs in Quinn's paper where he
writes that "harmful negative agency" involves "harm occurring
because of . . . the noninstantiation of some kind of action that
[the person] might have performed." Quinn used "positive" and
"negative" as I do "making" and "allowing," merely to label the
analysandum; evidently he thought he did not need these terms
in his analysans and so did not need to get them clear. He did,
though, as part of an account of what kinds of actions there are.
If he set no limits to those, we could say that *not* pushing a vehicle
is a kind of action; then in Push the disaster occurs because of the
*non*instantiation of that kind of action, which puts the Push scenario, absurdly, on the allowing side of the line. Of course Quinn
would reject this, declaring that not pushing the vehicle is not a
kind of action. Then he should explain why; and that, I believe,
would force him to confront the notion of negativeness.

In several places, Quinn comes dangerously close—as have
others—to the attractively simple idea that when someone allows
U to come about, it comes about "because of something he
doesn't do." It's simple all right, and I slipped it past you in my
introductory lists of locutions; but taken literally it is wrong. The
disaster in Stayback occurred because Agent did not interpose the
rock; if it occurred because of *something he didn't do,* what is that
something? In fact there is nothing such that he didn't do it and
the disaster occurred because of it. Interposing the rock? He didn't
do that, but the disaster didn't occur because of his interposing
the rock. Well, then, *not* interposing the rock? It's true that the
disaster occurred because of his not interposing the rock, but that
is something he did, not something he didn't do. Of course there
is nothing wrong with "It happened because of something he
didn't do" when this is taken as an idiom. If we want clarity,
however, we should replace it by a literal statement of its meaning,
which is provided by "It happened because of a negative fact about
his behavior."

It is interesting to see what lengths philosophers will go to in
avoiding the concept of a negative fact. Donald Davidson remarks, "We often seem to count among the things an agent does

things that he does *not* do: his refrainings, omissions, avoidances."[10] It must be a mistake to count things I don't do among the things I do! It isn't a mistake to include my omissions, but they are not things I don't do. What Davidson should have said is that in describing a person's behavior we often include negative facts about it.

XI. THE MORALITY OF THE TWO DISTINCTIONS

I have remarked that the positive/negative distinction obviously lacks basic moral significance. That was based on one metric for the possibility space, but I have not been able to find any plausible alternative that does better; so the result seems to stand. Donagan's active/passive distinction, on the other hand, is not so obviously devoid of moral significance. Still, it is not obvious, either, that it *does* have any, so there is something to be thought about here.

If the active/passive distinction carries basic moral weight, then something like this is right:

> If someone's ϕing would have a bad consequence *U,* that fact counts morally against his ϕing. Its weight as a reason against his ϕing is lessened if the following is true: If in this situation the person had not exercised his agency at all, *U* would have come about.

I can find no reason to accept this. When some bad state of affairs *U* comes about, this implies nothing about the morality of my behavior if my agency was not involved: there is an unbreakable link between

> My agency was not involved in the causation of *U,*

and "I did not act wrongly." The moral force of that, however, does not carry over to

> *U would* have obtained even if my agency *had* not been involved.

Nothing but muddle could lead anyone to think that "I could have prevented it, but I didn't" is significantly like "I had nothing to do with it." With that muddle set aside, I see no way of finding moral significance in the active/passive distinction. This is not to say that it obviously hasn't any, as I do say about positive/negative when that is based on my specificity metric; but I do contend that those who think that it is morally significant owe us reasons.

There is evidence that Alan Donagan himself had no great faith in the power of his analysis to invest making/allowing with moral significance. Later on in *The Theory of Morality,* when he is defending moral absolutism against an attack of mine,[11] he does not point out that my attack avowedly depends on the positive/negative analysis of making/allowing and therefore collapses if that is rejected. Given the weakness of what he does say in defense of absolutism, it is striking that he does not counterattack using the weapon he has forged earlier in the book—his active/passive analysis of the making/allowing distinction. Indeed, he seems to have underrated that analysis in every way. The pages of his book in which it is presented are nowhere referred to in the index; and in correspondence with him I found him to be less interested in it than I was.

NOTES

1. For discussion, see Jonathan Bennett, "Positive and Negative Relevance," *American Philosophical Quarterly,* 20 (1983), 185–94.

2. Jonathan Bennett, "Whatever the Consequences," *Analysis,* 26 (1965–66): 83–102, this volume, Chapter 10. A greatly improved version of the analysis is presented in Jonathan Bennett, "Killing and Letting Die," lecture 1 (pp. 47–72) in "Morality and Consequences," in *The Tanner Lectures on Human Values,* II, ed. S. McMurrin (Salt Lake City: University of Utah Press, 1981), pp. 47–116.

3. Gottlob Frege, "Negation," in *The Philosophical Writings of Gottlob Frege,* ed. P. Geach and M. Black (Oxford: Blackwell, 1952), pp. 117–35, at pp. 125–26.

4. Roderick M. Chisholm, *The First Person* (Minneapolis: University of Minnesota Press, 1981), pp. 124–25.

5. Immanuel Kant, *Critique of Pure Reason* (London: Macmillan, 1929), A 72f = B 97f. See also A. J. Ayer, "Negation," in his *Philosophical Essays* (London: Macmillan, 1954), pp. 36–65.

6. John Locke, *An Essay Concerning Human Understanding,* 2.8.6; G. W. Leibniz, *New Essays on Human Understanding,* trans. and ed. P. Rem-

nant and J. Bennett (Cambridge: Cambridge University Press, 1981), p. 130.

7. Alan Donagan, *The Theory of Morality* (Chicago: The University of Chicago Press, 1977), pp. 42–43, lightly edited.

8. Jeremy Bentham, *An Introduction to the Principles of Morals and Legislation* (1780), Chapter 8, sec. 8.

9. Warren S. Quinn, "Actions, Intentions, and Consequences: The Doctrine of Doing and Allowing," *Philosophical Review*, 98 (1989), 287–312; this volume, Chapter 20.

10. Donald Davidson, "Reply to Bruce Vermazen," in *Essays on Davidson: Actions and Events*, ed. Bruce Vermazen and Merrill Hintikka (Oxford: Clarendon Press, 1985), pp. 217–21, at p. 217.

11. Donagan, *The Theory of Morality*, pp. 157–58.

15

The Survival Lottery

John Harris

LET US SUPPOSE that organ transplant procedures have been perfected; in such circumstances if two dying patients could be saved by organ transplants then, if surgeons have the requisite organs in stock and no other needy patients, but nevertheless allow their patients to die, we would be inclined to say, and be justified in saying, that the patients died because the doctors refused to save them. But if there are no spare organs in stock and none otherwise available, the doctors have no choice, they cannot save their patients and so must let them die. In this case we would be disinclined to say that the doctors are in any sense the cause of their patients' deaths. But let us further suppose that the two dying patients, Y and Z, are not happy about being left to die. They might argue that it is not strictly true that there are no organs which could be used to save them. Y needs a new heart and Z new lungs. They point out that if just one healthy person were to be killed his organs could be removed and both of them be saved. We and the doctors would probably be alike in thinking that such a step, while technically possible, would be out of the question. We would not say that the doctors were killing their patients if they refused to prey upon the healthy to save the sick. And because this sort of surgical Robin Hoodery is out of the question we can tell Y and Z that they cannot be saved, and that when they die they will have died of natural causes and not of the neglect of their doctors. Y and Z do not however agree; they insist that if the doctors fail to kill a healthy man and use his organs to save them, then the doctors will be responsible for their deaths.

Many philosophers have for various reasons believed that we

Reprinted from *Philosophy*, 50, no. 191 (January 1975), 81–87 by permission of Cambridge University Press.

must not kill even if by doing so we could save life. They believe that there is a moral difference between killing and letting die. On this view, to kill A so that Y and Z might live is ruled out because we have a strict obligation not to kill but a duty of some lesser kind to save life. A. H. Clough's dictum "Thou shalt not kill but need'st not strive officiously to keep alive" expresses bluntly this point of view. The dying Y and Z may be excused for not being much impressed by Clough's dictum. They agree that it is wrong to kill the innocent and are prepared to agree to an absolute prohibition against so doing. They do not agree, however, that A is more innocent than they are. Y and Z might go on to point out that the currently acknowledged right of the innocent not to be killed, even where their deaths might give life to others, is just a decision to prefer the lives of the fortunate to those of the unfortunate. A is innocent in the sense that he has done nothing to deserve death, but Y and Z are also innocent in this sense. Why should they be the ones to die simply because they are so unlucky as to have diseased organs? Why, they might argue, should their living or dying be left to chance when in so many other areas of human life we believe that we have an obligation to ensure the survival of the maximum number of lives possible?

Y and Z argue that if a doctor refuses to treat a patient, with the result that the patient dies, he has killed the patient as sure as shooting, and that, in exactly the same way, if the doctors refuse Y and Z the transplants that they need, then their refusal will kill Y and Z, again as sure as shooting. The doctors, and indeed the society which supports their inaction, cannot defend themselves by arguing that they are neither expected, nor required by law or convention, to kill so that lives may be saved (indeed, quite the reverse) since this is just an appeal to custom or authority. A man who does his own moral thinking must decide whether, in these circumstances, he ought to save two lives at the cost of one, or one life at the cost of two. The fact that so called "third parties" have never before been brought into such calculations, have never before been thought of as being involved, is not an argument against their now becoming so. There are, of course, good arguments against allowing doctors simply to haul passers-by off the streets whenever they have a couple of patients in need of new organs. And the harmful side-effects of such a practice in terms of terror and distress to the victims, the witnesses and society generally, would give us further reasons for dismissing the idea. Y and Z realize this and have a proposal, which they will shortly produce, which would largely meet objections to placing such power in the hands of doctors and eliminate at least some of the harmful side-effects.

In the unlikely event of their feeling obliged to reply to the reproaches of Y and Z, the doctors might offer the following argument: they might maintain that a man is only responsible for the death of someone whose life he might have saved, if, in all the circumstances of the case, he ought to have saved the man by the means available. This is why a doctor might be a murderer if he simply refused or neglected to treat a patient who would die without treatment, but not if he could only save the patient by doing something he ought in no circumstances to do—kill the innocent. Y and Z readily agree that a man ought not to do what he ought not to do, but they point out that if the doctors, and for that matter society at large, ought on balance to kill one man if two can thereby be saved, then failure to do so will involve responsibility for the consequent deaths. The fact that Y's and Z's proposal involves killing the innocent cannot be a reason for refusing to consider their proposal, for this would just be a refusal to face the question at issue and so avoid having to make a decision as to what ought to be done in circumstances like these. It is Y's and Z's claim that failure to adopt their plan will also involve killing the innocent, rather more of the innocent than the proposed alternative.

To back up this last point, to remove the arbitrariness of permitting doctors to select their donors from among the chance passers-by outside hospitals, and the tremendous power this would place in doctor's hands, to mitigate worries about side-effects and lastly to appease those who wonder why poor old A should be singled out for sacrifice, Y and Z put forward the following scheme: they propose that everyone be given a sort of lottery number. Whenever doctors have two or more dying patients who could be saved by transplants, and no suitable organs have come to hand through "natural" deaths, they can ask a central computer to supply a suitable donor. The computer will then pick the number of a suitable donor at random and he will be killed so that the lives of two or more others may be saved. No doubt if the scheme were ever to be implemented a suitable euphemism for "killed" would be employed. Perhaps we would begin to talk about citizens being called upon to "give life" to others. With the refinement of transplant procedures such a scheme could offer the chance of saving large numbers of lives that are now lost. Indeed, even taking into account the loss of the lives of donors, the numbers of untimely deaths each year might be dramatically reduced, so much so that everyone's chance of living to ripe old age might be increased. If this were to be the consequence of the adoption of such a scheme, and it might well be, it could not be dismissed lightly. It might of course be objected that it is likely that more old people will need transplants to prolong their lives than will the young, and so the scheme would inevitably lead to a society dominated by the old. But if such a society is thought objectionable, there is no reason to suppose that a programme could not be designed for the computer that would ensure the maintenance of whatever is considered to be an optimum age distribution throughout the population.

Suppose that inter-planetary travel revealed a world of people like ourselves, but who organized their society according to this scheme. No one was considered to have an absolute right to life or freedom from interference, but everything was always done to ensure that as many people as possible would enjoy long and happy lives. In such a world a man who attempted to escape when his number was up or who resisted on the grounds that no one had a right to take his life, might well be regarded as a murderer. We might or might not prefer to live in such a world, but the morality of its inhabitants would surely be one that we could respect. It would not be obviously more barbaric or cruel or immoral than our own.

Y and Z are willing to concede one exception to the universal application of their scheme. They realize that it would be unfair to allow people who have brought their misfortune on themselves to benefit from the lottery. There would clearly be something unjust about killing the abstemious B so that W (whose heavy smoking has given him lung cancer) and X (whose drinking has destroyed his liver) should be preserved to over-indulge again.

What objections could be made to the lottery scheme? A first straw to clutch at would be the desire for security. Under such a scheme we would never know when we would hear *them* knocking at the door. Every post might bring a sentence of death; every sound in the night might be the sound of boots on the stairs. But, as we have seen, the chances of actually being called upon to make the ultimate sacrifice might be smaller than is the present risk of being killed on the roads, and most of us do not lie trembling a-bed, appalled at the prospect of being dispatched on the morrow. The truth is that lives might well be more secure under such a scheme.

If we respect individuality and see every human being as unique in his own way, we might want to reject a society in which it appeared that individuals were seen merely as interchangeable units in a structure, the value of which lies in its having as many healthy units as possible. But of course Y and Z would want to know why A's individuality was more worthy of respect than theirs.

Another plausible objection is the natural reluctance to play God with men's lives, the feeling that it is wrong to make any attempt to re-allot the life opportunities that fate has determined, that the deaths of Y and Z would be "natural," whereas the death of anyone killed to save them would have been perpetrated by men. But if we are able to change things, then to elect not to do so is also to determine what will happen in the world.

Neither does the alleged moral difference between killing and letting die afford a respectable way of rejecting the claims of Y and Z. For if we really want to counter proponents of the lottery, if we really want to answer Y and Z and not just put them off, we cannot do so by saying that the lottery involves killing and object to it for that reason, because to do so would, as we have seen, just beg the question as to whether the failure to save as many people as possible might not also amount to killing.

To opt for the society which Y and Z propose would be then to adopt a society in which saintliness would be mandatory. Each of us would have to recognize a binding obligation to give up his own life for others when called upon to do so. In such a society anyone who reneged upon this duty would be a murderer. The most promising objection to such a society, and indeed to any principle which required us to kill A in order to save Y and Z, is, I suspect, that we are committed to the right of self-defense. If I can kill A to save Y and Z then he can kill me to save P and Q, and it is only if I am prepared to agree to this that I will opt for the lottery or be prepared to agree to a man's being killed if doing so would save the lives of more than one other man. Of course there is something paradoxical about basing objections to the lottery scheme on the right of self-defense since, *ex hypothesi,* each person would have a better chance of living to a ripe old age if the lottery scheme were to be implemented. None the less, the feeling that no man should be required to lay down his life for others makes many people shy away from such a scheme, even though it might be rational to accept it on prudential grounds, and perhaps even mandatory on utilitarian grounds. Again, Y and Z would reply that the right of self-defense must extend to them as much as to anyone else; and while it is true that they can only live if another man is killed, they would claim that it is also true that if they are left to die, then someone who lives on does so over their dead bodies.

It might be argued that the institution of the survival lottery has not gone far to mitigate the harmful side-effects in terms of terror and distress to victims, witnesses and society generally, that would be occasioned by doctors simply snatching passers-by off the streets and disorganizing them for the benefit of the unfortunate. Donors would after all still have to be procured, and this process, however it was carried out, would still be likely to prove distressing to all concerned. The lottery scheme would eliminate the arbitrariness of leaving the life-and-death decisions to the doctors, and remove the possibility of such terrible power falling into the hands of any individuals, but the terror and distress would remain. The effect of having to apprehend presumably unwilling victims would give us pause. Perhaps only a long period of education or propaganda could remove our abhorrence. What this abhorrence reveals about the rights and wrongs of the situation is however more difficult to assess. We might be inclined to say that only monsters could ignore the promptings of conscience so far as to operate the lottery scheme. But the promptings of conscience are not necessarily the most reliable guide. In the present case Y and Z would argue that such promptings are mere squeamishness, an over-nice self-indulgence that costs lives. Death, Y and Z would remind us, is a distressing experience whenever and to whomever it occurs, so the less it occurs the better. Fewer victims and witnesses will be distressed as part of the side-effects of the lottery scheme than would suffer as part of the side-effects of not instituting it.

Lastly, a more limited objection might be made, not to the idea of killing to save lives, but to the involvement of 'third parties'. Why, so the objection goes, should we not give X's heart to Y or Y's lungs to X, the same number of lives being thereby preserved and no one else's life set at risk? Y's and Z's reply to this objection differs from their previous line of argument. To amend their plan so that the involvement of so called 'third parties' is ruled out would, Y and Z claim, violate their right to equal concern and respect with the rest of society. They argue that such a proposal would amount to treating the unfortunate who need new organs as a class within society whose lives are considered to be of less value than those of its more fortunate members. What possible justification could there be for singling out one group of people whom we would be justified in using as donors but not another? The idea in the mind of those who would propose such a step must be something like the following: since Y and Z cannot survive, since they are going to die in any event, there is no harm in putting their names into the lottery, for the chances of their dying cannot thereby be increased and will in fact almost certainly be reduced. But this is just to ignore everything that Y and Z have been saying. For if their lottery scheme is adopted they are not going to die anyway—their chances of dying are no greater and no less than those of any other participant in the lottery whose number may come up. This ground for confining selection of donors to the unfortunate therefore disappears. Any other ground must discriminate against Y and Z as members of a class whose lives are less worthy of respect than those of the rest of society.

It might more plausibly be argued that the dying who cannot themselves be saved by transplants, or by any other means at all, should be the priority selection group for the computer programme. But how far off must death be for a man to be classified as "dying"? Those so classified might argue that their last few days or weeks of life are as valuable to them (if not more valuable) than the possibly longer span remaining to others. The problem of narrowing down the class of possible donors without discriminating unfairly against some sub-class of society is, I suspect, insoluble.

Such is the case for the survival lottery. Utilitarians ought to be in favour of it, and absolutists cannot object to it on the ground that it involves killing the innocent, for it is Y's and Z's case that any alternative must also involve killing the innocent. If the absolutist wishes to maintain his objection he must point to some morally relevant difference between positive and negative killing. This challenge opens the door to a large topic with a whole library of literature, but Y and Z are dying and do not have time to explore it exhaustively. In their own case the most likely candidate for some feature which might make this moral difference is the malevolent intent of Y and Z themselves. An absolutist might well argue that while no one intends the deaths of Y and Z, no one necessarily wishes them dead, or aims at their demise for any reason, they do mean to kill A (or have him killed). But Y and Z can reply that the death of A is no part of their plan, they merely wish to use a couple of his organs, and if he cannot live without them . . . *tant pis!* None would be more delighted than Y and Z if artificial organs would do as well, and so render the lottery scheme otiose.

One form of absolutist argument perhaps remains. This involves taking an Orwellian stand on some principle of common decency. The argument would then be that even to enter into the sort of "macabre" calculations that Y and Z propose displays a blunted sensibility, a corrupted and vitiated mind. Forms of this argument have recently been advanced by Noam Chomsky (*American Power and the New Mandarins*) and Stuart Hampshire (*Morality and Pessimism*). The indefatigable Y and Z would of course deny that their calculations are in any sense "macrabre," and would present them as the most humane course available in the circumstances. Moreover they would claim that the Orwellian stand on decency is the product of a closed mind, and not susceptible to rational argument. Any reasoned defence of such a principle must appeal to notions like respect for human life, as Hampshire's argument in fact does, and these Y and Z could make comfortable to their own position.

Can Y and Z be answered? Perhaps only by relying on moral intuition, on the insistence that we do feel there is something wrong with the survival lottery and our confidence that this feeling is prompted by some morally relevant difference between our bringing about the death of A and our bringing about the deaths of Y and Z. Whether we could retain this confidence in our intuitions if we were to be confronted by a society in which the survival lottery operated, was accepted by all, and was seen to save many lives that would otherwise have been lost, it would be interesting to know.

There would of course be great practical difficulties in the way of implementing the lottery. In so many cases it would be agonizingly difficult to decide whether or not a person had brought his misfortune on himself. There are numerous ways in which a person may contribute to his predicament, and the task of deciding how far, or how decisively, a person is himself responsible for his fate would be formidable. And in those cases where we can be confident that a person is innocent of responsibility for his predicament, can we acquire this confidence in time to save him? The lottery scheme would be a powerful weapon in the hands of someone willing and able to misuse it. Could we ever feel certain that the lottery was safe from unscrupulous computer programmers? Perhaps we should be thankful that such practical difficulties make the survival lottery an unlikely consequence of the perfection of transplants. Or perhaps we should be appalled.

It may be that we would want to tell Y and Z that the difficulties and dangers of their scheme would be too great a price to pay for its benefits. It is as well to be clear, however, that there is also a high, perhaps an even higher, price to be paid for the rejection of the scheme. That price is the lives of Y and Z and many like them, and we delude ourselves if we suppose that the reason why we reject their plan is that we accept the sixth commandment.

NOTE

Thanks are due to Ronald Dworkin, Jonathan Glover, M. J. Inwood and Anne Seller for helpful comments.

16

The Problem of Abortion and the Doctrine of the Double Effect

Philippa Foot

ONE OF THE REASONS why most of us feel puzzled about the problem of abortion is that we want, and do not want, to allow to the unborn child the rights that belong to adults and children. When we think of a baby about to be born it seems absurd to think that the next few minutes or even hours could make so radical a difference to its status; yet as we go back in the life of the foetus we are more and more reluctant to say that this is a human being and must be treated as such. No doubt this is the deepest source of our dilemma, but it is not the only one. For we are also confused about the general question of what we may and may not do where the interests of human beings conflict. We have strong intuitions about certain cases; saying, for instance, that it is all right to raise the level of education in our country, though statistics allow us to predict that a rise in the suicide rate will follow, while it is not all right to kill the feeble-minded to aid cancer research. It is not easy, however, to see the principles involved, and one way of throwing light on the abortion issue will be by setting up parallels involving adults or children once born. So we will be able to isolate the "equal rights" issue, and should be able to make some advance.

I shall not, of course, discuss all the principles that may be used in deciding what to do where the interest or rights of human beings conflict. What I want to do is to look at one particular theory, known as the "doctrine of the double effect," which is invoked by Catholics in support of their views on abortion but supposed by them to apply elsewhere. As used in the abortion

---

From the *Oxford Review*, No. 5 (1967). Reprinted by permission of the author.

argument this doctrine has often seemed to non-Catholics to be a piece of complete sophistry. In the last number of the *Oxford Review* it was given short shrift by Professor Hart.[1] And yet this principle has seemed to some non-Catholics as well as to Catholics to stand as the only defence against decisions on other issues that are quite unacceptable. It will help us in our difficulty about abortion if this conflict can be resolved.

The doctrine of the double effect is based on a distinction between what a man foresees as a result of his voluntary action and what, in the strict sense, he intends. He intends in the strictest sense both those things that he aims at as ends and those that he aims at as means to his ends. The latter may be regretted in themselves but nevertheless desired for the sake of the end, as we may intend to keep dangerous lunatics confined for the sake of our safety. By contrast a man is said not strictly, or directly, to intend the foreseen consequences of his voluntary actions where these are neither the end at which he is aiming nor the means to this end. Whether the word "intention" should be applied in both cases is not of course what matters: Bentham spoke of "oblique intention," contrasting it with the "direct intention" of ends and means, and we may as well follow his terminology. Everyone must recognize that some such distinction can be made, though it may be made in a number of different ways, and it is the distinction that is crucial to the doctrine of the double effect. The words "double effect" refer to the two effects that an action may produce: the one aimed at, and the one foreseen but in no way desired. By "the doctrine of the double effect" I mean the thesis that it is sometimes permissible to bring about by oblique intention what one may not directly intend. Thus the distinction is held to be relevant to moral decision in certain difficult cases. It is said for instance that the operation of hysterectomy involves the death of the foetus as the foreseen but not strictly or directly intended consequence of the surgeon's act, while other operations kill the child and count as the direct intention of taking an innocent life, a distinction that has evoked particularly bitter reactions on the part of non-Catholics. If you are permitted to bring about the death of the child, what does it matter how it is done? The doctrine of the double effect is also used to show why in another case, where a woman in labour will die unless a craniotomy operation is performed, the intervention is not to be condoned. There, it is said, we may not operate but must let the mother die. We foresee her death but do not directly intend it, whereas to crush the skull of the child would count as direct intention of its death.[2]

This last application of the doctrine has been queried by Professor Hart on the ground that the child's death is not strictly a means to saving the mother's life and should logically be treated as an unwanted but foreseen consequence by those who make use of the distinction between direct and oblique intention. To interpret the doctrine in this way is perfectly reasonable given the language that has been used; it would, however, make nonsense of it from the beginning. A certain event may be desired under one of its descriptions, unwanted under another, but we cannot treat these as two different events, one of which is aimed at and the other not. And even if it be argued that there are here two different events—the crushing of the child's skull and its death— the two are obviously much too close for an application of the doctrine of the double effect. To see how odd it would be to apply the principle like this we may consider the story, well known to philosophers, of the fat man stuck in the mouth of the cave. A party of potholers have imprudently allowed the fat man to lead them as they make their way out of the cave, and he gets stuck, trapping the others behind him. Obviously the right thing to do is to sit down and wait until the fat man grows thin; but philosophers have arranged that flood waters should be rising within the cave. Luckily (luckily?) the trapped party have with them a stick of dynamite with which they can blast the fat man out of the mouth of the cave. Either they use the dynamite or they drown. In one version the fat man, whose head is *in* the cave, will drown with them; in the other he will be rescued in due course.[3] Problem: may they use the dynamite or not? Later we will find parallels to this example. Here it is introduced for light relief and because it will serve to show how ridiculous one version of the doctrine of the double effect would be. For suppose that the trapped explorers were to argue that the death of the fat man might be taken as a merely foreseen consequence of the act of blowing him up. ("We didn't want to kill him . . . only to blow him into small pieces" or even ". . . only to blast him out of the mouth of the cave.") I believe that those who use the doctrine of the double effect would rightly reject such a suggestion, though they will, of course, have considerable difficulty in explaining where the line is to be drawn. What is to be the criterion of "closeness" if we say that anything very close to what we are literally aiming at counts as if part of our aim?

Let us leave this difficulty aside and return to the arguments for and against the doctrine, supposing it to be formulated in the way considered most effective by its supporters, and ourselves bypassing the trouble by taking what must on any reasonable definition be clear cases of "direct" or "oblique" intention.

The first point that should be made clear, in fairness to the theory, is that no one is suggesting that it does not matter what you bring about as long as you merely foresee and do not strictly intend the evil that follows. We might think, for instance, of the (actual) case of wicked merchants selling, for cooking, oil they knew to be poisonous and thereby killing a number of innocent people, comparing and contrasting it with that of some unemployed gravediggers, desperate for custom, who got hold of this same oil and sold it (or perhaps *they* secretly gave it away) in order to create orders for graves. They strictly (directly) intend the deaths they cause, while the merchants could say that it was not part of their *plan* that anyone should die. In morality, as in law, the merchants, like the gravediggers, would be considered as murderers; nor are the supporters of the doctrine of the double effect bound to say that there is the least difference between them in respect of moral turpitude. What they are committed to is the thesis that *sometimes* it makes a difference to the permissibility of an action involving harm to others that this harm, although foreseen, is not part of the agent's direct intention. An end such as earning one's living is clearly not such as to justify *either* the direct or oblique intention of the death of innocent people, but in certain cases one is justified in bringing about knowingly what one could not directly intend.

It is now time to say why this doctrine should be taken seriously in spite of the fact that it sounds rather odd, that there are difficulties about the distinction on which it depends, and that it seemed to yield one sophistical conclusion when applied to the problem of abortion. The reason for its appeal is that its opponents have often *seemed* to be committed to quite indefensible views.

Thus the controversy has raged around examples such as the following. Suppose that a judge or magistrate is faced with rioters demanding that a culprit be found for a certain crime and threatening otherwise to take their own bloody revenge on a particular section of the community. The real culprit being unknown, the judge sees himself as able to prevent the bloodshed only by framing some innocent person and having him executed. Beside this example is placed another in which a pilot whose aeroplane is about to crash is deciding whether to steer from a more to a less inhabited area. To make the parallel as close as possible it may rather be supposed that he is the driver of a runaway tram which he can only steer from one narrow track on to another; five men are working on one track and one man on the other; anyone on the track he enters is bound to be killed. In the case of the riots the mob have five hostages, so that in both the exchange is supposed to be one man's life for the lives of five. The question is why we should say, without hesitation, that the driver should steer for the less occupied track, while most of us would be appalled at the idea that the innocent man could be framed. It may be suggested that the special feature of the latter case is that it involves the corruption of justice, and this is, of course, very important indeed. But if we remove that special feature, supposing that some private individual is to kill an innocent person and pass him off as the criminal we still find ourselves horrified by the idea. The doctrine of the double effect offers us a way out of the difficulty, insisting that it is one thing to steer towards someone foreseeing that you will kill him and another to aim at his death as part of your plan. Moreover there is one very important element of good in what is here insisted. In real life it would hardly ever be certain that the man on the narrow track would be killed. Perhaps he might find a foothold on the side of the tunnel and cling on as the vehicle hurtled by. The driver of the tram does not then leap off and brain him with a crowbar. The judge, however, needs the death of the innocent man for his (good) purposes. If the victim proves hard to hang he must see to it that he dies another way. To choose to execute him is to choose that this evil *shall come about,* and this must therefore count as a *certainty* in weighing up the good and evil involved. The distinction between direct and oblique intention is crucial here, and is of great importance in an uncertain world. Nevertheless this is no way to defend the doctrine of the double effect. For the question is whether the difference between aiming at something and obliquely intending it is *in itself* relevant to moral decisions; not whether it is important when correlated with a difference of certainty in the balance of good and evil. Moreover we are particularly interested in the application of the doctrine of the double effect to the question of abortion, and no one can deny that in medicine there are sometimes certainties so complete that it would be a mere quibble to speak of the "probable outcome" of this course of action or that. It is not, therefore, with a merely philosophical interest that we should put aside the uncertainty and scrutinize the examples to test the doctrine of the double effect. Why can we not argue from the case of the steering driver to that of the judge?

Another pair of examples poses a similar problem. We are about to give to a patient who needs it to save his life a massive dose of a certain drug in short supply. There arrive, however, five other patients each of whom could be saved by one-fifth of that dose. We say with regret that we cannot spare our whole supply of the drug for a single patient, just as we should say that we could not spare the whole resources of a ward for one dangerously ill individual when ambulances arrive bringing in the victims of a multiple crash. We feel bound to let one man die rather than many if that is our only choice. Why then do we not feel justified in killing people in the interests of cancer research or to obtain, let us say, spare parts for grafting on to those who need them? We can suppose, similarly, that several dangerously ill people can be saved only if we kill a certain individual and make a serum from his dead body. (These examples are not over fanciful considering present controversies about prolonging the life of mortally ill patients whose eyes or kidneys are to be used for others.) Why cannot we argue from the case of the scarce drug to that of the body needed for medical purposes? Once again the doctrine of the double effect comes up with an explanation. In one kind of case but not the other we aim at the death of the innocent man.

A further argument suggests that if the doctrine of the double effect is rejected this has the consequence of putting us hopelessly in the power of bad men. Suppose for example that some tyrant should threaten to torture five men if we ourselves would not torture one. Would it be our duty to do so, supposing we believed him, because this would be no different from choosing to rescue five men from his tortures rather than one? If so anyone who wants us to do something we think wrong has only to threaten that otherwise he himself will do something we think worse. A mad murderer, known to keep his promises, could thus make it our duty to kill some innocent citizen to prevent him from killing two. From this conclusion we are again rescued by the doctrine of the double effect. If we refuse, we foresee that the greater number will be killed but we do not intend it: it is he who intends (that is strictly or directly intends) the death of innocent persons; we do not.

At one time I thought that these arguments in favour of the doctrine of the double effect were conclusive, but I now believe that the conflict should be solved in another way. The clue that we should follow is that the strength of the doctrine seems to lie in the distinction it makes between what we do (equated with direct intention) and what we allow (thought of as obliquely intended). Indeed it is interesting that the disputants tend to argue about whether we are to be held responsible for what we allow as we are for what we do.[4] Yet it is not obvious that this is what they should be discussing, since the distinction between what one does and what one allows to happen is not the same as that between direct and oblique intention. To see this one has only to consider that it is possible *deliberately* to allow something to happen, aiming at it either for its own sake or as part of one's plan for obtaining something else. So one person might want another person dead, and deliberately allow him to die. And again one may be said to do things that one does not aim at, as the steering driver would kill the man on the track. Moreover there is a large class of things said to be brought about rather than either done or allowed, and either kind of intention is possible. So it is possible to *bring about* a man's death by getting him to go to sea in a leaky boat, and the intention of his death may be either direct or oblique.

Whatever it may, or may not, have to do with the doctrine of the double effect, the idea of *allowing* is worth looking into in this context. I shall leave aside the special case of giving permission, which involves the idea of authority, and consider the two main

divisions into which cases of allowing seem to fall. There is firstly
the allowing which is forbearing to prevent. For this we need a
sequence thought of as somehow already in train, and something
that the agent could do to intervene. (The agent must be able to
intervene, but does not do so.) So, for instance, he could warn
someone, but *allows* him to walk into a trap. He could feed an
animal but *allows* it to die for lack of food. He could stop a leaking
tap but *allows* the water to go on flowing. This is the case of
allowing with which we shall be concerned, but the other should
be mentioned. It is the kind of allowing which is roughly equivalent to *enabling;* the root idea being the removal of some obstacle
which is, as it were, holding back a train of events. So someone
may remove a plug and *allow* water to flow; open a door and
allow an animal to get out; or give someone money and *allow* him
to get back on his feet.

The first kind of allowing requires an omission, but there is no
other general correlation between omission and allowing, commission and bringing about or doing. An actor who fails to turn
up for a performance will generally spoil it rather than allow it
to be spoiled. I mentioned the distinction between omission and
commission only to set it aside.

Thinking of the first kind of allowing (forebearing to prevent),
we should ask whether there is any difference, from the moral
point of view, between what one does or causes and what one
merely allows. It seems clear than on occasions one is just as bad
as the other, as is recognized in both morality and law. A man
may murder his child or his aged relatives, by allowing them to
die of starvation as well as by giving poison; he may also be
convicted of murder on either account. In another case we would,
however, make a distinction. Most of us allow people to die of
starvation in India and Africa, and there is surely something
wrong with us that we do; it would be nonsense, however, to
pretend that it is only in law that we make a distinction between
allowing people in the underdeveloped countries to die of starvation and sending them poisoned food. There is worked into our
moral system a distinction between what we owe people in the
form of aid and what we owe them in the way of non-interference.
Salmond, in his *Jurisprudence,* expressed as follows the distinction
between the two.

A positive right corresponds to a positive duty, and is a right that he on whom the duty lies shall do some positive act on behalf of the person entitled. A negative right corresponds to a negative duty, and is a right that the person bound shall refrain from some act which would operate to the prejudice of the person entitled. The former is a right to be positively benefited; the latter is merely a right not to be harmed.[5]

As a general account of rights and duties this is defective, since not all are so closely connected with benefit and harm. Nevertheless for our purposes it will do well. Let us speak of negative duties when thinking of the obligation to refrain from such things as killing or robbing, and of the positive duty, e.g., to look after children or aged parents. It will be useful, however, to extend the notion of positive duty beyond the range of things that are strictly called duties, bringing acts of charity under this heading. These are owed only in a rather loose sense, and some acts of charity could hardly be said to be owed at all, so I am not following ordinary usage at this point.

Let us now see whether the distinction of negative and positive duties explains why we see differently the action of the steering driver and that of the judge, of the doctors who withhold the scarce drug and those who obtain a body for medical purposes, of those who choose to rescue the five men rather than one man from torture and those who are ready to torture the one man themselves in order to save five. In each case we have a conflict of duties, but what kind of duties are they? Are we, in each case, weighing positive duties against positive, negative against negative, or one against the other? Is the duty to refrain from injury, or rather to bring aid?

The steering driver faces a conflict of negative duties, since it is his duty to avoid five men and also his duty to avoid injuring one. In the circumstances he is not able to avoid both, and it seems clear that he should do the least injury he can. The judge, however, is weighing the duty of not inflicting injury against the duty of bringing aid. He wants to rescue the innocent people threatened with death but can do so only by inflicting injury himself. Since one does not *in general* have the same duty to help people as to refrain from injuring them, it is not possible to argue to a conclusion about what he should do from the steering driver case. It is interesting that, even where the strictest duty of positive aid exists, this still does not weigh as if a negative duty were involved. It is not, for instance, permissible to commit a murder to bring one's starving children food. If the choice is between inflicting injury on one or many there seems only one rational course of action; if the choice is between aid to some at the cost of injury to others, and refusing to inflict the injury to bring the aid, the whole matter is open to dispute. So it is not inconsistent of us to think that the driver must steer for the road on which only one man stands while the judge (or his equivalent) may not kill the innocent person in order to stop the riots. Let us now consider the second pair of examples, which concern the scarce drug on the one hand and on the other the body needed to save lives. Once again we find a difference based on the distinction between the duty to avoid injury and the duty to provide aid. Where one man needs a massive dose of the drug and we withhold it from him in order to save five men, we are weighing aid against aid. But if we consider killing a man in order to use his body to save others, we are thinking of doing him injury to bring others aid. In an interesting variant of the model, we may suppose that instead of killing someone we deliberately let him die. (Perhaps he is a beggar to whom we are thinking of giving food, but then we say "No, they need bodies for medical research.") Here it does seem relevant that in allowing him to die we are aiming at his death, but presumably we are inclined to see this as a violation of negative rather than positive duty. If this is right, we see why we are unable in either case to argue to a conclusion from the case of the scarce drug.

In the examples involving the torturing of one man or five men, the principle seems to be the same as for the last pair. If we are bringing aid (rescuing people about to be tortured by the tyrant), we must obviously rescue the larger rather than the smaller group. It does not follow, however, that we would be justified in inflicting the injury, or getting a third person to do so, in order to save the five. We may therefore refuse to be forced into acting by the threats of bad men. To refrain from inflicting injury ourselves is a stricter duty than to prevent other people from inflicting injury, which is not to say that the other is not a very strict duty indeed.

So far the conclusions are the same as those at which we might arrive following the doctrine of the double effect, but in others they will be different, and the advantage seems to be on the side of the alternative. Suppose, for instance, that there are five patients in a hospital whose lives could be saved by the manufacture of a certain gas, but that this inevitably releases lethal fumes into the room of another patient whom for some reason we are unable to move. His death, being of no use to us, is clearly a side effect, and not directly intended. Why then is the case different from that of the scarce drug, if the point about that is that we foresaw but did not strictly intend the death of the single patient? Yet it surely is different. The relatives of the gassed patient would presumably be successful if they sued the hospital and the whole story came out. We may find it particularly revolting that someone should be *used* as in the case where he is killed or allowed to die in the interest of medical research, and the fact of *using* may even determine what we would decide to do in some cases, but the principle seems unimportant compared with our reluctance to bring such injury for the sake of giving aid.

My conclusion is that the distinction between direct and oblique intention plays only a quite subsidiary role in determining what we say in these cases, while the distinction between avoiding injury and bringing aid is very important indeed. I have not, of course, argued that there are no other principles. For instance it clearly makes a difference whether our positive duty is a strict duty or rather an act of charity: feeding our own children or feeding those in far away countries. It may also make a difference whether the person about to suffer is one thought of as uninvolved in the threatened disaster, and whether it is his presence that constitutes the threat to the others. In many cases we find it very hard to know what to say, and I have not been arguing for any general conclusion such as that we may never, whatever the balance of good and evil, bring injury to one for the sake of aid to others, even when this injury amounts to death. I have only tried to show that even if we reject the doctrine of the double effect we are not forced to the conclusion that the size of the evil must always be our guide.

Let us now return to the problem of abortion, carrying out our plan of finding parallels involving adults or children rather than the unborn. We must say something about the different cases in which abortion might be considered on medical grounds.

First of all there is the situation in which nothing that can be done will save the life of child and mother, but where the life of the mother can be saved by killing the child. This is parallel to the case of the fat man in the mouth of the cave who is bound to be drowned with the others if nothing is done. Given the certainty of the outcome, as it was postulated, there is no serious conflict of interests here, since the fat man will perish in either case, and it is reasonable that the action that will save someone should be done. It is a great objection to those who argue that the direct intention of the death of an innocent person is never justifiable that the edict will apply even in this case. The Catholic doctrine on abortion must here conflict with that of most reasonable men. Moreover we would be justified in performing the operation whatever the method used, and it is neither a necessary nor a good justification of the special case of hysterectomy that the child's death is not directly intended, being rather a foreseen consequence of what is done. What difference could it make as to how the death is brought about?

Secondly we have the case in which it is possible to perform an operation which will save the mother and kill the child or kill the mother and save the child. This is parallel to the famous case of the shipwrecked mariners who believed that they must throw someone overboard if their boat was not to founder in a storm, and to the other famous case of the two sailors, Dudley and Stephens, who killed and ate the cabin boy when adrift on the sea without food. Here again there is no conflict of interests so far as the decision to act is concerned; only in deciding whom to save. Once again it would be reasonable to act, though one would respect someone who held back from the appalling action either because he preferred to perish rather than do such a thing or because he held on past the limits of reasonable hope. In real life the certainties postulated by philosophers hardly ever exist, and Dudley and Stephens were rescued not long after their ghastly meal. Nevertheless if the certainty were absolute, as it might be in the abortion case, it would seem better to save one than none. Probably we should decide in favour of the mother when

weighing her life against that of the unborn child, but it is interesting that, a few years later, we might easily decide it the other way.

The worst dilemma comes in the third kind of example where
to save the mother we must kill the child, say by crushing its
skull, while if nothing is done the mother will perish but the child
can be safely delivered after her death. Here the doctrine of the
double effect has been invoked to show that we may not intervene, since the child's death would be directly intended while the
mother's would not. On a strict parallel with cases not involving
the unborn we might find the conclusion correct though the reason given was wrong. Suppose, for instance, that in later life the
presence of a child was certain to bring death to the mother. We
would surely not think ourselves justified in ridding her of it by
a process that involved its death. For in general we do not think
that we can kill one innocent person to rescue another, quite apart
from the special care that we feel is due to children once they have
prudently got themselves born. What we would be prepared to
do when a great many people were involved is another matter, and
this is probably the key to one quite common view of abortion on
the part of those who take quite seriously the rights of the unborn
child. They probably feel that if *enough* people are involved one
must be sacrificed, and they think of the mother's life against the
unborn child's life as if it were many against one. But of course
many people do not view it like this at all, having no inclination
to accord to the foetus or unborn child anything like ordinary
human status in the matter of rights. I have not been arguing for
or against these points of view but only trying to discern some
of the currents that are pulling us back and forth. The levity of
the examples is not meant to offend.

NOTES

1. H. L. A. Hart, "Intention and Punishment," *Oxford Review,* 4 (Hilary 1967). Reprinted in H. L. A. Hart, *Punishment and Responsibility*
(Oxford, England: Oxford University Press, 1968). I owe much to this
article and to a conversation with Professor Hart though I do not know
whether he will approve of what follows.

2. For discussion of the Catholic doctrine on abortion see Glanville

Williams, *The Sanctity of Life and the Criminal Law* (New York, 1957); also N. St. John-Stevas, *The Right to Life* (London, 1963).

3. It was Professor Hart who drew my attention to this distinction.

4. See, e.g., J. Bennett, "Whatever the Consequences," *Analysis* (January 1966), 83–102, this volume, Chapter 10, and G. E. M. Anscombe's reply in *Analysis* (June 1966). See also Miss Anscombe's "Modern Moral Philosophy" in *Philosophy*, 33 (January 1958).

5. J. Salmond, *Jurisprudence*, ed. G. Williams (London, 1957), p. 283.

17

Killing and Letting Die

Philippa Foot

Is THERE a morally relevant distinction between killing and allowing to die? Many philosophers say that there is not, and further insist that there is no other closely related difference, as for instance that which divides act from omission, whichever plays a part in determining the moral character of an action. James Rachels has argued this case in his well-known article on active and passive euthanasia, Michael Tooley has argued it in in his writings on abortion, and Jonathan Bennett argued it in the Tanner Lectures given in Oxford in 1980.[1] I believe that these people are mistaken, and this is what I shall try to show in this essay. I shall first consider the question in abstraction from any particular practical moral problem, and then I shall examine the implications my thesis may have concerning the issue of abortion.

The question with which we are concerned has been dramatically posed by asking whether we are as equally to blame for allowing people in Third World countries to starve to death as we would be for killing them by sending poisoned food? In each case it is true that if we acted differently—by sending good food or by not sending poisoned food—those who are going to die because we do not send the good food or do send the poisoned food would not die after all. Our agency plays a part in what happens whichever way they die. Philosophers such as Rachels, Tooley, and Bennett consider this to be all that matters in determining our guilt or innocence. Or rather they say that although related things are morally relevant, such as our reasons for acting as we do and the cost of acting otherwise, these are only contin-

Reprinted from *Abortion and Legal Perspectives*, Jay L. Garfield and Patricia Hennessey, eds. (Amherst: University of Massachusetts Press, 1984), copyright © 1984 by the University of Massachusetts Press.

gently related to the distinction between doing and allowing. If we hold *them* steady and vary only the way in which our agency enters into the matter, no moral differences will be found. It is of no significance, they say, whether we kill others or let them die, or whether they die by our act or our omission. Whereas these latter differences may at first seem to affect the morality of action, we shall always find on further enquiry that some other difference—such as a difference of motive or cost—has crept in.

Now this, on the face of it, is extremely implausible. We are not inclined to think that it would be no worse to murder to get money for some comfort such as a nice winter coat than it is to keep the money back before sending a donation to Oxfam or Care. We do not think that we might just as well be called murderers for one as for the other. And there are a host of other examples which seem to make the same point. We may have to allow one person to die if saving him would mean that we could not save five others, as for instance when a drug is in short supply and he needs five times as much as each of them, but that does not mean that we could carve up one patient to get "spare parts" for five.

These moral intuitions stand clearly before us, but I do not think it would be right to conclude from the fact that these examples all seem to hang on the contrast between killing and allowing to die that this is precisely the distinction that is important from the moral point of view. For example, having someone killed is not strictly *killing* him, but seems just the same morally speaking; and on the other hand, turning off a respirator might be called killing, although it seems morally indistinguishable from allowing to die. Nor does it seem that the difference between 'act' and 'omission' is quite what we want, in that a respirator that had to be turned on each morning would not change the moral problems that arise with the ones we have now. Perhaps there is no locution in the language which exactly serves our purposes and we should therefore invent our own vocabulary. Let us mark the distinction we are after by saying that one person may or may not be 'the agent' of harm that befalls someone else.

When is one person 'the agent' in this special sense of someone else's death, or of some harm other than death that befalls him? This idea can easily be described in a general way. If there are difficulties when it comes to detail, some of these ideas may be best left unsolved, for there may be an area of indefiniteness reflecting the uncertainty that belongs to our moral judgments in some complex and perhaps infrequently encountered situations. The idea of agency, in the sense that we want, seems to be composed of two subsidiary ideas. First, we think of particular effects as the result of particular sequences, as when a certain fatal sequence leads to someone's death. This idea is implied in coroners' verdicts telling us what someone died of, and this concept is not made suspect by the fact that it is sometimes impossible to pick out a single fatal sequence—as in the lawyers' example of the man journeying into the desert who had two enemies, one of whom bored a hole in his water barrel while another filled it with brine. Suppose such complications absent. Then we can pick out the fatal sequence and go on to ask who initiated it. If the subject died by poisoning and it was I who put the poison into his drink, then I am the agent of his death; likewise if I shot him and he died of a bullet wound. Of course there are problems about fatal sequences which would have been harmless but for special circumstances, and those which although threatening would have run out harmlessly but for something that somebody did. But we can easily understand the idea that a death comes about through our agency if we send someone poisoned food or cut him up for spare parts, but not (ordinarily) if we fail to save him when he is threatened by accident or disease. Our examples are not problem cases from *this* point of view.

Nor is it difficult to find more examples to drive our original point home, and show that it is sometimes permissible to allow a certain harm to befall someone, although it would have been wrong to bring this harm on him by one's own agency, i.e., by originating or sustaining the sequence which brings the harm. Let us consider, for instance, a pair of cases which I shall call Rescue I and Rescue II. In the first Rescue story we are hurrying in our jeep to save some people—let there be five of them—who are imminently threatened by the ocean tide. We have not a moment to spare, so when we hear of a single person who also needs rescuing from some other disaster we say regretfully that we cannot rescue him, but must leave him to die. To most of us this seems clear, and I shall take it as clear, ignoring John Taurek's interesting if surprising argument against the obligation to save the greater number when we can.[2] This is Rescue I and with it I contrast Rescue II. In this second story we are again hurrying to the place where the tide is coming in in order to rescue the party of people, but this time it is relevant that the road is narrow and rocky. In this version the lone individual is trapped (do not ask me how) on the path. If we are to rescue the five we would have to drive over him. But can we do so? If we stop he will be all right eventually: he is in no danger unless from us. But of course all five of the others will be drowned. As in the first story our choice is between a course of action which will leave one man dead and five alive at the end of the day and a course of action which will have the opposite result. And yet we surely feel that in one case we can rescue the five men and in the other we cannot. We can allow someone to die of whatever disaster threatens him if the cost of saving him is failing to save five; we cannot, however, drive over *him* in order to get to *them*. We cannot originate a fatal sequence, although we can allow one to run its course. Similarly, in the pair of examples mentioned earlier, we find a contrast between on the one hand refusing to give to one man the whole supply of a scarce drug, because we can use portions of it to save five, and on the other, cutting him up for spare parts. And we notice that we may not originate a fatal sequence even if the resulting death is in no sense our object. We could not knowingly subject one person to deadly fumes in the process of manufacturing some substance that would save many, even if the poisoning were a mere side effect of the process that saved lives.

Considering these examples, it is hard to resist the conclusion that it makes all the difference whether those who are going to die if we act in a certain way will die as a result of a sequence that we originate or one that we allow to continue, it being of course something that did not *start* by our agency. So let us ask how this could be? If the distinction—which is roughly that between killing and allowing to die—*is* morally relevant, because it sometimes makes the difference between what is right and what is wrong, how does this work? After all, it cannot be a magical difference, and it does not satisfy anyone to hear that what we have is just an ultimate moral fact. Moreover, those who deny the relevance can point to cases in which it seems to make no difference to the goodness or badness of an action having a certain result, as, for example, that some innocent person dies, whether due to a sequence we originate or because of one we merely allow. And if the way the result comes about *sometimes* makes no difference, how can it ever do so? If it sometimes makes an action bad that harm came to someone else as a result of a sequence we *originated,* must this not always contribute some element of badness? How can a consideration be a reason for saying that an action is bad in one place without being at least a reason for saying the same elsewhere?

Let us address these questions. As to the route by which considerations of agency enter the process of moral judgment, it seems to be through its connection with different types of rights. For there are rights to noninterference, which form one class of rights; and there are also rights to goods or services, which are different. And corresponding to these two types of rights are, on the one hand, the duty not to interfere, called a 'negative duty', and on the other the duty to provide the goods or services, called a 'positive duty'. These rights may be in certain circumstances be overridden, and this can in principle happen to rights of either kind. So, for instance, in the matter of property rights, others have in ordinary circumstances a duty not to interfere with our property, though in exceptional circumstances the right is overridden, as in Elizabeth Anscombe's example of destroying someone's house to stop the spread of fire.[3] And a right to goods or services depending, for example, on a promise will quite often be overridden in the same kind of case. There is, however, no guarantee that the special circumstances that allow one kind of right to be overridden will always allow the overriding of the other. Typically, it takes more to justify an interference than to justify the withholding of goods or services; and it is, of course, possible to think that nothing whatsoever will justify, for example, the infliction of torture or the deliberate killing of the innocent. It is not hard to find how all this connects with the morality of killing and allowing to die—and in general with harm which an agent allows to happen and harm coming about through his agency, in my special sense having to do with originating or sustaining harmful sequences. For the violation of a right to noninterference consists in interference, which implies breaking into an existing sequence and initiating a new one. It is not usually possible, for instance, to violate that right to noninterference, which is at least part of what is meant by 'the right to life' by failing to save someone from death. So if, in any circumstances, the right to noninterference is the only right that exists, or if it is the only right special circumstances have not overridden, then it may not be permissible to initiate a fatal sequence, but it *may* be permissible to withhold aid.

The question now is whether we ever find cases in which the right to noninterference exists and is not overridden, but where the right to goods or services either does not exist or *is* here overridden. The answer is, of course, that this is quite a common case. It often happens that whereas someone's rights stand in the way of our interference, we owe him no *service* in relation to that which he would lose if we interfered. We may not deprive him of his property, though we do not have to help him secure his hold on it, in spite of the fact that the balance of good and evil in the outcome (counting his loss or gain and the cost to us) will be the same regardless of how they come about. Similarly, where the issue is one of life and death, it is often impermissible to kill someone—although special circumstances having to do with the good of others make it permissible, or even required, that we do not spend the time or resources needed to save his life, as for instance, in the story of Rescue I, or in that of the scarce drug.

It seems clear, therefore, that there are circumstances in which it makes all the difference, morally speaking, whether a given balance of good and evil came about through our agency (in our sense), or whether it was rather something we had the ability to prevent but, for good reasons, did not prevent. Of course, we often have a strict duty to prevent harm to others, or to ameliorate their condition. And even where they do not, strictly speaking, have a *right* to our goods or services, we should often be failing (and sometimes grossly failing) in charity if we did not help them. But, to reiterate, it may be right to allow one person to die in order to save five, although it would not be right to kill him to bring the same good to them.

How is it, then, that anyone has ever denied this conclusion, so sympathetic to our everyday moral intuitions and apparently so well grounded in a very generally recognized distinction between different types of rights? We must now turn to an argument first *given,* by James Rachels, and more or less followed by others who think as he does. Rachels told a gruesome story of a child drowned in a bathtub in two different ways: in one case someone pushed the child's head under water, and in the other he found the child drowning and did not pull him out. Rachels says that we should judge one way of acting as bad as the other, so we have an example in which killing is as bad as allowing to die. But how, he asks, can the distinction ever be relevant if it is not relevant here?[4]

Based on what has been said earlier, the answer to Rachels should be obvious. The reason why it is, in ordinary circumstances, "no worse" to leave a child drowning in a bathtub than to push it under, is that both charity and the special duty of care that we owe to children give us a positive obligation to save them, and we have no particular reason to say that it is "less bad" to fail in this than it is to be in dereliction of the negative duty by being the agent of harm. The level of badness is, we may suppose, the same, but because a different kind of bad action has been done, there is no reason to suppose that the two ways of acting will always give the same result. In other circumstances one might be worse than the other, or only one might be bad. And this last result is exactly what we find in circumstances that allow a positive but not a negative duty to be overridden. Thus, it could be right to leave someone to die by the roadside in the story of Rescue I, though wrong to run over him in the story of Rescue II; and it could be right to act correspondingly in the cases of the scarce drug and the "spare parts."

Let me now consider an objection to the thesis I have been defending. It may be said that I shall have difficulty explaining a certain range of examples in which it seems permissible, and even obligatory, to make an intervention which jeopardizes people not already in danger in order to save others who are. They following case has been discussed. Suppose a runaway trolley is heading toward a track on which five people are standing, and that there is someone who can possibly switch the points, thereby diverting the trolley onto a track on which there is only one person. It seems that he should so this, just as a pilot whose plane is going to crash has a duty to steer, if he can, toward a less crowded street than the one he sees below. But the railway man then puts the one man newly in danger, instead of allowing the five to be killed. Why does not the one man's right to noninterference stand in his way, as one person's right to noninterference impeded the manufacture of poisonous fumes when this was necessary to save five?

The answer seems to be that this is a special case, in that we have here the *diverting* of a fatal sequence and not the starting of a new one. So we could not start a flood to stop a fire, even when the fire would kill more than the flood, but we could divert a flood to an area in which fewer people would be drowned.

A second and much more important difficulty involves cases in which it seems that the distinction between agency and allowing is inexplicably irrelevant. Why, I shall be asked, is it not morally permissible to allow someone to die deliberately in order to use his body for a medical procedure that would save many lives? It might be suggested that the distinction between agency and allowing is relevant when what is allowed to happen is itself aimed at. Yet this is not quite right, because there are cases in which it does make a difference whether one originates a sequence or only allows it to continue, although the allowing is with deliberate intent. Thus, for instance, it may not be permissible to deprive someone of a possession which only harms him, but it may be reasonable to refuse to get it back for him if it is already slipping from his grasp.[5] And it is arguable that nonvoluntary passive euthanasia is sometimes justifiable although nonvoluntary active euthanasia is not. What these examples have in common is that *harm* is not in question, which suggests that the 'direct', i.e., deliberate, intention of *evil* is what makes it morally objectionable to allow the beggar to die. When this element is present it is impossible to justify an action by indicating that no *origination* of evil is involved. But this special case leaves no doubt about the relevance of distinguishing between originating an evil and allowing it to occur. It was never suggested that there will *always and everywhere* be a difference of permissibility between the two.

Having defended the moral relevance of the distinction which roughly corresponds to the contrast between killing and allowing to die, I shall now ask how it affects the argument between those who oppose and those who support abortion. The answer seems to be that this entirely depends on how the argument is supposed to go. The most usual defense of abortion lies in the distinction between the destruction of a fetus and the destruction of a human person, and neither side in *this* debate will have reason to refer to the distinction between being the agent of an evil and allowing it to come about. But this is not the only defense of abortion which is current at the present time. In an influential and widely read article, Judith Jarvis Thomson has suggested an argument for allowing abortion which depends on denying what I have been at pains to maintain.[6]

Thomson suggests that abortion can be justified, at least in certain cases, without the need to deny that the fetus has the moral rights of a human person. For, she says, no person has an absolute right to the use of another's body, even to save his life, and so the fetus, whatever its status, has no right to the use of the mother's body. *Her* rights override *its* rights, and justify her in removing it if it seriously encumbers her life. To persuade us to agree with her she invents an example, which is supposed to give a parallel, in which someone dangerously ill is kept alive by being hooked up to the body of another person, without that person's consent. It is obvious, she says, that the person whose body was thus being used would have no obligation to continue in that situation, suffering immobility or other serious inconvenience, for any length of time. We should not think of him as a murderer if he detached himself, and we ought to think of a pregnant woman as having the same right to rid herself of an unwanted pregnancy.

Thomson's whole case depends on this analogy. It is, however, faulty if what I have said earlier is correct. According to my thesis, the two cases must be treated quite differently because one involves the initiation of a fatal sequence and the other the refusal to save a life. It is true that someone who extricated himself from a situation in which his body was being used in the way a respirator or a kidney machine is used could, indeed, be said to kill the other person in detaching himself. But this only shows, once more, that the use of "kill" is not important: what matters is that the fatal sequence resulting in death is not initiated but is rather allowed to take its course. And although charity or duties of care could have dictated that the help be given, it seems perfectly reasonable to treat this as a case in which such presumptions are overridden by other rights—those belonging to the person whose body would be used. The case of abortion is of course completely different. The fetus is not in jeopardy because it is in its mother's womb; it is merely dependent on her in the way children are dependent on their parents for food. An abortion, therefore, originates the sequence which ends in the death of the fetus, and the destruction comes about "through the agency" of the mother who seeks the abortion. If the fetus has the moral status of a human person then her action is, at best, likened to that of killing for spare parts or in Rescue II; conversely, the act of someone who refused to let his body be used to save the life of the sick man in Thomson's story belongs with the scarce drug decision, or that of Rescue I.

It appears, therefore, that Thomson's argument is not valid, and that we are thrown back to the old debate about the moral status of the fetus, which stands as the crucial issue in determining whether abortion is justified.

NOTES

1. James Rachels, "Active and Passive Euthanasia," *New England Journal of Medicine*, 292 (January 9, 1975), 78–80; this volume, chapter 5: Michael Tooley, "Abortion and Infanticide," *Philosophy and Public Affairs*, 2, no. 1 (Fall 1972), 37–65; Jonathan Bennett, "Morality and Consequences," in *The Tanner Lectures on Human Values*, II, ed. Sterling McMurrin (Cambridge: Cambridge University Press, 1981), pp. 47–16.

2. John Taurek, "Should the Numbers Count?" *Philosophy and Public Affairs*, no. 4 (Summer 1977): 293–316.

3. G. E. M. Anscombe, "Modern Moral Philosophy," *Philosophy*, 33 (1958): 1–19.

4. Rachels, "Active and Passive Euthanasia."

5. Cf. Philippa Foot, "Killing, Letting Die, and Euthanasia: A Reply to Holly Smith Goldman," *Analysis*, 41, no. 4 (June 1981).

6. Judith Jarvis Thomson, "A Defense of Abortion," *Philosophy and Public Affairs*, 1 (1971), 44.

18

Saving Life and Taking Life

Richard Trammell

*The purpose of this paper is to examine the distinction between "nega-
tive" and "positive" duties. Special attention will be given to certain
criticisms raised against this distinction by Michael Tooley.*

A Paradigm Case

IF SOMEONE THREATENED to steal $1000 from a person if he did not
take a gun and shoot a stranger between the eyes, it would be
very wrong for him to kill the stranger to save his $1000. But if
someone asked from that person $1000 to save a stranger, it would
seem that his obligation to grant this request would not be as
great as his obligation to refuse the first demand—even if he had
good reason for believing that without his $1000 the stranger
would certainly die. Refraining from the action of killing is a kind
of "inaction" which it seems appropriate to call a "negative" duty.
Saving is a kind of "action" which it seems appropriate to call a
"positive" duty.[1] In this particular example, it seems plausible to
say that a person has a greater obligation to refrain from killing
someone than to save someone, even though the effort required
of him ($1000) and his motivation toward the stranger be assumed
identical in both cases. None of this is meant to exact analysis, but
rather as an initial indication of what seems to be a plausible view.

According to Tooley, one reason we intuitively feel greater
responsibility not to intervene harmfully than to aid is that harmful intervention usually implies a malicious motive whereas failure

Richard Trammell, "Saving Life and Taking Life," *Journal of Philosophy*, LXXII,
no. 5 (March 13, 1975), 131–37. Reprinted by permission of publisher and
author.

to aid often involves only indifference. Also it usually requires greater effort to perform positive action to save someone than to refrain from killing. Tooley[2] asks us to consider the following illustration:

> (1) Jones sees that Smith will be killed by a bomb unless he warns him. Jones's reaction is: "How lucky, it will save me the trouble of killing Smith myself." So Jones allows Smith to be killed by the bomb, even though he could easily have warned him. (2) Jones wants Smith dead, and therefore shoots him. Is one to say there is a significant difference between the wrongness of Jones's behavior in these two cases? Surely not. This shows the mistake of drawing distinction between positive and negative duties and holding that the latter impose stricter obligations than the former.

In some respects Tooley's illustration is misleading. For example, Jones's extreme hatred for Smith and his cynical joy at seeing Smith blown to bits have a "masking" or "sledgehammer" effect, which makes it difficult to evaluate the significance of the distinction between negative and positive duties. The fact that one cannot distinguish the taste of two wines when both are mixed with green persimmon juice does not imply that there is no distinction between the wines.

In addition, Tooley sets up his procedures in such a way that he arbitrarily excludes consideration of those cases where the prima facie claim for the moral relevance of the distinction between negative and positive duties is strongest. He stipulates that the cases of negative and positive duties considered must involve "minimal effort," thus eliminating from consideration cases in which effort is more than minimal *but still a constant.*

Suppose Tooley's example is modified as follows: Jones's attitude toward Smith is neutral in both cases. It costs Jones $1000 to save Smith from the bomb. It costs Jones $1000 to avoid shooting Smith. *Without introducing any new variables,* we have made Tooley's example parallel to the paradigm case; and now it ceases to appear that Jones has the same obligation to save Smith as not to kill Smith.

The paradigm case (or Tooley's, as modified above) provides *prima facie* justification for the claim that in some cases we are under greater obligation to avoid taking a life than to save a life, even though effort and motivation are constants. Anyone wishing to defend the moral equivalence of negative and positive duties should avoid introducing the ad hoc requirement of "minimal effort," since precisely one of the reasons for doubting the universal moral equivalence of negative and positive duties is that we feel obligated to go to almost any length to avoid killing someone, but not under equally great obligation to save someone.

Suppose it is granted that, in cases involving great effort, we are under greater obligation not to kill than to save—i.e., the distinction between positive and negative duties is morally significant. But it is also held that this distinction does not apply in cases of minimal effort. (This is perhaps Tooley's position, although he does not explicitly say so.) Then the following questions need to be answered. Does the distinction cease to hold gradually or suddenly? If suddenly, at what point in decrease of effort does the distinction cease to hold, and why? If gradually, why should the distinction cease to hold altogether at any point?

DISCHARGEABILITY OF DUTY

A number of factors underlie the distinction between negative and positive duties, one of which is the dischargeability of a duty. It is an empirical fact that in most cases it is possible for a person not to inflict serious physical injury on any other person. It is also an empirical fact that in no case is it possible for a person to aid everyone who needs help. The positive duty to love one's neighbor or help those in need sets a maximum ethic which would never let us rest except to gather strength to resume the battle. But it is a rare case when we must really exert ourselves to keep from killing a person.

In short, the negative duty of not killing can be discharged completely. The statement, "For every x, if x is a person, then y does not kill x" is true for many y's. But the positive duty of saving can never be discharged completely. The statement "For every x, if x is a person and x needs aid, y aids x" is not true for any y in the world.

Denial of the distinction between negative and positive duties leads straight to an ethic so strenuous that might give pause even to a philosophical John the Baptist. Compare the following two cases: (1) by spending a dollar (say to make a minor but essential repair on his car) Smith can avoid harming a person *(x)*; (2) by giving a dollar to charity, Smith can help a person *(y)* avoid harm. Suppose that Smith's motivation toward the people is the same, the effort is minimal and identical in amount, and each person will be saved from an equivalent amount of harm. Now suppose that Tooley is right and that Smith is as obligated to spend the dollar to help *y* as he is to spend the dollar to avoid hurting *x*. So Smith gives a dollar to charity. But the poor are always with Smith. Before he has a chance to fix his car, Smith notes that another dollar to this charity would have the same beneficial effect. Now perhaps giving this second dollar would come harder than the first. But still it would come no harder than the unspent dollar for the car repair; and thus Smith gives his second dollar to charity. Bit by bit, Smith gives away all his resources—reminding himself from time to time that he is just as obligated to give another dollar to charity as to fix his car. The problem is that, even though fulfillment of one particular act of aid involves only minimal effort, it sets a precedent for millions of such efforts. If one maintains as a general principle that we have equal duty not to kill as to save, then either one must uphold an ethic so strenuous that asceticism is the only morally defensible way of life; or else one must be willing to allow Smith to harm someone with his car for lack of a simple repair.

P. J. Fitzgerald, in his article "Acting and Refraining,"[3] makes a point related to what has been said above. Fitzgerald says that the duty to refrain from a certain action "merely closes off one avenue of activity," whereas the duty to perform a certain action "closes off all activities but one." Now it might seem that Fitzgerald is overlooking an essential point. Even though a negative duty is something we should not do, and hence involves a kind of inaction, there may be great effort involved in carrying out this inactivity. For example, someone may have to wreck his car to avoid running over someone else. The inaction involved in a negative duty does not necessarily imply freedom to do whatever we please. Sometimes to avoid killing someone might close off "all activities but one."

However, this apparent exception really proves the rule. There are billions of people whom we have a duty not to kill. It is an exceptional case indeed when fulfillment of this duty for any particular person imposes one specific action (like swerving a car to avoid hitting a pedestrian). Even in such exceptional cases, the specific action required can usually be quickly discharged, without recurrent obligation. As a rule, fulfilling the duty not to kill leaves us free to carry out a vast range of activities without constraint. The case is very different when it comes to the duty to save. The duty to save is "distractive" (Santayana's term) and demands of us the "one thing needful," preventing us from doing anything else. Thus P. J. Fitzgerald's formulation, even though there are various kinds of exceptional situations, gives overwhelming statistical support to the distinction between negative and positive duties.

THE OPTIONALITY PRINCIPLE

"Optionality" is a second important factor underlying the distinction between negative and positive duties. Some actions either destroy a good or make it impossible for anyone else to realize a certain good; whereas other actions do not destroy and perhaps leave open to others the option of realizing the good in question. Suppose that the continuation of x's life is good. Then obviously if someone kills x, not only does the killer fail to contribute toward the realization of this good; he also closes everyone else's option to do so. But if a Levite or priest merely passes by on the other side of x, then at least the option is left open for some Good Samaritan to come along and provide x the aid he needs to live.

A negative duty is a duty not to do an action that closes all options, not only for oneself but for everyone else, to realize a certain good that would (or might) have been realized if one had done nothing. A positive duty is the duty to do an action to bring about a certain good, which someone else might also have the option to bring about.

It should be noted that there is an essential difference between negative and positive duties in regard to the probability of the good being realized in case the duty is not met. There is a logical equivalence between y failing to meet the negative duty of not causing x to suffer at time z, and a probability of I that x suffer at time z; whereas there is *no* logical equivalence between y failing to meet the positive duty of relieving x from suffering at time z, and a probability of I that x suffer at time z. If x kills y, it is certain that y will not live; but if x fails to save y, someone else may still have the option of saving y.

RESPONSIBILITY

Still another factor underlying the distinction between negative and positive duties is responsibility. To illustrate this factor, consider the following case. A fire is started by Miller. Both Miller and Thompson, who also happens on the scene, witness a woman on the third floor crying for help. According to the responsibility factor, if everyone else is equal, Miller is more obligated to try to save the woman than Thompson, because Miller is responsible for the woman being in the situation of needing to be saved, whereas Thompson is not. In general, if x kills y, then x is responsible for y's death.[4] But if x fails to save y, then x may or may not be responsible for y being in the situation in which y needs to be saved. The more directly involved x is for y's needing to be saved, the more responsible x is for helping to rescue y. If, for example, x accidentally gave y poison, we might expect x to spend as much effort to save y as we would expect x to spend to avoid poisoning y to begin with. Certainly more would be required from x to save y than from uninvolved neighbor z. In the paradigm case, it was clear that, if the person shot the stranger between the eyes, he would be responsible for the stranger's death. But there was no reason for believing that the person was responsible for the other stranger's being in a position of needing to be saved. In the charity-versus-car-repair case, x is clearly responsible for hurting someone with his car through negligence; but x may very well not be responsible for the plight of the unfortunate administered to by charity.

To summarize, we have suggested three factors that underlie the distinction between negative and positive duties. The negative duty not to kill can be fully discharged, whereas the duty to save cannot. Failure to meet the duty of not killing cuts off any possibility of realizing the good connected with the life in question, whereas failure to save leaves open the option for someone else to save. Finally, a person is not necessarily responsible for someone else's needing to be saved; but he is responsible for the life of anyone he kills.

Tooley Again

In order to test the analysis developed in this paper, two additional illustrations from Tooley will be considered, beginning with his diabolical-machine[5] example:

> Imagine a machine which contains two children, John and Mary. If one pushes a button, John will be killed, but Mary will emerge unharmed. If one does not push the button, John will emerge unharmed, but Mary will be killed. In the first case one kills John, while in the second case one merely lets Mary die. Does one really wish to say that the action of intentionally refraining from pushing the button is morally preferable to the action of pushing it, even though exactly one person perishes in either case?

Failure to meet a negative duty makes the realization of some good impossible which would have been realized if one had not acted at all. But in evaluating whether or not an action prevents the realization of a "good," one must consider the over-all results of the action. In the case given by Tooley, whether one does or does not push the button, one person lives and one person dies. Therefore regardless of which action one chooses, there is no over-all good to be realized and no negative nor positive duty involved.

Tooley also raises the question why killing an infant is wrong, if refraining from conception is not wrong, since in both cases a potential human being is kept from coming to maturity. For x to kill an infant is to act in such a way that it closes out all options for anyone to realize the good involved in the infant's continued life. But if x acts to prevent his conceiving children, x does not take away any good the world would have had if x had done nothing.[6] Also, the duty to have all the children potentially involved in one's genes is a nondischargeable duty, since, regardless of how many children one had, one would be obligated to try to have some more. But the duty not to kill infants is a duty that can in the great majority of cases be easily discharged. No doubt other important principles differentiate the morality of contraception from infanticide. The distinction between negative and positive duties is one of these principles.

NOTES

1. Philippa Foot defends the view that we are more obligated to meet negative duties of not injuring people than to meet positive duties of helping them. See "The Problem of Abortion and the Doctrine of the Double Effect," *The Oxford Review*, 5 (1967), 5–15 (in this volume, chapter 16).

2. Michael Tooley, "Abortion and Infanticide," *Philosophy and Public Affairs*, 2, no. 1 (Fall 1972), 59–60.

3. *Analysis*, 37, no. 4 (March 1967), 133–39.

4. If y's death was unforeseeable and unavoidable, then x is not responsible in a moral sense. In this case one might wish to say that no negative duty has been violated, just as no positive duty would be violated if x had no way of knowing that y needed to be saved, or knew it but had no way of helping x.

5. Taken from a paper delivered by Michael Tooley at the American Philosophical Association Meeting, Eastern Division, held in Atlanta, Georgia, December 27–29, 1973. The paper is entitled "Abortion and Infanticide Revisited." The example is from pages 19–20. Tooley's original article, "Abortion and Infanticide," has been revised and published in a collection of essays entitled *The Problem of Abortion*, ed. Joel Feinberg (Belmont, Cal.: Wadsworth, 1973).

6. The case would be different if x had donated sperm for artificial insemination and then without justification tried to interfere with the conception process afterward.

19

The Priority of Avoiding Harm

N. Ann Davis

MANY NON-CONSEQUENTIALIST[1] philosophers have advanced views which involve or presuppose the claim that it is morally worse to (actively) bring about a bad outcome than it is to (merely) allow an equally bad outcome to obtain.

There are many variants of such a view. One of these, the Doctrine of the Double Effect (henceforth, DDE), is often employed by those whose moral principles take the form of absolute prohibitions. The DDE involves the claim that it is morally significant whether a bad outcome was *intended* by the agent or was *merely foreseen* as a side effect of his otherwise morally acceptable course of action. It is often applied in cases of performance of an action which results in a death. While it is held to be impermissible to aim at the death of another either as a means or as an end in itself, it may be permissible in certain circumstances for an agent to pursue a course of action which has the death of another as a foreseen consequence.[2] Many of those who defend the DDE have maintained that it is impermissible for a doctor to crush the skull of a fetus to save the life of the pregnant woman who will otherwise die in childbirth, even when the fetus could not be delivered alive in any case. In such a case, it is maintained, allowing the woman to die in labor is merely foreseeing her death, while crushing the skull of the fetus in order to save the woman's life would be intending to kill the fetus as a means to saving the woman. Defenders of the DDE have maintained in contrast to this that it is permissible for a doctor to perform a hysterectomy upon a pregnant woman who has a cancerous uterus; for even though the removal of the uterus would have the death of the fetus as a

Printed by permission of author.

foreseen consequence, the death of the fetus is not sought as a means of the saving of the woman.

Other philosophers, while certainly concerned with the agent's mental state with respect to the outcome of his[3] course of action, have not thought that the difference between what is intended and what is foreseen as a certain consequence is as important or as clear as proponents of the DDE suggest. They have been interested in other features of the agent's role in the production of the outcome. Many legal theorists and philosophers have claimed that it is significant whether an agent is actively doing harm or is merely passively failing to benefit. Thus Lord Macaulay has said

> It is, indeed, most highly desirable that men should not merely abstain from doing harm to their neighbours, but should render active service to their neighbours. In general, however, the penal law must content itself with keeping men from doing positive harm, and must leave to public opinion, and to the teachers of morals and religion the office of furnishing men with motives for doing good.[4]

Similarly, Sir David Ross maintains that while we have a duty to (actively) do others good, we have a stricter duty not to do others harm: "the duty of nonmaleficence is recognized as a distinct [duty] and as *prima facie* more binding" than the duty of beneficence. He illustrates this with these examples:

> We should not, in general, consider it justifiable to kill one person in order to keep another alive, or to steal from one in order to give alms to the other.[5]

Many people believe that it is morally significant whether a bad outcome is the result of an agent's act or the result of his omission to act. Thus two lines of A. R. Clough's (satirical) poem, "The Latest Decalogue"

> Thou shalt not kill, but need'st not strive
> Officiously to keep alive

are often solemnly quoted by medical personnel in support of allowing a suffering individual to die, but in opposition to actively killing him.[6] Thus it is held to be permissible to refrain from attaching a severely deformed neonate to a life-support system, or to refrain from performing the surgery that would enable him to survive, but impermissible to actively kill him (e.g.) by injecting him with a fatal dose of morphine.

Some of those who think that there is a significant difference between acting and omitting think this because they believe that to act and to thereby bring about a bad outcome is to harm, while to omit to act (or, differently, to "do nothing") is merely to fail to benefit. And they believe—with Macaulay and Ross—that duties not to harm are more stringent than duties to benefit. Others think that the significance of the distinction between acting and omitting is more derivative: it is of moral importance only when the agent would have different intentions or motives in omitting than he would in acting.[7] If, for example, the doctor who refrains from attaching the deformed infant to the life-support system does so because she wants the infant's suffering to be minimal (and so, given the prognosis, wants him dead), then her refraining from attaching him to the life-support system would be morally on a par with her injecting him with morphine. Still others feel that the difference between acting and omitting is morally important even when there is no substantive difference in motivation: since injecting the infant with morphine is a positive act, it is, they claim, in itself worse than refraining from attaching the infant to the life-support system.

Whichever form it takes, the belief that there is a morally significant asymmetry between actively causing a bad outcome and merely allowing a bad outcome to obtain lies at the heart of recent criticism of consequentialist moral theories (such as utilitarianism). What I shall suggest is that these moral asymmetry views face serious difficulties. They employ or presuppose various distinctions—acts versus omissions, harms versus mere failures to benefit, negative duties versus positive duties—which are unclear in themselves and equivocal in their application. We cannot examine here all extant forms of the moral asymmetry view, or all of the arguments and counterarguments concerning the viability of those forms which we do consider. But I believe that we may learn what sorts of problems confront moral asymmetry views (as a group) by examining one philosopher's view in some detail. Accordingly, I shall focus on Philippa Foot's elaboration and defense of the claim that negative duties (—duties not to actively harm—) are more stringent than positive duties (—duties to actively benefit).[8]

I

In "Abortion and the Doctrine of the Double Effect," Foot advances a principle which allows us to "reject the doctrine of the double effect" but "not [be] forced to the conclusion that the size of the evil must always be our guide" (p. 276). What she offers us is (what I shall call) a principle of the Priority of Avoiding Harm *(PAH)* which tells us:

> Other things equal, the obligation not to harm people is more stringent than the obligation to benefit people.[9]

The PAH is put forward as a rival to the (crude) consequentialist principle that "the size of the evil[10] must always be our guide," and as a replacement for the DDE. And it is touted as an improvement on both.

To see why Foot believes the PAH to be superior to consequentialism, we must look at some of her examples (which are presented here in a rather abbreviated and schematized form):

1. A: There is a runaway tram headed down a track with five people on it; if it continues down this track it will kill the five. The driver cannot stop the tram, but he can steer it. His choice is to continue down this track (and thereby kill the five) or to steer onto another track with one person on it, and kill that one.

   B: Unless we frame someone—declare him guilty and punish him for a crime that he did not commit—an angry mob will take revenge on five innocent people.

2. A: We have only five grains of a scarce medicine. We can use it to save five people, each of whom needs only a one-grain dose, or else use it to save one person who needs a five-grain dose.

   B: We can save five people if (and only if) we kill a sixth person and make a serum out of his body.

3. A: We send a rescue party to save people from a wicked tyrant's tortures. We can either save group *a*, which consists of five people, or group *b*, which consists of one (different) person.

B: Same wicked tyrant: unless we agree to torture one person, he threatens to torture five others.

Prima facie, the consequentialist would have us adopt the "numbers" solution to *all* of the above dilemmas. Nor is such a suggestion entirely counterintuitive. Most of us would concur with the consequentialist's solution to the A cases and agree that we should (e.g.) distribute the scarce medicine so that more rather than fewer people are saved (2A). But many of us would not espouse the 'numbers' solution in the B cases; we would agree with Foot that the 'size of the evil' should not be our *only* guide. Foot's PAH is supposed to allow us to escape the counterintuitive conclusion that we must adopt the 'numbers' solution in the B cases if we are to adopt it in the A cases. It is supposed to allow us to adopt the 'numbers' solution in the A cases but to reject it in the B cases.

According to Foot, the A cases involve only one kind of duty (the duty to benefit in 2A and 3A, and the duty not to harm in 1A), while the B cases involve conflicts between different kinds of duties (viz. duties to benefit and duties not to harm). Foot thinks that this is an important disanalogy between the A and B cases: "Since one does not *in general* have the same duty to help people as to refrain from injuring them" (p. 274) we may not argue from the A cases to the B cases. We can perhaps agree that we ought to act on some sort of restricted 'numbers' principle: other things equal, we should seek to benefit five rather than one when faced with the impossibility of benefiting all six, and to harm one rather than five when faced with the impossibility of harming none at all. But—according to Foot and the PAH—if there is a conflict between benefiting five and not harming one, it is not the (mere) numbers that determines the morally correct course of action.

But how does Foot arrive at the PAH? Why does she suggest that it is a good (non-consequentialist) replacement for the DDE? Foot thinks that in seeking a viable alternative to consequentialism

The clue that we should follow is that the strength of the doctrine [i.e., the DDE] seems to lie in the distinction it makes between what we do . . . and what we allow . . . [p. 272].

Accordingly, it is this distinction between "what one does or causes and what one merely allows" (p. 273) that Foot seeks to exploit as the basis for her claim that there is a difference between "what we owe people in the form of aid and what we owe them in the way of non-interference" (p. 273). And it is this latter difference which Foot takes Salmond to be expressing in his distinction between positive and negative duties, and to be embodied in the PAH.[11] Salmond characterizes positive duties as duties to "do some positive act[12] on behalf of the person entitled"—as duties to positively benefit someone—and negative duties as duties to "refrain from some act that would operate to the prejudice of the person entitled"[13]—as duties not to positively harm.

Thus the important contrasts, and those I shall discuss, are:

- The distinction between positive duties and negative duties.
- The distinction between duties to benefit and duties not to harm.
- The distinction between doing (or causing)[14] and merely allowing.

It is not easy to see what relations Foot believes to hold among these various distinctions. Nor is it easy to formulate and assess Foot's line of argument, for it is not clear which distinctions she means to be using to ground or explain others and which (if any) she takes to be strictly equivalent. Before going on to consider these distinctions and the relations among them, however, it is important that certain preliminary points be clarified.

(i) Whichever distinction (if any) is taken to be the fundamental basis of the PAH, it must be exclusive. If it is not exclusive, then a principle based on it will be inadequate, and when applied to cases, contradictory.

Consider the PAH understood as a principle about the relative stringency of negative and positive duties (as: other things equal, negative duties are more stringent than positive duties). If some duty d could be both a negative and a positive duty, then we could not, in a conflict situation, determine whether the PAH directed us to act in accord with d or to refrain from so doing. Suppose that the conflict were between (the double-aspect) d and some negative duty d'. We could not determine whether the PAH enjoined us to act in accord with d' or whether we could instead appeal to the restricted 'numbers' principle and go on to consider the number of people affected in each alternative. The same point can be expressed a bit differently. If d could be both a positive and a negative duty, then there could arise a situation in which one was instructed by the PAH to behave in accord with d (in so far as d is regarded as a negative duty—i.e., a duty not to actively harm), yet also *not* to behave in accord with d, but rather to behave in accord with some competing negative duty d' (in so far as d is regarded as a positive duty—i.e., a duty to positively benefit).

(ii) It seems reasonable to add a stiffer requirement, that we be able, in practice, to determine whether a given duty is a positive or a negative duty.[15] If the PAH is to be presented as a candidate for a moral principle, a principle which could guide our practice, then we must be able, in practice, to make the distinctions needed to employ it.

In fact it may be difficult to do this. A course of action may admit of one description that makes it seem a fulfillment of a duty to benefit while also admitting of another description that makes it seem a transgression of a duty not to harm. Suppose that we rig a Bingo game, and thus insure that the rich man will lose the $100 jackpot (which he would have won had we not tampered with the numbers) and the poor man will win it. Are we violating the (negative) duty not to harm the rich man, or are we acting in accord with the (positive) duty to benefit the poor man? Both? Neither? How is the answer to be determined?

(iii) In discussing the PAH, the view that we do not "*in general* have the same duty to help people as to refrain from injuring them" (p. 274), we must take care to distinguish Foot's non-consequentialist claim from a consequentialist rule of thumb which could be expressed in the same words. It might turn out in a particular case that violating a negative duty results in greater disutility than violating a positive duty. For example, Smith's stealing $50 may have worse consequences than her failing to pay a $50 debt or her failing to give the $50 to a charitable organization. But even if it were *generally* true that violating negative duties resulted in greater disutility than violating positive duties, this is not what Foot is claiming, and such a result would not support her principle of the Priority of Avoiding Harm. Since Foot is appealing to the PAH to support non-consequentialist solutions to (some of) her example cases, she cannot be advocating the view that *consequentialist* considerations provide the basis for the claim that negative duties are more stringent than positive duties.

(iv) If we are to be able to assess the claim that negative duties are more stringent than positive duties, then we must be able to determine independently whether doing x is violating a negative duty and whether doing x is (more) reprehensible. If the claim is to have force, then we should not be able to conclude that doing x offends against a negative duty rather than a positive duty simply on the ground that we think that doing x is (more) reprehensible. Sometimes it seems that Foot does just this:

> we may suppose that instead of killing someone we deliberately let him die. (Perhaps he is a beggar to whom we are thinking of giving food, but then we say "No, they need bodies for medical research.") Here it does seem relevant that in allowing him to die we are aiming at his death, but presumably we are inclined to see this as a violation of negative rather than positive duty [p. 275].

These remarks are puzzling and problematic. Why does Foot think that *this* letting-die is a violation of a negative duty when her remarks about the example cases suggest that she thinks that letting the tyrant torture the five (3B) and letting the five die at the hands of the angry crowd (1B) are not? A defender of the Doctrine of Double Effect might claim that the case of the beggar was not on a par with the other two, for in the case of the beggar we intend the death, while in the other two we merely foresee it. In Foot's language, in the beggar case we 'aim at' the death of the innocent man, while in 1B and 3B we do not. But if 'aiming at' an innocent man's death is transgressing a negative duty while foreseeing the death of the five is transgressing a positive duty, then it seems that the view that negative duties are more stringent than positive duties is merely the DDE couched in different language. If Foot's principle of the Priority of Avoiding Harm is not merely to reduce to the DDE, then it does not seem that Foot can maintain that letting the beggar die is violating a negative duty while letting the five be tortured by the tyrant or killed by the angry crowd is violating (only) a positive duty.

Perhaps if we look more closely at the distinctions that Foot employs we can find out what the difference between the cases is supposed to be and so get a sense of how Foot's view differs from consequentialism on the one hand, and the nonconsequentialist DDE on the other.

II

What I have called Foot's principle of the Priority of Avoiding Harm, the view that

> Other things equal, the obligation not to harm people is more stringent than the obligation to benefit people

admits of different interpretations, depending on whether it employs the distinction between negative and positive duties or the distinction between duties not to harm and duties to benefit. I shall discuss two interpretations of the PAH:

I. The Negative/Positive Duty Doctrine *(NPD)*: Other things equal, negative duties, understood as duties not to perform some positive act which harms, are more stringent than positive duties understood as duties to perform some positive act which benefits.

II. The Harm/Benefit Doctrine *(HBD)*: Other things equal, duties not to harm are more stringent than duties to benefit.

It may seem that we can treat the HBD as a special case of the NPD. It may seem that we can reason as follows: if negative duties are more stringent than positive duties, then one of the former—a duty not to harm—will be more stringent than one of the latter—a duty to benefit. But if we look more closely at the definitions of negative and positive duties, we shall see why we cannot reason in this way.

The NPD employs a double use of 'positive' that may be confusing. *Both* negative duties and positive duties concern (only) *positive acts*. (A positive act is, according to legal usage, either an act of commission or a bodily act.) A positive duty is positive in that it is a duty to *do* some positive act which benefits. A negative duty is negative in that it is a duty *not* to do some positive act which harms. In order to avoid confusion, I shall speak of negative duties as duties not to *actively* harm and of positive duties as duties to *actively* benefit. (By "Smith actively harmed Jones" I shall mean

"Smith performed some positive act which harmed Jones.") There are, then, *two* components in the definition of positive and negative duties. If Smith has a positive duty toward Jones, Smith is not merely bound to benefit Jones, she is bound to *actively* benefit Jones, to do some positive act which benefits Jones. Similarly, a negative duty is not a quite general duty to refrain from harming someone, but the narrower and more specific duty to refrain from *actively* harming someone. Thus if it is possible to harm or benefit someone by allowing—i.e., harm or benefit someone without doing some positive act—then the HBD *cannot* be merely a special case of the NPD. (And if one cannot benefit by allowing, then Salmond's phrase "positively benefit" is otiose.) In particular, someone could hold the HBD while denying that the distinction between doing and allowing is, as such, morally significant.

Since Foot thinks that "the strength [of the DDE] seems to lie in the distinction it makes between what we do . . . and what we allow" (p. 272) it seems reasonable to think that the NPD is a better interpretation of her PAH than the HBD is. The NPD explicitly concerns itself with the question of how the harm or benefit is produced. Thus the NPD leaves open the possibility of treating in-actively harming or benefiting (i.e., harming or benefiting by allowing or refraining) differently from the way we treat actively harming or benefiting. But the HBD embodies no such grounds for discrimination. Still, as we proceed, we shall see that it is far from obvious that the NPD is the interpretation of the PAH that Foot is seeking to defend.

This may give us some sense of what the DDE and the NPD have in common (that the DDE and the HBD do not). But it is more important—especially if the NPD is the more plausible interpretation of Foot's PAH—for us to have a sense of how the DDE and the NPD *differ*. Foot contends that "it is possible *deliberately* to allow something to happen, aiming at it either for its own sake or as part of one's plan for obtaining something else" (p. 272). If she is correct, then the distinction between what one does and what one allows to happen is not the same as (or co-extensive with) the distinction between what one intends and what one merely foresees. Since the difference between actively harming and in-actively harming seems to be a difference between doing and allowing rather than a difference between intending and merely foreseeing, the NPD and the DDE differ.

I claimed that if one can harm (or benefit) by allowing, then the HBD and the NPD differ. And I suggested that if it is possible to harm (or benefit) by allowing, the difference between them is that the NPD treats the distinction between doing and allowing as itself morally significant while the HBD does not. Suppose that it were said that our duties not to actively harm are more stringent than our duties to actively benefit, but our duties not to in-actively harm (to harm by allowing) are not more stringent than our duties to actively benefit. Then, unless it were maintained that the difference is to be explained by logical or pragmatic considerations, the distinction between doing and allowing would be thought to be, in itself, morally significant.

Though we cannot pursue them at any length, it is worthwhile looking at some of the nonmoral—pragmatic and purely conceptual—considerations that might incline someone to advance the NPD rather than the HBD. What we will look at, then, are considerations which suggest that it is preferable to advance the narrower NPD, but which do not depend on the view that the distinction between doing and allowing is in itself morally significant.

First, the restriction in scope to actively harming and actively benefiting could be based on the belief that it is easier to see that harm or benefit has been done, and to see who is responsible for it, when it is the result of some positive act than when it is the result of some 'negative act' (or allowing). Or such a restriction could be based on the belief that it is usually easier for us to refrain from acts which we believe will be harmful than it is to attempt acts which we believe will be beneficial. Or it could be based on the belief that we are more likely to be morally successful, or to be happy, if we refrain from performing positive acts which we believe will be harmful than if we undertake positive acts which we believe will be beneficial. It is worth noting, however, that these would be good rules of thumb just in case there seldom are cases in which it is clear who is responsible for the harm, and clear that it would have been more difficult for that person to have undertaken the positive action that would have prevented it.

Second, it might be maintained that there is a conceptual connection between positive acts (or doings) and benefits, or between positive acts and harms, which is such that we *cannot* speak of benefiting or harming unless there is a positive act. Such a view might be put forward by someone who reasoned as follows: To harm someone is to cause him to be worse off (and to benefit someone is to cause him to be better off) than he otherwise would have been. But if we are, in fact, doing nothing, then we cannot be said to have affected the way things would have been at all. To affect someone for the worse (better) is to cause him to be worse (better) off. But if we do nothing, then there is nothing (no event) that is our causing someone to be worse (better) off. Hence, we cannot harm (benefit) someone by doing nothing.

There is, I think, much to object to in this brief argument. One might wish to attack the tacit assumption that causes must be 'active forces' or (in more modern dress) the view that causal relations must be relations among events.[16] Or one might incline towards accepting the view that causal relations must be relations among events but object to the narrowness of the notion of harm that is being employed, the notion that *causing* harm to someone is the only way of harming him. One might maintain instead that to harm someone is not necessarily to *cause* harm to him, but is rather to be responsible for his suffering harm,[17] or (more barbarously) to have one's behavior be the best explanation for his suffering the harm that he does suffer. Resolution of these issues—particularly the issue of what sorts of causal relations are involved in ascriptions of responsibility for harm—is very important to legal thinking, to moral philosophy, and to other subjects concerned with questions of and about agency. But pursuit of these issues would take us too far afield. Hence the strategy that I shall follow here will be to suggest, by the use of (what I hope are) persuasive examples, that we do in fact believe that there are cases in which it is (properly) said that we have harmed another by 'doing nothing.' Consider the following:

> We are rock climbing. You ask me to drive in another piton so that you, who have a shorter reach than I, can execute a particularly difficult part of the climb. I agree, but in fact do not drive in the piton. Instead I remain seated in my safe position and watch you tumble down the mountain.

And the following:

> I am ice-fishing, and (since I am rather bored) I am putting a new notch in my harpoon. You skate up to me, not seeing the harpoon, which is angled directly at you. Though I believe that you will not see the harpoon until it is too late (you will either skate into the harpoon, or else fall through the ice in trying to avoid it), I do not move at all. You skate directly into my harpoon.

These examples should help defuse the claim that there is a conceptual connection between positive acts and harms that is such that we *cannot* speak of harming unless there is a positive act. And even if someone steadfastly refuses to allow that one's doing nothing can be said to *cause* harm, still the examples suggest that we regard people as harming when they are *responsible* for the harm whether or not they have actively caused the harm. And barring an argument to the effect that one is responsible only for harm that one has actively caused, that is all that is required. The pragmatic and conceptual considerations in favor of the NPD (in preference to the HBD) seem to me to be inconclusive and far from compelling. But in any case—whatever our assessment of the non-moral considerations' success—we need to determine which doctrine, the NPD or the HBD, is more in accord with Foot's PAH.

Which doctrine, the NPD or the HBD *is* more in accord with Foot's PAH? Unfortunately it is not easy to see what Foot is endorsing when she says that "one does not *in general* have the same duty to help people as to refrain from injuring them." She might be endorsing the conjunctive (two-tier) claim that:

(i) In most cases of conflict, the duty to benefit will be morally outweighed by the duty not to harm; and
(ii) In most cases in which the duty not to harm does outweigh the duty to benefit, not-harming would not involve performing a positive act, while benefiting would involve performing a positive act.

To make this conjunctive claim is not yet to propound the NPD. It is rather to propound the HBD and to maintain that there is a strong empirical correlation between fulfilling a positive duty and performing a positive act, and between violating a negative duty and performing a positive act.

Alternatively, Foot might be endorsing the claim that the duty not to harm *understood as* the duty to refrain from some positive act outweighs the duty to benefit *understood as* the duty to perform some positive act. (It is left an open question whether there is thought to be a conceptual connection between harming (or benefitting) and performing a positive act, or whether there is some other rationale for the restriction of scope.) On this second interpretation, the distinction between performing a positive act (doing) and allowing is treated as morally significant—for one has not, *a fortiori*, acted in accord with a duty to benefit unless one has performed a positive act—though it may not be morally overriding.[18]

III

In order to get clearer on Foot's view, we must consider more closely her remarks about allowing,

> the allowing which is forbearing to prevent. For this we need a sequence thought of as somehow already in train, and something that the agent could do to intervene [pp. 272–73].

And we need to consider

> whether there is any difference, from the moral point of view, between what one does or causes and what one merely allows [p. 273].

We must also bear in mind Foot's remarks to the effect that we must make sure that we concern ourselves with the question of whether a distinction is *itself* relevant to moral decisions and evaluations, not with whether it is relevant *when accompanied by* different degrees of certainty (p. 271). So the sort of cases we must compare are those in which the allowing and the doing are thought to issue equally certainly in their respective outcomes.

Foot says that sometimes an allowing is as bad as a doing and sometimes it is not. If a man kills his children[19] by allowing them to starve to death it is as bad as if he poisons them, but if we fail to send food to children in distant countries and so allow them to starve to death it is not as bad as if we send them poisoned food.[20] But what is the difference? When is allowing morally on a par with doing? And, when allowing *is* morally on a par with doing, is it harming rather than merely failing to benefit?

That Foot does not undertake to explain the difference between the two is not itself a criticism, for a complete account of when it is that allowing is as bad as doing and when it is not is quite beyond the scope of her article. But without some idea of what the asymmetry is supposed to be we cannot address satisfactorily the question of whether there is a moral difference between doing and allowing, and so cannot assess Foot's principle of the Priority of Avoiding Harm. So I shall offer some speculations on what the asymmetry between the two cases might be thought to be.

The asymmetry might be held to lie in the fact that we merely foresee the death of the distant children whom we allow to starve to death, while the man intends the death of the children—his children—whom he does not feed. Presumably Foot would not wish to embrace *this* as the basis of the difference, for to do so would be merely to reaffirm the DDE.

Alternatively, the ground of the difference might lie in the fact that the children whom we allow to starve are not our own children, while the ones whom the man allows to starve are his children. Parents (it might be pointed out) have special responsibilities and so prior obligations to prevent their children from coming to grief for want of necessities. But we have no special responsibility for or prior obligation to children in distant lands. When someone occupies a role in virtue of which he is specially responsible for seeing to it that a certain outcome does not obtain, allowing that outcome is—or is as bad as—harming. So the parent harms his children by allowing them to die of starvation, but we, who occupy no role vis-à-vis the children in distant lands, do not harm them by allowing them to starve to death.

This reply—the appeal to roles—would give Foot the required asymmetry. But it would do so at a high cost: the abandonment or restriction of the claim that the distinction between doing and allowing is of moral import, and the abandonment of the NPD in favor of the (wider) HBD. The claim that one has a more stringent duty not to harm than to benefit will not, in role cases, be in any generally specifiable way correlated with the distinction between doing and allowing. And so it will not correspond to and should not be expressed as the NPD. If it is held to be as bad to allow one's children to starve to death as it is to poison them even though the duty to feed one's children is alleged to be only a positive duty, then we have no alternative but to conclude that negative duties are *not* more stringent than positive duties. For here is a (supposed) positive duty that is every bit as stringent as a negative duty.

But perhaps we need not be faced with this difficulty. Perhaps—since the duty to bring one's children food seems to be as strict as the duty not to poison them—allowing one's children to starve to death is violating a negative duty and not, as was suggested above, violating a positive duty. This is, however, a less satisfactory solution. If we say that allowing one's children to starve is violating a negative duty, we have conceded that one may be violating a negative duty when one is not actively harming anyone—violating a negative duty merely by allowing harm to obtain. We have conceded that a negative duty may enjoin us to perform a positive act. And this either contradicts the definition of a negative duty as a duty not to actively harm, or else employs the wide notion of harm that is the notion involved in the HBD. (The HBD is silent on whether duties not to harm may be duties to some positive act.)

These considerations do not completely undermine the NPD, but they do drastically restrict its sphere of application. We cannot apply the NPD in cases in which the obligations associated with one role conflict with those associated with another: if, in role cases, positive duties are as stringent as negative duties, then in comparing the negative duty affiliated with one role to the positive duty affiliated with another role, we are comparing a negative duty with a duty that is as stringent as a negative duty, which is like comparing two negative duties. And so, presumably, we would be driven to adopt a consequentialist solution—to consider the 'size of the evil'—every time two role duties conflict. (There may be similar difficulties in cases in which role obligations conflict with non-role obligations.)

This is an important concession to consequentialism in several respects. First, of course, it allows us to adopt consequentialist solutions in a wider range of cases. But—more important—it seems to weaken the ground needed to withstand further consequentialist encroachment. Once it is conceded that allowing can be harming (or as bad as harming), it cannot simply be assumed that role cases will prove to be the only cases in which allowing can be harming (or as bad as harming). An explanation-cum-defense is required for the claim that role and non-role obligations differ so significantly. And it may well turn out that some non-role cases share a sufficient number of features with role cases, and consequently that allowing can be harming (or as bad as harming) in non-role cases as well.

This point is important, and so worth expanding. The claim that the agent's occupying a role determines whether his allowing a harm to come about is to be considered harming or merely failing to benefit is not convincing as a reply to the consequentialist challenge. To attribute such significance to roles is, in effect, to say that the stringency (or perhaps just the existence) of prior obligation determines whether allowing is harming or merely failing to benefit. But the consequentialist will be quick to point out that the sense in which it is true that one has a more stringent obligation to do something if one has a prior (or a role) obligation to do it is trivial, and irrelevant to the case at hand. One is more obligated to do something if one has a prior obligation to do it than if one has *no* obligation to do it. But what is in question is whether the obligations generated by a role are overriding—e.g., whether the special responsibility that attaches to someone in virtue of his occupying a role overrides the general utilitarian requirement of beneficence. To call allowings that are failures to meet special (or role) responsibilities *harms* and the allowings that are failures to meet the duty of beneficence *mere failures to benefit,* and then to maintain that duties not to harm are more stringent than duties to benefit is simply to evade (or beg) the difficult questions. We need to know *why* role obligations are to be accorded moral precedence when they conflict with non-role obligations, even if more people stand to benefit by our choosing to act in accord with the non-role obligation (and in particular, the utilitarian obligation of beneficence). Why is it morally significant whether the harm is brought about or merely allowed to come about? Why is this less significant when the agent occupies some special role?

Let us return to Foot's view in the light of this discussion of roles. Since one of Foot's declared interests is in the distinction between doing (or causing) and merely allowing, it would seem that the interpretation of the PAH that she would wish to put forward would be the NPD rather than the HBD, for the HBD does *not* employ or depend on the distinction between doing and allowing. But as we have seen, Foot believes that allowing can be as bad as doing, that allowing can harm or be as bad as harming. And so it appears that she would not be willing to put forward the NPD: for the NPD seems to assign too much significance to the distinction between doing and allowing. Thus, if her view is to be practicable, and plausible as an alternative to consequentialism, we must have some way of determining when an allowing is as bad as a doing (other than by appealing to our pre-critical beliefs about the reprehensibility of a particular case of allowing harm to occur). The proposal that an allowing is as bad as a doing when the agent occupies a role does not accomplish these ends.

In fact, it does not seem that Foot wishes to put much weight upon roles. Though she says that it is possible for a man to murder his children by allowing them to die of starvation, and that to do so is as bad as to give them poison, she suggests that one has only a positive duty rather than a negative duty to bring one's starving children food:

> It is interesting that, even where the strictest duty of positive aid exists, this still does not weigh as if a negative duty were involved. It is not, for instance, permissible to commit a murder to bring one's starving children food [pp. 274–75].

Though this might solve some difficulties, it raises more formidable ones. Either when the man murders his children by allowing them to starve he violates only a positive duty, or it is the difference of intentions between Jones, the man who murders his children, and Smith, the woman who refuses to murder to feed her children, that explains the difference in stringency: how it can be that Jones violates a negative duty while Smith violates only a positive duty. For, *ex hypothesi,* the difference does not lie in the gravity of the consequences (the 'size of the evil') or the method of their coming about: in both cases an allowing is involved which results in the death of the children.

If Foot were to say that Jones violates a negative duty, her position would still be problematic. She would need either to qualify her notions of negative and positive duty (abandoning Salmond's account)—perhaps replace them with the wider notions of harm and benefit that are incorporated in the HBD—or else go into greater detail on the question of just how her PAH differs from the DDE. For it would otherwise look as if her view were that when a bad outcome (e.g., the death of the children) is merely foreseen, only a positive duty is violated; while when a bad outcome is intended, a negative duty is violated: it would no longer be the distinction between doing and allowing that was carrying the weight. Instead, the relevant distinction would seem to be that between allowing-where-the-outcome-is-intended and allowing-where-the-outcome-is-merely-foreseen, and the result would seem to be some sort of higher-level DDE.

The best conjecture is that Foot would opt for the first horn of the dilemma and say that both Smith and Jones violate positive duties. We would then wish to ask: But what is the basis for the claim that Jones murders and Smith does not, that Jones' behavior is so much worse than Smith's?

Foot (or a hypothetical Foot, for we have moved quite a way beyond the text of the article) might offer the following reply: When you can feed your children without violating a negative duty, to violate the positive duty to feed your children is morally unjustifiable. Indeed, in some cases it is so bad morally that we call it murder. Though negative duties outweigh positive duties, positive duties—at least the strictest ones—still have a strong claim upon us.

Such a reply seems a plausible one. But it is still problematic, particularly for someone who wishes to espouse some version of Foot's principle of the Priority of Avoiding Harm. Which positive duties are the strictest and why? The hypothetical reply should not, of course, be expected to provide a ready answer to this; still, unless we can get a grip on some of the difficulties it raises, the hypothetical reply cannot even offer us the basis for an answer. If we say: One positive duty is stricter than another if failure to act in accord with the first results in greater harm than failure to in accord with the second, then a lot of weight must be put on whether the harm comes about through a doing or through an allowing, for otherwise the distinction between positive and negative duties will threaten to collapse. If a failure to fulfill a positive duty can be a harm (as well as a failure to benefit), then what distinguishes negative duties from positive duties? (For a failure to fulfill a negative duty can be a failure to benefit as well as a harm.) If failure to fulfill a negative duty results in n amount of harm, and failure to fulfill a positive duty results in n amount of harm, then, in the case of the negative duty, it must be the fact that the harm came about through a doing (rather than through an allowing) that accounts for the negative duty's greater stringency.

There is a more promising line. One might say that one positive duty is stricter than another if it is permissible for us to fail to fulfill the first for reasons other than that it conflicts with a negative duty, but permissible to fail to fulfill the second only when it conflicts with a negative duty. I have a positive duty to return the dollar that I borrow from you, but if it would produce great disutility for me to do so it is not worth worrying about: I may fail to fulfill this positive duty for a reason other than that it conflicts with a negative duty. On the other hand, it is permissible for me to fail to feed my children only when I would have to violate a negative duty in order to feed them; the fact that it would produce great disutility to get them fed does not (itself) lessen the obligation. But this way of describing the difference between the two cases seems neither illuminating nor satisfying. We seem merely to be appealing to our pre-critical beliefs about the moral stringency of our various obligations, not systematizing or defending these beliefs.

There is, however, a more pressing problem. Is it being maintained that *any* negative duty outweighs *any* positive duty? Why does Foot (in the passage quoted) compare such a strict negative duty with the strict(est) positive duty to bring one's starving children food? Surely if her intention were to show that negative duties (as such) outweigh positive duties (as such) then her point would be more forcefully made if she compared a rather weak negative duty with the strong positive duty to bring one's children food. But in fact, such a comparison would undermine rather than underscore her thesis. Though we might be inclined to agree that one may not violate very strict negative duties to act in accord with positive duties, we would surely allow that it is permissible to violate *some* negative duties in order to act on strict positive duties. Though we might be inclined to agree that one may not commit a murder in order to bring one's starving children food, we tend to think that it is permissible to steal a loaf of bread (or perhaps even break an arm) to get the starving children fed.

This is a damaging criticism. Since it is so damaging, we should consider the possibility that some misinterpretation of the claim that negative duties are more stringent than positive duties is involved. Perhaps what Foot means is that negative duties outweigh their *corresponding* positive duties, where a negative duty and a positive duty are said to correspond when failure to fulfill one results in the same sort of harm as failure to fulfill the other. Thus the negative duty not to kill Brown (by a positive act— e.g., shooting her) would correspond to the positive duty to save Green (by a positive act—e.g., giving him the antidote to a poison). In each case the outcome of transgressing the duty could be said to be a death, and we could speak of this negative duty and this positive duty as 'corresponding duties concerning death.'

Interpreting the claim in this way would enable us to understand why Foot compares the strict positive duty to bring one's children food with the strict negative duty not to murder (by a positive act). It would also render the position more plausible, for the unqualified thesis that negative duties outweigh positive duties seems doubtful especially in cases in which we harm the very well off just a little in order to benefit those badly off a great deal.

But even this restricted thesis faces problems. Though it is, in the case of death, reasonably clear what the corresponding duties are, it is not so clear in the case of other sorts of harm. Even when the actual injuries differ, we may feel that there is an equal amount of harm done (or not prevented). For example, we may think that a composer suffers as much harm by being deafened as a sculptor does by being blinded; that a dancer would suffer greater harm by losing a toe from frostbite than a sedentary academic would suffer by losing a foot. It may be that when we try to determine what duties correspond, we are appealing to the 'size of the evil' that would come about—appealing, that is, precisely to a consequentialist notion of harm or disutility.

But even if we can solve this problem of commensurability (without having to appeal to a consequentialist measure), a more serious problem remains for the restricted thesis. If Foot's view is that negative duties outweigh positive duties when the negative duties and positive duties correspond, then it will not underwrite refusal to inflict some harm to procure greater benefit. Though we will not be permitted to inflict *serious* harm on someone in order to prevent serious harm to someone else, we may be permitted to inflict less serious harm on one person to prevent graver injury to another (or others). But on this reasoning, it would seem to be permissible for us to choose the 'numbers' solution to at least some of the B cases; to frame the one in order to prevent the savage murder of the five (1B), and perhaps to kill the one to save the five from a more horrible death (3B). This would weaken the position considerably.

We seem to be confronted by a dilemma. If the NPD is to be understood as a view about corresponding negative and positive duties, then, if only the same types of harm can be compared, it is so restricted as to be virtually useless, and it will yield conclusions which Foot would not accept. On the other hand, if different types of harm can be compared, the restricted form of the NPD seems to presuppose a view of how serious different harms are, a catalogue of comparison which can (and perhaps must) be made before the fact, thus enabling us to say before the fact which negative duties and which positive duties are corresponding duties.

Clearly it is the second horn of the dilemma which is the more attractive. But what would be, on such a view, the basis for the claim that a given negative duty is more stringent than its corresponding positive duty? It cannot be the belief that greater harm obtains (this either violates the definition of corresponding duties, or threatens to collapse into consequentialism). It must be the belief that it is worse to harm by doing than it is to allow an equal amount of harm, that it is worse to actively harm than it is to in-actively harm. This raises the obvious question: *Why* would someone think that it is worse to actively harm than it is to allow an equal amount of harm to come about? The belief that it is worse to actively harm might be based on a foundational belief in the moral importance of the distinction between doing and allowing: it just *is* worse to harm by doing. In the light of our earlier discussion of the difficulties in formulating and defending this claim, the view seems both dogmatic and not very plausible.

A more plausible suggestion is that the concern with whether harm was produced by an agent's positive act reflects concern with the agent's intention, motive, and responsibility for the harmful outcome. When a bad outcome is not connected with or realized through an agent's positive act, there is greater likelihood that the agent was indifferent to, or even oblivious of, the harm's coming about than there is in the case in which it is his positive act that is responsible for the harm. Conversely, if harm comes about through an agent's positive acts (where it would have been possible for him to have refrained from so acting), there is greater reason to think that he welcomed the bad outcome, and that he was willing to expend some energy in order to see that it was realized.

Several things should be pointed out. First, if this were correct, it might suggest that there was a statistical correlation between bad motives or intentions and *positive* acts that is not so strong in the case of bad motives or intentions and *negative* acts (e.g., allowings and refrainings). It might suggest that there was a greater empirical likelihood that bad motives and intentions would be associated with the agent's actively bringing about the harm, but it would not suggest that there is any sort of tight conceptual connection between bad motives and positive acts. Where we do not think that allowing or refraining is a sign of reluctance, or that it is evidence of the agent's ignorance of the fact that harm will result unless he takes steps to prevent it; where we do not think that the agent's mere allowing or refraining is a pre-condition of his engaging in some other worthwhile activity; and where we are reasonably sure of the causal relations between his allowing and the bad outcome's coming about, then we do not regard the difference between doing and allowing as morally significant. If I know that my ferocious dog will attack you if I (continue to) do nothing—he has been trained to do such things— is this any different morally from my giving the dog the command to attack, or from my otherwise not preventing him from attacking? I do not believe that many people would think so.

In so far as the belief that it is worse to actively harm than it is to merely allow harm to come about is plausible, I think that it is likely to be either a reflection of a statistical view along the lines of the one just discussed, or else a belief based on views about justice or about agency. The root intuition might be one about justice: that it is *unfair* to inflict n amount of harm on one person (or group of persons) simply in order to bring about n (on even $n + m$) amount of benefit to others.[21] Or the root intuition might be one about agency: that it is wrong (or incoherent) to treat some agents merely as means to achieving benefits for other agents, wrong to *use* one person's suffering to benefit another person. We shall touch upon some of these views in greater depth later.

IV

More difficulties beset allowing.

We noted that allowing requires the notion of "a sequence thought of as somehow already in train, and something the agent could do to intervene." But it seems plausible that what people see as constituting a sequence depends upon their beliefs about what usually follows what. Different people will have different expectations and so will see different things as constituting sequences. In consequence, not everyone will identify the same not-doings as allowings. This is important, for whether or not we see something as a sequence, or a particular not-$x$ing as an allowing, may well affect our moral beliefs about whether people act wrongly in not doing x. And conversely, our beliefs about what people are morally obligated to do may well affect our expectations about what people will do, and so affect our views about what is a sequence and what is not.

Most of us do not, in fact, expect that people will sacrifice their comforts in order to help improve conditions in Indian villages, and so do not, in fact, regard them as *allowing* the Indians to languish. (Yet most of us believe that the Indians will languish unless they are helped, and believe that our aid could prevent the Indians' suffering.) Whether this is because we do not see slow death from overwork and undernourishment as a sequence, or because we do not, in fact, expect that people will 'intervene,' is a moot point. Our purpose here is met if we note that what we view as a sequence, and what our expectations are, may not be independent of our unscrutinized or uncritical beliefs about what people can do and ought to do to prevent undesirable outcomes. Unless there are other ways of deciding whether someone *allows* a particular outcome to obtain, and whether he harms by allowing that outcome to obtain, then it seems that the language of harming and allowing may inescapably embody an uncritical view of the limits of obligation, and so should not simply be called upon to try to determine the limits of moral obligation.

Foot tells us that (this kind of)

> allowing requires an omission, but there is no other general correlation between omission and allowing, commission and bringing about or doing. An actor who fails to turn up for a performance will generally spoil it rather than allow it to be spoiled [p. 273].

The actor spoils the play by not turning up. Though his not showing up does not seem to be a doing, he can spoil the play without doing anything else. It might seem, then, that there are two senses of 'do' or 'act' involved here: a sense to which the allowing (or omitting) is contrasted, and a sense under which it is to be subsumed.

But this suggestion seems to bring us little advantage. The sense in which the actor is not doing anything else (the narrower sense) is neither that he is making no bodily movement nor that he is performing no intentional actions. Though the actor could be sleeping soundly at curtain time (and so be motionless and engaged in no intentional action), he need not be. All that 'he spoiled the play by not turning up' seems to mean is that the play was spoiled and his not turning up was the cause or the best explanation of it.

In fact, 'spoils,' like some other doing verbs, sometimes imputes neither intention nor foresight, nor opportunity or ability to do otherwise. Sometimes it may mean no more than 'causes (or is the best explanation for) the spoiling of.' If it turns out that the actor was twenty miles away from the theater at curtain time, changing a flat tire, it will not be any less true that he spoiled the play, though we will probably add "but it was not his fault." Roughly the same can be said of 'kills.' The driver of a car that has gone out of control kills the people that she crashes into, though she could not avoid doing so. We may often want to refrain from saying that Smith killed Jones or that Green spoiled the play, for such allegations usually impute (more than just causal) responsibility. But since 'kills' and 'spoils' focus on the *terminus* of a causal process rather than on the initial or mid-stages of it, an agent may be said to have killed or to have spoiled even though the conditions required for his being responsible for the killing or the spoiling—ability, opportunity to do otherwise, knowledge of what he was doing, etc.—may be absent.

These doings—spoiling and killing—are one kind of second-level doings. One difference between first- and second-level doings is illustrated by the remark that in certain contexts one can do some second-level doing simply in virtue of not doing a first-level doing of a certain type (e.g., embarrass the speaker by handing him the microphone). 'Spoils' and 'kills' should be contrasted to 'murders' and 'starves to death.' Though the latter two may seem to be classifiable with the former, they are not. One cannot murder *simply* in virtue of not doing something else, one must have seen one's not-doing in a certain light. Though 'murders' and 'starves to death' include reference to the terminus of a causal process (and so are what I am calling a kind of second-order act or doing), they impute agency; indeed, action or behavior designed to compass that terminus.

It is noteworthy that 'he allowed the play to be spoiled' and 'he allowed Green to be killed' may be stronger than 'he spoiled the play' and 'he killed Green.' According to Foot, allowing requires the possibility of prevention or intervention; and there is no point in citing the possibility of prevention unless it is supposed that the agent had (or was responsible for having had) knowledge that would have prevented the unwanted outcome. Neither 'spoiled' nor 'killed' makes such demands. A morality that forbade allowing people to spoil things or forbade allowing people to be killed would be a more lenient, and, on the face of it, more reasonable morality than one which forbade spoilings or killings.

Foot's actor example is intended to show that since one can be said to do something by omitting, the distinction between doing or causing (or bringing about) and allowing does not correspond to the distinction between acting and omitting. But when we look at the example of the man who murders his children by allowing them to die of starvation, we see that this conclusion is not warranted.

The murder-by-starvation example is supposed to show that allowing may be morally as bad as doing. But what it seems to show is that sometimes allowing *is* (or is said to be) doing or causing, that sometimes allowing to die *is* killing.

Consider the following argument:

(1) Jones murdered his children by allowing them to starve to death.

(2) If one murders, one kills.

(3) If one kills, one causes or brings about a death.

∴ (4) Jones killed his children by allowing them to starve.

∴ (5) Jones caused the death of his children by allowing them to starve.

∴ (6) This (Jones's) causing a death is a case of allowing.

∴ (7) This (Jones's) allowing is a causing or bringing about.

Foot seems to face a dilemma. Either she must concede that the distinction between doing (or causing) and allowing is not exclusive, or she must attack either (2) or (3) or the implications that depend upon (2) and (3).[22] Though it is open to Foot to argue that Jones has not caused the death of his children, or that we may kill people whose deaths we do not cause, or that murdering is not always killing, it seems most plausible to think that it is the distinctions between doing (or causing) and allowing that is suspect.

What the two examples—the actor and Jones' children—taken together seem to show is that one can be said to do something by allowing and to act by omitting. This is, of course, not conclusive support for the claim that the two distinctions overlap. But it is sufficient to undermine Foot's suggestion that they must be distinct, for she assumes that they are distinct because one can *do* something by omitting. But we have seen that in the (slippery) sense in which one can 'do' something by omitting, one can also do something by allowing.

I suspect that the distinction between doing and allowing will break down in those cases in which roughly the same moral judgment attaches to the allowing as to the doing. Often those will be cases in which we think that the outcome ought not to obtain (however it would be brought about), or think that the agent in question has an obligation to see to it that the outcome does not obtain, and that he can fulfill that obligation without incurring greater moral cost.

But if there is a disagreement about who has the obligation, conflict between the morality of self-reliance ('I am not my brother's keeper') and the morality of cooperation ('We are all in this together'), then there is also likely to be disagreement about whether the allowing is a mere allowing or is as bad as a doing, disagreement about whether the man (or the many) who has *let* someone die has killed him. The same is true, *pari passu,* of disagreement about what constitutes greater moral cost.

If our distinction between doing and allowing is strongly influenced by our beliefs about what ought to be done or about who ought to do it, then we can hardly expect to appeal to the distinction between doing and allowing (or doing and mere allowing) to *defend* a view about the relative stringency of different obligations to do and allow. By appealing to it we may well find out what our moral beliefs and biases are, but this does not vindicate the distinction if our search is for theory rather than for mere (quasi-systematic) description.

V

Even if it is not question-begging or futile to appeal to our unscrutinized beliefs about allowing, when we appeal to our beliefs about allowing we find that allowing (as such) cannot carry much moral weight. We can see this by considering variations on Foot's runaway tram example.

> S is the driver of a runaway tram which can be steered but not stopped. At *j* there is a junction at which S must either steer the tram down track *a* or steer the tram down track *b*. Track *a* has two men working on it who are bound to be killed if S steers down it, and track *b* has one man who will be killed if S steers down it.

Case one

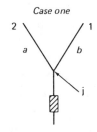

T is the driver of a runaway tram which can be steered but not stopped. The tram's route is down track *a*; track *b* is an out-of-use but still functioning service route. T is able to switch the course from *a* to *b*. Again, there are two men on *a* and one on *b*; the two will die if he stays on *a*, and the one will die if he switches the course to *b*.

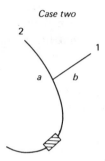

Case two

Presumably the difference between Case one and Case two is morally trivial: in either case the driver should see to it that the tram goes down *b* rather than down *a*. But if the NPD is appealed to, with its weight on allowing as such, we reach different answers in the two cases.

In Case two there is a sequence in train and there is something T could do to intervene. So if he forbears he allows two to die but kills no one, whereas if he acts and alters the course, he kills one man. Since he has a negative duty to the man on *b* to refrain from some act that would harm him but (presumably) only a positive duty to the two men on *a* to do some positive act that would benefit them, he ought to stay on track *a* and allow the two men to die.[23]

Foot might try to deny this counterintuitive asymmetry by appealing to the role of tram driver as making one specially responsible for (e.g.) keeping the number of deaths from accidents or mishaps as low as possible. Or she could say that when one is the driver or controller of a vehicle, the vehicle is, or is to be regarded as an extension of the person in control of it. If T were a runner, it would be preposterous for him to say that since he had already decided to take course *b*, to switch to course *a* would be to intervene in a sequence, for the 'sequence' was (and is) merely the result of his decision and is changeable without 'intervention'. The same is true of one who is in control of a vehicle.

In fact, this is a plausible suggestion. So our earlier reply that the appeal to roles involves abandonment of the NPD in favor of the HBD; and that it is probable that allowings that are not associated with a role may share a sufficient number of features with allowings that are associated with a role (and so may also count as harms) brings about a stalemate where an advance is needed. Let us then consider a variant of Case two.

V is a railway enthusiast out for a walk. She can see that the tram is out of control (perhaps there is a red flag that indicates this). V can see that there are two men on *a* and that there is one man on *b*. She is knowledgeable, the points are mere yards away; she could switch the points and send the tram down *b*, though to do so would be to kill the man on *b* (and to save the two on *a*), while to refrain would be to kill no one, but to let the two on *a* die. V can harm one to benefit two, or can refrain from both benefiting and harming.

May V switch the points? Most of us would say not only that it is morally permissible for her to do so, but that it would be wrong for her *not* to do so.

Case three

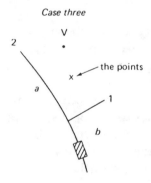

Foot encounters a difficulty whichever version of the PAH she endorses, the NPD or the HBD: both enjoin V's inaction. And the appeal to roles cannot be made with any plausibility. To claim that it is not permissible for V to switch the points is to adopt a counterintuitive position. But to maintain that she may or that she ought to switch the points is to abandon or trivialize the PAH.

In order to uphold the view that V may switch the points and maintain the PAH (either in the form of the NPD or in the form of the HBD), one would have to modify the PAH: it would have to be modified so that it applies only to cases in which the same number of persons stand to be killed (e.g.).

This is a damaging concession. It robs the PAH of most of its power and interest, for it is left with mere tie-breaking weight, and we are left wondering *what* justification is to be summoned for allowing it that much (and that little) weight. And it will now no longer preclude our adopting the "numbers" solution to the *B* cases; in particular, it will not deliver the answers Foot wants in the cases of the framer and the evil tyrant (1B and 3B). Although Foot is not driven to the conclusion that "the size of the evil must always be our guide," unless she offers us other principles—those about the distribution rather than the balancing or weighting of harms and benefits seem good candidates—it does appear that the 'size of the evil' will be our more frequently applicable and more decisive court of appeal.

VI

Let us review (and refurbish) the argument so far:

We considered two interpretations of Foot's principle of the Priority of Avoiding Harm, the Negative/Positive Duty Doctrine and the Harm/Benefit Doctrine. The NPD requires that negative duties (duties not to perform some positive act which harms) and positive duties (duties to perform some positive act which benefits) be distinct and distinguishable; the HBD requires that duties not to harm and duties to benefit be distinct and distinguishable. Properly understood, the HBD is wider and more general than the NPD: the NPD does, while the HBD does not, treat the distinction between doing and allowing as itself morally significant.

Foot takes "the strength of the [DDE] to lie in the distinction it makes between what we do . . . and what we allow . . ." (p. 272). She seeks to exploit this distinction as the basis for her claim that there is a difference between "what we owe people in the form of aid and what we owe them in the way of noninterference" (p. 273). Since the NPD embodies the distinction between doing and allowing, it—and not the HBD—seems to be the better interpretation of Foot's PAH. But the grounds—both philosophical and textual—for preferring the NPD to the HBD are inadequate.

It is unhelpful and problematic simply to insist that there is a (fundamental) *moral* difference between doing and allowing. And the logical (conceptual) and pragmatic arguments for the distinction are not compelling: they are weak, confused and inconclusive.

Foot wants to maintain that there is a difference between doing (or causing) harm and merely allowing it, but she also wants (quite properly) to maintain that allowing is sometimes as bad as doing, that allowing harm to come about is sometimes harming (or as bad as harming) and not merely failing to benefit. This creates a number of difficulties for her position.

It cannot be helpfully maintained that we decide whether a particular allowing counts as a harm by appealing to the moral badness of the result, or to roles and special responsibilities to produce (or prevent) a certain outcome. What we see as a sequence, and what we recognize as a role, depend in part upon our expectations, and often upon our prior beliefs about what people are required to do. But the justification of our previous beliefs about the ordering of obligations is just what is in question when we ask why it is that allowing harm to obtain is thought to be harming in role cases but not in non-role cases.

The appeal to roles also represents a move away from the NPD, or reduces the scope of the NPD, robbing it of significant application. Further, if it is admitted that allowing can harm in role cases, the theoretical basis of the NPD is threatened, as is Foot's professed rationale for holding the PAH: that it exploits the distinction between doing and allowing. Finally, it becomes questionable whether the restriction of allowing-as-harming to role cases can be maintained in the face of the consequentialist's objections and complaints that such a restriction is (unless itself argued for) *ad hoc*.

To advance the NPD (rather than the HBD) as the interpretation of the PAH is, as noted, to be committed to the view that whether an outcome obtains through a positive act or through an allowing is itself a morally significant fact, and to be faced with the difficult task of trying to specify just *how* significant a fact it is. But there is not much room for play if one is to avoid endorsing counterintuitive conclusions (e.g., that V should not switch the points—case three above). And if one takes the steps that seem to be necessary to avoid such conclusions, it is not clear that one can prevent the PAH (in either form) from collapsing into some form of consequentialism.

Foot does not, of course, intend the PAH to be a form of consequentialism. What lies behind Foot's endorsement of the PAH is a fundamentally non-consequentialist view. I suggested earlier that it was a view about justice or about using. On that interpretation, Foot's view about how harms and benefits are to be *weighted*—i.e., the PAH—stems largely from her views about how they should be *distributed:* her view is non-consequentialist in its very core.

If these suggestions are correct, then Foot's concern should *not* be focused on the question of whether a harm accrues to someone 'actively' or 'passively.' What is morally significant is whether the harm's accruing to him in the way that it does is an unjust violation of his interests, or a compromise of his status as a moral agent, an autonomous member of the moral community.

I shall try to make these suggestions more plausible (both in themselves and as an interpretation of the motivation behind Foot's endorsement of the PAH) by considering some of the examples that Foot discusses in connection with the DDE.

VI

The first of these examples is (what I shall call) the case of the trapped potholer:

> A group of people go potholing (cave-exploring). One of them— the fat man—gets stuck in the mouth of the cave and thereby blocks the exit. The cave is flooding rapidly, and all of the potholers are bound to be drowned—the fat man is stuck facing *into* the cave— unless the fat man is dynamited out of the exit.

The second case, which Foot says is parallel to the case of the trapped potholer (p. 277), is a case we (briefly) considered earlier, the case of the doomed fetus:

A woman will die in labor unless the skull of the fetus is crushed. Even if the craniotomy is not performed, the fetus will die, for there is nothing that can be done to save the life of the fetus.

The DDE forbids the doctor's performing the craniotomy on the doomed fetus as well as the potholers' dynamiting the (doomed) fat man out of the exit. To perform the craniotomy and to dynamite would be to intend the deaths of the fetus and the fat man; but the DDE forbids aiming at any (innocent) person's death either as an end in itself or (as in these two cases) as a means.

Foot does not think (as of course defenders of the DDE do think) that an agent always acts wrongly in intending a death (or in killing instead of letting die). She says of the case of the doomed fetus:

It is a great objection to those who argue that the direct intention of the death of an innocent person is never justifiable that the edict will apply even in this case [p. 277].

And she says of the potholders' situation:

Given the certainty of the outcome, as it was postulated, there is no serious conflict of interests here, since the fat man will perish in either case, and it is reasonable that the action that will save someone should be done [p. 277].

Foot is here advancing a substantive (i.e., not a purely conceptual) objection to the DDE. The objection is that the DDE forbids our intending a death (or killing) in cases in which nothing is to be gained—and indeed, additional life is to be lost—if we refrain from killing, cases in which no one's interests are being unjustly neglected or overridden (and others' interests are being justly taken account of, and preserved) if we do intend a death. The DDE is unreasonable.

This is an interesting and *prima facie* plausible objection. But it is, in the context of Foot's other remarks and examples, somewhat problematic. In particular, the view that Foot seems to be advancing here is *not* one which employs the distinction between doing and allowing or even the distinction between harming and merely failing to benefit. What it seems to be, rather, is a view about *justice:* a view about how harms and benefits should be distributed.

The principle that Foot seems to be appealing to here—what I shall call the interest principle *(IP)*—is (roughly) the following:

> When there is no serious conflict of interests in our doing so, it is reasonable that we follow the course of action that will benefit someone. We may (from the standpoint of morality) and we should (from the standpoint of reasonableness) take action to benefit someone.

Does the IP—or the rationale behind it—lend plausibility to the PAH? It does not appear so. To begin with, unless we are told what Foot means by the phrase "no serious conflict of interests," we do not know when the IP applies. Foot's remarks suggest that this is what she has in mind:

> (a) If someone's suffering harm is imminent and—practically speaking—inevitable, and we can bring about a great benefit (or prevent a great harm) to someone else only by inflicting the injury upon the first person ourselves, then there is no serious conflict of interests: we do not seriously violate the first person's interests if we inflict the injury upon him ourselves.

Further, the IP and the PAH do not even seem to be consistent unless we make another substantive assumption, that in cases in which there is, in Foot's sense, 'no serious conflict of interests,' we do not harm the person on whom we inflict the injury, and so do not violate a negative duty or a duty not to harm. To render them consistent, that is, we should have to agree to (something like) the following:

> (b) When there is no serious conflict of interests (and so no serious violation of someone's interests if we inflict the injury on him), then we do not *harm* the person on whom we inflict the injury.

But both (a) and (b) are questionable.

Let us consider yet another evil tyrant case, which I shall call the third tyrant case (in order to distinguish it from Foot's two tyrant cases, 3A and 3B):

> The evil tyrant informs us that he intends to kill both Y and W by (e.g.) shooting them to death. But, he tells us, if we are willing to

kill W, then he will refrain from killing Y. Our choices then, are these: either we kill W, or we refrain, and the tyrants kills W and Y.

What should we do in such a case?

According to (a), there is no serious conflict of interests, and so no serious violation of W's interests if we kill him in order to save Y. And so, if we interpret 'no conflict of interests' in accord with Foot's remarks, the IP would recommend that we shoot and kill W. Would Foot's PAH recommend the same?

In order to answer these questions fully, we would have to answer some others: When there is 'no serious violation of interests' it is the case that we do not *harm* the person on whom we conflict the injury: is it the case that the PAH does not apply? Or is it rather that although we do indeed *harm* the person, the IP supersedes the PAH?

Complete answers to these questions would require a thorough investigation of the notions of harm and interest and the connection between them, something quite beyond the scope of Foot's essay and this commentary on it. But the short answer is, I believe, that we do indeed harm W if we shoot and kill him. Whether this is because there *is* a conflict of interests and we *do* seriously violate W's interests—*pace* (a)—or because we think that we may harm people even when there is no serious conflict of interests—*contra* (b)—is not clear. But we do not need for our purposes to be clear on this. If I am correct in claiming that in the third tyrant case, if we were to shoot and kill W we would be harming him, then the PAH would seem to proscribe our shooting W while the IP—assuming (a)—would recommend it.

Foot therefore faces a trilemma:

(1) If she is advancing the IP and assuming (a) as the interpretation of 'no serious conflict of interests,' then her solution to the doomed fetus case and the trapped potholer case are acceptable, but she would be obliged in the interest of consistency to recommend that we shoot and kill W: assuming (a), that is the solution that the IP yields when it is applied to the third tyrant case.

(2) We may think that the problems with the IP stem primarily from (a); that (a) is not a plausible rendering of the notion 'no serious conflict of interests'. This may well be true. But if Foot were to replace (a) with a significantly different interpretation of

'no serious conflict of interests', it is unlikely that she would get a more acceptable result: she might no longer be obliged to recommend that we shoot W, but it is doubtful that she could (go on to) defend killing the fetus or the trapped potholer.

(3) Finally, if Foot were to maintain that it is impermissible for us to kill W on the ground that it is a violation of the PAH, then she could not consistently propose that we kill the doomed fetus or the trapped potholer. For the PAH is supposed to preclude our actively causing harm to one person in order to benefit another.

But perhaps there is a fourth possibility. It might be claimed that the case of the trapped potholer and the case of the third tyrant are not analogous, and that a simple qualification of (a) would remove the appearance of implausibility, and so allow us to maintain that the IP does not require our shooting W. Perhaps we may call upon the IP only when *we* are the ones facing the danger; perhaps it is permissible to appeal to the IP only in cases of self-defense. On this understanding, the potholers would be allowed to kill the fat man because they would die if they were to refrain, while the fat man will die in either case. But we, as mere bystanders of the cave disaster, not ourselves at risk, would not be allowed to dynamite the fat man out of the mouth of the cave. Likewise, *we* may not shoot and kill W, who is in no sense a threat to us, but Y might be permitted to kill W in order to prevent his being killed by the tyrant. This will not do. Even if we choose to ignore Foot's claim that the case of the trapped potholers is parallel to the case of the doomed fetus, the self-defense requirement is unsatisfactory. It is too stiff a requirement, for it debars the doctor's killing the fetus who will die anyway to save the woman who need not. The doctor does not kill the fetus in self-defense. And if she is allowed to 'assist' in self-defense killings, then it becomes difficult to say why we should not be allowed to 'assist' Y by killing W.

Thus the IP will not, as it stands, suit Foot's purposes (or ours). If it were to be restricted to cases of self-defense, then it would rule out the doctor's killing the doomed fetus in order to save the woman. If it were unrestricted, it would allow (and perhaps require) us to kill W.

What then is the underlying rationale behind Foot's suggested solutions to the different example cases? Is there *any* set of principles or any theory that underlies (and so helps unify) these suggested solutions? It may be helpful to start by reviewing Foot's proposed solutions:

- It is permissible to adopt the 'numbers' solution to the A cases: to steer the tram over the one rather than over the five; to give the five rather than the one the scarce medicine; to save the five rather than the one from the evil tyrant's tortures.
- It is permissible for the doctor to kill the doomed fetus, and for the trapped potholders to kill the (doomed) fat man who is blocking their exit.
- It is impermissible to adopt the 'numbers' solution to the B cases: to frame the innocent man in order to save the five from the angry crowd; to make a serum out of one man's body in order to keep five others alive; to torture one person ourselves to appease a tyrant who will otherwise torture five others.
- It is impermissible for us to allow a beggar to starve in order that his body may be used for medical research.
- It is impermissible for a parent to poison his children, and just as impermissible for him to allow his children to die of starvation.
- It is impermissible for us to send poisoned food to children in distant lands, but it is not as impermissible (if impermissible at all) for us to allow these children to starve to death.
- Presumably: it is impermissible for us to kill W (who will die in either case) in order to appease the third tyrant and thereby save Y's life.
- Presumably: it is permissible (and perhaps even obligatory) for V (in Case three) to change the points, and thereby bring it about that the tram kills one man rather than two.

We have seen that the PAH will not do in either of its forms. And the IP, which was initially put forward as the rationale or intuition behind the PAH, will not do either. Yet the conviction persists that there is *something* in (or behind) the PAH (that 'connects' all these different examples). What is it? This is a large question, and I can offer here only an indication of the direction that a reply might take.

VIII

It matters to us *how* a harm comes about: whether it 'just happens' in the course of things, or whether it is inflicted. And when it is inflicted, it matters to us *why* it is inflicted: for what purpose, by whom, and with what motivation. These are considerations that are relevant both to the question of whether someone is being used in an objectionable fashion. The IP (unsuccessfully) tries to capture the importance of the first sort of consideration, the consideration of justice. But it is, I believe, the second consideration— the consideration about using—that is of greater importance.

When harm and death are inevitable, it matters to us *why* they are inevitable. But this may not have anything to do with the question of whether there is (in Foot's sense) a serious conflict of interests. When we are told that someone's suffering or death cannot be avoided, we want to know what sort of inevitability is involved, and we care why the harm is inevitable. Is it physical inevitability *sans phrase,* inevitability that is the result of a problem in the coordination of the desires and actions of many people, or inevitability that is the result of mere stubbornness? Is it physically impossible to prevent[24] the harm, psychologically impossible to prevent the harm, or merely 'adventitiously' impossible?

Some examples may help to illustrate these differences.

> (i) A driver discovers that her brakes have failed. Her car is careening down the mountain towards a crowd of people. She can steer off the road and thereby kill only one or two people, or she can continue down the road with the result that others—more—will die. In either case, it is inevitable that some lives be lost.
>
> (ii) A crowd of tense and angry people have gathered in the square. Someone reveals to them that they are all about to be arrested, and that they will, as 'subversives,' face stiff prison sentences. It is inevitable that some get hurt in the panic that ensues when many of the people try to flee.
>
> (iii) An evil tyrant assures us that he will torture five people unless we cooperate by torturing one person (3B). It is inevitable that someone suffer.

In case (i), no course of action that we could follow would prevent a death. (We cannot prevent a death without contravening the laws of nature.) In case (ii), though we might be lucky enough to be in a position to try to calm the crowd and to get the people to cooperate and leave in an orderly fashion, it is most unlikely that our attempts would meet with success, and most unlikely that any one person's decision, taken independently, would be effective in preventing panic and subsequent death or injury. The 'inevitability' here is really 'high probability, given the exigencies of the situation and the workings of human psychology'; but if we *could* coordinate peoples' actions, no one need be hurt. In case (iii), the 'inevitability' is the product of human cruelty, or perversity, or mere whim that the evil shall come about. One person's decision would obviate the harm.

We are loath to treat a willful human demand as we treat the physical limitations of a situation, or as we treat the difficulties of achieving successful coordination. Though it must surely be horrible to find ourselves in a situation in which nothing that we can do will prevent great harm (or death), we do not, in such situations, think of ourselves as instruments of evil (even if we incline toward melodrama, and think of ourselves as mere victims of circumstance). But we do think of ourselves as instruments of evil when we are 'blackmailed' to inflict pain or cause deaths at the bidding of evil men. And we find the role 'instrument of evil' an especially repugnant one, an assault on our dignity, and a threat to our status as autonomous moral agents. Those who have the misfortune to be used twice over—the victims of our acting as instruments—suffer a double indignity.

Thus it may matter very much to us how a bad outcome comes about, and we may feel very differently about causing harm to others in natural disaster or coordination situations than about harming others in 'human disaster' situations. But if this is right, the important distinction is not that between killing people and allowing them to die (or between harming and merely failing to benefit); the important distinction seems rather to be that between killing and allowing to be killed (or harming and allowing to be harmed). And the important cases are those in which the harms or deaths obtain because another agent deliberately brings them about, or is foreseeably and culpably responsible for them. Thus we may feel that the case of the doomed fetus and the case of the trapped potholer differ significantly from the case of the third tyrant and the case in which we are being 'invited' to frame an innocent man (1B). Killing the fetus is killing in a natural disaster situation, as is killing the fat man struck in the mouth of the cave. But the third tyrant's threat and the angry crowd's threat (1B) are human disasters: the victims are the victims of human wickedness or willfulness, not the victims of mere circumstance.

These remarks are regrettably both promissory and imprecise. They have, however brought us close to (if not actually upon) a doctrine familiar from the law (which I shall refer to here as the *doctrine of the intervening agent*)[25]:

> The free, deliberate and informed intervention of a second person, not acting in concert with the first, and intending to bring about the harm which in fact occurs or recklessly courting it, is normally held to relieve the first actor of . . . responsibility.[26]

Even when we believe that he will do harm, we are not responsible for the outcome of the free action of another agent (so long as the above conditions are met). Even when we believe that another agent would not undertake some particular wrongful act but for some lawful (and morally neutral) act of our own, we are not responsible for the harm that ensues if we act and the other agent then proceeds to perform the wrongful act and so bring about the harm. We are not obliged to refrain from following our chosen course of action, one we regard as reprehensible (or unlawful), in order thereby to prevent the other agent from performing his nasty deed.[27]

This doctrine is not as uncompromising as it may sound to laymen. The law is more often willing to hold one agent responsible for the consequences of another's action than the actual wording of the doctrine may suggest. First, the law has provisions for treating 'first agents' as vicariously responsible (and even, in a very restricted set of circumstances, as strictly liable) for the harm produced by other agents. A parent may be held (vicariously) responsible for the mischief perpetrated by his child, an employer for the negligence of her employee. Second, where the 'intervening action' of the 'second agent' was 'automatic' (or close to it: 'typical' behavior counts for the law's purposes as automatic) and hence such that the 'first agent' ought to have foreseen it (i.e., was negligent), then the 'first agent' may not be relieved of responsibility for the harm. Suppose that someone—for a joke— shouts 'Fire!' in a crowded theater and the ushers are injured when the patrons run for the exit. It is the 'first agent' who shouted (and not the 'second agents' who panicked) who is responsible for the harm. Third (relatedly), the notion of a free or voluntary action is given a rather restricted interpretation by legal theorists. According to Hart and Honoré, an agent's action does not count as free unless he was, in the circumstances, presented with a 'fair choice':

> An act done [by an 'intervening agent'] to preserve a right will . . . not count as free, the actor not being presented with a fair choice. . . . The defence [by an 'intervening agent'] of an interest not amounting to a recognized legal right may have the same effect.[28]

Further,

> when we take a step reluctantly, as the lesser of two evils, our act is something less than voluntary.[29]

These qualifications of the legal doctrine make it clear that there is significant convergence between the doctrine of the intervening agent and the set of concerns that we have been discussing, *viz.* using other agents as means or treating them as victims, and being used oneself as an instrument of evil. Both the doctrine of the intervening agent and the considerations about using require that we distinguish cases in which one agent's course of action leads to a bad result only because of another agent's voluntary harmful actions (e.g., the third tyrant case and the case of the angry crowd [1B]) from cases in which his inaction leads to a bad result "naturally" (e.g., the cases of the [first] tram driver [1A] and of the doomed fetus). Both require us to see the deliberately or recklessly harmful actions[30] of (other) agents as different from mere events or from mere behavior. And—more in keeping with our purposes—both seem *prima facie* to accord with the proposed solutions to Foot's example cases. But before it could be said with confidence that these considerations do underlie Foot's intuitions[31] (or ours), or that they could plausibly be advanced as a moral principle or as a basis for one, they must be clarified and rendered more precise. This is (again) a substantial task, and my remarks will be largely preliminary. We shall find, I believe, that in spite of its initial promise, not even the set of considerations about using succeeds in yielding the differential obligations that Foot seeks.

I suggested above that when great harm is inevitable, it matters to us what sort of disaster it is that faces us, a natural disaster—one in which the harm is attributable to "natural" causes, or a human disaster—one in which it is attributable to malign human agency. And I suggested that when it is impossible for us to prevent the harm, it matters to us whether it is physical impossibility or mere human obstinacy that is at issue, harm that it is physically impossible for us to prevent, or harm that could be prevented by a mere softening of an agent's will: a change of plan. I said that we feel ourselves to be instruments of another's will when we are faced with a human disaster, when a wicked agent threatens that if we will not do something bad (harmful), he will do something worse. But, in fact, two different sorts of concerns are being run together here: first, whether or not there is a wicked agent who can change his plan, and whose action in accord with his change of plan would obviate the harm; and second, whether or not a harmful outcome is the result of malign human agency. And these considerations often come apart: it will often be true that an agent who has engineered a human disaster cannot prevent the harmful outcome merely by changing his plans and his subsequent course of action.[32] Consider, for example, an airplane hijacker who threatens to kill the pilots unless his (wicked) demands are met, and who carries out his threat just as the plane is crossing mountainous terrain. No subsequent change of his plans will remove the need for our deciding (e.g.) whether we should attempt to land the plane (and thereby lose some lives) or to abandon the plane (and thereby lose others). Indeed, it may even come about that an agent who has masterminded a disaster has engineered things in such a way that his own (future) actions *could not* be effective in preventing (or decreasing) the harm. A wicked agent may so arrange things that harm could only be prevented by an innocent agent's doing some dastardly deed. Consider, for example, a variation on 2B. Suppose that there is a wicked agent who has deliberately injected five people with a lethal drug, and suppose that they can be saved if (and only if) a sixth is killed, and a serum made from his body. If an innocent agent—a bystander—is the only one who possesses the requisite chemical knowledge and medical expertise to make the serum from the victim's body, then he alone can mitigate the harm. Thus there are human disasters which *cannot* be prevented by the wicked agent's change of plans. And even in those cases in which a human disaster can be *mitigated* by a wicked agent's change of plans, it may be that it is an innocent agent who can more effectively mitigate the harm, and *most* effectively mitigate the harm by acceding to the wicked agent's will.

This raises a number of questions. In those cases in which we seek to uncover (or generate) differential obligations by employing considerations about using and in which the two strands of these considerations come apart, which is the more important? Is either in itself morally significant? Does either capture the notion of using, or help us to see just what is so objectionable about being the instrument of another's will?

We cannot pursue these questions at any length. But the short answer is, I believe, that the question of whether the wicked agent could prevent the harm simply by changing his plans does not capture the notion of using. Nor is it of any special moral significance. The third tyrant case helps clarify this. It seems implausible to claim that our obligations would be any different if the evil tyrant had so arranged things that it was (now) impossible for *him* to prevent W's death. If we thought before that we ought to shoot and kill W in order that Y might be saved, we should not be inclined to think otherwise in this revised third tyrant case. And if we thought before that we ought not to shoot W, I do not believe that we would be persuaded that we should do otherwise in the revised case.

Two interesting points emerge from this. If we thought that we should in the unrevised case refuse to shoot W on the ground that we are being pressured to be the instrument of another agent's will in the execution of a truly horrible deed, our objection to shooting W would be even stronger in the revised third tyrant case. For here the manipulation of our will is even more contrived, and more total. If this is correct, then it seems reasonable to conclude that in so far as we object to being the instrument of another's will, our feeling is not predicated upon the belief that the situation is one in which the latter's decision to avoid (or reduce) the harm would be efficacious. In brief, the distinction between the physical impossibility and the 'adventitious' impossibility of preventing harm does not express what it is that is so objectionable about using and being used. We do not regard ourselves as 'less used' (or less abused), or as obliged to kill W, if the third tyrant has engineered things so that only *our* decision and action would prevent Y's death. Whether the impossibility of preventing harm is 'adventitious' is not in itself of moral significance. (Nor is it of help in determining the proper solutions to our puzzle cases.)

Consideration of the revised third tyrant case will also undercut another view that is *prima facie* attractive, but mistaken. One might be inclined to use (alleged) difference of certainty of about the harm's obtaining to account for the (supposed) moral signifi- cance of the distinction between harm that is physically inevitable and harm that is 'adventitiously' inevitable, to claim that we are more certain that the harmful outcome will come about when it is physically impossible to prevent it than when it is 'adventitiously' impossible to do so. And, the claim continues, this helps explain why being used as an instrument of another's will is so repugnant to us. Having to do something awful is that much worse and that much more upsetting when the necessity for it is that much weaker, and the necessity *is* that much weaker when the harm that one takes objectionable action to avoid is (relatively) less certain to come about.

This argument is confused, and, as consideration of the revised third tyrant case reveals, it is implausible as well. In the revised third tyrant case we feel that we are being used, yet we recognize that the harm is not 'adventitiously' inevitable. So, even if harmful outcomes that are 'adventitiously' inevitable *are* less certain than those which are (physically) inevitable, our feelings of repugnance at being used cannot simply be based on the difference in certainty.

Is it, then, the distinction between natural disasters and human disasters that is the relevant distinction? I think not: the distinction between natural and human disasters is artificial, and too arbitrary to serve as the ground for differential obligations.

First of all, natural disasters are often the result of human wickedness or human recklessness. An unscrupulous politician with real estate interests may see to it that drilling for oil is contin- ued in a particular spot, even though he knows that continued drilling in that place is certain to precipitate a landslide which will destroy houses in the town nearby. It may suit his purposes financially and politically to have a 'natural' disaster clear the land that he hopes to develop. And natural events can become disastrous because of men's deliberate or reckless actions. A minor earthquake may kill or injure school children because a corrupt official approves buildings that he knows to be sub-standard (while planning to make earthquake safety an election issue).

Conversely, some human disasters are brought about by natural events. A flood may drive the starving and impoverished victims to desperation, and they may threaten and even harm others in their attempts to get enough food to keep their families alive. I believe that it is simply a mistake to regard as morally different in kind a harmful outcome which results from a "natural" disaster that accords with human design or recklessness, and a harmful outcome which is more directly the result of an agent's (malign) will. The same applies when the contrast is between a harmful outcome which is the result of a human disaster that is itself the response to a merely 'natural' disaster, and a harmful outcome which is more immediately the result of a 'natural' disaster. In general, it is a mistake to underestimate the extent to which human actions are part of the natural order of events.

Upon consideration, the distinction between 'natural' and 'human' disasters is not one which is useful for our purposes. It is not a clear distinction; and it is not, I believe, relevant to the question of what it is that we ought to do. Suppose that someone has sabotaged the brakes of the runaway tram, or that someone has pushed the fat potholer into the mouth of the cave, or maliciously tricked him into going first. It does not seem to me that this would have any bearing on our view about what we ought to do in those situations. Whether this is because the distinction between 'natural' and 'human' disasters is not the basis for (or the expression of) our repugnance at using and being used, or because we do not regard the question of whether someone is being used as morally overriding, is not clear.

Thus it seems that neither the contrast between 'physical' and 'adventitious' inevitability of a harmful outcome, nor the contrast between a harmful outcome's resulting from a human disaster and a harmful outcome's resulting from a 'natural' disaster is tightly connected with the question of whether someone is being used as the instrument of another's will. The significance of this conclusion should not be overestimated: it may be that the first contrast is relevant to the question of whether we are being used when it is taken in tandem with either the second contrast or with still other considerations (perhaps the intentions with which the agent acts). And it may be that the second contrast does express what we find objectionable in being used, but that considerations about using are, finally, not morally overriding. Nor should the significance of our conclusion be underestimated: what our discussion reveals is that it is quite difficult to explain why we object to being used as instruments of another's will, and not easy to say just what such an objection comes to. And the discussion helps to direct us, to suggest what sort of path we should follow if we are to continue to try to explain and defend the view that considerations about using are of great moral significance.

IX

We touched upon the legal doctrine of the intervening agent in the course of the discussion of using because it seemed that the views were closely related. Both presuppose some of the same distinctions and attitudes and—notably—some of the same assumptions about agency and responsibility. And both are—at least *prima facie*—plausible and promising. But what our discussion suggests is that the notion of agency that these views share may be seriously flawed, and that we may find them persuasive precisely to the extent that we share that misconception (what we might call) the common-sense (mis)conception about what is involved in our being and seeing others as moral agents.

It is widely believed that it is defensible to hold a person responsible for his actions only if he acted freely, and only to the extent to which he acted freely. (As it used to be put, 'Moral responsibility presupposes freedom of the will'.) And it is also believed that the acknowledgement of another's free agency requires the acknowledgement that we cannot ever really know what that person's actions will be in a given situation. The possibility of successful prediction of an agent's actions is thought somehow to preclude their being 'really' free actions. This is sometimes the reasoning that lies behind the belief that there is a relevant moral difference between cases in which it is 'physically' impossible for us to prevent the harm and cases in which it is (merely) 'adventitiously' impossible, behind the view which we considered earlier that harmful outcomes which are 'adventitiously' inevitable are less certain than harmful outcomes which are 'physically' inevitable. It is pointed out—quite correctly—that the runaway tram cannot decide not to plow into people, but that the evil tyrant can often simply change his plans (and so not harm the five). And it is claimed (or assumed) that the fact that the evil tyrant can change his mind is reason to believe that we do not really know that he will not change his mind. This skepticism is not usually the manifestation of a radical doubt about whether we can *ever* really know what will happen. Nor is it a reflection of a (slightly more modest) general worry about the adequacy of our techniques of formulating estimates of the probability of the occurrence of 'mere' events. Rather it proceeds from (what I believe are mistaken) views about the nature of and requirements for free agency. The confusions involved are ones about the connection of questions of free agency and questions of responsibility, and about the relation of determination to prediction. In particular, the issue of whether or not an action is determined is confused with the issue of whether or not it is predictable. Thus what I am suggesting is that non-consequentialist defenders of views like Foot's should— if they wish to make use of considerations about using (considerations expressed in a somewhat different form by the legal doctrine of the intervening agent)—seek to explicate the notion of agency which underlies these considerations. The continued attempt to formulate principles to capture the notion of using (or to exploit some other (related) notions) in order to provide the solutions we want in the various example cases, is misguided. But I am also claiming that the 'common sense' account of agency which seems to underlie the considerations about using is confused in several important respects. And so I believe that developing a cogent account of agency will ultimately lead us to doubt the very plausibility of views like Foot's, and to reject the PAH.

X

We arrived at questions about agency and autonomy (using) by trying to determine what Foot's view is, and what the basis might be for her view (or for a view like hers). What we have seen—to put it briefly—is that neither of these issues admits of an easy resolution. It is not clear what Foot's view is; nor is it clear what its underlying basis is. In so far as espousal of the PAH is to be understood as espousal of the NPD, and so to reflect the belief that the distinction between doing and allowing is both clear and itself significant, it is unsatisfactory. The distinction between doing and allowing will not, either morally or conceptually, bear the weight that Foot seeks to place upon it. But construing the PAH as the HBD is only slightly less problematic. It is difficult to specify (in a way that is neither circular nor question-begging) what counts as harming and what counts as merely failing to benefit. And the HBD, like the NPD, yields counterintuitive conclusions.

Further, it is not clear how the PAH in either form is to be reconciled with other considerations that Foot seems to think important, in particular with considerations of justice that surface in the form of the Interest Principle. This is, of course, the sort of problem that faces any moral pluralist, not one that is uniquely Foot's. But it is especially troublesome for Foot, for if we do not know what is the basis of the PAH—what its rationale is, or what values it is meant to reflect—then it will be difficult to assess the PAH, and still more difficult to adjudicate conflicts between the PAH and other moral considerations, particularly considerations about justice and using.

In trying to spell out the relation between the PAH and the IP what we found was that certain cases emerged as special—namely those cases in which an agent is being used as an instrument of another agent's will.[33] It may therefore seem that principles proscribing using others or being the instrument of their will are superior to both the PAH and the IP. For our repugnance at using and being used cannot be adequately explained by either the PAH or the IP. And it seems that principles about using could give us better solutions to Foot's (and the other related) example cases than either the PAH or the IP does. But we also found that it is difficult to capture just what it is that is so objectionable about using, and difficult to formulate principles about using.

I believe that it is considerations about using (or relatedly, belief in the fundamental importance of the autonomy of the individual) that are the principal considerations moving those non-consequentialists who share Foot's intuitions.[34] And I believe that the plausibility of such considerations and intuitions is largely the result of their presupposing or employing our 'common-sense' notion of agency (a notion that they share with the doctrine of the intervening agent). Hence, what we must do if we are to explain (and to have any hope of defending) our intuitions about the wrongness of using persons is to articulate the notion of agency and the conception of the person embedded in our 'common sense' view. But if I am correct in the claim that the 'common-sense' view embodies serious confusions, *articulation* of the 'common-sense' view of agency will not be sufficient. What will be required is no less than defense and repair (or else replacement). And, as I suggested, I do not believe that the PAH would survive such repairs.

In any case, we are now in a position to see more clearly why moral asymmetry views are, as a class, inadequate. They face difficulties on a number of levels. First, there are problems of application. The distinctions upon which the various moral asymmetry views depend—acting versus allowing; acting versus omitting; harming versus merely failing to benefit; intending harm versus merely foreseeing harm—are unclear, equivocal, or question-begging. Second, there are problems of scope. No one of these moral asymmetry views is likely to yield answers that accord with our clearer intuitions across the wide range of the problem cases. But even if—as I believe is not the case—these problems could be surmounted, moral asymmetry views would not *thereby* be vindicated. A more significant problem remains. Moral asymmetry views are merely moral *principles;* and what I have been suggesting is that the mere proffering of moral principles is insufficient. Without a theoretical base—a theory of agency in the case of principles about using—a moral principle can claim—at best—plausibility. But it cannot claim authority. Though we have no guarantee that an adequate account of agency would in the end vindicate the non-consequentialist's intuitions, we have seen that the mere presentation of plausible moral principles is inadequate. It is inadequate in itself, inadequate as a representation of the nature of non-consequentialist moral thinking, and inadequate as a basis upon which to formulate (or advance) non-consequentialist criticism of consequentialist moral thought.[35]

NOTES

Much of the material in this paper is drawn from several unpublished essays written in 1974–75, and from Chapter 2 of my dissertation, "Acts, Omissions, and Integrity" (University of California at Berkeley: 1976).

I am indebted to Philippa Foot, Bernard Williams, and Barry Stroud for the helpful discussions that led to the writing of the essays and the chapter. I owe a special debt to Derek Parfit, whose insight into the issues, sustained interest in how I would discuss them, and suggestions as to how I might better discuss them have been invaluable.

I was helped greatly in writing this paper by Paolo Dau's numerous and detailed suggestions.

Were I to approach these issues in the philosophical climate of the 1990s, I would write this paper differently. The argument has many strands and tentacles, and it would be helpful to identify them more clearly and to disentangle them a bit more. But I believe that the paper's central claims remain both true and relevant. People continue to assign great normative and theoretical significance to 'the' distinction between killing and letting die, and to its associated distinctions, in spite of the fact that the practice continues to have demonstrably bad implications in both normative and theoretical domains. Discussions of euthanasia, in particular, illustrate this with great clarity.

Thus, though the path to the paper's argument is more tortuous and complex than one would like, I continue to believe both that my conclusions are important, and that it is worth articulating them and investigating why they are important, in some detail.

1. A *consequentialist* moral theory is, roughly, one that involves the claim that the moral value of a course of action is determined by the goodness of its consequences: the right course of action is that which (of all of those open to the agent) produces the best consequences. *Utilitarianism*—the view that the right course of action is that which produces the most *happiness*—is a *form* of consequentialism. *Non-consequentialist* views are those which deny what the consequentialist views affirm: according to the non-consequentialist, there are factors other than the value of the consequences—e.g., considerations about justice, autonomy, or

agent's motivation—that are relevant to the determination of the moral value of a course of action.

2. For a formulation of the DDE see *The Catholic Encyclopedia*, p. 48. See also Aquinas, II-II Q 64 Art. 6; Kenny, Antony, "Intention and Purpose in the Law" in *Essays in Legal Philosophy*, ed. R. Summers (Oxford: 1968), pp. 146–63, and "The History of Intention in Ethics," Appendix to Kenny, *The Anatomy of the Soul* (Oxford: 1973). The DDE is discussed in G. E. M. Anscombe, "Modern Moral Philosophy," *Philosophy*, 33 (1958), 1–19; reprinted in *Ethics*, ed. J. J. Thomson and G. Dworkin (New York: 1968), 186–210 and "War and Murder" in *War and Morality*, ed. R. Wasserstrom (Belmont: 1970), 42–53; Jonathan Bennett, "Whatever the Consequences," *Analysis*, 26 (1966) [in this book, Chapter 10]; Daniel Callahan, *Abortion: Law, Choice and Morality* (New York: 1970), pp. 424–28; Campbell, A. V., *Moral Dilemmas in Medicine* (London: 1972), pp. 100–103; Duff, R. A., "Intentionally Killing the Innocent," *Analysis*, 33 (1973), 93–98 and "Absolute Principles and Double Effect," *Analysis*, 36 (1976), 68–80; H. T. Engelhardt, Jr., "Ethical Issues in Aiding the Death of Young Children" in *Beneficent Euthanasia*, ed. M. Kohl (Buffalo: 1975) 180–92; Geddes, L., "On the Intrinsic Wrongness of Killing Innocent People," *Analysis*, 34 (1974), 16–19; H. L. A. Hart, "Intention and Punishment" in *The Oxford Review*, 4 (Hilary: 1967), 5–22; J. G. Murphy, "The Killing of the Innocent," *Monist*, 57 (1973), 525–50; Glanville Williams, *The Sanctity of Life and the Criminal Law* (London: 1958), in his chapters on abortion and euthanasia.

3. I use "he" and "his" in conjunction with subjects like "the agent," "someone," and "one." This should be understood as a way of abbreviating "he or she" and "hers or his" and not as a restriction on the referents of "the agent," etc.

4. Lord Macaulay, "Notes on the Indian Penal Code, 1937" in Trevelyan (ed.), *Works* 7, 497.

5. Sir David Ross, *The Right and the Good* (Oxford: 1930), pp. 21–22; see also Ross, *Foundations of Ethics* (Oxford: 1939), p. 75.

6. Clough is also solemnly quoted by lawyers. See Cross and Jones, *An Introduction to Criminal Law*, 3rd ed. (London: 1953), p. 263: "the words 'thou shalt not kill but needst not strive officiously to keep alive' present a tolerably accurate picture of the English law of homicide, which seldom punishes omissions."

7. See P. J. Fitzgerald, "Acting and Refraining," *Analysis*, 27 (1967), 133–39; Judith Jarvis Thomson, "A Defense of Abortion," *Philosophy and Public Affairs*, 1 (1971), 47–66 and "Individuating Actions," *Journal of Philosophy*, 68 (1971), 774–81; Michael Tooley, "A Defense of Abortion and Infanticide" in *The Problem of Abortion*, ed. J. Feinberg (Bel-

mont: 1973), 51–92; Richard J. Trammell, "Saving Life and Taking Life," *Journal of Philosophy*, 72 (1975), 131–37 [in this book, chapter 18].

8. Philippa Foot, "Abortion and the Doctrine of the Double Effect," published in *The Oxford Review*, 5 (1967), and reprinted in *Moral Problems*, J. Rachels (New York: 1971), pp. 28–41, and in this book, chapter 16. (All page numbers in parentheses refer to Foot's article in this text.)

9. Foot never states such a principle explicitly, but the PAH is based on Foot's remarks; in particular on her claim that "one does not *in general* have the same duty to help people as to refrain from injuring them" (p. 274). I have chosen to substitute 'harm' and 'benefit' for 'injure' and 'help' on the ground that they are less restricted terms, and hence more in accord with the spirit of Foot's view.

10. It is clear in context that the 'size of the evil' is to be determined by employing a (rough) consequentialist standard of measurement. E.g., if an alternative results in a greater number of deaths, the 'size of the evil' is greater. I shall use scare quotes to signal employment of Foot's notion, and I shall speak of the 'numbers' solution (i.e., the proposal that it is the number of people harmed or benefited that is the determinant of what we ought to do).

It should be kept in mind, however, that consequentialist views are not *as such* committed to adopting the 'numbers' solution or thinking that the 'size of the evil' should be our final guide. Any refined consequentialist view will allow the possibility that, e.g., disutility is not proportional to the 'size of the evil'—e.g., the number of deaths. Thus it is not clear that the consequentialist need adopt the solutions (to Foot's example cases) that Foot's 'numbers' consequentialist would. And so Foot's anti-'numbers' remarks are not compelling criticisms of consequentialism (in any but its crudest form). I ignore this complication in the text since it does not really bear on my arguments against Foot.

11. Salmond, *Jurisprudence*, 11th ed., ed. G. Williams (London: 1957); 12th ed., ed. P. J. Fitzgerald (London: 1966), p. 283, cited in Foot, p. 37 [in this book, pp. 273–74]. Others draw the distinctions a bit differently; see, e.g., M. Singer, "Positive Duties and Negative Duties," *Philosophical Quarterly*, 15 (1965), 97–103. Also relevant are John Casey, "Actions and Consequences" in *Morality and Moral Reasoning*, ed. John Casey (London: 1971), p. 191; Phillip E. Davis, *Moral Duty and Legal Responsibility* (New York: 1966), p. 143; Daniel Dinello, "On Killing and Letting Die," *Analysis*, 31 (1971), p. 83 [in this book; pp. 192–96]; Fitzgerald, "Acting and Refraining," *Analysis*, 27 (1967), p. 133; George P. Fletcher, "Legal Aspects of the Decision Not to Prolong Life" in *The Journal of the American Medical Association* 203:1 (1968), reprinted in *Moral Problems in Medicine*, S. Gorovitz, et al. (Englewood Cliffs, N.J.:

Prentice-Hall, 1976), p. 262; Alvin Goldman, *A Theory of Human Action* (Englewood Cliffs, N.J.: Prentice-Hall, 1970), p. 48; Gilbert Harman, "Moral Relativism Defended," *Philosophical Review*, 83 (1974), pp. 12–13; *Freedom and Responsibility*, ed. Herbert Morris (Stanford: 1961); Paulsen and Kadish, *Criminal Law and Its Processes*, 3rd ed. (Boston: 1962), pp. 223–28.

12. I argue in Chapter 1 of my dissertation that the notions of a 'negative act' and a 'positive act' are seriously confused, and I suggest that we would do better not to employ them (unless we are willing to regard them as terms of art and to lay down careful directions about how to use them). I reluctantly ignore such advice here, and more reluctantly follow the legal usage that derives from Bentham. Bentham says in *An Introduction to the Principles of Morals and Legislation* (Oxford, 1892), p. 72–3: "By positive [acts] are meant such as consist in motion or exertion: by negative, such as consist in keeping at rest; that is in forbearing to move or exert oneself in such and such circumstances. . . . Positive acts are styled also acts of commission; negative, acts of omission or forbearance." See also John Austin, *Lectures on Jurisprudence* (London: 1873) v. I Lecture XII, pp. 346, 426–40; Salmond in Morris, *Freedom and Responsibility*, p. 111.

13. Foot pp. 273, 274 from Salmond, *Jurisprudence*, p. 283.

14. Foot sometimes yokes together doing and causing (and sometimes doing and bringing about) in drawing the contrast to allowing. This is apt to be misleading, for doing causing. Further discussion of this occurs later in the text.

15. The claim is not that we must *all* possess the requisite expertise, but is rather the minimal claim that unless the distinction is exclusive, etc., then even the most subtle and well-intentioned moral agent will run into difficulties of inadequacy/contradiction.

16. See J. S. Mill, *A System of Logic* in *Collected Works of John Stuart Mill* ed. J. M. Robson (Toronto: 1973), v. 8, Book III, ch. 5, sec. 3, pp. 330–33; Hart, H. L. A. and Honoré, A. M., *Causation in the Law*, (Oxford: 1959), *passim;* John Mackie, "Causation and Conditions," *American Philosophical Quarterly*, 2 (1965), 245–64 and *The Cement of The Universe* (Oxford: 1974); Donald Davidson, "Causal Relations," *Journal of Philosophy*, 64 (1967), 691–703 and "Agency" in *Agent, Action and Reason* ed. Binkley et al. (Oxford: 1971), 3–26.

17. Hart and Honoré, *Causation in the Law, passim.*

18. It need not, of course, be thought to be overriding. Perhaps the distinction between doing and allowing is thought to come into play only after some other (morally and 'lexically') prior factor is considered.

19. Foot speaks of the man as *murdering* his child by allowing it to

starve. I prefer to speak of his *killing* his children, for that makes the example cases more nearly parallel.

20. In speaking of *murdering* in this context, Foot concurs with what the legal writers say. E.g., Cross and Jones *(Introduction to Criminal Law)* say on p. 34: "The prohibited state of affairs may be caused by an omission rather than an act. If a person deliberately refrains from feeding his child with the object of starving it to death, he will be guilty of murder if it dies in consequence." But if 'murders' suggests intention and malice, then starving one's children to death differs from allowing the children in distant lands to starve to death out of sheer indifference. But the cases must be kept parallel if it is to be the difference between allowing and doing that is under scrutiny, rather than that difference accompanied by others.

21. But is it fair to let someone suffer? Is the view here that it is wrong to 'create' injustices, but that there is no obligation to correct 'natural' injustices that 'arise' (when we could prevent them from arising, or correct them)? See the discussion in the text of 'natural' and 'human' disasters.

22. Since she accepts (1), Foot would presumably not want to attack its implications.

23. I am, in considering the tram variations, using 'kill' and 'allow to die' as Foot does, and so treating them as if they were exclusive and could be distinguished in the way that Foots seeks to distinguish them. That I disagree with both of these aspects of Foot's account should be clear from my discussion in the text.

24. My use of 'it is physically impossible for us to prevent the harm' and related expressions may be confusing. As I am using the terms, we cannot infer 'the harm will occur' from 'it is physically impossible for us to prevent the harm'; or 'x cannot occur without contravening the laws of nature' from 'we cannot prevent x without contravening the laws of nature.' It may be that there is nothing that we can do to prevent harm from occurring, but that—through a piece of good luck, or a miracle, or an act of God—the harm does not occur. E.g., the careening car may inexplicably go into reverse, and then stop dead without hitting anyone.

25. What I am calling the 'doctrine of the intervening agent' is called, in law, the doctrine of *novus actus interviens*.

26. Hart and Honoré, *Causation in the Law*, p. 292.

27. This is a vague and highly general characterization. See *ibid., passim*, for a more detailed characterization.

28. *Ibid.*, p. 138.

29. *Ibid.*, p. 147. It should be emphasized that the legal notion of a

voluntary act is an evaluative (or value-laden) one. Hart and Honoré continue: "[there is] a point at which the concept of a fully voluntary action incorporates judgments of value. A man who hands over his purse to a highwayman to save his life, and one who hands over strategic plans to the enemy to save his life, are treated differently because the value of the interest sacrificed is different. In the first case one would readily say that the man was 'bound', 'obliged', or 'forced' to act as he did, but not in the second."

30. We see negligent action as different from both deliberately harmful action and recklessly harmful action (though like each one in important respects in which it is not like the other). Negligence is a fascinating topic, and it is problematic both in law and in morals. But it is a large topic, and one that cannot be pursued here.

31. What I am suggesting is that considerations of using may, *pace* Foot, underlie Foot's intuitions. Though she claims that "To refrain from inflicting injury ourselves is a stricter duty than to prevent other people from inflicting injury . . ." (p. 275)—which we should note is a principle distinct from the PAH—Foot considers and rejects the possibility that considerations of using are what underlie her intuitions about the example cases. She says on p. 276: "We may find it particularly revolting that someone should be *used* as in the case where he is killed or allowed to die in the interest of medical research, and the fact of *using* may even determine what we would decide to do in some cases, but the principle seems unimportant compared with our reluctance to bring such injury for the sake of giving aid." I am maintaining just the opposite.

32. Nor is it having the later opportunity to prevent a bad outcome (and not taking such opportunity) that makes one agent (more) responsible for a bad outcome. If it were, then the Levite who passed by the man lying wounded on the Jericho road could excuse his not stopping to render aid if he saw the priest following him in the distance. (And the priest could excuse *his* not stopping if he saw the Samaritan following *him*.)

33. See Bernard Williams, "The Idea of Equality," in *Problems of Self* (Cambridge: 1973), especially pp. 233–34.

34. I have (silently) stopped talking about considerations of justice because I believe that considerations about justice are subsidiary to considerations about using, that using is the more fundamental notion. But this is a substantive—and a controversial—claim, and not one that can be discussed or defended here. See *ibid.*, especially pp. 233–34.

35. When I wrote this paper, I believed that it was not feasible to write a clear paper without frequent use of a third-person singular pronoun. I also believed that, though clearly less than optimal, the common conven-

tion of using 'he' and 'his' to refer to both males and females was not objectionable. I no longer believe either of these things. Were I to rewrite the paper, I would correct what I now regard as its unfortunate and avoidable overuse of masculine pronouns.

I have continued to write on issues related to those discussed in this paper. Here is a list of some relevant work: "Abortion and Self-Defense," *Philosophy and Public Affairs*, 13 (1984): 175–207; "The Doctrine of Double Effect: Problems of Interpretation," *Pacific Philosophical Quarterly*, 65 (1984); "Contemporary Deontology," in *A Companion to Ethics*, ed. Peter Singer (Oxford: Blackwell, 1981), pp. 205–18; "Moral Theorizing and Moral Practice: Reflections on the Sources of Hypocrisy," in *The Applied Ethics Reader*, eds. Winkler and Coombs (Oxford: Blackwell, 1993), pp. 164–80; "Intention, Motivation and the Decision Not to Live" (under consideration), and "The Three Strands of 'Killing': Some Reflections on Euthanasia" (under consideration).

20

Actions, Intentions, and Consequences: The Doctrine of Doing and Allowing

Warren S. Quinn

SOMETIMES WE CANNOT BENEFIT one person without harming, or failing to help, another; and where the cost to the other would be serious—where, for example, he would die—a substantial moral question is raised: would the benefit justify the harm? Some moralists would answer this question by balancing the good against the evil. But others deny that consequences are the only things of moral relevance. To them it also matters whether the harm comes from action, for example, from killing someone, or from inaction, for example, from not saving someone. They hold that for some good ends we might properly allow a certain evil to befall someone, even though we could not actively bring that evil about. Some people also see moral significance in the distinction between what we intend as a means or an end and what we merely foresee will result incidentally from our choice. They hold that in some situations we might properly bring about a certain evil if it were merely foreseen but not if it were intended.

Those who find these distinctions morally relevant think that a benefit sufficient to justify harmful choices of one sort may fail to justify choices no more harmful, but of the other sort.[1] In the case of the distinction between the intentional and the merely foreseen, this view is central to what is usually called the Doctrine of Double Effect (DDE). In the case of the distinction between action and inaction, the view has no common name, so for convenience we may call it the Doctrine of Doing and Allowing

From *Philosophical Review* 98, no. 3 (July 1989). Copyright 1991 Cornell University. Reprinted by permission of the publisher.

(DDA). (Because harm resulting from intentional inaction has, typically, been allowed to occur.) Absolutist forms of either doctrine would simply rule out certain choices (for example, murder or torture) no matter what might be gained from them. Nonabsolutist forms would simply demand more offsetting benefit as a minimum justification for choices of one sort than for equally harmful choices of the other sort.

In this paper I shall examine the Doctrine of Doing and Allowing.[2] My aim is twofold: first, to find the formulation of the distinction that best fits our moral intuitions and second, to find a theoretical rationale for thinking the distinction, and the intuitions, morally significant. Both tasks are difficult, but the former will prove especially complex. What we find in the historical and contemporary literature on this topic is not a single clearly drawn distinction, but several rather different distinctions conforming roughly but not exactly to the distinction between what someone does and what he does not do. Special cases of inaction may be treated by an author as belonging, morally speaking, with the doings, and special cases of doing as belonging with the inactions. So in searching for the proper intuitive fit, we shall have to be alert to the possibility that the distinction between action and inaction (or between doing and allowing) is only a first approximation to the distinction we really want.

In evaluating various formulations of the doctrine I shall need special test cases. These will often involve improbable scenarios and repetitive structural elements. This is likely to try the reader's patience (he or she may begin to wonder, for example, whether we are discussing the morality of public transportation). But it may help to recall that such artificialities can hardly be avoided anywhere in philosophy.[3] As in science, the odd sharp focus of the test cases is perfectly compatible with the general importance of the ideas being tested. And the DDA is, I think, of the greatest general significance, both because it enters as a strand into many real moral issues and because it stands in apparent opposition to that most general of all moral theories, consequentialism.

Before beginning, I should emphasize that both the DDE and, especially, the DDA apply more directly to moral justification than to other forms of moral evaluation. It is therefore open to a defender of the DDA to admit that two *unjustified* choices that cause the same degree of harm are equally *bad*, even though one choice is to harm and the other not to save. I note this only because some writers have looked for such pairs in hope of refuting the doctrine.[4] Take the well-known example of an adult who deliberately lets a child cousin drown in order to inherit a family fortune.[5] The act seems so wicked that we understand the point of saying that it is no better than drowning the child. But if so, how can we hold that the difference between killing and letting die matters morally?

This objection seems to presuppose that if letting someone die is ever more acceptable, *ceteris paribus*, than killing someone, it must be because some intrinsic moral disvalue attaches to killing but not to letting die. And if so, this intrinsic difference must show up in all such cases.[6] But the doctrine may, and I shall argue should, be understood in a quite different way. The basic thing is not that killing is intrinsically worse than letting die, or more generally that harming is worse than failing to save from harm, but that these different choices run up against different kinds of rights—one of which is stronger than the other in the sense that it is less easily defeated. But its greater strength in this sense does not entail that its *violation* need be noticeably worse.

Such relations between rights are possible because moral blame for the violation of a right depends very much more on motive and expected harm than on the degree to which the right is defeasible. Your right of privacy that the police not enter your home without permission, for example, is more easily defeated than your right that I, an ordinary citizen, not do so. But it seems morally no better, and perhaps even worse, for the police to violate this right than for me to. So there is nothing absurd in saying that the adult acts as badly when he lets the child drown as when he drowns the child, while insisting that there are contexts in which the child would retain the right not to be killed but not the right to be saved.

I

The Doctrine of Doing and Allowing has been most notably defended in recent moral philosophy by Philippa Foot.[7] It will be convenient, therefore, to begin with two of the examples she uses to show the intuitive force of the doctrine.[8] In Rescue I, we can save either five people in danger of drowning at one place or a single person in danger of drowning somewhere else. We cannot save all six. In Rescue II, we can save the five only by driving over and thereby killing someone who (for an unspecified reason) is trapped on the road. If we do not undertake the rescue, the trapped person can later be freed. In Rescue I, we seem perfectly justified in proceeding to save the five even though we thereby fail to save the one. In Rescue II, however, it is far from obvious that we may proceed. The doctrine is meant to capture and explain pairs of cases like these in which consequential considerations are apparently held constant (for example, five lives versus one) but in which we are inclined to sharply divergent moral verdicts.

The first order of business is to get clearer on the crucial distinction that the doctrine invokes. In effect, the DDA discriminates between two kinds of agency in which harm comes to somebody. It discriminates *in favor of* one kind of agency (for example, letting someone drown in Rescue I) and it discriminates *against* the other kind (for example, running over someone in Rescue II).[9] That is, it makes these discriminations in the sense of allowing that the pursuit of certain goods can justify the first kind of harmful agency but not the second. I shall call the favored kind of agency *negative*, since on any plausible account it is usually a matter of what the agent does *not* do. For parallel reasons, I shall call the disfavored kind of agency *positive*. But, as indicated earlier, the distinction between positive and negative agency may or may not line up exactly with the ordinary distinction between doing and allowing or action and inaction. We may discover, as we consider various special circumstances, that certain actions function morally as allowings and certain inactions as doings. So let us begin by sifting various proposals for spelling out the nonmoral difference between the two kinds of agency.

One such proposal comes from some brief passages in the *Summa Theologiae* where Aquinas could be taken to suggest that the difference between the two forms of agency is one of voluntariness.[10] In harmful positive agency, the harm proceeds from the will of the agent while in harmful negative agency it does not.[11] St. Thomas seems to think that foreseeable harm that comes from action is automatically voluntary. But he thinks that foreseeable harm coming from inaction is voluntary only when the agent could and *should* have acted to prevent it. Positive agency would therefore include all foreseeably harmful actions and those foreseeably harmful inactions that could and should have been avoided. And negative agency would include the foreseeably harmful inactions that could not or need not have been avoided.

But what kind of "should" (or "need") is this? If we take it to be moral, the doctrine becomes circular.[12] Inactions falling under positive agency are harder to justify than inactions falling under negative agency. Why? Because by definition the latter need not have been avoided while the former, if possible, should have been.

We could, however, avoid the circularity by taking the "should" to be premoral, reflecting social and legal conventions that assign various tasks to different persons. And we might think that these conventions play a central role in an important premoral, but morally relevant, notion of causality.[13] The helmsman's job is to steer the ship, and this is why we say that it foundered *because* of his careless inaction. The loss of the ship would thus be like the death in Rescue II, which happens because of what we do. And both cases would contrast with the death in Rescue I, which we do not, in the relevant sense, bring about. Voluntariness would thus be seen as a distinctive kind of causal relation linking agency and its harmful upshots in the cases of action and conventionally proscribed inaction (positive agency), but not in the case of conventionally permitted inaction (negative agency). So formulated, the doctrine not only would be clear but would have an obvious rationale. Harmful negative agency is easier to justify because in such cases the harm cannot, in the relevant causal sense, be laid at the agent's door.

I have two objections to this proposal. First, there is little reason to treat most instances of the neglect of conventional duty as positive agency. We can usually explain in other ways just why morality takes these tasks so seriously. If human communities are to thrive, people will have to perform their social roles. That is why, in a variant of Rescue I, the private lifeguard of the lone individual might not be morally permitted to go off to save the five, even though a mere bystander would be. To explain this difference, we would not also need to suppose that the private lifeguard and bystander stand in different causal relations to the person's death. There is, moreover, room to think that the special duty of the private lifeguard should be put aside, especially if his employer is a pampered rich man, and the five are too poor to afford personal attendants. But this kind of circumstance would have no justificatory force where death was the upshot of clearly positive agency. In Rescue II, for example, it would not matter that the man trapped on the road was rich and spoiled while the five were poor and worthy.

My second objection is more general. The type of proposal we are examining relationalizes the special moral opprobrium attaching to positive agency by reference to its special causal properties. Since negative agency is not, in the intended sense, the cause of its unfortunate upshots, the moral barriers against it are lower. But this leaves the doctrine open to a serious criticism. For there are other conceptions of causality according to which we are in (the original) Rescue I every bit as much a cause of death as in Rescue II. What matters, according to these conceptions, is whether a nonoccurrence necessary for a given effect was, relative to a certain standard background, surprising or noteworthy. In this sense, we may say that a building burns down because its sprinklers failed to work, even though their failure was traceable to the diversion of water to another more important fire. That the diversion was quite proper is nothing against the claim that the failure of the sprinklers helped cause the loss of the building. And something similar holds for Rescue I. The fact that we did not save the one because we quite properly saved the others would not show that his death was not in part due to our choice.

So even if there is a causal notion that corresponds to Aquinas's idea of the voluntary, it is in competition with other causal notions that may seem better to capture what is empirically important in scientific and ordinary explanation. And it is arguable that the defense of the doctrine should not depend on a causal conception that we would otherwise do without. If the doctrine is sound it ought to remain plausible on an independently plausible theory of causation. In any case, this is what I shall assume here. So I shall grant opponents of the doctrine that the permissible inactions we are considering, no less than the impermissible actions, are partial causes of their harmful upshots. This will force me to try to make sense of the doctrine on other grounds.

But this still leaves the task of stating the nonmoral content of the distinction between harmful positive and harmful negative agency. Perhaps the difference should, after all, be put in the most simple and straightforward way, as the difference between action that produces harm and inaction that produces harm. If we think of action along the lines proposed by Elizabeth Anscombe and taken up by Donald Davidson—a conception whose basic outline I proposed to adopt—individual actions are concrete particulars that may be variously described.[14] To say that John hit Bill yesterday is to say that there was a hitting, done by John to Bill, that occurred yesterday. To say that John did not hit Bill, on the other hand, is to say that there was no such hitting. Taking things this way, the distinction between harmful positive agency and harmful negative agency would be the distinction between harm occurring because of what the agent does (because of the existence of one of his actions) and harm occurring because of what the agent did not do but might have done (because of the noninstantiation of some kind of action that he might have performed).[15]

Surprisingly, most moral philosophers who write on these matters reject this way of drawing the distinction. Jonathan Bennett, a severe critic of the DDA, dismisses Davidson's conception of action without argument.[16] Most likely he minds its failure to provide a clear criterion for distinguishing action from inaction in all cases, one that would tell us, for example, whether observing a boycott (by not buying grapes) or snubbing someone (by not acknowledging his greeting) consists in doing something by way of inaction or simply in deliberately not doing something. Bennett is reluctant to assign moral work to any distinction that leaves some cases unclear, especially where there is no theoretically compelling reductionistic theory for the clear cases. But I am disinclined to adopt such a standard. Almost no familiar distinction that applies to real objects is clear in all cases, and theoretical reducibility is a virtue only where things really are reducible. In any case, the imposition of such a standard would shut down moral theory at once, dependent as it is on the as yet unreduced and potentially vague distinctions between what is and is not a person, a promise, an informed consent, etc.

But Bennett is not simply negative. He proposes an ingenious and, for limited applications, clearly drawn distinction between positive and negative *facts* about agency as a respectable way of formulating the doctrine.[17] (Not of course to save it, but to expose it.) Roughly speaking, an event is brought about by someone's positive instrumentality, as Bennett calls it, when the event is explained by a relatively strong fact about the agent's behavior— for example, that he moved in one of a limited number of ways. Negative instrumentality, on the other hand, explains by reference to relatively weak facts about behavior—for example, that the agent moved in any one of a vast number of ways.

The trouble is that this distinction gets certain cases intuitively wrong. Bennett imagines a situation in which if Henry does nothing, just stays where he is, dust will settle and close a tiny electric circuit which will cause something bad—for example, an explosion that will kill Bill.[18] If Henry does nothing, he is by Bennett's criterion positively instrumental in Bill's death. (For only one of Henry's physical actions, staying still, will cause the death, while indefinitely many will prevent the death.) But suppose Henry could save five only by staying where he is—suppose he is holding a net into which five are falling. Surely he might then properly refuse to move even though it means not saving Bill. For his agency in Bill's death would in that case seem negative, much like that in Rescue I.

Bennett also misses the opposite case. Suppose the device will go off only if Henry makes some move or other. In that case his instrumentality in the death would, for Bennett, be negative. But those who would rule out Rescue II would surely not allow Henry to go to the rescue of five if that meant setting off the device. For his agency in the death of Bill would in that case seem positive.[19] Bennett's distinction, however admirable in other ways, is not the one we seem to want. Perhaps this is already clear when we reflect that, according to him, the instrumentality of someone who intentionally moves his body (in, for example, following the command "Move in some way or other—any way you like!") is negative.

Philippa Foot also rejects the idea that the distinction between positive and negative agency is that between action and inaction.[20] She claims that it would not make any interesting moral difference if respirators (presumably sustaining patients who would otherwise die) had to be turned on again each day. Active turning off and passive not turning on would be morally the same. To be relevant to the present issues, her idea must be that this would not make a difference even in cases where some great good could come about only if a particular respirator were not running. Let us see whether this is right. Suppose there are temporary electrical problems in a hospital such that the five respirators in Ward B can be kept going only if the one in Ward A is off. On Foot's view it should not matter whether a hospital attendant keeps the five going by shutting down the one or, in case it is the kind that needs to be restarted, by simply not restarting it.

It would be very odd to think that if the single respirator were already off, the attendant would be required to restart it even if that meant shutting down the five in Ward B. So Foot's idea must imply that if the single respirator were running, the attendant could just as properly shut it down to keep the others running. Now while there seems something more objectionable about shutting the respirator down, I think that all things considered it might be permitted. One reason is that we could perhaps see it as a matter of the hospital's allocating something that belongs to it, a special kind of circumstance that we shall consider later. But suppose the hospital is an unusual one in which each patient must provide his own equipment and private nursing care. Suppose further that you are an outsider who happens for some reason to be the only person on the scene when the electrical problem arises. In this case, it seems to matter whether you keep the respirators in Ward B going by not restarting the one in Ward A (it being of the type that needs restarting and the private nurse having failed to show up that day) or whether you actually shut it down. The first case seems rather like Rescue I and the second uncomfortably like Rescue II.

Foot goes on to offer what she takes to be a different and better interpretation of the distinction. She thinks what matters is not the difference between action and inaction but the difference between two relations an agent can have to a sequence of events that leads to harm. It is one thing to *initiate* such a sequence or to *keep it going,* but quite another to *allow it to complete itself* when it is already in train.[21] Agency of the first two kinds is positive, while agency that merely allows is negative. One problem with this account arises when we try to explain the difference between allowing a sequence to complete itself and keeping it going when it would otherwise have stopped. We might have thought that the former was a matter of doing nothing to stop it and the latter was a matter of doing something to continue it. But that would seem to take us back to the rejected distinction between action and inaction.

Another problem concerns forms of help and support which do not seem to consist in keeping already existing dangerous sequences at bay. Suppose I have always fired up my aged neighbor's furnace before it runs out of fuel. I haven't promised to do it, but I have always done it and intend to continue. Now suppose that an emergency arises involving five other equally close and needy friends who live far away, and that I can save them only by going off immediately and letting my neighbor freeze. This seems to be more like Rescue I than Rescue II, but it doesn't appear to be a case in which I merely allow an already existing fatal sequence to finish my neighbor off. For he was not already freezing or even, in some familiar sense, in danger of freezing before the emergency arose. Of if we think he was in danger, that danger was partly constituted by what I might fail to do. We might simply stipulate, of course, that any fatal sequence that appears to arise from a *failure* to help someone is really the continuation of a preexisting sequence. But then we seem to be falling back on the notion of inaction as fundamental.

II

I am therefore inclined to reject Bennett's and Foot's positive suggestions, despite their obvious attractions. May we then return to the simple and straightforward way of drawing the distinction, as between harm that comes from action and harm that comes from inaction? I think not. Cases involving the harmful *action of objects or forces* over which we have certain powers of control seem to demand a more complex treatment. Consider, for example, the following variant of Rescue II (call it Rescue III). We are off by special train to save five who are in imminent danger of death. Every second counts. You have just taken over from the driver, who has left the locomotive to attend to something. Since the train is on automatic control you need do nothing to keep it going. But you can stop it by putting on the brakes. You suddenly see someone trapped ahead on the track. Unless you act he will be killed. But if you do stop, and then free the man, the rescue mission will be aborted. So you let the train continue.

In this case it seems to me that you make the wrong choice. You must stop the train. It might seem at first that this is because you occupy, if only temporarily, the role of driver and have therefore assumed a driver's special responsibility to drive the train safely. But, upon reflection, it would not make much moral difference whether you were actually driving the train or merely had access to its brake. Nor would it much matter whether you were in the train or had happened upon a trackside braking device.[22] The important thing from the standpoint of your agency is that you *can* stop the train and thereby prevent it from killing the one.

But this is not the only thing that matters, as can be seen in a different kind of case. Suppose, in a variant of Rescue I (Rescue IV), you are on a train on which there has just been an explosion. You can stop the train, but that is a complicated business that would take time. So you set it on automatic forward and rush back to the five badly wounded passengers. While attending to them, you learn that a man is trapped far ahead on the track. You must decide whether to return to the cabin to save him or stay with the passengers and save them.

May you stay? I think you may.[23] We would be more tolerant of inaction here than in Rescue III. And this is because of your intentions. In Rescue III you intend an action of the train that in fact causes the man's death, its passing over the spot where he is trapped.[24] Not, of course, because he is trapped there. But because the train must pass that spot if the five are to be saved. In Rescue IV, however, things are different. In that case you intend no action of the train that leads to the man's death. The purposes for which you act would be just as well served if the train's brakes were accidentally to apply themselves.

In Rescue III, but not in Rescue IV, the train kills the man *because* of your intention that it continue forward. This implicates you, I believe, in the fatal action of the train itself. If you had no control, but merely wished that the rescue would continue—or if, as in Rescue IV, you had control but no such wish—you would not be party to the action of the train. But the combination of control and intention in Rescue III makes for a certain kind of complicity. Your choice to let the train continue forward is strategic and deliberate. Since you clearly *would* have it continue for the sake of the five, there is a sense in which, by deliberately not stopping it, you *do* have it continue. For these reasons your agency counts as positive.

The surprise in this is that we must bring the distinction between what is intended and merely foreseen into the DDA. But the two doctrines do not therefore merge. As I shall try to show in another paper, the DDE depends on something different—on whether or not a victim is *himself* an intentional object, someone whose manipulation or elimination will be useful. But the victim is not in that way involved in the special kind of positive agency we find in Rescue III. What is intended there is not something for him—that he be affected in a certain way—but some action of an object that (foreseeably but quite unintentionally) leads to his death.

To the idea of positive agency by action, we must therefore add positive agency by this special kind of inaction. But this is, I think, the only complication we need to build into the doctrine itself (Other more minor qualifications will be discussed in the next section.) We may now construct the doctrine in stages, starting with some definitions. An agent's *most direct contribution* to a harmful upshot of his agency is the contribution that most directly explains the harm. And one contribution explains harm more directly than another if the explanatory value of the second is exhausted in the way it explains the first.

In the absence of special circumstances involving the actions of objects, an agent's contributions to various effects in the world are those of his voluntary actions and inactions that help produce the effects. So in ordinary cases, his most direct contribution to any effect is the action or inaction that most directly explains the effect. In Rescue I, for example, our most direct contribution to the death of the one is our failure to save him. Our going off to save the five contributes less directly. For it explains the death precisely by explaining the failure to save.[25] In Rescue II, on the other hand, our most direct contribution to the death of the man trapped on the road is our act of running him over.

In special circumstances, that is, where harm comes from an active object or force, an agent may by inaction contribute the harmful action of the object itself. This, as we have seen, happens just in case the object harms because the agent deliberately fails to control it and he fails to control it because he wants some action of the object that in fact leads to the harm. Having defined this much, the rest is straightforward. Harmful positive agency is that in which an agent's most direct contribution to the harm is an action, whether his own or that of some object. Harmful negative agency is that in which the most direct contribution is an inaction, a failure to prevent the harm.

III

We should now look briefly at certain kinds of cases in which common-sense morality seems to qualify the doctrine as I have just described it, permitting us to harm or even kill someone in order to help others. I am not thinking here of the avoidance of great catastrophes. The doctrine, as already indicated, need not be absolutist. And even in its nonabsolutist form, it cannot contain everything of moral relevance. Special rights to do that which produces harm and special duties to prevent harm must also be factored in. In this way the doctrine has the force of one important *prima facie* principle among others. Rights of competition, to give a familiar example, legitimate certain kinds of harmful positive agency—such as the shrewd but honest competition in which you take away another person's customers. The right to punish is another familiar example. On the other side, special duties to aid may arise from jobs, contracts, natural relations, or from the fact that someone's present predicament was of your making.[26] These special duties explain why some instances of negative agency seem no easier to justify than active harmings.

These familiar rights and duties do not require that the doctrine be qualified. They merely oppose it in particular cases. But other situations seem either to require special amendments to my definitions of positive and negative agency or to show that in certain

situations the doctrine lacks its usual *prima facie* force. Qualifications of the first sort sometimes seem required where harm arises
from the active *withdrawal* of aid. In one kind of case you actively
abort a project of rescuing or helping that, knowing what you
now know, it would have been wrong to undertake. For example,
you stop the train in Rescue III, and the five therefore die. In
another kind of case, you remove something from where it would
help fewer to where it would help more, for example, a raft that
is presently within the reach of one drowning victim but that
could be moved to the vicinity of several other victims.[27] The
object might be your body. You might, for example, cushion the
fall of one baby if you stay where you are, but cushion the fall of
several others if you move. In all these cases harm comes to someone because you decide to act rather than to do nothing. But
because your action is a certain kind of withdrawing of aid, it
naturally enough seems to count as negative agency.

In other cases, harmful positive agency seems to lack some of
the *prima facie* opprobrium that usually attaches to it. Sometimes
this is because the harm would have been avoided but for some
blameable fault of the person harmed. Suppose, for example, that
the person in Rescue II who blocks the road had been repeatedly
warned not to stray where he might interfere with important
rescue efforts. If so, we might feel somewhat more justified in
proceeding with the rescue (although never, I think, as justified
as we feel in Rescue I). People must, after all, accept some responsibility for the predicaments they stupidly and wrongly bring
upon themselves.[28]

In a quite different kind of case, someone may have a special
liability to be harmed by a physical or psychological interaction
that is generally innocuous and, therefore, of no general moral
significance. He might have a rare disease that makes any kind
of physical contact very harmful to him. Or he might become
dangerously hysterical if we yell in his presence. In such cases we
might feel that we could try to save other people from some
serious danger even if it would mean brushing up against him or
yelling. For, unlike standard instances of harmful positive agency,
the attempt would not seem to count as an aggression against the
victim, since he does not suffer because of any *general or typical*

liability to harm. And this seems sensible. Morality must to some degree reflect the standard human condition. In particular, it must be capable of defining a class of presumptively innocent actions.[29]

Another qualification concerns large public and private projects, like the building of skyscrapers, highways, and dams. We are clearly permitted to help initiate such projects even though we know that in their course some deaths or injuries are practically inevitable. For one thing, the harm is usually remote from what we do. And, more important, the actual harm will generally have been preventable, and its occurrence will be much more directly traceable to the wrongful agency of persons more immediately concerned. It is of course essential that we do not in any way intend the harm that may occur, and take reasonable precautions to prevent it.

In the celebrated Trolley Problem, we seem to find yet another exception to the doctrine's strictures against harmful positive agency.[30] In this case a runaway trolley threatens five who are trapped on the track where it is now moving. If the driver does nothing the five will die. But he can switch to a side-track where only one person is trapped. Most people think the driver may switch tracks. But switching is positive agency while doing nothing appears to be negative agency. So the case looks like a counterexample.

But if we look again, we can see that the driver's passive option, letting the train continue on the main track, is really a form of positive agency. This is because the only possibly acceptable reasons for him not to switch would be to prevent the death of the man on the side-track or to keep clean hands. But the clean-hands motive begs the question; it presupposes that the doctrine does not also speak against not switching. So in deciding the status of his possible inaction we must put this motive aside. This leaves the aim of preventing the death of the man on the side-track. But if the driver fails to switch for this reason, it is because he intends that the train continue in a way that will save the man. But then he intends that the train continue forward past the switch, and this leads to the death of the five. So, by my earlier definitions, his choice is really between two different positive options—one passive and one active.[31] And that is why he may pick the alterna-

tive that does less harm. Properly understood, Trolley Cases are
no exception to the doctrine.

IV

Perhaps we have found the basic form of the doctrine and the
natural qualifications that, when combined with other plausible
moral principles, accurately map our moral intuitions. But someone will surely object that intuitiveness and correctness are different things and that intuitions about particular kinds of cases may
reflect nothing more than conditioning or prejudice. What we
need, therefore, is a more philosophical defense of the doctrine,
a rationale that can be called upon to support the intuitions. Foot
locates a kind of rationale in the distinction, borrowed from the
law but applied to morality, between negative and positive rights.
Negative rights are claim rights against harmful intervention, interference, assault, aggression, etc. and might therefore naturally
seem to proscribe harmful positive agency, whether by action of
the agent himself or by action of some object to which, by strategic inaction, he lends a hand. Positive rights, on the other hand,
are claim rights to aid or support, and would therefore seem to
proscribe harmful negative agency. Foot's idea seems to be that
general negative rights are, *ceteris paribus*, harder to override than
general positive rights.[32] And while this seems intuitively correct,
it is not obvious why it should be so.

The thesis that negative rights are harder to override immediately implies that negative rights take precedence over positive
rights. And it is the thesis of precedence that matters most to us,
since it applies directly to circumstances, such as the ones we have
been considering, in which the two kinds of rights compete with
each other—situations in which the positive rights of one person
or group can be honored just in case the negative rights of another
person or group are infringed. In Rescue II, for example, the
positive rights of the five to be saved from death compete in this
way with the negative right of the trapped person not to be killed.

The weakest thesis of precedence would hold that in such oppo-
sitions the negative rights prevail just in case the goods they protect (the goods that would be lost if they were overridden) are at

least as great as the goods protected by the positive rights (the goods that would be lost if they were overridden.) The goods in questions are life, health, freedom from injury, pleasure *de facto* liberty, etc.—goods that do not include or presuppose the moral good of respect for any of the rights in conflict.[33] All other things being equal, the weakest thesis of precedence would forbid us to kill one person to save another, but would permit us to kill one in order to save two.

A very strong thesis of precedence, on the other hand, would rule out any infringement of certain very important negative rights (for example the right not to be killed or the right not to be tortured) no matter what positive rights were in competition with them. This would still allow positive rights protecting more important goods to prevail over negative rights protecting less important goods—would permit us, for example, to knock one person down in order to save another from serious injury. But it would not permit us, for example, to kill or torture one to save any number of others even from death or torture.

A perhaps more plausible intermediate thesis would hold that no negative rights are absolute, but would accord to the most important ones considerably more force than they have on the weakest thesis. Such a view might well accommodate the ordinary thought that while someone may not be killed to save five, he might be killed to stave off the kinds of disasters that consequentialists dream up. It might go on to state some kind of criterion for when negative rights must give way; or it might, in Aristotelian fashion, leave the matter to moral perception.[34]

If, on the other hand, negative rights do not take precedence over positive rights, then either the reverse is true or neither takes precedence over the other. If positive rights actually take precedence, then we might, as seems absurd, kill two to save one. Suppose one person is drowning and two are trapped on the road. A morality that permitted us to run over and kill the two in order to save the one seems not only odious but incoherent. For once we have decided to kill the two, we have placed them in at least as much danger as the one was in originally. And that would presumably activate their positive rights to be saved from their predicament—rights that would collectively outweigh the positive rights of the one who is drowning.

If there is going to be precedence, it clearly has to be precedence of negative rights. But this leaves open the possibility that neither kind of right takes precedence over the other, that is, that in the competitions we are considering the rights protecting the greater balance of good should, *ceteris paribus*, prevail. In such a moral system the person trapped on the road in Rescue II could not with moral authority object to our running over and killing him. For we shall be saving five others each of whom values his life just as much as he values his. This moral system is perfectly coherent. But it has unappealing aspects.

In such a morality the person trapped on the road has a moral say about whether his body may be destroyed only if what he stands to lose is greater than what others stand to gain. But then surely he has no real say at all. For, in cases where his loss would be greater than the gain to others, the fact that he could not be killed would be sufficiently explained not by his authority in the matter but simply by the balance of overall costs. And if this is how it is in general—if we may rightly injure or kill him whenever others stand to gain more than he stands to lose—then surely his body (one might say his person) is not in any interesting moral sense *his*. It seems rather to belong to the human community, to be dealt with according to its best overall interests.

If it is morally his, then we go wrong if, against his will, we destroy or injure it simply on the ground that his loss will be less than the gains of others. The same is true of his mind. If we may rightly lobotomize or brainwash him whenever others will gain more than he will lose, then his mind seems to belong not to him but to the community. There is an obvious parallel here with his different, and much less important, relation to his property. An object does not belong to him if he may have and use it, and others may not take it from him, only as long as his keeping it would be better for him than his losing it would be for them.[35] Whether we are speaking of ownership or more fundamental forms of possession, something is, morally speaking, his only if his say over what may be done to it (and thereby to him) can override the greater needs of others.[36]

A person is constituted by his body and mind. They are parts or aspects of him. For that very reason, it is fitting that he have primary say over what may be done to them—not because such an arrangement best promotes overall human welfare, but because any arrangement that denied him that say would be a grave indignity. In giving him this authority, morality recognizes his existence as an individual with ends of his own—an independent *being*.[37] Since that is what he is, he deserves this recognition. Were morality to withhold it, were it to allow us to kill or injure him whenever that would be collectively best, it would picture him not as a being in his own right but as a cell in the collective whole.[38]

This last point can be illustrated not by thinking of bodies or minds but of lives. The moral sense in which your mind or body is yours seems to be the same as that in which your life is yours. And if your life is yours then there must be decisions concerning it that are yours to make—decisions protected by negative rights. One such matter is the choice of work or vocation. We think there is something morally amiss when people are forced to be farmers or flute players just because the balance of social needs tips in that direction. Barring great emergencies, we think people's lives must be theirs to lead. Not because that makes things go best in some independent sense but because the alternative seems to obliterate them as individuals. This obliteration, and not social inefficiency, is one of the things that strikes us as appalling in totalitarian social projects—for example, in the Great Cultural Revolution.

None of this, of course, denies the legitimate force of positive rights. They too are essential to the status we want as persons who matter, and they must be satisfied when it is morally possible to do so. But negative rights, for the reasons I have been giving, define the terms of moral possibility. Their precedence is essential to the moral fact of our lives, minds, and bodies really being ours.

But it might be objected that the weakest thesis of precedence would give us some degree of moral independence, and at the same time would let us do the maximum good, honoring as many positive rights as possible. On that thesis, it would not be proper to kill one person to save another who is equally happy and useful—it would not be proper, say, to flip a coin. But it could be right to kill one to save two or even five to save six. Why then adopt a stronger thesis? The answer, I think, depends on how important the relevant forms of legitimate control are to us—the extent to which we wish to belong, in the sense under discussion, to ourselves.[39] And this might depend on the aspect of ourselves in question.

We feel, I believe, most strongly about assaults on our minds. Here most of us are far from minimalists about the precedence of negative rights. The idea that against our will we could justifiably be brainwashed or lobotomized in order to help others cuts deeply against our sense of who and what we are. Here it seems the sense of our own rightful say leads almost to absolutism. We feel less strongly about our persons (at least those parts that do not directly affect our minds) and labor. But even here we wish, I think, to have a kind of defensive say that goes far beyond the weakest thesis of precedence. A system that gave you some authority over what might be done to you but allowed us to kill or injure you whenever that would even slightly maximize the overall good would seem a form of tokenism.

It must be said that something like the precedence of negative rights can be accepted by a certain kind of consequentialist—one who thinks that a person's having an effective say over what is done to him (but not over what is done to others) is, in itself, a kind of good that can be added to the more familiar goods of life or happiness.[40] This kind of consequentialism would grant each of us a kind of special authority against interference. But it is unclear that it would thereby give us the moral image of ourselves we think fitting. For it locates the ultimate ground of proper deference to a person's will in the fact that such deference maximizes the general balance of good. In such a system, it is not so much his right to have his way that really matters as the general goodness of letting him have his way.

A consequentialist might reply that anything other than a consequentially grounded system of rights leads to absurdities, and that in praising the virtues of a rights-based morality I can be saying no more than that there is value in the social influence of such a system—that it is good if people's rights are respected and bad if they are violated. But circumstances can arise in which respecting someone's negative rights will lead to an abuse of the negative rights of others. And in at least this kind of case it would be incoherent, the consequentialist will insist, to suppose that negative rights can override their positive counterparts.[41] Suppose

B and C will be murdered unless we murder A. A has a negative right against our murdering him, and B and C have positive rights that we help prevent their being murdered. If the ground of the system of rights lies in the value of respect for (or at least nonviolation of) rights, then surely the positive rights of B and C must prevail. For only by murdering A can we maximize the value that the entire system aims at.

But his objection misses the mark. The value that lies at the heart of my argument—the appropriateness of morality's recognizing us as independent beings—is in the first instance a virtue of the moral design *itself*. The fittingness of this recognition is not a goal of action, and therefore not something that we could be tempted to serve by violating or infringing anybody's rights. It is also true, of course, that we think it good if people actually respect each other's rights. But this value depends on the goodness of the moral design that assigns these rights. It is not that we think it fitting to ascribe rights because we think it a good thing that rights be respected. Rather we think respect for rights a good thing precisely because we think people actually have them—and, if my account is correct, that they have them because it is fitting that they should. So there is no way in which the basic rationale of a system of rights rules it out that a person might have a right not to be harmed even when harming him would prevent many others from being harmed in similar ways.

The rationale that I have proposed is anticonsequentialist not only in its assignment of priority to negative rights, but also, and more fundamentally, in its conception of the basic social function of morality. For consequentialism, it seems fair to say, the chief point of morality is to make things go better overall—to increase average or total welfare within the human community. But on the view presented here, an equally basic and urgent moral task is to define our proper powers and immunities with respect to one another, to specify the mutual authority and respect that are the basic terms of voluntary human association. The doctrine we have been discussing addresses this task directly. And this is why it is far more than a casuistical curiosity. Whether we ultimately agree with it or not, we should recognize that, in giving each person substantial authority over what can rightly be done to him, the doctrine conveys an important and attractive idea of what it is to be a citizen rather than a subject in the moral world.

NOTES

Thanks to Rogers Albritton, Tyler Burge, Phillippa Foot, Matthew Hanser, Thomas Nagel, Michael Thomson, Derek Parfit, T. M. Scanlon, and to the editors of *The Philosophical Review* for valuable suggestions and criticisms.

1. Harm here is meant to include any evil that can be the upshot of choice, for example, the loss of privacy, property, or control. But to keep matters simple, my examples will generally involve physical harm, and the harm in question will generally be death.
2. I shall examine the DDE in a subsequent paper, "Actions, Intentions, and Consequences: The Doctrine of the Double Effect."
3. Think of Gettier cases, brain transplants, teletransporters, etc.
4. For example, Michael Tooley in "Abortion and Infanticide," *Philosophy and Public Affairs* 2 (1972), p. 59.
5. From James Rachels, "Active and Passive Euthanasia," *The New England Journal of Medicine,* 292 (1975), p. 79; this volume, pp. 115–16.
6. In "Harming, Not Aiding, and Positive Rights," (*Philosophy and Public Affairs,* 15 [1986], pp. 5–11), Frances Kamm rightly makes us distinguish between two ways in which killing might be intrinsically worse than letting die: a) killing might have some bad essential feature that cannot attach to letting die or b) killing might have some bad essential feature that, while not essential to letting die, can nevertheless be present in cases of letting die. If (b) is true then the moral equivalence of the two cases in which the child drowns would not establish a general moral equivalence between killing and letting die. For letting the child drown might be a special case in which letting die has the bad feature essential to killings but not to lettings die. And even apart from Kamm's point, the idea that intrinsically nonequivalent parts must always make an overall evaluative difference when embedded in identical contexts seems wrong. Consider aesthetics. There may certainly be important intrinsic aesthetic differences between two lampshades even though they create an equally bad overall impression when placed on a certain lamp.
7. In "The Problem of Abortion and the Doctrine of the Double Effect," in *Virtues and Vices and Other Essays* (Berkeley, Calif.: University of California Press, 1978), pp. 19–32 (this volume, pp. 266–79), Foot argued that the distinction between doing and allowing could do all the

work usually credited to the distinction between the intentional and the merely foreseen. In "Killing and Letting Die," Jay Garfield, ed., *Abortion: Moral and Legal Perspectives* (Amherst, Mass.: University of Massachusetts Press, 1984), pp. 178–85 (this volume, chapter 17) and even later in "Morality, Action and Outcome," in Ted Honderich, ed., *Morality and Objectivity* (London, England: Routledge and Kegan Paul, 1985), pp. 23–38, she withdraws this claim, arguing instead that any intuitively adequate morality must assign an independent moral significance to the distinction between doing and allowing.

8. From "Killing and Letting Die," p. 179, this volume, p. oo.

9. It seems clear than an agent's *not* doing something (for example, not saving someone from drowning) can be morally evaluated as justified, unjustified, right, or wrong, in precisely the sense in which these terms apply to actions. I shall therefore speak of assessing the justification or the rightness of someone's *agency* in some matter, meaning by this an evaluation of his knowingly acting or not acting.

10. *Summa Theologiae XVII* (Cambridge, England: Blackfriars, 1970), 1a2ae Q. 6 article 3, pp. 15–16. The terms "positive agency" and "negative agency" are not, of course, St. Thomas's. This is the interpretation that he might give to them.

11. In speaking of an inaction as harmful or as producing harm (or in speaking of harm as coming from it) I am not begging the question against Aquinas. For I mean these expressions only in the weak sense of connecting the inaction with a harmful upshot, and not in any sense that would imply that the harm was voluntary.

12. It may be, of course, that Aquinas's account of the voluntary is not meant as part of the theory of justification and is therefore not directed to the distinction between positive and negative agency. It might instead be part of the theory of praiseworthiness and blameworthiness, which presupposes an independent account of what can and cannot be justified. If so, there could be no charge of circularity. For harmful inaction clearly does deserve blame only if it could and should, morally speaking, have been avoided.

13. I am indebted here to Michael Thompson, who thinks that something like this is suggested in the work of Elizabeth Anscombe.

14. G. M. A. Anscombe, *Intention,* 2nd ed. (Oxford, England: Blackwell, 1963), especially sec. 26, pp. 45–47. See also Donald Davidson, *Essays on Actions and Events* (Oxford, England: Clarendon Press, 1980). See there "The Logical Form of Action Sentences," pp. 105–22; "Criticism, Comment and Defence," pp. 122–44, esp. pp. 135–37; and "The Individuation of Events." pp. 163–80.

15. What I see as right in the Anscombe-Davidson view is the sug-

gested metaphysics—the claim that action is a matter of the presence of something and inaction a matter of its absence. And I think that our intuitions about whether something is an action or inaction as we think about it morally are metaphysically relevant. So I am not greatly worried that someone pursuing the Anscombe-Davidson line might discover criteria of action and inaction that would radically conflict with our judgments in moral thought.

16. "Morality and Consequences," *The Tanner Lectures on Human Values* II (Salt Lake City, Utah: University of Utah Press, 1981), pp. 54–55.

17. *Ibid.*, pp. 55–69.

18. *Ibid.*, pp. 66–68. If Henry's body were *activating* the device—if he were depressing a trigger or conducting a current—we might see his agency as positive despite his motionlessness. But Bennett doesn't assign any such role to Henry's body.

19. That Bill's death would in this case be a side-effect of the rescue does not distinguish it from Rescue II. For in neither case is the death of the one intended. It might be objected that here but not in Rescue II the killing would not be *part* of the rescue. But if Henry's movement sets off the explosion (for example, by triggering a fuse sensitive to movement) then Henry's killing Bill does seem part of the rescue, at least in the sense that he kills Bill by the very movements that form part of the rescue attempt. Of course there could be circumstances in which Henry's movement would not so much set off the explosion as allow it to be set off. Suppose, for example, Henry's remaining where he is prevents dust from settling upon and thereby triggering an explosive device below him. In such a case, I agree that he might go off to save the five. For although he will be active in Bill's death, his agency will involve taking his body from where it would save Bill to where he can make use of it to save the five, a special circumstance that I shall discuss later.

20. "Morality, Action and Outcome," p. 24.

21. *Ibid.*, p. 24, including note 2 on p. 37.

22. Suppose that you and a friend are off, by car, on a rescue mission that unexpectedly turns into Rescue II. You are sitting in the passenger seat, and your friend is driving. For some reason he hasn't noticed the trapped person, but you have. If you do nothing, your friend will inadvertently run over and kill the man. Can you really think that the end of rescuing the five would *not* justify your friend the driver in deliberately killing the man, but *would* justify you in keeping silent (or in not pulling up the hand brake)? I find this implausible. And it seems equally implausible to suppose that your obligation to yell or pull the brake comes from your having, temporarily, assumed the role of driver. What

matters is that the mission has become illicit precisely because, as you can see, it requires that someone be killed. So it has also become illicit to try to *further* the mission, whether by deliberate action or omission.

23. At least if you are not the driver or his designated replacement—that is, someone charged with a special moral responsibility to see to it that the train kills no one. If you have that responsibility but lack a special duty toward the injured people (you are not also their doctor), then there would be something extra on the moral balance in favor of stopping. But we should not build this complication into our account of the difference between positive and negative agency. For the force of this extra factor seems independent of facts about agency. If does not seem to derive from any supposition that, if you stay with the passengers, you will really be taking the train forward or will somehow be party to the fatal action of the train itself.

24. In Rescue III you intend an action of the train that immediately kills the man. But it would make no difference if, in a variant of the case, you did not intend that the train pass over the spot where the man was trapped, but merely intended that it pass over some nearer part of the track (where that would foreseeably lead to its passing over the fatal spot). Nor would it matter, in a further variant of the case, if the intended action of the train would lead to the man's being killed by some immediate cause other than the train. All that is essential is that you intend some action of the train that you can foresee will cause the man's death.

25. We fail to rescue the one *because* we rescue the five instead. But notice that this account implies, in the previously mentioned puzzle cases of boycotting and snubbing (cases where we are unsure whether there is a genuine action by way of an inaction or merely a deliberate inaction), that the agent's most direct contribution to the upshot is an inaction. Grape sales decline because we don't buy grapes, and we don't buy them *because* we are boycotting. Happily, this means that we do not have to decide whether boycotting is a genuine action in order to determine the boycotter's agency in the intended upshot. It will turn out on either hypothesis to be negative.

26. If you have advertently or inadvertently poisoned someone who can yet be saved by an antidote that you actually have, then you seem to be in no moral position to go to the rescue of five others rather than staying to save him.

27. It seems important in this kind of case that those who are saved by your action have just as much right to the raft as the one who suffers. Removing it from the reach of its owner would, for example, be very questionable. It also seems important that the person from whom the

raft is taken is not already using the raft to save himself. It is one thing to remove it from his reach and quite another to push him off it.

28. The responsibility of others also comes in when we know that an action will occasion aggression by a third party—for example, if I know that Jones will murder you if I rescue five of his enemies who are drowning. If it seems that I may proceed with the rescue in this case it is because we shall, quite sensibly, attribute the blame for your death to Jones and not to me. In this kind of situation it is important that the action I undertake is morally pressing. Had Jones threatened to murder you in case I mowed my lawn, my ignoring the threat might well seem a kind of active provocation.

29. But this qualification does not apply to special liabilities created by *external* features of a situation. If driving by Smith's house would set off an explosive device that would blow him up, then driving by, even when it would be necessary to rescue five others, would count as an aggression rather than a failure to help. And this also makes sense. For there seems to be no way in which we can define the class of presumptively innocent actions by prescinding from unusual external circumstances. Removing a ladder is not presumptively innocent when someone is high up on it. And driving down a public road is not presumptively innocent when someone is trapped on it. But entering someone's field of vision (where that sets off no devices, etc.) seems quite different, even where the person will, because of a rare mental illness, be harmed by it.

30. I believe the case was introduced by Foot in "The Problem of Abortion and the Doctrine of the Double Effect," p. 27, this volume p. 270. See also Judith Jarvis Thomson, "The Trolley Problem," in *Rights, Restitution, and Risk: Essays in Moral Theory* (Cambridge, Mass.: Harvard University Press, 1986), pp. 94–116. And Jonathan Glover discusses a fascinating real-life trolley case in *Causing Death and Saving Lives* (Harmondsworth, England: Penguin Books, 1977), pp. 102–103. During World War II British intelligence apparently had the power to deceive the German command about the accuracy of rocket attacks on London. Had they chosen to do so—and they did not—they could have redirected the rockets to less densely populated areas outside the city.

31. This solution to the trolley problem works equally well for versions in which the choice belongs to someone who happens upon a trackside switch.

32. See "The Problem of Abortion and the Doctrine of the Double Effect," p. 27, this volume p. 270. Foot does not actually speak of "general" positive and negative rights. But I think that is what she means. For natural or contractually acquired "special" positive rights may some-

times bind as strongly as general negative rights. We saw, for example, that a private lifeguard in Rescue I might not be permitted to leave to save the five.

33. In presenting versions of the precedence thesis, I am supposing (*contra* John Taurek in "Should the Numbers Count?" *Philosophy and Public Affairs*, 6 [1977]) that the numbers do count—for example, that saving two lives generally does twice as much good as saving one. I am also supposing that goods of different kinds (for example, preservation of life and relief from suffering) can be compared and at least roughly summed up, and that in cases of conflicting rights we can make at least a rough comparison of the overall good protected by the rights on each side of the conflict.

34. Or it might include a criterion that itself requires intuition to apply—by claiming, for example, that a negative right may be justifiably infringed just in case it would be contemptible of its possessor to insist on it. That is the kind of criterion that I find attractive.

35. And something similar holds for damage. You don't own something if others may damage it whenever that is best for all concerned.

36. Reference to the specific moral relation that I have in mind (in saying that someone's body and mind are his and not the community's) is made most naturally by a particular moral use of the possessive pronoun. This makes repeated reference awkward, and tempts me to talk in ways that are potentially misleading. I have spoken of a person's mind as belonging to him and have drawn an analogy with property. But both moves are dangerous. The intended sense of "belong" derives from the special use of the possessive. And the analogy with property is, as indicated, inexact. Both relations ground rights of say in what is to be done, but a person's mind or body are definitely not property—not even his property.

37. I mean here to invoke the ordinary sense of "being," in which human persons, gods, angels, and probably the higher animals—but not plants, cells, rocks, computers, etc.—count as beings.

38. It would make no difference, I think, if the overall good of the whole were thought to be a mere sum of the good of its parts—that is, if the whole were regarded as a mere colony without a morally significant higher-order function of its own. To deny the precedence of negative rights would still be to limit a person's moral protections precisely by this test: whether or not granting the protections would best serve the collective good. It would be to suppose that he may rightly be killed or injured if the cost to him does not outweigh the sum of the benefits to others. And this seems to me a clear enough way in which he would be regarded, morally, as a cell in the collective whole.

39. I am not claiming that any person or persons have actually designed morality with an eye to giving themselves the degree of say they find fitting. But I do think that light can be shed on the (timeless) content of morality by considering the importance to us of what would be realized or unrealized in the design of various moral systems.

40. Amartya Sen makes room for what he calls goal rights in "Rights and Agency," *Philosophy and Public Affairs*, 11 (1982), pp. 3–39.

41. Samuel Scheffler develops such an argument in *The Rejection of Consequentialism* (Oxford, England: Clarendon Press, 1982), pp. 80–114. Sen, in "Rights and Agency," Section VI and VII, tries to make room within a consequentialist framework for kinds of agent-relativity that would undermine the argument. But I find these agent-relative features poorly motivated as elements of a possible consequentialism.

21

Killing, Letting Die, and Withdrawing Aid

Jeff McMahan

INTRODUCTION

THE CONCEPTS OF killing and letting die are not evaluatively neutral. Yet their use, while reflecting certain moral beliefs, is nevertheless governed primarily by empirical criteria. This is in part because they both exemplify broader categories that are clearly defined largely if not exclusively in nonmoral terms. Thus killing is an instance of *doing,* or directly causing an event to occur, while letting die is an instance of *allowing* an event to occur. Because our use of the concepts of killing and letting die is both largely governed by empirical criteria and expressive of certain moral beliefs, the uncovering of the empirical criteria is particularly important. For, since the empirical criteria determine a way of applying the concepts that we recognize as having moral significance, it seems that the criteria themselves must have moral significance. Mapping our use of the concepts helps to reveal the contours of commonsense morality. Discovering the criteria for their use helps to reveal the deeper foundations of that morality.

One of the aims of this article is to contribute to the identification of the empirical criteria governing the use of the concepts of killing and letting die. I will not attempt a comprehensive analysis of the concepts but will limit the inquiry to certain problematic cases—namely, cases involving the removal or withdrawal of life-supporting aid or protection.[1] The analysis of these cases will,

Reprinted from *Ethics,* 103 (January 1993), 250–279, with permission of the author and the publisher. © 1993 by The University of Chicago. All rights reserved.

however, shed light on the criteria for distinguishing killing and letting die in other cases as well.

My overall aims in the article are partly constructive and partly skeptical. I hope to advance our understanding of the nature of the distinction between killing and letting die. This, I believe, will enable us to defend the moral relevance of the distinction against certain objections—in particular, objections that claim that the distinction fails to coincide with commonsense moral intuitions. Yet I will suggest that, as we get clearer about the nature of the distinction and the sources of its intuitive appeal, it may seem that the intuitions it supports are not so well grounded as one could wish.

WITHDRAWING AID

Let us assume, as I have suggested, that the distinction between killing and letting die exemplifies the broader distinction between doing and allowing. How should the broader distinction be analyzed? Perhaps the most influential analysis is the one advanced by Philippa Foot. Focusing specifically on doing harm and allowing harm to occur, Foot contends that the relevant distinction is between, on the one hand, initiating a threatening sequence of events or keeping it going and, on the other hand, allowing a threatening sequence that is already in train to continue.[2] She then distinguishes further between two ways of allowing an existing sequence to continue, one of which involves "forbearing to prevent" the sequence from continuing while the other involves "the removal of some obstacle which is, as it were, holding back a train of events."[3]

Two points about Foot's analysis should be noted. First, Foot's distinction does not coincide with the distinction between action and inaction, or that between action and omission. She notes that "The first kind of allowing requires an omission, but there is no other general correlation between omission and allowing, commission and bringing about or doing."[4] This, I believe, is right—at least as regards the claim that there is no correlation between allowing and inaction. Consider the following example.

The Aborted Rescue.—Two persons are in the water when one begins to drown. The other attempts to haul the drowning man to shore but the latter, in a panic, begins to claw and encumber his rescuer in a way that threatens to drown him as well. To extricate himself from this peril, the erstwhile rescuer has to push the drowning man off and swim away from him while the drowning man goes under.

The erstwhile rescuer clearly does not kill the other man when he leaves him to drown. He merely lets him die, or fails to save him (for there was some possibility that, had he continued to try, he might have succeeded in saving him). Yet in order to allow the drowning man to die, the erstwhile rescuer had to *do* something— namely, actively prevent the drowning man from trying to save himself at his rescuer's expense.[5]

The second noteworthy point is that Foot believes that the distinction between killing and letting die exemplifies her broader distinction only imperfectly. For she believes that there are certain cases in which one kills by allowing a threatening sequence to continue. The example she cites is:

The Involuntary Donor.—One has been involuntarily hooked up to a patient with a normally fatal disease who can survive only if he continues to draw life-support from one's body for a number of months. If one removes the tubes connecting one's body to his, he will die. One removes the tubes.[6]

Since what the agent does in this case is to withdraw a barrier that stands in the way of the patient's death, Foot's distinction implies that this is a case of allowing harm to occur. Thus she describes it as a "refusal to save a life."[7] Yet she also says that the agent who removes the tubes kills the patient who is thereby removed from his source of life-support. But this, she writes, shows only "that the use of 'kill' is not important: what matters is that the fatal sequence resulting in death [i.e., the disease] is not initiated but is rather allowed to take its course."[8]

Since, however, this is a case in which, according to Foot's own distinction, the agent allows the patient to die, Foot here commits herself to the position that the agent both kills the patient and allows him to die—indeed, that the agent kills the patient by allowing him to die. I believe that this is a mistake. To refuse to save a life is not normally to kill. The exceptions are cases in which the act of killing has the death of the victim as a delayed effect which the agent could prevent during the period between the performance of the act and the occurrence of the effect, but does not. In cases of this sort, in which the victim requires saving because of something the agent has previously done, the agent both kills the victim and allows him to die—both kills him and fails to save him from the effect of the earlier act. Clearly, however, the case of the Involuntary Donor is not a case of this sort. If it is—as it certainly seems to be—a case of allowing the patient to die from a preexisting threat, then it is not also a case of killing. I suspect that Foot acquiesces in the claim that the agent in this case kills the patient because removing the tubes is an *act* that leads immediately to the patient's death. Thus, if we ignore the background conditions, this seems more like a killing. But, as we have just noted, Foot herself is aware that there are cases in which one can let another die only by vigorous action that results immediately in the person's death.

One critic of Foot's distinction is Warren Quinn, who argues that the distinction between action and inaction has a critical role in defining the broader distinction of which the distinction between killing and letting die is one exemplification. "Harmful positive agency," he writes, "is that in which an agent's most direct contribution to the harm is an action, whether his own or that of some object [that he intends to manipulate for some purpose]. Harmful negative agency is that in which the most direct contribution is an inaction, a failure to prevent the harm."[9] Quinn then goes on to suggest that certain cases may require "special amendments" to his definitions, citing as the only examples cases involving "the active *withdrawal* of aid."[10] Of these he writes that "harm comes to someone because you decide to act rather than to do nothing."[11] Thus it seems that, by his definitions, one's agency must be positive in these cases since one's most direct contribution to the harm is an act rather than inaction. But his next sentence is: "But because your action is a certain kind of withdrawing of aid, it naturally enough seems to count as negative agency." This seems right: intuitively, one's agency *is* negative in at least some of these cases.

How can Quinn's definitions be modified to accommodate

these cases? As noted, Quinn mentions these cases in the context of conceding that the definitions may require "special amendments." But the amendments are never made and the cases are left hanging as counterexamples that cannot obviously be accommodated without giving up the basic idea behind Quinn's way of drawing the distinction. Certain cases of actively withdrawing aid seem to present a fundamental challenge to all accounts of the relevant distinction, such as Quinn's, that focus essentially on the distinction between doing and not doing, or action and inaction.

How, then, is the relevant distinction to be drawn? Is Foot's analysis the right one? I believe that it too is defective and that, like Quinn's proposal, it is undermined by cases involving the active withdrawal of aid or protection from a threat. Consider:

> Respirator.— A person is stricken with an ailment that would normally be fatal but is given mechanical life-support to sustain him until the condition can be cured. While the patient is on a respirator, his enemy surreptitiously enters the hospital and turns the machine off. The patient dies.[12]

Since the agent in this case simply removes a barrier that is, as it were, holding death at bay, his action falls on the negative side of Foot's distinction. It counts as allowing harm to occur rather than doing harm. If we believe, with Foot, that her distinction marks an intuitively morally important difference, then I think that we must conclude that it misclassifies this case. If we believe, as I have suggested we should, that the distinction between killing and letting die exemplifies the broad distinction that she is trying to capture and derives its moral significance from that broader distinction, then Foot's distinction classifies Respirator as a case of letting a patient die and suggests that there is a presumption that the agent's action is less objectionable than it would be in an otherwise comparable case involving killing. But it is more natural to describe this as a case of killing; and we certainly evaluate it as such.[13]

Another case of this sort is:

> Burning Building.—A person trapped atop a high building that is on fire leaps off. Seeing this, a firefighter quickly stations a self-standing net underneath and then dashes off to assist with other work. The imperiled person's enemy is, however, also present and,

seeing his opportunity, swiftly removes the net so that the person hits the ground and dies.

Here too Foot's distinction implies that the agent merely allows his enemy to die by removing a barrier to a threat. Yet again it seems more natural to describe this as a case of doing harm rather than allowing harm to occur—of killing rather than letting die— and we certainly evaluate it as such.

It is significant that the cases that resist assimilation into the categories established by both Foot's and Quinn's distinctions are all cases involving the active withdrawal of aid or protection against a threat. Foot's distinction locates all such cases on the negative side of the divide, classing them as instances of allowing harm to occur or, in cases in which the harm is death, as instances of letting die (provided, of course, that I am right that the distinction between killing and letting die exemplifies the broader distinction). Yet at least some of these cases seem to belong on the positive side; they are cases of killing rather than letting die. Quinn agrees with the implications of Foot's distinction, saying that cases of withdrawing aid should be classified as instances of negative agency. Yet his distinction seems to class them all as instances of positive agency. Other writers have, moreover, thought that they *should* be classed as instances of doing harm rather than allowing harm to occur, or as cases of killing rather than letting die. Frances Myrna Kamm, for example, explicitly claims that "a case in which one removes a barrier to the cause of death [is] a killing, not a letting die."[14]

A review of the cases we have considered so far should convince us that all of these views are mistaken. For some cases of withdrawing aid or protection are cases of killing, while others are cases of letting die. As we have just noted, the agent's withdrawal of the patient's life-support mechanism in Respirator seems a clear instance of killing, as does the agent's removal of the protective net in Burning Building. By contrast, the rescuer's withdrawing his aid to the drowning man in the Aborted Rescue is uncontroversially an instance of letting die. And, though this may seem less obvious, disconnecting oneself from the patient for whom one has been involuntarily providing life-support is also best understood as allowing the dependent patient to die of the disease from the effects of which one has been protecting him (albeit involuntarily).

What is the basis of our classing some of these cases as killings and others as instances of letting die? One suggestion is that whether an act of withdrawing aid or protection counts as killing or letting die depends on whether the barrier to death that one removes is a barrier that one has oneself provided. Thus it might be argued that, in general, if one withdraws a barrier that protects a person from death, one's action counts as letting the person die if the barrier is one that one has oneself interposed or provided, whereas it counts as killing if the barrier was not interposed or provided by oneself.[15] If, in other words, one temporarily intervenes to block a threat and then withdraws, one simply allows the threat to continue, thereby allowing its victim to die. Withdrawing one's own previous aid or protection simply nullifies one's initial intervention: the net effect is tantamount to nonintervention (apart from any benefit that the initial intervention may have provided). But to remove a barrier that exists independently of anything one has done is totally unlike nonintervention. While in many cases it may be infelicitous to characterize action of this sort as creating a threat, since the threat already exists but is blocked, it is relevantly like the creation of a new threat in that the victim would have been entirely safe independently of any intervention by oneself.

I believe that this suggestion is on the right track. It gives what seem to be the right descriptions in the Aborted Rescue, Involuntary Donor, Respirator, and Burning Building cases. Nevertheless, it is, as it stands, too crude. For consider:

> The Pipe Sealer.—An earthquake cracks a pipe at a factory, releasing poisonous chemicals into the water supply. Before a dangerous amount is released, a worker seals the pipe. But a year later he returns and removes the seal. As a result, numerous people die from drinking contaminated water.[16]

In this case the worker removes a barrier or protection against a threat that he himself has provided. Yet clearly he does not merely allow the victims to die but instead kills them. Thus the suggested ground for distinguishing between cases involving the withdrawal of aid or protection must be refined.

It seems that what makes the pipe sealer's action an instance of killing is that, although he removes a protection that he himself has provided, the barrier that he has created was both complete and self-sustaining, requiring no further contribution from him in order to keep the threat at bay. Indeed, because the barrier he interposed was operative, complete, and self-sustaining, it may seem appropriate in this case to say that the threat was not merely blocked but eliminated. If so, his action in removing the barrier he interposed may be said to have created a new threat rather than merely unblocking or releasing an existing threat. In this respect his action is analogous to that of a person who rescues a drowning man from the water but then throws him back—a clear case of killing, in contrast to the action of a person who merely abandons an attempt at rescue, as in the Aborted Rescue.

Now contrast the case of the Pipe Sealer with a variant of the classic tale of the little Dutch boy.

> *The Dutch Boy.*—A little Dutch boy, seeing that the dike is beginning to crack, valiantly sticks his finger in the crack to prevent the dike from breaking and flooding the town. He waits patiently but after many hours no one has come along who can help. Eventually succumbing to boredom and hunger, the boy withdraws his finger and leaves. Within minutes the dike bursts and a flood engulfs the town, killing many.

Whereas it seems clear that the pipe sealer causes rather than merely allows the poisonous chemicals to be released into the water supply, it is equally clear that the Dutch boy merely allows rather than causes the town to be flooded. Thus, while the pipe sealer kills the victims of the poison, the Dutch boy merely lets the inhabitants of the town die, or allows them to be killed. Yet both remove or withdraw a barrier that they themselves have provided. The difference seems to be that, while the barrier provided by the pipe sealer is complete and self-sustaining, the protection provided by the Dutch boy is, when withdrawn, still in progress and requires further and indeed continuous contributions from the boy to be sustained. This suggests that the original proposal should be refined in the following way: when an agent withdraws aid or protection from a lethal threat that he has not himself provided, or when he withdraws aid or protection that he has provided but which was complete and self-sustaining, his action counts as killing; but when an agent withdraws aid or protection that he himself has provided but which requires further contributions from him to be effective, then his action counts as letting the victim die.

This way of distinguishing between different instances of withdrawing aid or protection appears to follow our general sense of linguistic propriety in classifying instances of doing and allowing rather than merely following our moral intuitions about the different examples. Thus the pipe sealer does not allow the poisons to escape but instead releases them, whereas the Dutch boy does not cause the flood but merely allows it to occur. The same descriptions would be appropriate even if each's action were expected to have good consequences rather than bad. Yet this proposal yields the intuitively correct classifications of all of the cases so far considered. In Respirator and Burning Building, each agent removes a barrier that was provided by someone else and each seems intuitively to be guilty of killing. In Pipe Sealer, the agent removes a barrier that he himself has provided but which was complete and self-sustaining; he too seems to be guilty of killing. But in the cases of the Aborted Rescue, the Involuntary Donor, and the Dutch Boy, each agent withdraws aid or protection that he has himself provided but which is in progress and requires more from the agent to be finally effective. In these cases it seems clear that the agents merely allow people to die and are not guilty of killing.

OPERATIVE AND AS-YET INOPERATIVE AID

The proposed way of distinguishing among cases of withdrawing aid or protection seems thus far to account quite well for our intuitions about how certain cases should be classified. There is, however, a further range of cases to which the proposal may not seem to apply or to which, if it does apply, it may seem to give the wrong answers. Consider, for example, the following case cited by Jonathan Bennett:

> *The Impoverished Village.*—One is threatened with a 10% loss of income but can recover this sum by pressing a claim against a trust

fund. If one does not press one's claim, the fund will be used to save the lives of people in a remote impoverished village. One presses one's claim.[17]

In Bennett's view, the agent's action in this case falls on the positive side of the relevant positive-negative distinction, which he draws in a way that is different from the proposals of Foot and Quinn. According to Bennett, if an event occurs because one has moved one's body in one of the few ways that would have resulted in the occurrence of that event, one is positively instrumental in its occurrence. If, by contrast, most of the ways in which one could move one's body at a given time would all result in the occurrence of some event, and if one moves one's body in one of those ways, then one is negatively instrumental in the occurrence of the event. Bennett claims that, with few exceptions, killing involves positive instrumentality, while letting die involves negative instrumentality.[18]

Bennett argues that comparing Impoverished Village with another, similar case shows that the broader positive-negative distinction is devoid of moral significance. The other case is:

> *The Impoverished Village 2.*—If one were to donate 10% of one's income one could save the same number of lives in the same village. One does not do this.

Since in Impoverished Village 2 one is negatively instrumental in the deaths of the villagers (i.e., one lets them die) while one is positively instrumental in their deaths in Impoverished Village, there should be a detectable moral difference between one's action in the two cases if the positive-negative distinction is morally significant. But Bennett contends that there is no discernible moral difference. To emphasize the point, he present one further instance of positive instrumentality:

> *The Impoverished Village 3.*—Having given one's accountant full power of attorney, one learns that because of a misunderstanding he is preparing to sign away 10% of one's income to be sent to the village. One phones to instruct him not to do it.[19]

Again, although Impoverished Village 2 and Impoverished Village 3 differ with regard to Bennett's positive-negative distinction, it is hard to believe that there could be an important moral difference between them.

This same form of argument appears in the more recent work of Shelly Kagan.[20] Kagan is concerned to attack the idea that there is a special constraint against doing harm that does not apply to allowing harm to occur. He presents a series of cases intended to show that the constraint against doing harm prohibits forms of behavior that commonsense morality accepts as permissible—an especially damaging form of objection. Beginning with a case in which it seems plausible to suppose that doing harm is forbidden, he progresses by a series of seemingly trivial alterations to cases in which it seems that what the agent does is permissible. Here is a series of cases.[21]

>*Abdul.*—Food is being sent to the starving inhabitants of a remote village but Abdul intercepts the supplies and steals them.
>
>*Abdul 2.*—A check that can be used to buy food is on its way to the village but Abdul intercepts and steals the check.
>
>*Abdul 3.*—Abdul himself writes a check and mails it to the village. Later, however, he intercepts the check and tears it up.
>
>*Abdul 4.*—Abdul writes a check for the village and gives it to a friend to mail. A moment later he changes his mind and asks the friend to return it to him.

In each of these cases, Kagan claims, Abdul does something that prevents aid from reaching its intended beneficiaries. He interferes in a sequence of events in such a way that people die who would not otherwise have died. He therefore violates the constraint against doing harm. Yet commonsense morality holds that what Abdul does in Abdul 3 and in Abdul 4 is permissible. Thus, Kagan concludes, the idea that there is a constraint against doing harm is excessively restrictive and cannot account for our intuitions.

Bennett's argument depends on the assumption that the agent's action in both Impoverished Village and Impoverished Village 3 is properly located on the positive side of the relevant distinction—that is, that his action is an instance of doing harm, or killing. Similarly, Kagan's argument depends on the assumption that Abdul's action in both Abdul 3 and Abdul 4 counts as doing harm. How does the way I have proposed of drawing the relevant distinction classify these cases? In each of these cases, the agent withdraws aid that he has himself provided (for even in Impoverished Village the money in the trust fund rightfully belongs to the agent); yet the aid seems to be self-sustaining, since no further action on the part of the agent is required for the aid to block the threat that the starving villagers face. Thus in each case the villagers would not die if the agent were simply to drop dead. These considerations suggest that my distinction counts these cases as instances of killing and that it is correct to do so.

This, however, would be a mistake. Intuitively, the agent in each of these four cases (i.e., Impoverished Village, Impoverished Village 3, Abdul 3, and Abdul 4) seems merely to let the villagers die. In each case there is an antecedent threat to the victims the existence of which is independent of any action by the agent. The agent then initiates a process that, if continued, would eventually block or eliminate the threat. But before this process intervenes to eliminate the threat, the agent acts to abort it. Intuitively we regard this as an instance of allowing a preexisting lethal threat to continue—that is, as an instance of letting die. It is true that, in this case, the agent does begin to intervene to eliminate the threat but then withdraws his intervention before it becomes effective. But, while stopping oneself from intervening may be an active form of nonintervention, it *is* a form of nonintervention. In more figurative terms, preparing a barrier to interpose between onrushing death and its potential victim but then withdrawing the barrier before it blocks death's path amounts to no more than allowing death to pass.

I believe that the way I have proposed of drawing the relevant distinction captures this. For, while in each of these cases the villagers do not depend on further *action* by the agent, they do depend on further aid or protection from the agent, for the aid that the agent has provided has not yet become operative. These cases should therefore be classed with the earlier cases involving withdrawing aid that I have identified as cases of letting die, and for the same reason: namely, that the victims are still dependent for their survival on aid from the agent that the agent fails to provide. The unifying thought here is this: if a person requires or is dependent for survival on further aid from or protection by an agent, and if the person dies because the agent fails to provide further aid or withdraws his own aid either while it is in progress or before it becomes operative, and if the agent is not causally responsible for the person's need for aid or protection, then the agent lets the person die.

The distinction that I have drawn therefore yields what I believe is the intuitively correct classification of the cases cited by Bennett and Kagan involving the withdrawal of one's own as-yet-inoperative aid. Since these cases turn out to be cases of letting die, they do not, as Bennett and Kagan claim, undermine the claim that the relevant positive-negative distinction is morally significant. Rather, they undermine the ways in which Bennett and Kagan believe that the distinction should be drawn. Or, to be more precise, they show that the distinctions on which Bennett's and Kagan's arguments depend do not coincide with the distinction that that underlies our commonsense moral intuitions.

It might be suggested, as an alternative to my proposal, that it is whether aid is operative or as-yet-inoperative that determines whether the withdrawal of aid counts as killing or letting die and that who has provided the aid that is withdrawn is irrelevant. Focusing on whether the aid is operative or inoperative might be thought to restore plausibility to the distinction proposed by Foot, since it might be held that, while to remove operative aid is to create a threatening sequence where none existed, to remove as-yet-inoperative aid is to allow a threatening sequence to continue.[22] I believe, however, that matters are more complicated than this. For there are cases of letting die and cases involving the withdrawal of operative aid that are clearly cases of letting die and cases involving the withdrawal of as-yet-inoperative aid that are clearly cases of killing. The cases of the Aborted Rescue, the Involuntary Donor, and the Dutch Boy are all cases of the former sort, while the Burning Building is an example of the latter.

What does seem true is that, if aid or protection against a lethal threat is both operative and self-sustaining, withdrawing it appears to count as killing irrespective of whether the person who withdraws it is also the person who provided it. But, when aid that is as-yet-inoperative is withdrawn, it seems to make a difference to whether this counts as killing or letting die whether the person who withdraws it is also the person who provided it. Thus compare Burning Building with:

Burning Building 2.—A person trapped atop a high building that is on fire leaps off. Seeing this, a firefighter quickly stations a self-standing net underneath. But he then immediately notices that two other persons have jumped from a window several yards away. He therefore repositions the net so that it catches the two. The first jumper then hits the ground and dies.

In this case, it seems absurd to say that the firefighter kills the one; rather, he merely allows him to die. A similar contrast is evident in the comparison between, on the one hand, Abdul and Abdul 2 and, on the other, Abdul 3 and Abdul 4.[23]

In cases in which aid is operative but ongoing rather than self-sustaining, it is less clear that it matters whether the person who withdraws the aid also provided it, but there is some support for the claim that it does. Consider:

The Involuntary Donor 2.—The same as Involuntary Donor except that it is a person who wanders in off the street who removes the tubes so that the patient dies.

and

The Dutch Boy 2.—The same as Dutch Boy except that it is the Dutch boy's father, annoyed because his son is late for dinner, who yanks the boy's finger out of the dike.

In both of these cases the agent who terminates the aid or protection is not the person who has been providing it. And in both it seems natural to say that the agent kills the victims rather than merely allowing them to die.

It seems, therefore, that various factors are relevant in determining whether an instance of withdrawing aid or protection from a threat counts as killing or letting die. Among these are whether the person who terminates the aid or protection is the person who has provided it, whether the aid or protection is self-sustaining or requires more from the agent, and whether the aid or protection is operative or as yet inoperative. Thus matters are already quite complex. In the next section, I will introduce further complications.

PROBLEM CASES

It might be objected that Burning Building and Burning Building 2 do not differ only with respect to whether the person who terminates the aid is also the person who provided it. For in Burning Building the agent acts with malice and intends the death of the victim, whereas the agent in Burning Building 2 is motivated by reasons of beneficence to move the net and does not intend the death of the victim. Comparable claims might be made with regard to the comparison between Involuntary Donor and Involuntary Donor 2. And this may suggest that our inclination to class Burning Building and Involuntary Donor 2 as cases of killing is not a response to a way in which these cases differ from their counterparts in terms of a broader distinction between doing and allowing but simply reflects a tendency to label as killing any acts with lethal consequences of which we strongly morally disapprove.

Some theorists have, indeed, held that in some cases our moral beliefs directly determine whether the withdrawal of a barrier to death counts as an instance of killing or letting die.[24] But, while I concede that our moral intuitions do exert an influence on our classificatory impulses, I believe that this is an influence that should be resisted. For there is a distinction between killing and letting die which, like the broader distinction it exemplifies, is based on nonmoral criteria—though it nevertheless has moral significance. Because the distinction normally has moral significance, we are disposed to identify particularly objectionable instances of letting die as acts of killing. But this is a result of our failure to bear in mind that the relevance of the distinction between killing and letting die may sometimes be overshadowed by other factors (e.g., when a letting die that is intentional and malicious is compared to a killing that is a side effect of benevolently motivated action) or that there may be contexts in which the distinction between killing and letting die lacks its normal significance.[25] (I will return to these matters in the penultimate section.)

Having said this, I am aware that there is a challenge that remains to be met. It is based on such cases as the following:

Burning Building 3.—A person trapped atop a high building that is on fire leaps off. Seeing this, a firefighter quickly stations a self-standing net underneath and then dashes off to assist with other work. A second firefighter sees that two other persons have also jumped from an adjacent window. He therefore moves the net

over to catch the two, with the consequence that the first jumper
hits the ground and dies.

The Involuntary Donor 3.—The same as in Involuntary Donor
except that it is a doctor acting at the donor's request who removes
the tubes connecting the donor to the dependent patient.

These cases appear to be counterexamples to my proposed way
of distinguishing among cases of withdrawing aid. In Burning
Building 3, the agent withdraws a self-sustaining though as-yet-
inoperative barrier that someone else has provided. So my proposed distinction should classify it as a case of killing; but intuitively we regard it as a case of letting die. It is hard to believe
that the firefighter in Burning Building 3 kills the falling person
while the firefighter in Burning Building 2 merely lets him die,
especially if this alleged difference is thought to make a moral
difference. In Involuntary Donor 3, the agent terminates operative
aid that is being provided by someone else (the donor). Hence
my proposal should classify it as a case of killing; yet it too may
seem to be a case of letting die. Again, it is hard to believe that
the doctor in Involuntary Donor 3 kills the patient while the donor
in Involuntary Donor merely allows him to die, especially if this
alleged difference is thought to make a moral difference.

Perhaps one could try to defend my proposal by claiming that
these two most recent cases are in fact cases of killing that we are
mistakenly disposed to regard as instances of letting die because
we believe that what the agent does in each case is permissible in
the same way that it would be if it were done by the person who
provided the aid that is terminated (as is the case in Burning
Building 2 and Involuntary Donor). I think, however, that this is
the wrong response. These cases show that my proposal requires
further refinements.

When a person withdraws aid or protection from a lethal threat
that is either in progress or as yet inoperative, it is not strictly
necessary in order for his action to count as letting die that he
should be the very same person who provided the aid or protection. In some cases of this sort, the agent who provides the aid
or protection acts in a capacity that is role-based. Indeed, it may
be his occupancy of the role that makes his provision of aid or
protection possible. In cases in which an agent provides aid or

protection against a lethal threat not in his capacity as an individual but in his capacity as the occupant of a role, the withdrawal of that aid or protection by his partners or successors in the role he fills will count as letting die. This is because we interpret the provision of aid in these cases as an act by a person-in-a-role; if the action is undone by a different person occupying the same role, we regard individual identity as irrelevant. This, I believe, is what allows us to regard the second firefighter's action in Burning Building 3 as an instance of letting die.

Suppose the second firefighter in Burning Building 3 is accused of killing the first jumper. His accuser might argue as follows: "You didn't let him die; for he was quite safe independently of you. It's not as if you were saving him but then withdrew to save the other two instead. Rather, you killed him in order to be able to save the other two." It seems to me that the firefighter could appropriately respond that "it's not true that the jumper would have been safe if not for me. If it looked as if he would be safe, that is because *we,* the team of firefighters, were there in our role as firefighters. When the first firefighter placed the net under the first jumper, he was fulfilling the requirements of his role. When I moved the net, I was fulfilling the requirements of the same role. It makes no difference which individual does what when they are all acting in a role-based capacity. If I had moved the net out of malice, then of course I could be accused of killing—not because my action would have been wrong (though it would have been) but because I would then have been acting in my capacity as a private individual and not in the role of a firefighter." This seems a cogent reply.

Involuntary Donor 3 requires a different response. To understand why this is a case of letting die rather than killing, we must distinguish between the decision to withdraw aid and the execution of that decision. What is important, in determining whether an act of terminating aid or protection counts as killing or letting die, is who decides to terminate it, not who physically implements the decision. In Involuntary Donor 3, it is the person who has been providing the aid who decides to terminate it. And it is this fact, together with the fact that the aid was in progress rather than self-sustaining, that makes this a case of letting die. When the doctor removes the tubes, he acts as an agent whose principal is the donor herself. His action thus counts as action by proxy, or vicarious action, on behalf of the donor.

These two refinements should be read back into the earlier claim that it makes a difference, in cases of withdrawing aid, whether the person who withdraws the aid is also the person who provided it. We see now that this was only a crude approximation to the truth. Doubtless there are other subtle refinements that are necessary but which I have overlooked.

There is one further matter that should be addressed in this section. I have argued that the removal of aid or protection that is both operative and self-sustaining counts as killing irrespective of whether the person who terminates it is also the person who provided it, but that the termination of aid or protection that is operative but *not* self-sustaining, in that it requires more from the agent, counts as letting die if the person who terminates it is also the agent who has provided it.[26] Thus the question whether aid that an agent has provided is self-sustaining or whether it requires more from the agent is a critical question; yet the relevant notions here are vague, and this can lead to uncertainties about how certain cases should be classified.

Return to the case I have called Respirator. In this case the agent terminates life-supporting aid that he has had no part in providing. Hence his action counts as killing. This seems intuitively right; and it would seem right even if the agent did not have a discreditable motive but intended his act as an instance of euthanasia—that is, an act intended to benefit the person who dies. Now consider:

> *Respirator 2.*—A person is stricken with an ailment that would normally be fatal but is given mechanical life-support to sustain him. Eventually, however, the doctor who ordered that the patient should receive life-support concludes that the patient will never regain consciousness and so turns the respirator off.

Many people regard this as a case in which the doctor lets the patient die.[27] And the fact that the doctor was himself responsible for providing the aid he discontinues supports this assessment. Other people, however, have doubts and suspect that the act of turning off or disconnecting a life-support machine must always count as killing.

Perhaps this uncertainty derives from a lack of clarity about whether or not a life-support machine counts as a self-sustaining form of aid. Clearly the provision of a life-support machine does not require continuous intervention and effort in the way that hauling a drowning man to shore or keeping one's finger in the dike does. Compared to these forms of aid or protection, the provision of a life-support mechanism seems a relatively self-sustaining form of aid—hence the temptation to call its withdrawal, even by its provider, an act of killing. Yet a life-support machine requires monitoring and maintenance, and keeping it functioning draws continuously on the provider's resources and exacts opportunity costs from him. In these respects it falls far short of being self-sustaining in the way that, for example, the pipe sealer's patch is; hence the temptation to call its withdrawal by its provider an instance of letting die. (Note that it seems appropriate to describe what the doctor does in Respirator 2 as *discontinuing* the patient's life-support—implying that he—the doctor—would otherwise be continuing it. It would, by contrast, be inappropriate to describe what the agent does in Respirator in this way.) If I am right that whether the withdrawal of operative aid or protection by its provider counts as killing or letting die depends on whether the aid is self-sustaining, then it should not be surprising that vagueness as to what kinds of aid count as self-sustaining should lead to the sorts of taxonomical and moral uncertainties that surround cases involving the termination of mechanical life-support.

I have argued that whether or not life-supporting aid or protection is self-sustaining is only one of a number of factors that may determine whether an instance of withdrawing aid counts as killing or letting die. And, just as there may be uncertainty about whether or not aid or protection is self-sustaining, so there may be uncertainty about other factors—for example, about what counts as having provided aid or protection, whether aid is operative or as yet inoperative, when action is role-based or who qualifies as an occupant of a role, and so on. If I am right that all of these various factors have to be taken into account, then the full analysis of the distinction between killing and letting die (which I will not endeavor to give here) will be complicated, messy, and seemingly ad hoc. Moreover, since there may be vagueness or uncertainty about certain relevant factors, and since the various factors may be present in different combinations and to different degrees in different cases, we should expect that there will be numerous cases that we are uncertain how to classify or that we disagree about how to classify.

It is, perhaps, surprising that what most people have taken to be simple, basic distinctions (doing and allowing, killing and letting die) should turn out to be complex and multifaceted. This confusion, is, I think, readily explicable. Our intuitions about killing and letting die are indeed based on considerations that are relatively simple, as I will suggest in the final section. But, because of the unruly complexity of reality, it is often difficult to determine what these considerations imply about the classification of a particular case. Thus, while there are clear paradigm cases of killing and letting die in which the relevant considerations appear in relatively pure forms, there are also numerous gray areas in which these same considerations are more difficult to discern or interpret. We have, nevertheless, somehow evolved unexplicit rules for the classification even of most of the cases in the gray areas. But, because the function of these rules is to sort a welter of diverse and heterogeneous cases into two apparently simple categories, the rules are necessarily intricate, involving distinctions that are subtle and nuanced.

Implications for Abortion

If my proposal for distinguishing cases of withdrawing aid that count as instances of killing from those that count as instances of letting die is correct, this will have important implications for the moral problem of abortion. It is often claimed that the morality of abortion cannot be decided simply by weighing the interests (if any) of the fetus against those of the pregnant woman on the ground that performing an abortion involves forms of action that are inherently morally objectionable while the nonperformance of an abortion does not. In particular, abortion is said to involve killing, and perhaps intentional killing, while the nonperformance of an abortion merely involves foreseeably but unintentionally allowing the pregnant woman to be harmed or, in the worst case, to die.

It cannot reasonably be denied that some abortions kill the fetus. These are abortions in which the procedure itself injures the fetus' body in a way that directly causes its death. But abortions need not be, and sometimes are not, carried out in this way. To achieve the aim that most women have in aborting a pregnancy, all that is necessary is that the fetus should be removed from the woman's womb, and this can be done without mangling or damaging the fetus's body in a way that causes its death.[28] Let us call abortions that are carried out in this way "merely extractive abortions."

A merely extractive abortion involves the active withdrawal of life-supporting aid from the fetus. It is important to notice, moreover, that the aid that is terminated was, though operative, not self-sustaining but required continuous provision. Hence it is appropriate to describe a merely extractive abortion as the discontinuation of life-supporting aid to the fetus. I have argued that the discontinuation of ongoing life-supporting aid by the person who has been providing it counts as allowing the dependent person to die. Therefore when a pregnant woman has a merely extractive abortion, thereby withdrawing life-supporting aid that she herself has been providing to a fetus, she does not kill the fetus but merely allows it to die.

There are three rather obvious objections to this claim. I will attempt to answer each in turn. The first and perhaps most obvious objection is that, even if we concede that withdrawing aid in progress that one has oneself been providing counts as an instance of letting die, the agent who performs an abortion is typically not the pregnant woman herself but is instead her doctor. Since the doctor terminates life-support that someone else has provided, he kills the fetus rather than lets it die.

To answer this objection we need to recall the second refinement of the proposal made in the previous section. There I contended that what is necessary for the withdrawal of aid to count as an instance of letting die is that the withdrawal should occur as the result of a decision taken by the person who has provided it. It makes no difference if the actual implementation of the decision is done by proxy, or through an agent. Thus, provided that a merely extractive abortion is undertaken at the initiative of the pregnant woman herself, she and the doctor through whose agency she acts allow the fetus to die.

The second objection is that even a merely extractive abortion is an instance of doing something that results in the fetus's death—namely, actively removing the fetus from the environment that supports its life. Hence it is odd to describe it as merely allowing death to occur.

This objection has also already been answered. As cases such as the Aborted Rescue and the Dutch Boy show, it is often necessary to do some quite specific act in order to let a person die.

The third and final objection is more interesting and will take longer to answer. The source of this objection is Philippa Foot, who argues that, in order for one to allow a person to die, there must be some preexisting threatening sequence of events that one fails to arrest or to which one removes some barrier by which it has been blocked. But in the case of a merely extractive abortion, there is no threat to the fetus which the abortion allows to continue by failing to arrest it or by unblocking it. Foot therefore concludes that the abortion itself "originates the sequence which ends in the death of the fetus, and the destruction comes about 'through the agency' of the mother who seeks the abortion."[29] A merely extractive abortion, is therefore, an act of killing rather than an instance of allowing the fetus to die.

This objection appeals to Foot's analysis of the broader distinction between doing and allowing, which I have rejected. Yet, while I have rejected her claim that unblocking or releasing a preexisting lethal threat always counts as allowing death to occur, I have not repudiated the assumption of her analysis that is most relevant here—namely, the assumption that in cases of allowing a person to die there must be a preexisting threatening sequence to which the victim's death may be attributed. This assumption may seem obviously correct, but I believe it can be successfully challenged. For there are cases in which, although an individual is not *under threat,* in the sense of being threatened by a clearly distinguishable and perhaps deviant sequence of events that is leading to his or her death, the individual may nevertheless be naturally dependent on assistance or aid from others in order to survive. We might say that, in these cases, the individual is under a *latent* rather than an active threat of death. The notion of a latent threat captures the fact that there is a sense in which anyone who is chronically unable to satisfy his or her essential needs without assistance from others is threatened by his or her own helplessness and dependency. In these cases, the threat does not stand out as a distinct causal sequence since it is a chronic condition—in the case of the fetus, one that is a natural and universal condition of that stage of life.

Foot herself supplies what I believe to be the best counterexample to her own assumption. "The fetus," she writes, "is not in jeopardy because it is in its mother's womb; it is merely dependent on her in the way children are dependent on their parents for food."[30] If parents fail to feed their baby, they do not create a threat or initiate a threatening causal sequence; hence they do not, by her definition, kill the baby. This is clearer than in the case of abortion, in which the pregnant woman, or her agent, does something to the fetus that brings about its death. By contrast, parents who fail to feed their baby do not do anything to the baby at all; they simply allow its basic needs to go unmet. Yet, as Foot notes, the baby is not threatened by a preexisting sequence of events; hence the parents cannot, by her definition, be said to allow it to die. But the failure to feed one's baby, so that it starves, is either to kill it or to allow it to die. And, unless the parents take action that prevents others from feeding the baby, it seems clear that what they do is to allow death to occur. Therefore it is not necessary in order to allow someone to die that the victim should be antecedently threatened by some distinct sequence of events.[31]

There is, of course, a temptation to say, as Foot in fact says, that parents may murder their baby by allowing it to die of starvation.[32] If this assumes that only killing can count as murder, then I would suggest that the reason we are tempted to class the failure to feed one's own baby as a case of killing is that we regard the failure to feed one's baby as morally comparable to typical cases of killing. In short, the categorization is being influenced by moral considerations, as is evidenced by Foot's choice of the term "murder." But this is a mistake. The reason that the failure to feed one's own baby is at least as wrong as typical instances of wrongful killing is not that it is an instance of killing but is instead that it involves the violation of a special duty to care for one's own children.

The claim that there is no threatening sequence that is allowed to continue when parents fail to feed their baby might be challenged by the suggestion that the threatening sequence which the parents allow to continue is the gradual impairment of the baby's functions from lack of nourishment. By allowing this threatening sequence to continue, the parents allow the baby to die.[33] While this challenge concedes that the failure to feed one's baby is a case of letting die, it supports Foot's assumption that letting die requires a preexisting threatening sequence. It therefore challenges my claim that a merely extractive abortion merely lets the fetus die, since the gradual impairment of the fetus's functions might also be identified as a threatening sequence in the case of abortion and in that case the sequence may seem to be caused directly by the abortion itself.

This challenge does not, however, refute the claim that there can be cases of allowing harm to occur in which there is no preexisting threatening sequence. For suppose that it is right that the gradual impairment of the baby's functions is a threatening sequence that the parents allow to continue. The impairment of the baby's functions is also itself a harm. Moreover, it is a harm that the parents have allowed to occur. But, in allowing it to occur, the parents did not allow some preexisting threatening sequence to continue. This, therefore, is a case of allowing harm to occur in which there was no preexisting threatening sequence. Since there clearly can be such cases, it is reasonable to include failing to feed one's baby, and merely extractive abortions, among them.[34]

GENERAL REFLECTIONS

I have argued that certain cases of withdrawing aid or protection count as acts of killing while others count as instances of letting die. This does not, however, imply that all instances of withdrawing aid that let the victim die must be morally just like other instances of letting die, if other things are equal. It is possible, for example, that letting a person die by actively withdrawing aid in progress is generally more objectionable than letting a person die by simply failing to intervene at all to arrest a sequence of events by which he is threatened. We may feel that letting a person die by withdrawing aid in progress is more like killing than simple nonintervention is (perhaps because withdrawing aid may involve action, or because releasing a threat that has been blocked is more like initiating a threat than simply failing to block a threat is).

Similarly, killing by withdrawing aid or protection may seem generally less objectionable, and perhaps more like letting die, than killing by initiating a lethal threat, other things being equal. There are certainly precedents for drawing a moral distinction in this way between different ways of killing. It has been plausibly suggested, for example, that we distinguish morally between killing via the creation of a lethal threat where none previously existed and killing via the redistribution or redirection of a preexisting threat, holding that the latter is less objectionable than the former, other things being equal.[35] Some have, moreover, sought to explain the plausibility of this distinction between ways of killing in a way that resembles standard explanations of why letting die is in general less bad than killing.[36] And just as killing via redistributing a threat may be less bad than killing via the creation of a threat because the former has more in common with letting die than the latter, so killing via withdrawing aid may be less bad than killing via the creation of a threat for much the same reason.

These claims are, of course, speculative; and limitations of space preclude a thorough defense of them here. But they suggest a conclusion that I believe to be true. This is that, because the distinction between killing and letting die is not a simple distinction, but is, as I noted earlier, based on a variety of subfactors, it is not the case that all instances of killing differ morally from all instances of letting die in exactly the same way, at least with respect to the difference that is marked by the distinction between killing and letting die. Instead, rather than distinguishing two simple and opposed categories, the distinction between killing and letting die marks a rough division along a spectrum of cases. Within each of the two subspectra, there are yet further morally relevant subdivisions.[37] Cases at opposite ends of each subspectrum are maximally dissimilar in terms of the empirical criteria for distinguishing between killing and letting die. If other things are equal, cases at these extremes will also be maximally different morally. By contrast, cases at the near end of each spectrum, where the two subspectra begin to converge, may differ very little in terms of the relevant empirical criteria. In comparisons between these cases, not only are our taxonomical intuitions likely to be weak or confused but also the moral differences are less easily discernible.[38]

It is also important to note that there are, in commonsense morality, numerous factors that may affect the moral status of a course of conduct that has lethal consequences other than the distinction between killing and letting die. The most commonly noted among these further considerations is whether a person's death is an intended effect of an agent's action; but there are others as well. The relevance of these other nonconsequentialist factors for present purposes is that they may interact in complex and perhaps as yet unidentified ways with the fact that an act is one of killing or letting die to determine the overall moral status of an agent's conduct. The presence (or absence) of a certain factor or combination of factors may outweigh, alter, or even nullify the significance of considerations deriving from the distinction between killing and letting die.[39]

These two facts—that the relevance of the distinction between killing and letting die may vary depending on where a particular case of killing or letting die lies along its subspectrum and that the presence of other factors may outweigh or otherwise affect the significance of the fact that an act is one of killing or letting die—together indicate that an ethical theory that aims to unify and systematize the intuitive elements of common moral thought will have to be quite complex. Such a theory cannot consist of simple principles of the sort that have hitherto been thought to capture the central elements of commonsense morality—for example, the principle that there is an agent-centered or deontological constraint against killing (or, more generally, doing harm) that does not apply to letting die (or allowing harm to occur), or the principle that there is a constraint against intentional killing or letting die (or intentionally harming or allowing harm to occur) that does not apply to unintended killing or letting die (or unintentionally harming or allowing harm to occur).[40]

The recognition of these facts may also help to explain how it can be that in certain comparisons the difference between killing and letting die may seem to make no intuitive difference. In these instances, the cases of killing and letting die that are being compared with one another may be relevantly similar, lying near the intersection of the two subspectra. Or the significance of the difference between killing and letting die may simply be outweighed by, or even perhaps nullified by, the presence (or absence) of other factors. In many cases, both these things may be true.[41]

The range of factors that influence our moral judgments may be very great and may include factors the significance of which we have not yet identified. One often finds that there is broad intuitive agreement that there is a moral difference between two cases even when we are unable to discern the source of that difference. Our intuitive moral discriminations are, on these occasions, sensitive to nuances so subtle as to elude identification.

Consider, for example, the following familiar case.

> *The Tactical Bomber.*—A pilot fighting in a just, defensive war can significantly enhance the prospect of victory by his country by destroying an enemy munitions factor. But, because the factory is located in the center of a city and because his country lacks the capacity for precision bombing, he foresees that his bombing the factory will have as an unintended effect the killing of civilians. He can also reasonably predict that the benefits that the bombing will achieve, even when assessed impartially, and giving due priority to the interests of the innocent over those of the noninnocent, will greatly outweigh the harms inflicted on the civilians. He bombs the factory.

Most people believe that the Tactical Bomber acts permissibly. Indeed, anyone who condemns his action would seem to be committed to at least a contingent form of pacifism, since the conditions of this case exemplify the nature of modern warfare. In virtually all cases, modern warfare inevitably involves harm to civilians, usually on a massive scale. Because most of us believe in the possibility of a just modern war, we had better be able to defend the intuition that the Tactical Bomber acts permissibly.

Yet, given the relevance of the factors cited, it should be quite surprising that we find the Tactical Bomber's action permissible. He kills his victims rather than letting them die. He kills them, moreover, through the creation of a new threat rather than through the redirection of a preexisting threat or through the removal of a barrier provided by someone else. And, although it seems that he kills them unintentionally, their deaths occur as it were en route to the good effect rather than being a further effect of the production of the good. These factors normally combine to produce an act that is impermissible, as is illustrated by another familiar case that was first introduced in Foot's seminal paper.

> *The Poison Gasser.*—"There are five patients in a hospital whose lives could be saved by the manufacture of a certain gas, but . . . this inevitably releases lethal fumes into the room of another patient whom for some reason we are unable to move."[42] An agent manufactures the gas.

This case appears to have the same structure as that of the Tactical Bomber. The Poison Gasser kills by creating a new threat, he kills unintentionally but en route to his intended good effect, and the expected good effect of his action impartially outweighs the bad.[43] Yet intuitively we condemn the Poison Gasser's action.

The comparison between Tactical Bomber and Poison Gasser illustrates the claim that there are instances in which we intuitively discern an important moral difference between cases but are unable to determine what the difference is. Perhaps, in this comparison, the relevant difference is that the Tactical Bomber acts in self– and other-defense whereas the Poison Gasser's act is one of self– or other-preservation. Or perhaps it is that we feel that ordinary restraints that apply in the case of the Poison Gasser are relaxed or weakened in the context of war. Or perhaps we feel that what the Tactical Bomber does is permissible because we believe that even many civilians in a country that is fighting an unjust war are not fully innocent, while the victim in Poison Gasser clearly is. (This latter suggestion draws support from the fact that we would be more reluctant to endorse the Tactical Bomber's action if the unintended victims of his action were civilian citizens of a neutral country, or citizens of the bomber's own country.) The important point, however, is that *something* is at work here that causes us to distinguish morally between these cases. Before we can learn much about the significance of the distinction between killing and letting die from comparisons between cases, we must locate and identify the various other factors that influence our intuitive reactions and attempt to determine how the distinction between killing and letting die interacts with these factors to determine the morality of a course of action.

CONCLUSION

Does the foregoing discussion of cases that involve the withdrawal of life-supporting aid reveal anything about the plausibility of distinguishing morally between killing and letting die? In closing, I will consider one possible conclusion one might draw.

The proposal I have advanced for distinguishing between instances of withdrawing aid that count as killing and those that count as letting die follows a central intuition behind the distinction between killing and letting die. This intuition may be articulated in rough and general terms as follows. If the situation is such that a person will live in the absence of any further intervention in his life by a certain agent, then, if the person nevertheless dies, the agent has killed him. In these cases, we identify the agent's intervention as the primary cause of the person's death. If, by contrast, a person dies who would not have lived without some present or future intervention in his life by a certain agent, and if the agent neither caused the person's need for aid nor caused a further, independent threat to his life, then the agent has let the person die. In these cases, we trace the cause of the person's death to conditions that are independent of any intervention by the agent.

In short, the fundamental intuitive difference between killing and letting die is that in cases of killing we assign primary causal responsibility for a person's death to an agent's intervention in the person's life, whereas, in cases of letting die, primary responsibility for the death is attributed to factors other than any intervention by the agent. It has to be conceded, of course, that there are analyses of the concept of causation that allow that the failure to prevent a death can count as the cause of the death. According to these accounts, the cause of an event is whatever positive or negative condition of the event is of most interest to us, perhaps because it explains why the event occurred in these circumstances but not in other relevantly similar circumstances, or because it is a factor that we can manipulate in order to bring about or suppress this type of event in the future, or perhaps for other reasons.[44] Accounts of causation of this sort clearly reflect certain dispositions of ordinary language and may be no less defensible than the core notion of causation as an active force. But our moral intuitions have been shaped by the latter. Thus even when we recognize the causation of death by omission, we evaluate it differently from the causation of death by active intervention.

Suppose that this is right—that our tendency to distinguish morally between killing and letting die as well as our tendency to distinguish morally within the two categories themselves both reflect a concern with the form and degree of an agent's causal responsibility for a person's death. We should ask whether these considerations are really sufficiently important to support the full moral significance that we attribute to the distinction.

Our aversion to being causally implicated in the death of an innocent person shows up in contexts in which its rationality is open to question. It influences us, for example, in cases in which killing an innocent person would not be worse for that person— for example, in the well known case devised by Bernard Williams in which a military officer who is about to have twenty innocent persons shot offers to free nineteen of them if a bystander agrees to kill the remaining one.[45] It also lies behind many people's reluctance to accept voluntary euthanasia in cases in which it is clear that death for the person concerned would not only not be a harm but would also be a benefit.

The aversion further manifests itself in cases in which one kills an innocent person but in which one cannot be held responsible or blamable for doing so. Again, a case of Bernard Williams's illustrates this point.[46] If a person who is driving carefully and alertly runs into a small child who has darted unexpectedly from behind a parked car, we expect the driver to feel an agonizing form of regret that other passengers in the car will not feel, even though the driver is not at fault because there was nothing that he or she could have been expected to do to avoid the accident. The aversion even extends to cases in which one is causally implicated in the killing of an innocent person but in which not only is one blameless but also one's causal role is not even that of agent. If, for example, one is blown off a rooftop by a sudden gust of wind so that one falls on and kills an innocent bystander, one will again feel an acute form of regret that a mere observer of the incident would not.

When we reflect on these cases, we may find that our intuitive responses, while deeply ingrained and difficult to repudiate, nevertheless strike us as primitive or atavistic impulses that critical moral thinking might enable us to rise above. On reflection, the importance we intuitively attribute to mere causal responsibility for a death may seem excessive. Similarly, the significance that we attribute to differences in the form and degree of causal responsibility for a death when we distinguish between killing and letting die may also seem excessive.

More generally, it is difficult to believe that the way in which an agent is instrumental in the occurrence of an outcome could be more important than the nature of the outcome itself. Consider the value of an entire human life—of all the good that the life contains. Now suppose that one must choose between killing one person to save two and allowing the two to die. Is it really credible to suppose that how one acts on that single occasion matters more in moral terms than the whole of the life that will be lost if one lets the two die rather than killing the one?

Doubtless this poses the question in terms that are excessively crude. It nevertheless helps to make vivid a particularly acute dilemma. One of the aims of moral theory is to illuminate the considerations that underlie our common moral intuitions. Yet it may happen that these deeper considerations, when exposed, seem not to be especially cogent or compelling. When this happens, we face a choice between retaining intuitions that are apparently ungrounded and abandoning them. Yet the intuitions may be central to any morality that we could bring ourselves to accept— indeed to any system of norms that we could genuinely recognize as a morality at all. I think it possible that a dilemma of this sort arises with our intuitions about killing and letting die.

Notes

I have been greatly helped in writing this paper by comments on earlier drafts by Heidi Malm, Shelly Kagan, Michael Gorr, and N. Ann Davis and by discussions with Robert McKim.

1. I use the terms 'withdrawal' and 'removal' interchangeably. However, on p. 389, I draw a distinction that might be articulated by distinguishing between withdrawing and removing (see n. 15 below).

2. Philippa Foot, "The Problem of Abortion and the Doctrine of Double Effect" in her *Virtues and Vices* (Oxford: Blackwell, 1978), p. 26; this volume, p. 272. Also see her "Morality, Action, and Outcome," in *Morality and Objectivity,* ed. Ted Honderich (London: Routledge & Kegan Paul, 1985), p. 24, and "Killing and Letting Die," in *Abortion: Moral and Legal Perspectives,* ed. Jay L. Garfield and Patricia Hennessey (Amherst: University of Massachusetts Press, 1984), pp. 178–80; this volume, pp. 280–97.

3. Foot, "The Problem of Abortion and the Doctrine of Double Effect," p. 26; this volume, pp. 272, 273.

4. *Ibid.*; this volume, p. 273.

5. See the similar case presented by H. M. Malm in her "Killing, Letting Die, and Simple Conflicts," *Philosophy and Public Affairs,* 18, no. 3 (1989), 254–55.

6. This is the well-known case introduced by Judith Thomson as an analogue of abortion in "A Defense of Abortion," *Philosophy and Public Affairs,* 1, no. 1 (1971), 47–66. Foot's reference to it is on pp. 184–85 of "Killing and Letting Die"; this volume, pp. 288–89.

7. Foot, "Killing and Letting Die," p. 184; this volume, p. 288.

8. *Ibid.,* p. 185; this volume, p. 288.

9. Warren S. Quinn, "Actions, Intentions, and Consequences: The Doctrine of Doing and Allowing," *Philosophical Review,* 98 (1989), 301–2; this volume, 367.

10. *Ibid.,* p. 302; this volume, p. 367.

11. *Ibid.,* p. 303; this volume, p. 368.

12. Compare Shelly Kagan, *The Limits of Morality* (Oxford: Oxford University Press 1989), p. 101.

13. In fairness to Foot, it should be noted that she focuses (in "The Problem of Abortion and the Doctrine of Double Effect") her initial discussion on the contrast between doing and allowing in the first of her two senses—i.e., allowing as "forbearing to prevent." Respirator, however, is a case involving allowing in her second sense—allowing as "enabling." Thus, if her claims about the contrast between doing and allowing were restricted to comparisons between doing and allowing in the first sense, Respirator as a counterexample might miss its target. But in the later paper ("Killing and Letting Die," p. 185; this volume, p. 288), she contends that the agent's action in Involuntary Donor is "completely different" from normal instances of killing since "the fatal sequence resulting in death is not initiated but is rather allowed to take its course."

Since Involuntary Donor is a case involving enabling rather than forbearing to prevent, this passage shows that she intends her claims about the contrast between doing and allowing to apply to both forms of allowing.

14. Frances Myrna Kamm, "Harming, Not Aiding, and Positive Rights," *Philosophy and Public Affairs,* 15 (1986), 310, n. 5.

15. One might articulate this suggestion by drawing a distinction between withdrawing and removing. Withdrawing might be understood as a subspecies of removing in that removing aid, protection, or, more generally, a barrier counts as an instance of withdrawing only if the agent who removes the aid, protection, or barrier is also the agent who provided it. Given this understanding of the terms, the suggestion in the text is that, while withdrawing life-supporting aid or protection counts as letting die, all other instances of removing life-supporting aid or protection count as killing. I have not adopted this use of the terms in the text because the dictionary recognizes a sense of withdrawing such that one can withdraw what one has not oneself provided.

16. I owe this case, and the objection it raises, to Heidi Malm.

17. Jonathan Bennett, "Morality and Consequences," in *The Tanner Lectures on Human Values,* II, ed. S. McMurrin (Salt Lake City: University of Utah Press, 1981), p. 89.

18. Bennett's exceptions are "positive lettings die, such as letting a climber fall to his death by cutting his rope, or letting a terminal patient die by unplugging his respirator," and "negative killings, such as killing your baby by not feeding it. . . . In these cases," he claims, "the very same conduct is both a killing and a letting die" (*ibid.,* p. 70). As will become evident, I would challenge the first and third of these classifications. It is perhaps revealing that it seems implausible to class the agent's action in Impoverished Village as an act of killing.

19. *Ibid.,* p. 91.

20. Kagan, *The Limits of Morality,* pp. 106–11.

21. *Ibid.,* pp. 106–107.

22. This was suggested by Heidi Malm.

23. It is not clear that in the first two cases Abdul kills the villagers. He may neither kill them nor let them die, perhaps because the causal connection between his action and their deaths seems too remote to warrant the claim that he kills them.

24. Anthony Woozley, e.g., claims that "I allow something to happen if I do not put in the way an obstacle which would prevent its happening or if I remove an obstacle which is now preventing its happening" ("A Duty to Rescue: Some Thoughts on Criminal Liability," *Virginia Law Review,* 69 [1983], 1295). Thus, he notes, a doctor who turns off a patient's life-support system merely allows the patient to die. Woozley

stipulates, however, that, for the removal of an obstacle to death to count as allowing a person to die, the removal must be done legitimately. Thus if a patient's life-support system is turned off "against the declared wishes of parents or guardian," or "by somebody who has no authority in the case at all, e.g., an enemy agent or a hospital orderly," then this instance of removing a barrier to death counts as killing rather than allowing to die (p. 1297).

25. On this latter possibility, see Francis Myrna Kamm, "Killing and Letting Die: Methodological and Substantive Issues," *Pacific Philosophical Quarterly*, 64 (1983), 297–312, and "Harming, Not Aiding, and Positive Rights"; Shelly Kagan, "The Additive Fallacy," *Ethics*, 99 (1988), 5–31; and H. M. Malm, "Directions of Justification in the Negative-Positive Duty Debate," *American Philosophical Quarterly*, 27 (1990), 315–24.

26. Here and elsewhere one should read in the refinements suggested above.

27. See, e.g., George P. Fletcher, "Prolonging Life: Some Legal Considerations," *Washington Law Review*, 42 (1967), 999–1016; this volume, chapter 3. Others have objected to this classification of Respirator 2 on the ground that it is "structurally similar" to Respirator, which seems a clear case of killing. Shelly Kagan, e.g., suggests that the similarity challenges the idea that the intuitive difference between the two cases can be explained by appealing to the claim that one is a case of killing and the other a case of letting die (*The Limits of Morality*, p. 101). Also see Christopher Boorse and Roy A. Sorensen, "Ducking Harm," *Journal of Philosophy*, 85 (1988), 126.

28. Compare Sissela Bok, "Ethical Problems of Abortion," in *The Problem of Abortion*, ed. Joel Feinberg, 2nd ed. (Belmont, Calif.: Wadsworth, 1984), pp. 189–90.

29. Foot, "Killing and Letting Die," p. 185; this volume, p. 289. Foot's argument takes the form of a reply to Judith Thomson's argument for the permissibility of abortion ("A Defense of Abortion") that appeals to the analogy between an abortion and the case of the Involuntary Donor. Foot rejects the analogy on the ground that, while there is a preexisting threat (i.e., the disease) from which the agent in Involuntary Donor removes the victim's protection, there is no preexisting threat in the case of an abortion. There are other failures of analogy besides this— e.g., that the donor in Involuntary Donor is not responsible for the patient's need for aid while a pregnant woman may be partially responsible for the fact that the fetus requires her aid; that the patient in Involuntary Donor is a stranger to the donor while the fetus is the pregnant woman's biological offspring (except perhaps in certain cases of in vitro fertilization); and so on. (I discuss this in a book provisionally entitled

Killing at the Margins of Life [New York: Oxford University Press, in press].)

30. Foot, "Killing and Letting Die," p. 185; this volume, pp. 288–89.

31. Warren Quinn has also objected to Foot's assumption that one can let a person die only if the person is already faced with a threatening sequence of events. He cites as a counterexample a case in which one's elderly neighbor freezes to death because one is called away to an emergency and thus fails to fuel his furnace as one customarily does ("Actions, Intentions, and Consequences," p. 298; this volume, p. 364). It is not clear, however, that this counterexample succeeds, since it might be argued with some plausibility that the freezing weather constitutes the threatening sequence from which one fails to protect the victim. This raises difficult questions about the individuation of causal sequences that are best avoided here.

32. Foot, "The Problem of Abortion and the Doctrine of Double Effect," p. 26; this volume, p. 273.

33. This challenge was posed by Heidi Malm.

34. Earlier I noted that there may be grounds for claiming that the parents kill their baby by failing to feed it if, in addition to not feeding it themselves, they take action that prevents others from feeding it. It is worth noting that, prior to the time at which the fetus becomes viable, there is nothing a pregnant woman can do that could prevent others from providing the support she withdraws in having a merely extractive abortion, for the simple reason that no one else can provide what the fetus requires. After viability, the claim that a merely extractive abortion involves only letting the fetus die assumes that no further steps are taken to prevent the fetus from surviving.

35. See, e.g., Judith Thomson, "The Trolley Problem," in her *Rights, Restitution, and Risk,* ed. William Parent (Cambridge, Mass.: Harvard University Press, 1986).

36. Eric Mack, e.g., argues that "when generally perilous and inevitably injurious forces confront a person such that, no matter how that person acts, some nonaggressor(s) will be injured, the antecedent perilous forces bear the predominant causal responsibility for the subsequent injuries" ("Three Ways to Kill Innocent Bystanders," *Social Philosophy and Policy,* 3 [1985]: 17). In other words, responsibility for the harm is traced, as it is in cases in which one fails to arrest a harmful sequence, to the preexisting sequence of events rather than to the agent.

37. The image of the spectrum should not be interpreted too literally. It should not, e.g., be understood to imply that cases can be ordered along a single dimension.

38. The following cases illustrate this point. Both are variants of The

Aborted Rescue. In the first case (suggested by Shelly Kagan as an objection to my proposal), the rescuer of a drowning man is exceptionally tall and is able to perform the rescue by carrying the drowning man on his shoulders, above the water. In this variant, there is no threat to the rescuer. Nevertheless before he reaches the shore he wearies of the effort, drops the drowning man back into the water, and wades to shore, leaving the victim to drown. In the second case, the rescuer carries the drowning man onto dry land but immediately regrets his action and heaves him back into the water. This is clearly a case of killing. Kagan believes that the first case is also a case of killing. Surely there is little to distinguish the two cases morally (except, perhaps, that the rescuer's motives and intentions are presumably more discreditable in the second case). Yet my analysis commits me to the view that the first case is an instance of letting die, since it involves the withdrawal or discontinuance of aid in progress by the person who has been providing it. I remain convinced that this is in fact right. The difference between the two cases that makes the one a case of letting die and the other an instance of killing is that in the first case the victim requires further aid from the rescuer in order to survive while in the second he does not. Yet the cases are otherwise so similar that it is not surprising that we evaluate them similarly (and hence, perhaps, are inclined to think that they must both count as instances of killing).

39. See Kamm, "Killing and Letting Die," and "Harming, Not Aiding, and Positive Rights"; Kagan, "The Additive Fallacy"; and Malm, "Directions of Justification in the Negative-Positive Duty Debate."

40. Kagan attacks commonsense morality by arguing that neither the idea that there is a constraint against doing harm nor the idea that there is a constraint against intending harm is capable of accounting for commonsense intuitions (*The Limits of Morality,* esp. Chapters 3 and 4). Eric Mack, whose concern is to defend commonsense intuitions, reviews and rejects a series of simple doctrines taken individually. He considers the doctrine that doing harm is worse than allowing harm to occur, the doctrine that intentionally causing harm is worse than causing harm voluntarily but unintentionally, and the idea that causing harm in self-preservation is less defensible than causing harm in self-defense. He finally settles on a doctrine based on the distinction between creating a threat and redistributing an existing threat (see his "Three Ways to Kill Innocent Bystanders," and "Moral Rights and Causal Casuistry," in *Moral Theory and Moral Judgments in Medical Ethics,* ed. Baruch Brody [Dordrecht: Kluwer, 1988], pp. 57–74). If what I have claimed is correct, however, commonsense morality has a structure that is far more compli-

cated than either of these writers recognizes, so that it cannot effectively be attacked or defended in these ways.

41. One comparison in which the distinction between killing and letting die appears to have no intuitive significance is suggested by the discussion in the previous section. When we compare a merely extractive abortion with an abortion that kills the fetus in the process of removing it from the womb, it may be difficult to detect a significant moral difference between them, except perhaps a contingent difference in the amount of pain that is caused to the fetus. (Hence even if I am right that a merely extractive abortion does not kill but merely lets the fetus die, the problem of abortion would not be solved by switching to the exclusive use of merely extractive abortifacient techniques.) Perhaps we fail to discern a difference in part because letting die by actively withdrawing aid is more like standard cases of killing. Or perhaps it is because the distinction between killing and letting die loses its ordinary significance in cases in which neither involves a serious harm, as I would argue is the case in most instances of abortion. (See my *Killing at the Margins of Life*.)

42. Foot, "The Problems of Abortion and the Doctrine of Double Effect," p. 29; this volume, p. 276.

43. It is perhaps worth noting that the two cases under discussion combine to cast doubt on a proposal recently advanced by Francis Myrna Kamm. Kamm defends what she calls the Principle of (Im)permissible Harm (PI/PH): "It is permissible to cause harm to some in the course of achieving the greater good of saving a greater number of others from comparable harm, if events which produce the greater good are not more intimately causally related to the production of harm than they are to the production of the greater good" ("Harming Some to Save Others," *Philosophical Studies*, 57 [1989], 232). The PI/PH does not permit (though, given its form, it also does not forbid) the action of the Tactical Bomber, since the event (the bombing) that produces the greater good (victory in a just war, which will presumably save innocent lives) is more intimately causally related to the production of the harm (the killing of civilians) than it is to the production of the greater good. The PI/PH does, however, permit the action of the Poison Gasser, since the event (the manufacture of the gas) that produces the greater good (saving the five) is at least as intimately causally related to the production of the production of the greater good as it is to the production of the lesser harm (killing the one). These claims seem true on any measure of causal intimacy. Thus the PI/PH gives the intuitively wrong answer in both cases.

44. See Joel Feinberg, *Harm to Others* (New York: Oxford University

Press, 1984), esp., pp. 171–86. And compare Bart Gruzalsi, "Killing By Letting Die," *Mind*, 90 (1981), 91–98, and "Death by Omission," in *Moral Theory and Moral Judgments in Medical Ethics*, ed. Baruch Brody (Dordrecht: Kluwer, 1988), pp. 75–85.

45. Bernard Williams, "A Critique of Utilitarianism," in *Utilitarianism: For and Against,* by J. J. C. Smart and Bernard Williams (Cambridge: Cambridge University Press, 1973), pp. 98–99.

46. Bernard Williams, "Moral Luck," in his *Moral Luck* (Cambridge: Cambridge University Press, 1981), p. 28.

SUGGESTED READINGS

I. BACKGROUND IN MEDICAL AND BIOETHICS

Callahan, Daniel. *Abortion: Law, Choice, and Morality.* New York: Macmillan, 1970.

Campbell, A. V. *Moral Dilemmas in Medicine.* Edinburgh: Churchill Livingston, 1975.

Contemporary Issues in Bioethics. Ed. Tom L. Beauchamp and Walters Leroy. Encino, Ca.: Dickenson, 1978.

Ethics and Public Policy. Ed. Tom L. Beauchamp. Englewood Cliffs, N.J.: Prentice-Hall, 1975.

Fletcher, Joseph. *Morals and Medicine.* Boston: Beacon, 1954.

Moral Problems in Medicine. Ed. Samuel Gorovitz. Englewood Cliffs, N.J.: Prentice-Hall, 1976.

O'Donnell, T. J. *Morals in Medicine.* 2nd ed. Westminster, Md.: Newman, 1960.

Veatch, Robert M. *Medical Ethics.* Boston: Jones and Bartlett, 1989.

Zucker, Arthur, et al. *Medical Ethics: A Reader.* Englewood Cliffs, N.J.: Prentice-Hall, 1991.

II. EUTHANASIA AND THE TERMINATION OF LIFE-PROLONGING TREATMENT

"Against Euthanasia." *Lancet,* 1 (1971), 220.

Behnke, John, and Sissela Bok. *Dilemmas of Euthanasia.* New York: Doubleday, 1975.

Beneficent Euthanasia. Ed. Marvin Kohl. Buffalo: Prometheus Books, 1975.

Brown, N. K., et al. "The Preservation of Life." *Journal of the American Medical Association,* 5 (January 1970), 76–82.

Byrn, Robert M. "Compulsory Lifesaving Treatment for the Competent Adult." *Fordham Law Review,* 44 (1975), 1–36.

Dagi, Theodore F. "The Paradox of Euthanasia." *Judaism,* 24 (1975), 157–67.

Engelhardt, H. Tristram. "Ethical Issues in Aiding the Death of Young Children." In *Killing and Letting Die,* 1st ed. Ed. B. Steinbock. Englewood Cliffs, N.J.: Prentice-Hall, 1980. Pp. 81–91.

———. "Fashioning An Ethic for Life and Death in a Post-Modern Society." *Hastings Center Report*, 19 (1989), 7–9.

Euthanasia: The Moral Issues. Eds. Robert M. Baird and Stuart E. Rosenbaum. Buffalo: Prometheus Books, 1989.

Euthanasia and the Right to Death. Ed. A. B. Downing. Los Angeles: Nash, 1969.

Feinberg, Joel. "Overlooking the Merits of the Individual Case: An Unpromising Approach to the Right to Die." *Ratio Juris*, 4, no. 2 (July 1991), 131–51.

Fenigsen, Richard, "A Case Against Dutch Euthanasia." *Hastings Center Report*, 19 (1989), 22–30.

Fletcher, G. P. "Legal Aspects of the Decision Not to Prolong Life." *Journal of the American Medical Association*, 203 (1968), 65–68.

Fletcher, J. "Ethics and Euthanasia." *American Journal of Nursing*, 73 (1973), 1228–31.

Gillett, G. R. "Why Let People Die?" *Journal of Medical Ethics*, 12 (1986), 83–86.

Guttman, F. M. "On Withholding Treatment." *Canadian Medical Association Journal*, 111 (1974), 520, 523.

Humphry, Derek, and Wickett, Ann. *The Right To Die: Understanding Euthanasia*. New York: Harper & Row, 1986.

Kübler-Ross, Elisabeth. *On Death and Dying*. New York: Macmillan, 1969.

———. "The Right to Die with Dignity." *Canadian Nurse*, 68 (1971), 31–35.

McCarrick, Pat Milmoe. "Active Euthanasia and Assisted Suicide." *Kennedy Institute of Ethics Journal*, 2 (1992), 79–100.

Platt, M. "On Asking to Die." *Hastings Center Report*, 5 (1975), 9–12.

Ramsey, Paul. "The Indignity of 'Death with Dignity.'" *Hastings Center Studies*, 2 (1974), 47–62.

———. "Prolonged Dying: Not Medically Indicated." *Hastings Center Report*, 6 (1976), 14–17.

Reich, Walter. "The Physician's Duty to Preserve Life." *Hastings Center Report*, 5 (1975), 14–15.

Robitscher, Jonas B. "The Right to Die." *Hastings Center Report*, 2 (1972), 11–14.

Rosner, F. "Jewish Attitudes Towards Euthanasia." *New York Journal of Medicine*, 67 (1972), 2499–2506.

Simons, S. M. "The Obligation to Live vs. the Option to Die." *Southern Medical Journal*, 65 (1972), 731.

Smith, David H. "On Letting Some Babies Die." In *Killing and Letting*

Die, 1st ed. Ed. B. Steinbock. Englewood Cliffs, N.J.: Prentice-Hall, 1980. Pp. 92–105.

St. John-Stevas, N. *Life, Death and the Law*. Cleveland: World, 1964.

Suicide and Euthanasia. Ed. Baruch A. Brody. Norwell, Kluwer, 1989.

Thomasma, David C. *Euthanasia: Toward an Ethical Social Policy*. New York: Continuum, 1990.

Williams, G. L. "Euthanasia and Abortion." *University of Colorado Law Review*, 38 (1966).

Wolf, Susan M. "Holding the Line on Euthanasia." *Hastings Center Report*, 19 (1989), 13–15.

―――. "Nancy Beth Cruzan: In No Voice At All." *Hastings Center Report*, 20 (1990), 38–41.

―――. "Final Exit: The End of Argument." *Hastings Center Report*, 22 (1992), 30–33.

Wreen, Michael. "The Definition of Euthanasia." *Philosophy and Phenomenological Research*, 48 (1988), 637–54.

III. Legal Background

Austin, John. *Lectures in Jurisprudence*. I. London: 1873. Lecture XII, 346; Lecture XVIII, 426–40.

Bentham, Jeremy. *An Introduction to the Principles of Morals and Legislation*. Oxford, 1892.

―――. *The Theory of Legislation*. London, 1931.

Davis, Phillip E., *Moral Duty and Legal Responsibility*. New York: Irvington, 1966.

Fletcher, George P. *Rethinking Criminal Law*. Boston: Little, Brown, 1978. Chapter 8.

Fletcher, Joseph. "Euthanasia in the Courts." *Euthanasia Review*, 2 (1987), 115–22.

Hall, Jerome. *General Principles of Criminal Law*. 2nd ed. Indianapolis: Bobbs-Merrill, 1960.

Hart, H. L. A., and A. M. Honoré. "Legal and Moral Obligation." In *Essays in Moral Philosophy*. Ed. A. Melden. Seattle: University of Washington Press, 1958.

―――. *Causation in the Law*. Oxford: Oxford University Press, 1959.

Kenny, Antony. "Intention and Purpose in the Law." In *Essays in Legal Philosophy*. Ed. R. Summers. Oxford: Oxford University Press, 1968.

―――. "Negligence and the General Problem of Criminal Responsibility." *Yale Law Journal*, 81 (1972), 949.

Wasserstrom, Richard. "H. L. A. Hart and the Doctrine of *Mens Rea* and Criminal Responsibility." *University of Chicago Law Review*, 92 (1967), 102–106.

Williams, Glanville. *Criminal Law: The General Part.* London: Stevens, 1953.

———. *The Sanctity of Life and the Criminal Law.* New York: Knopf, 1957.

IV. PHILOSOPHICAL PROBLEMS

Abrams, Natalie. "Active and Passive Euthanasia." *Philosophy*, 53 (1978), 257–63.

Anscombe, G. E. M. *Intention.* Oxford: Blackwell, 1957.

———. "Modern Moral Philosophy." *Ethics, Religion, and Politics.* Collected Philosophical Papers. III. Minneapolis: University of Minnesota Press, 1981. Pp. 26–42.

———. "Two Kinds of Error in Action." *Ethics, Religion, and Politics.* Collected Philosophical Papers. III. Minneapolis: University of Minnesota Press, 1981. Pp. 3–9.

———. "War and Murder." *Ethics, Religion, and Politics.* Collected Philosophical Papers. III. Minneapolis: University of Minnesota Press, 1981. Pp. 51–61.

Belliotti, Raymond. "Negative Duties, Positive Duties, and Rights." *The Southern Journal of Philosophy*, 14 (1978), 581–88.

Bennett, Jonathan. "Acting and Refraining." *Analysis*, 28 (1967), 30–31.

———. "Shooting, Killing, Dying." *Canadian Journal of Philosophy*, 2 (1973), 315–23.

———. "Morality and Consequences." *The Tanner Lectures on Human Values.* II. Ed. S. McMurrin. Salt Lake City: University of Utah Press, 1981. Pp. 47–116.

———. "Positive and Negative Relevance." *American Philosophical Quarterly*, 20 (1983), 185–94.

———. *The Act Itself.* Oxford: Oxford University Press, forthcoming.

Berkowitz, Leonard J. "Intention and Euthanasia." *Philosophical Forum*, 19 (1987), 54–62.

Boyle, Joseph M., Jr. "On Killing and Letting Die." *New Scholasticism*, 51 (1977), 433–52.

Brook, Richard. "Dischargeability, Optionality, and the Duty to Save Lives." *Philosophy and Public Affairs*, 8, no. 1 (Winter 1979), 194–200.

Callahan, Daniel. "Can We Return Death to Diseases?" *Hastings Center Report*, 19 (1989), 4–6.

Casey, John. "Killing and Letting Die: A Reply to Bennett." In *Killing and Letting Die,* 1st ed. Ed. B. Steinbock. Englewood Cliffs, N.J.: Prentice-Hall, 1980. Pp. 132–38.

Chandler, John. "Killing and Letting Die—Putting the Debate in Context." *Australasian Journal of Philosophy,* 68 (1990), 420–31.

Collinson, Diane, and Robert Campbell. *Ending Lives.* New York: Blackwell, 1988.

Conway, David. "Is Failing to Save Lives as Bad as Killing?" *Journal of Applied Philosophy,* 5 (1988), 109–112.

D'Arcy, Eric. *Human Acts.* Oxford: Oxford University Press, 1963.

Donagan, Alan, *The Theory of Morality,* Chicago: The University of Chicago Press, 1977.

Duff, R. A. "Intentionally Killing the Innocent." *Analysis,* 33 (1973), 93–98.

———. "Absolute Principles and Double Effect." *Analysis,* 36 (1976), 68–80.

Feinberg, Joel. *Doing and Deserving.* Princeton: Princeton University Press, 1970.

———. *Social Philosophy.* Englewood Cliffs, N.J.: Prentice-Hall, 1973.

Finnis, John. "The Rights and Wrongs of Abortion." *Philosophy and Public Affairs,* 2 (1973), 117–45.

Fitzgerald, P. J. "Acting and Refraining." *Analysis,* 27 (1967), 133–39.

Foot, Philippa. "Morality as a System of Hypothetical Imperatives." *Philosophical Review,* 81 (1972), 305–16.

———. "Euthanasia." *Philosophy and Public Affairs,* 6, no. 1 (Winter 1977), 85–112.

———. "Killing, Letting Die, and Euthanasia: A Reply to Holly Goldman." *Analysis,* 41 (1981), 159–60.

Fried, Charles. "Right and Wrong: Preliminary Considerations." *Journal of Legal Studies,* 5 (1976), 165–200.

Glover, Jonathan. "It Makes No Difference Whether or Not I Do It." *Proceedings of the Aristotelian Society,* 49 (1975), 171–90.

———. *Causing Death and Saving Lives.* London: Penguin, 1977.

Goldman, Alvin. *A Theory of Human Action.* Englewood Cliffs, N.J.: Prentice-Hall, 1970.

Hanink, J. G. "Some Light on Double Effect." *Analysis,* 35 (1975), 147–51.

———. "On the Survival Lottery." *Philosophy,* 51 (1976), 223–25.

Hare, R. M. "Euthanasia: A Christian View." *Philosophical Exchange,* 2 (1972), 43–52.

———. "Rules of War and Moral Reasoning." *Philosophy and Public Affairs,* 1, no. 1 (Winter 1972), 166–81.

————. *Moral Thinking: Its Levels, Method and Point.* Oxford: Oxford University Press, 1981.

Harman, Gilbert. "Moral Relativism Defended." *Philosophical Review,* 84 (1975), 3–22.

Harris, John. "The Marxist Conception of Violence." *Philosophy and Public Affairs,* 3, no. 1 (Winter 1974), 191–220.

————. "Williams on Negative Responsibility and Integrity." *Philosophical Quarterly,* 24 (1974), 265–73.

————. *Violence and Negative Responsibility.* Routledge & Kegan Paul, 1980.

Howard-Snyder, Frances. "The Heart of Consequentialism." *Philosophical Studies,* forthcoming.

Jordan, Jeff. "Why Negative Rights Only?" *Southern Journal of Philosophy,* 29 (1991), 245–55.

Kagan, Shelly, "The Additive Fallacy." *Ethics,* 99 (1988), 5–31.

————. *The Limits of Morality.* Oxford: Oxford University Press, 1989.

Kamm, Frances M. "Killing and Letting Die: Methodological and Substantive Issues." *Pacific Philosophical Quarterly,* 64 (1983), 297–312.

————. "Harming Some to Save Others." *Philosophical Studies,* 57 (1989). 227–60.

————. "The Doctrine of Double Effect: Reflections on Theoretical and Practical Issues." *Journal of Medical Philosophy,* 16 (1991), 571–85.

————. "Non-Consequentialism, the Person as an End-in-Itself, and the Significance of Status." *Philosophy and Public Affairs,* 21 (1992), 354–89.

Kuhse, Helga. *The Sanctity-of-Life Doctrine in Medicine: A Critique.* New York: Oxford University Press, 1987.

McCloskey, H. J. "The Right to Life." *Mind,* 84 (1975), 403–25.

Mackie, John. *The Cement of the Universe.* Oxford: Oxford University Press, 1974.

————. *Ethics: Inventing Right and Wrong.* London: Penguin, 1977.

Malm, H. M. "Killing, Letting Die, and Simple Conflicts." *Philosophy and Public Affairs,* 18, no. 3 (1989), 238–58.

————. "Directions of Justification in the Negative-Positive Duty Debate." *American Philosophical Quarterly,* 27 (1990), 315–24.

Montague, Philip. "The Morality of Active and Passive Euthanasia." *Ethics in Science and Medicine,* 5 (1978), 39–45.

Morillo, Carolyn. "As Sure as Shooting." *Philosophy,* 51 (1976), 80–89.

————. "Doing, Refraining, and the Strenuousness of Morality." *American Philosophical Quarterly,* 14 (1977), 29–39.

Morris, Herbert. *Freedom and Responsibility.* Stanford: Stanford University Press, 1961.

Nagel, Thomas. *The Possibility of Altruism*. Oxford: Oxford University Press, 1970.

———. *Mortal Questions*. Cambridge: Cambridge University Press, 1979.

Naylor, Margery Bedford. "The Moral of the Trolley Problem." *Philosophy and Phenomenological Research*, 48 (1988), 711–22.

Norcross, Alastair. "A Reply to Margery Naylor." *Philosophy and Phenomenological Research*, 49, no. 4 (June 1989), 715–19.

———. "Should Utilitarianism Accommodate Moral Dilemmas?" *Philosophical Studies*, forthcoming.

O'Neil, Richard. "Killing, Letting Die, and Justice." *Analysis*, 38 (1978), 124–25.

Otten, James. "Even If One Were Letting Another Innocent Person Die." *Southern Journal of Philosophy*, 14 (1976), 313–22.

Parfit, Derek. *Reasons and Persons*. Oxford: Oxford University Press, 1984.

Phillips, Michael. "Are 'Killing' and "Letting Die' Adequately Specified Moral Categories?" *Philosophical Studies*, 47 (1985), 151–58.

Quinn, Warren S. "Actions, Intentions, and Consequences: The Doctrine of Double Effect." *Philosophy and Public Affairs*, 18 (1989), 334–51.

Rachels, James. "Killing and Letting People Die of Starvation." *Philosophy*, 54, no. 208 (April 1979), 159–71.

Reichenbach, Bruce R. "Euthanasia and the Active-Passive Distinction." *Bioethics*, 1 (1987), 51–73.

Russell, Bruce, "Still a Live Issue." *Philosophy and Public Affairs*, 7, no. 2 (Spring 1978), 278–81.

———. "The Presumption Against Taking Life as Compared to that Against Failing to Save Life." *The Journal of Philosophy and Medicine*, 4, no. 3 (September 1979).

———. "On the Relative Strictness of Negative and Positive Duties." In *Killing and Letting Die*, 1st ed. Ed. B. Steinbock. Englewood Cliffs, N.J.: Prentice-Hall, 1980. Pp. 215–31.

Singer, Marcus. "Positive Duties and Negative Duties." *Philosophical Quarterly*, 15 (1965), 97–103.

Singer, Peter. "Famine, Affluence and Morality." *Philosophy and Public Affairs*, 1, no. 3 (1972), 229–43.

———. "Utility and the Survival Lottery." *Philosophy*, 52 (1977), 218–22.

Smart, R. N. "Negative Utilitarianism." *Mind*, 67 (1958), 542–43.

———. "An Outline of a System of Utilitarian Ethics." In J. J. C. Smart and Bernard Williams, *Utilitarianism For and Against*. Cambridge: Cambridge University Press, 1973. Pp. 3–74.

Steinbock, Bonnie. *Life Before Birth: The Moral and Legal Status of Embryos and Fetuses.* New York: Oxford University Press, 1992.

Stocker, Michael. "Intentions and Act Evaluations." *Journal of Philosophy,* 67 (1970), 589–602.

Strudler, Alan, and David Wasserman. "The First Dogma of Deontology: The Doctrine of Doing and Allowing and the Notion of a Say." *Philosophical Studies,* forthcoming.

Talmadge, R. S. "Utilitarianism and the Morality of Killing." *Philosophy,* 47 (1972), 55–63.

Thomson, Judith Jarvis. "Individuating Actions." *Journal of Philosophy,* 68 (1971), 774–81.

———. "A Defense of Abortion." In *Rights, Restitution, and Risk: Essays in Moral Theory.* Ed. W. Parent. Cambridge: Harvard University Press, 1986. Pp. 1–19.

———. "Killing, Letting Die, and the Trolley Problem." In *Rights, Restitution, and Risk: Essays in Moral Theory.* Ed. W. Parent. Cambridge: Harvard University Press, 1986. Pp. 78–93.

———. "The Trolley Problem." In *Rights, Restitution, and Risk: Essays in Moral Theory.* Ed. W. Parent. Cambridge: Harvard University Press, 1986. Pp. 94–116

——— *The Realm of Rights.* Cambridge: Harvard University Press, 1990.

Tooley, Michael. "Abortion and Infanticide." *Philosophy and Public Affairs,* 2, no. 1 (1972), 37–65.

Trammell, Richard. "Tooley's Moral Symmetry Principle." *Philosophy and Public Affairs,* 5 (1976), 305–13.

———. "The Presumption Against Taking Life." *The Journal of Medicine and Philosophy,* 3 (1978), 53–67.

———. "The Nonequivalency of Saving Life and Not Taking Life." *The Journal of Medicine and Philosophy,* 4, no. 3 (September 1979).

Williams, Bernard. *Morality: An Introduction to Ethics.* New York: Harper Torchbooks, 1972.

———. "A Critique of Utilitarianism." In J. J. C. Smart and Bernard Williams, *Utilitarianism For and Against.* Cambridge: Cambridge University Press, 1973.

———. *Problems of the Self.* Cambridge: Cambridge University Press, 1973.

———. "Moral Luck." *Proceedings of the Aristotelian Society,* supplementary vol. 50 (1976), 115–36.

———. "Persons, Character and Morality." In *The Identities of Persons.* Ed. A. Rorty. Berkeley: University of California Press, 1979. Pp. 197–216.

Winkler, Earl. "Is the Killing/Letting-Die Distinction Normatively Neutral?" *Dialogue,* 30 (1991), 309–25.

Notes on Contributors

JONATHAN BENNETT teaches philosophy at Syracuse University. He has written books on early modern philosophy, the philosophy of mind and language, and metaphysics. A work on ethics, *The Act Itself,* is forthcoming from Oxford University Press.

N. ANN DAVIS (formerly Nancy Davis) teaches philosophy at the University of Colorado at Boulder. Currently Director of the Center for Values and Social Policy (1993–1995), she focuses on moral theory, moral practice, and the connections between them. Among her publications are those on abortion, reproductive technologies, morality and technology, sexual harassment in the university, moral hypocrisy, and topics in moral theory.

DANIEL DINELLO is an independent filmmaker who also teaches film production and film theory at Columbia College in Chicago.

GEORGE P. FLETCHER is Charles Keller Beekman Professor of Law at Columbia University. He is the author of *Rethinking Criminal Law* (Little, Brown, 1978), *A Crime of Self-Defense: Bernhard Goetz and the Law on Trial* (Free Press, 1988), and *Loyalty: An Essay on the Morality of Relationships* (Oxford University Press, 1993).

PHILIPPA FOOT is Emeritus Professor of Philosophy at the University of California, Los Angeles, and Honorary Fellow of Somerville College, Oxford. She is the editor of *Theories of Ethics* (Oxford University Press, 1967) and *Morality and Action* (Cambridge University Press, 1993), the author of *Virtues and Vices* (Blackwell and the University of California Press, 1978), and a Fellow of the British Academy.

JOHN HARRIS is Professor of Philosophy and a Director of the Center for Social Ethics and Policy at the University of Manchester. He is the author of *Violence and Responsibility* (Routledge & Kegan Paul, 1980), and *The Value of Life* (Routledge & Kegan

Paul, 1985), and the editor (with Anthony Dyson) of *Experiments on Embryos* (Routledge & Kegan Paul, 1989).

JUDITH LICHTENBERG is Associate Professor in the Department of Philosophy and Senior Research Scholar at the Institute for Philosophy and Public Policy, University of Maryland at College Park. She has written many articles in the areas of ethics and political philosophy, and is the editor of *Democracy and the Mass Media* (Cambridge University Press, 1990).

JEFF McMAHAN is Associate Professor of Philosophy at the University of Illinois at Urbana-Champaign. He is currently working on two books, *Killing at the Margins of Life* and *The Ethics of War*, both forthcoming from Oxford University Press.

JEFFRIE G. MURPHY is Professor of Law and Philosophy at Arizona State University. His most recent books are *Forgiveness and Mercy* (Cambridge University Press, 1988) and *Retribution Reconsidered* (Kluwer, 1992).

ALASTAIR NORCROSS is Easterwood Assistant Professor of Philosophy at Southern Methodist University. His articles on theoretical and applied ethics have appeared in *The Journal of Philosophy, Analysis, Philosophy and Phenomenological Research, The Journal of Philosophical Research,* and *Philosophical Studies.*

WARREN QUINN was Professor of Philosophy at the University of California, Los Angeles, until his death in 1991. He published widely in theoretical and applied ethics. A collection of his papers, *Morality and Action* (Cambridge University Press, 1993), edited by Philippa Foot, appeared posthumously.

JAMES RACHELS is Professor of Philosophy at the University of Alabama in Birmingham. Specializing in ethics, he is the author of such articles as "Why Privacy Is Important," "On Moral Absolutism," and "Can Ethics Provide Answers?" He is also the author of *The Elements of Moral Philosophy* (Random House, 1986), *The End of Life: Euthanasia and Morality* (Oxford University Press, 1986), and *Created From Animals* (Oxford University Press, 1990).

BONNIE STEINBOCK is Professor of Philosophy at the University at Albany, State University of New York. She has published on a wide variety of topics in applied ethics and biomedical ethics. Her most recent book was *Life Before Birth: The Moral and Legal Status of Embryos and Fetuses* (Oxford University Press, 1992).

THOMAS D. SULLIVAN is Aquinas Professor of Philosophy and Theology at the University of St. Thomas in St. Paul, Minnesota. He is the author of "Between Thoughts and Things: The Status of Meaning" and "Adequate Evidence for Religious Assent" and the coauthor of "Benevolence and Absolute Prohibitions." He is also the author of an article on abortion, "In Defense of Total Regard."

MICHAEL TOOLEY is Professor of Philosophy at the University of Colorado at Boulder. A Fellow of the Australian Academy of the Humanities, he is the author of *Abortion and Infanticide* (Oxford University Press, 1983), and *Causation: A Realist Approach* (Oxford University Press, 1987), and coeditor, with Ernest Sosa, of *Causation* (Oxford University Press, 1993). He is currently working on books on the nature of time and on the epistemology of theistic belief.

RICHARD TRAMMELL is Associate Professor of Philosophy at Grove City College, Grove City, Pennsylvania. His articles on ethics and other topics have appeared in *Philosophy, Philosophy and Public Affairs, The Journal of Philosophy,* and *The Journal of Medicine and Philosophy.*

Media Center (Library)
Elizabethtown Community College
600 College Street Rd., KY 42701

O

M

OC

OC

M

Media Center (Library)
Elizabethtown Community College
Elizabethtown, KY 42701